A plain TeX Primer

A plain TEX Primer

Malcolm Clark

OXFORD · NEW YORK · TOKYO
OXFORD UNIVERSITY PRESS
1992

Oxford University Press, Walton Street, Oxford OX2 6DP

Oxford New York Toronto
Delhi Bombay Calcutta Madras Karachi
Kuala Lumpur Singapore Hong Kong Tokyo
Nairobi Dar es Salaam Cape Town
Melbourne Auckland Madrid

and associated companies in
Berlin Ibadan

Oxford is a trade mark of Oxford University Press

Published in the United States
by Oxford University Press Inc., New York

A catalogue record for this book is available from the British Library

Library of Congress Cataloging in Publication Data
Clark, Malcolm.
A plain TEX primer / Malcolm Clark.
1. TEX (Computer file).   2. Computerized typesetting–Computer
programs.   3. Mathematics printing–Computer programs.   I. Title.
Z253.4.T47C46   686.2' 2544536–dc20   92-25531
ISBN 0-19-853784-0 (Hbk)
ISBN 0-19-853724-7 (Pbk)

Text keyed and photoset by the author using TEX
Printed in Great Britain by
Bookcraft (Bath) Ltd
Midsomer Norton, Avon

I looked at him from the corner of my eye and said:
You can't beat a good pint.
He leaned over and put his face close to me in an earnest
manner.
Do you know what I am going to tell you, he said with
his wry mouth, a pint of `plain` is your only man.

When things go wrong and will not come right,
Though you do the best you can,
When life looks black as the hour of night —
A PINT OF PLAIN IS YOUR ONLY MAN.

from At Swim-Two-Birds
by Flann O'Brien

Preface

This book has evolved from courses which were first given at Imperial College, London, in 1984. These first courses were based around the Pascal version of TeX78 running on a CDC mainframe and outputting to an Autologic APS μ-5 phototypesetter. Now the course is based on the current version of TeX running on a variety of mainframes, minis, workstations, and micros, generating output for screens, laser printers, and phototypesetters. TeX has come a long way.

Many people have contributed; some directly, some obliquely, many unwittingly. It seems invidious to attempt to list them, although a few will find themselves embedded in the text. I trust the omission does not offend.

I am particularly grateful to P. J. Kavanagh and the Peters Fraser & Dunlop Group Ltd. for permission to reprint an extract from *The Perfect Stranger*. Acknowledgement is made to Russell Hoban for permission to quote from *The Medusa Frequency*, published by Cape.

June 27th, 1992

Contents

Introduction 1

TEX predates the current concern with microcomputers. This is both a boon and a bane. Its origins lie, in part, in a series of books, *The Art of Computer Programming*, written by Donald Knuth. This is a projected seven-volume work, as yet incomplete. The first volume was published in 1968, to be followed by Volume 2 in 1969, and Volume 3 in 1973. As might be inferred from the title of the series, the books contain an appreciable amount of mathematics, of one sort or another.

In the contemporary typesetting environment mathematics was described as 'penalty copy'. The author's text (perhaps typed, perhaps even longhand) was annotated by the publisher's copy editor to include information about the page layout, the typefaces to be used, and a myriad of other details traditionally part of the publisher's arcana. The job of the author is to write the text, the job of the copy editor is to begin the translation into type. The annotated copy or *markup* copy of the text is then presented to a human typesetter to be typeset. The position of line breaks is decided at this point. Page breaks may also be decided at this time, or entire chapters can be set as *galleys*, where the proof copy is in the form of long single-column strips; these galleys are then used to decide where page breaks will occur.

Writing a series like *The Art of Computer Programming* is similar to painting the Forth Rail Bridge. No sooner is it finished than the job must be started again. The revision to the first editions of the first three volumes was underway some time after 1973. This coincided with a change in printing technology, away from hot metal type to phototypesetting. Between the first editions of *The Art of Computer Programming*, using the old hot metal technology, and the second editions, Knuth detected a decline in the quality of typesetting. Although he might have made a valiant rearguard stand and insisted that the revised editions be set with the old technology, Knuth was a realist. There were to be a further four volumes, and since it would take some years to complete them he could hardly insist on the retention of hot metal to suit him. Technology was bound to change in the interim 'and the quality would go down each time'.

Frustration and dissatisfaction by themselves do not necessarily lead to the development of a new computerized system to set type. At about the same time, Knuth saw the proofs of a book on artificial intelligence which had been prepared on a digital photo-typesetter. He says 'it looked as good as any (book) I had ever seen done with metal'. In 1977 Knuth decided to spend one year developing a new computerized system which would be useful in producing his books, and then go back to *The Art of Computer Programming*. The design of T_EX started on Thursday, May 5th, 1977.

Setting mathematics is inherently difficult in traditional typesetting. If we regard a typesetter as a linear device – after all, *most* text is essentially linear, and text is what comprises most typesetting – coping with mathematics or other technical text, which is often two dimensional, must impose its own set of problems. Since mathematics is a minority interest, innovation to account for this particular area is unlikely to be embraced by the whole of the industry, especially if it requires significant relearning of skills. The excellence of any alternative does not ensure its adoption.

The variation in quality which was observable between the first and second editions of *The Art of Computer Programming* was not unique to books, as Knuth's examination of the changes which had taken place in the *Transactions of the American Mathematical Society* showed. He documents the fluctuations in typeset presentation in the essay *Mathematical Typography*, where he says that the reduction in quality culminated in his decision not to submit papers to the AMS 'since the finished product was just too painful for me to look at'.

How can such a problem be resolved: how can an author ensure that the end product is worthy of his or her efforts? Knuth's solution was straightforward, if ambitious: design and implement a form of markup which would be understood by a computer and which could generate the appropriate codes for a typesetting machine to produce the 'correct' forms on the page. It is probable that it seemed a simpler problem at the time. With hindsight it is easy to see the difficulties which were to lie ahead. After all, it took about a decade before a final version of this system was unveiled.

Tau Epsilon Chi

We must also consider the hardware available at the time too. No matter how good ideas are, they will not germinate and flower if they are completely outside the context of their time.

The principal computer hardware available was a minicomputer which could handle the computational side of things (a DEC-20 running the TOPS-20 operating system), and a raster (or dot matrix) plotter which could provide some representation of the results – in fact an obsolescent Xerox XGP printer, with a nominal resolution of 180–200 dpi (dots per inch). A fully fledged typesetter would have been convenient, and although these were uncommon at the time, especially outside the printing and publishing industry, Knuth was able to obtain access to a CRS AlphaType, with a resolution of 5333 lines per inch. Nevertheless, it is quite important to the development of the system that the output device used for development was one which created its characters by accumulating dots. In other words, it was a digital device, not an analogue one. Traditional 'hot metal' type, photosetting, and even typewriter type can all be regarded as involving the manipulation of analogue images.

It is also important to appreciate that the ultimate goal which Knuth set for TEX is that of publishing – *real* publishing, within the structure of the existing publishing world. TEX was not designed for memos, letters, and the like. Its aims were altogether loftier. That is not to say that it is inflexible. Having been designed for maximum scrutiny and exposure, the more mundane tasks are still accessible. It is probably also significant that Knuth's publishers were Addison Wesley. He certainly had some discussions with their technical staff, and some of the quirks of TEX can easily be laid to the desire to emulate the house style of this particular publisher.

A clue to Knuth's aims is provided by the name he chose to give to the software – TEX. Originally, TEX was subtitled 'Tau Epsilon Chi, a system for technical text'. The Greek $\tau\epsilon\chi$ is the first syllable of the word *tékhnē*, which is the root from which we obtain words like 'technology'. But to the Ancient Greeks, 'technology' was closer in meaning to 'art'. If we take art to imply 'craft', then we are probably getting closer to the sort of meaning both the Greeks and Knuth intended. The Greek origin of the name 'TEX' also helps to explain its pronunciation. The 'X' is really doing duty for a 'χ', and therefore has the same sort of sound as the 'ch' in loch. Naturally, if you cannot pronounce 'loch' properly, but say 'lock', this doesn't really help you. Pronouncing 'TₑX' correctly is really one of our lesser worries, except when it starts to confuse. In that case, you can always say 'Donald Knuth's TₑX'; everyone then knows what you are talking about, and Knuth gets the credit. This seems only fair.

Of course, TₑX was not isolated in its development. There were other efforts which were directed towards the same sorts of goals. The UNIX tools nroff and its variants and extensions eqn, tbl, grap, and pic were at an early stage of their development. Document description systems like Brian Reid's *Scribe* were in circulation, as well as others which were less public, but probably known to Knuth.

In developing TₑX, Knuth was assisted by many others. Equally important, the program was made available to others to port to other computing environments; this proved to be an excellent way of locating bugs and fixing them. Although originally written in SAIL (Stanford Artificial Intelligence Language), TₑX was rewritten in Pascal – a far more generally available language, and one uncannily popular with computer scientists, who were among the first groups to take up TₑX enthusiastically. (It has been said that TₑX is one of the finest tests of any Pascal compiler, and that it has found more bugs in Pascal compilers than any other piece of software.) So development of TₑX was not carried out in lofty isolation. This also meant the facilities in the program were open to criticism and review. Fortunately, the final word remained with Knuth, and the substance of the achievement is his. No committee decided what should or should not happen.

This public availability also meant that TₑX could be found running on a vast range of machines. It was not restricted to one computer range, or one operating system. Any computer which had a Pascal compiler could reasonably be expected to run TₑX. This also encouraged the production of interfaces from TₑX to a wide variety of output devices: not just typesetters, but impact dot matrix printers, and, perhaps more significantly, laser printers.

Friends of TₑX

All along, the American Mathematical Society had expressed interest in systems like TₑX. Quite early, their Advisory Committee on Composition Technology identified TₑX as a possible useful addition to the society's capabilities. The AMS concern is perhaps obvious. They produce a very large range of journals. Reducing the in-house overheads on their production could effect savings not only of money, but also of time. Anyone who submits an article to a scientific journal soon starts to wonder where the article has got to, and even when it is accepted, publication still seems to take aeons.

The AMS estimate that 30–40% of the time a paper spends at their offices in Providence is taken up by keyboarding and subsequent checking and correction of that work; similarly, composition costs are estimated to account for about 48% of the production costs at John Wiley & Sons Ltd. If an author could prepare a manuscript electronically (for example, using TeX), by the time it came to be accepted for publication, no rekeying would be needed. The same electronic manuscript (perhaps with referees' and editors' amendments) would suffice. Anyone who has submitted manuscripts with equations in them will be aware how a printer (even a good one) can attack those equations, requiring corrections to the proof. At least if authors prepare the equations themselves, the onus is theirs alone.

A measure of the AMS's belief in TeX is to be gained from their selection of it as their preferred language for the input of mathematics. They have been using TeX for the production of various internally created documents (like their membership lists, directories, and so on), and more recently the mainstream publications which require input from authors. The most notable recent development has been their 'Electronic Manuscript Program' to encourage the submission of papers in TeX.

Knuth asked the AMS to hold the trademark 'TeX'. He also devised a testing procedure to ensure that any implementation which describes itself as TeX meets certain minimum (but high) standards. Anyone, anywhere, who uses a system called TeX can be confident that it will be the same as other TeX systems in all essential details.

The AMS has also given consistent and determined assistance in promoting the use of TeX, through TUG (TeX Users Group). The group formed in February 1980, and produced its first newsletter, TUGBOAT, later that year. At first TUG sheltered under the AMS, but eventually it grew large enough to establish its own offices. TUG has consistently provided an umbrella for all TeX users. Membership confers benefits and TUG members are among the nicest bunch of people you are ever likely to meet. TUG's address, and that of other national or language-oriented groups, will be found at the end of this book, in Appendix C.

Public TEX

The first 'public' reference to TEX was in January 1978. The first major public release of TEX was the so-called TEX78, which is described in the book *TEX and Metafont*. This provided a widespread standard, especially since it was supported by adequate documentation. Knuth's writing style attracted many compliments; the general feeling seemed to be that at last someone had mastered the blend of fact, exposition, and structured development which made reading a manual a delight rather than a chore.

In the next few years TEX was rewritten. By and large, the changes made could be described as 'upwards compatible' – that is to say, features which were present in TEX78 are also present in TEX82 – although some details changed drastically. In general terms, TEX became more comprehensive, simpler, more consistent, and more coherent. The end product was TEX-(almost)-as-we-know-it-now, originally termed TEX82. And accompanying it was *The TEXbook*. Some idea of the changes made between TEX78 and TEX82 may be gauged from the fact that there were about 200 pages in the original manual, and about 500 in *The TEXbook*. The -(almost)- tag became necessary when, in 1989, Knuth agreed to make some changes in TEX, chiefly in order to enhance its capability in handling languages which use accents or diacriticals. Fortunately all the changes are upwards compatible, and if you write only in English, you are unlikely to notice the changes at all. At the time of the changeover, the 'new' TEX was being termed TEX3.

Other threads were present in TEX's development. Knuth was not completely satisfied with the typefaces which were available to him. The typefaces which were provided on the early digital devices tended to be emulations of typewriter characters rather than true typefaces. He therefore invented METAFONT – a language to describe fonts (also given its first public airing in 1978). This was no trivial task, especially since METAFONT was to describe a font in such a way that it was scale or resolution independent, an aspect which will be discussed later. METAFONT also went through a metamorphosis, between the original attempt and the final version, METAFONT84. The changes which took place were far more fundamental than those between TEX78 and TEX82. METAFONT provided the basis from which Knuth developed the Computer Modern family of typefaces.

Not content with inventing a typesetting system TEX, a font creation language, METAFONT, and the Computer Modern typeface family, Knuth also invented WEB. WEB is a structured program documentation system which combines a programming language *and* a document formatting language into a single language. As you might anticipate, TEX is the document formatting language. Pascal is the programming language. A WEB program without clear exposition would be unthinkable. In this way Knuth hoped that programs would become more portable, as well as becoming 'literate'. A post-processor could take a WEB program and WEAVE it to select the comment structure to produce documentation, or TANGLE it to extract the lower-level language. Diagrammatically, the process looks like:

$$\text{WEB document}$$
$$\text{TANGLE} \swarrow \qquad \searrow \text{WEAVE}$$
$$\text{Pascal source} \qquad \text{TEX document}$$

WEB itself is not a compiled language. Originally, the underlying programming language was Pascal, but equally, other languages could be substituted. There are currently several implementations of WEB which support a wider variety of programming languages, including C. One day there may even be AdaWEB. Similarly, the underlying document formatting language need not be TEX. And of course, work was still progressing on *The Art of Computer Programming*.

TEX grows up

The story does not end with the rewriting of TEX in WEB. The late 70s saw the rise of the microcomputer. To begin with these were rather limited devices, with restricted memory and rather primitive operating systems (of course, there were exceptions). TEX required, as a minimum, a 16-bit machine. These began to appear in quantity, and at a reasonable price, in the early 80s. In a relatively short time, TEX was running on 16-bit micros, such as the IBM pc. By an amazing coincidence, two independent commercial implementations appeared within a few months of one another in 1985. A fully fledged, inexpensive TEX system was now within the reach of anyone. This brings with it some important consequences: one of the most important is that the 'community' of TEX users becomes even more diffuse. While there are strong pockets of TEX users in various universities, industrial and commercial organizations (including publishers), there are also individual TEX users, completely separate from any sort of group support. More than

ever, TEX has to be able to stand on its own two feet. There is no
longer a guaranteed 'local expert' to whom tricky problems can
be assigned.

At the same time, we have seen the rise of *wysiwyg* (what you
see is what you get) text formatting systems: these come from at
least two directions. The first direction is a typewriter enhance-
ment, where the ability of a microcomputer to store files and
permit on-screen editing has encouraged the virtual replacement
of the typewriter by the micro. This is purely emulation. We
are simply replacing one technology for producing a typewritten
document with another. This has nothing to do with publishing.
In this context the micro has simply become a more sophisticated
typewriter. The other direction is much more micro dependent.
The development of the Apple Macintosh allowed the introduction of what Apple described as 'desktop publishing', when the
extremely integrated *wimp* (window, icon, mouse, and pull-down
menu) environment was coupled to a good crisp screen and a
laser printer. All these components had been around already –
Interleaf (a broadly similar system for the production of technical
documentation) and TEX both ran on the Sun workstation in just
that sort of environment, but to Apple must go the credit of the
new buzzwords. The accompanying software permitted a variety
of typefaces to be used, at a variety of sizes – something the
typewriter emulators could never achieve. In both environments,
however, the document was closely related to its operating system.
You could not really expect to sit down at some arbitrary keyboard
and use the same commands to achieve the same results. In fact,
you could not be sure which commands did achieve the results,
since they tended to be hidden (non-visible) codes which produced
effects like emboldening, superscripts, paragraphing, and so on.
Despite this, many people quickly become adept at the correct
sequence of keystrokes or menu selections which give a particular
effect. This is also true of human typesetters, who memorize even
more extensive keystroke sequences for printing effects.

The key difference between these systems and TEX is that TEX
does not hide the keystroke sequences. They are there for all to
see. This has some advantages: changing the sequences is easier.
They are there to be changed. And the same set of sequences work
on any implementation of TEX, running on any machine. On the
other hand, changes to the 'typeset' or 'TEXed' version can only
be effected by going back to the original, correcting it, and then
TEXing it again. To the printing and publishing industry this has

always been the natural order of things. You don't see the final product until you print it. To the 'office' environment, it seems unnatural. Typing is the original *wysiwyg* system where the person at the keyboard is accustomed to seeing their work develop as they enter it, and to making large-scale changes by retyping, rather than simple editing.

TEX was developed before there were screens with adequate resolution to make direct screen previewing a practical proposition. Since it used a fairly ordinary computing system, the special function keys of today's word processors were not available, nor were extra characters. In fact TEX uses a conventional keyboard to prepare text which will be typeset at arbitrary complexity. There never was any intention of viewing 'output' or some approximation of it on the screen – ordinary 'glass' or 'dumb' terminals had no powers of displaying anything other than their own limited range of fixed characters. In any case, given the breadth of possible TEX machines, it is still an impossibility to write a single program which could provide a sensible representation of TEX output on each and every terminal which might be linked up to a computer. TEX strives for a universality and standardization which is remarkable, especially in the computing industry.

The approach of embedding visible sequences of keystrokes within a document is by no means unique to TEX. The family of nroff formatters uses a similar approach, while SGML (the Standard Generalized Markup Language) also adopts this mechanism. In fact, looking back to how publishers would handle a manuscript, we can see that they would take it and *mark it up* with agreed codes which conveyed information to the typesetter. Few publishers actually do the typesetting and printing themselves, but subcontract these jobs to specialist typesetters and printers. The publishers' markup therefore has to be fairly standardized. All that TEX has done is intercept the publisher's markup stage and the interpretation by the human typesetter, replacing them by codes which talk directly to the printing machine. Again we come back to the view that TEX is a publishing engine.

Markup can permit enormous flexibility. Any arbitrary new sequence can be introduced, at the convenience of the author. At some point there must be a definition of what the markup 'means', but this might be in the hands of the author or the publisher. And altering the definition should affect only the finished appearance. The original document remains unchanged. Markup also allows the document to be prepared on any arbitrary system before being run through TEX. The widespread availability of microcomputers makes this a less vital attribute, but it is useful to know that wherever you are, whatever machine is available, you can at least prepare the text in a manner suitable for TEX, even though TEX itself may not be available. The actual transfer of files from one computer system to another is a well-trodden path by now.

There are many levels at which markup can be employed. At the very highest level, markup can be abstract: we can consider entities like 'Preface', 'Chapter', 'Section', and so on – in other words, the *logical* structure of the document. This is the sort of approach that SGML and *Scribe* adopt. The actual details of how the text looks on the page are not considered. This is simply an arbitrary realization of the overall concept *book*. This sort of markup is usually termed 'declarative', and contrasts with 'procedural' markup, where much more detailed and specific information is provided. At this lower 'procedural' level, we say that we want a certain typeface, we want subscripts to be a particular height, or the first line of a paragraph to be indented by a particular amount. TEX is capable of this degree of detail. There are strong arguments that authors should *not* be permitted this sort of control. Some of them seem valid. At the very least, authors should not really have to consider these minutiae whilst in the throes of composition. However, part of the beauty of TEX is that it can form the basis of an abstract description, adequately bridging the gulf between concept and realization. One way of doing this is through the use of LATEX (which itself sets out to emulate *Scribe*). Although written entirely in TEX, this encourages an author to concentrate on the text, without having to worry too much about the details of the structure on the page (or the details of TEX). It is a reflection of the intimate mixing of content, structure, and TEX that LATEX only partly succeeds in its aim.

Declaration of independence

The overhead of going straight from text to typeset output was obviously high, and Knuth introduced a very convenient way around the problem. He introduced the *device* independent (`dvi`) file: this was an intermediate file produced by TEX which contained an account of where everything was arranged on the pages, which fonts were being used, and so on. But this `dvi` file was not specific for any particular output device, whether laser printer, typesetter, or whatever. The output device selected might be at any of a number of resolutions (say from 100 dpi to 5333 dpi), or may use different technologies to represent its fonts (for example, bit-maps, vector or bézier outlines, run-length encoding). The dvi file is simply independent of the characteristics of the output device – it is a neutral file. It is a very powerful interchange standard for TEX. Every TEX program, presented with the same input information, produces an *identical* dvi file. The dvi file may then be interrogated by any of a number of 'printer driver' programs, each written specifically for a given output device:

TEX document

↓

dvi file

↙ ↓ ↘

a variety of output devices

TEX itself is concerned only with the creation of the dvi file. When a new output device comes along, TEX is not rewritten. It is sufficient to write a new device driver. This modular approach helps to distribute TEX widely. A benefit of the approach is that it is possible to examine the results on a low-resolution device (low resolution often also means 'cheap'), and, if these results seem good, then to process the dvi file again for a higher-resolution printer (like a phototypesetter). Higher-resolution printers tend to be more expensive, and access to them may not be so straightforward. The important aspect is that TEX does not have to be used again, and that you will be confident after examining the 'proof' that the end product will be the same, only better. No nasty surprises will lie in store.

Of course, the real world is never quite this simple. The main fly in the ointment is font information. Different phototypesetters use different fonts. Although Knuth designed the Computer Modern family of typefaces, which are publicly available, they were not embraced by all typeface manufacturers. Part of the problem lies in the fact that METAFONT is really designed as a 'pixel' or bit-map font generator, and not all phototypesetters use this system. Therefore they would have to generate Computer Modern fonts from scratch, using their own system. This takes time and money, and as suggested earlier, typesetting technical text is a minority interest. Of course, you could also use the manufacturers' own fonts. The major drawbacks here are that the typeface information that TEX requires, like the size of each character and so on, is often a rather jealously guarded secret; that no lower-resolution pixel representation may be available, so that proofing on a laser printer or whatever has to be done using those typefaces available to the laser printer – which may be a little different; and lastly, that manufacturers' typefaces may not contain the rich set of characters which TEX takes for granted.

We should also be a little wary in our interpretation of 'resolution'. What does resolution really mean in this context? It means the ability to address so many independent dots per linear inch. It does not necessarily imply what size the individual dots are, nor does it say anything about their shape. Let's take an example. Many laser printers are rated at 300 dpi. They are able to address 300 dots per inch, both horizontally and vertically. We can reasonably expect the 'grid' to be Cartesian; this carries with it the expectation of lots of little squares (pixels) – 90,000 for every square inch on the page. If the page being marked is an A4 page, and if each pixel requires 1 bit, then the total amount of information (or better, the total number of bytes) required is about 1 megabyte. Doubling the number of dots per inch would quadruple the number of bytes required. The 'marking engine', the device which places 'marks' on the page, will not create neat little squares. It will tend to create little blobs, approximately circular in shape (in fact they are rather fuzzy almost-circles, if the machine is a laser printer). The blobs will likely overlap – they may each have a diameter greater than our 'nominal' $1/_{300}$th of an inch. They have to overlap to provide the necessary continuity for a character built up of lots of discrete pixels. The characteristics of the blob's outline will determine how the edge of a character looks, and will contribute to the overall look of the page.

Different technologies give different characteristics, and even different laser printers give different results. Many laser printers are 'write-black', which is to say that they are concerned with placing overlapping blobs of ink (or toner) on the page. The other major group is 'write-white'. The page starts out 'black' and the shapes on the page are formed by removing overlapping blobs of 'black' so that only the letters are left. One of the consequences of write-white is that very thin lines are difficult to draw (or rather, it is difficult to leave the thin line). In Figure 1.1, the grid represents the resolution of the device, with the black circles representing the action of the printer. On the left, a write-black printer creates a blobby vertical line, while on the right, a write-white printer erodes the surrounding area to leave a rather slimmer, shorter zone which will attract toner and result in a rather different perceived line.

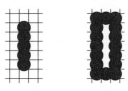

Figure 1.1
Write-black
(left) and write-
white (right)

The differences in technologies also help to explain why *wysiwyg* is so difficult to attain. The dots on a screen are much squarer than those on a laser printer and they do not overlap. On one of the Apple Macintosh implementations of TeX, for example, you can magnify the TeX characters so that you see the individual pixels which will be sent to the laser printer. This preview tends to make diagonal lines look very jagged (the staircase effect). On the laser printer, the same lines look much smoother, simply because of the shape of the individual pixels on the laser printer, and the smearing of the toner which takes place. The smearing or 'de-focusing' seems to help, and leads to a slightly more agreeable end product.

This does not imply that laser-printed output is perfect. Far from it. It can be good, and it can be quite suitable for many jobs. For books, it is generally agreed to be inadequate, although a fair number of books have been produced from laser-printed masters. With care, attention, and good-quality paper the end product can be quite tolerable. When the next generation of laser printers becomes generally available it should be possible to compete with traditional typesetting, which claims the capability of addressing from 700 to 5333 dots per inch.

Book notes

As the title of this book implies, it is a TeX *primer*. Its intention is to introduce TeX, and to provide the reader with sufficient information to get started with the majority of tasks which she or he wishes to tackle. It is in no way intended as a comprehensive discussion of all the nuances of TeX. Even Knuth's *The TeXbook* fails to cover all aspects of TeX. A major intention is to explain why TeX approaches its subject in the way it does, and to try to provide the 'context' into which it fits.

Not only is the book a 'primer', it is a 'plain' TeX primer. 'Plain' is not intended to imply 'straightforward or unadorned', it has a much more direct meaning than that. Wherever TeX is running, it comes with at least one basic style definition, called 'plain'.

This is a common starting point for many TeX users. It is a useful basic style, and lends itself to extension and modification to suit individual needs. There are of course other 'styles' like LaTeX and $\mathcal{AMS}$-TeX, but working with 'plain TeX' (plain, or plain TeX, as we will call it from now on) has its advantages.

Another thread will be the emphasis placed on document structure – and consequently on the 'declarative' side of markup, when this is appropriate. Naturally stress is laid on practical work. When the objective is to place marks on paper, placing marks on paper is an instructive way to illustrate points. It may be possible to obtain some impression of the scope of TeX by reading books on the subject, or looking closely at books prepared using TeX (a few of which are listed in Appendix B), but learning to use TeX, without the benefit of the software running on some sort of computer and an output device, would be to make learning an arduous task.

Just how arduous is it to learn TeX? That all depends. If you have a problem to solve – writing a book, a thesis, a paper – you probably won't find it very difficult. Remember that TeX is a typesetting system. Traditionally, to achieve competence in typesetting required an apprenticeship of many years. You do not become an expert typesetter overnight, or just because you have read the books. Some never become expert. We should not be surprised therefore if it takes some time to be at ease in TeX's company. Always bear in mind that we are emulating the setting of type, and not merely trying to improve on what a typewriter can do. Ultimately, we are following in the footsteps of Johann Gensfleisch zum Gutenberg and Aldus Manutius; the names of premier exponents of typewriting have not been handed down in the same way. The man credited with the design of the first practical typewriter, Christopher Sholes, is hardly a household name.

But not only is TeX a typesetting system, it aspires to the highest quality possible. Achieving quality demands some application too. If you come to TeX with very definite ideas of how you want things to look on the page, it will take some time before you see how to ease TeX into your own mould. Therefore, don't expect to do everything immediately. One of the minor problems associated with TeX is that many people come to it when all other packages have failed them – when they are doing something rather difficult. Not surprisingly, doing difficult things is sometimes difficult. There are things to learn about TeX before you start to do the really tricky things that it does to perfection. Let's assume that we can start close to the beginning. In that way the overall structure of TEX is much easier to grasp.

There is one terrible drawback to TEX that we must admit now: attempting to produce beautifully typeset documents through TEX can become compulsive. You end up using TEX for all documents, from shopping lists to books. Not only that, it becomes difficult to pick up a book without looking for clues to reveal the way it was produced, almost ignoring the content. Naturally this book was produced with TEX. Whatever is good in it is due to the excellence of TEX, and the far-sightedness of Donald Knuth. Whatever is less acceptable must be laid firmly to my account.

First last words

A book like this has a number of 'orthogonal' axes. On the face of it, it should be possible to lay out the material in a sequential fashion, introducing and developing concepts which slowly accrete to the whole body of knowledge. This is a rather naive and oversimplified expectation. Naturally the aim of any author is to make the obscure more straightforward, to sketch the grand design into which everything else fits more snuggly. And naturally, every author, despite the evidence, likes to hope that she or he has done so. There is a grand design to TEX. The more I work with it, the more convinced I am of it. But the closer I get to it, the more difficult it is to grasp. It is a huge world, and we see only facets of it. I suspect that even Knuth did not envisage the scope and breadth of TEX. This indicates to me that it really is a work of genius. It is more powerful than it was built to be. This does not mean it is without flaws. Nothing 'manufactured' ever is. Knuth has already discussed the 'Errors of TEX' in a paper presented to the TEX Users Group annual meeting in 1989. There are also some fundamental flaws and shortcomings.

There is another question lurking in the shadows. Ought we really to be teaching TEX at all? TEX is a markup language. In its rawest form it can be a very explicit form of typographic markup, more or less describing every movement of the hypothetical pieces of type. It is almost an environment in which Gutenberg or Manutius would have felt (fairly) comfortable. It seems to me that Knuth never really expected TEX to be used in its rawer forms. There are a number of places where he indicates that he expected TEX to be hidden under layers of a user interface. This is of course what $\mathcal{AMS}$-TEX and LATEX do. There are other examples around, but none has achieved the widespread currency of these two. The problem which arises with LaTeX (for example) is that to extend it beyond its present structures requires fairly advanced skills. Competence in LaTeX is not hard to acquire; even the most rushed can end up with something which is acceptable. Doing something which lies outside LaTeX's defaults requires much more than competence in LaTeX. So the answer to the question is 'Yes, we should be teaching TeX.' But we should not necessarily be promoting TeX as the tool for Everyman.

We should not lose sight of the objective. TeX is a typesetting tool. In our environment, it is a software tool, like a multitude of other software tools. In the final analysis, we are producing bits of paper (some sort of written communication); that is how we should be judged. Not for our craft with TeX; for our craft with words on the page.

Getting started 2

First steps

TEX can do all sorts of very clever things, but it seems sensible to try to do all sorts of ordinary things first, and then migrate to the more esoteric later.

Experience is a potential, if expensive, teacher; let us examine what happens when we run some text through TEX. An example input file, named **EXAMPLE**, is listed in Figure 2.1, and the result of running that file through TEX is shown in Figure 2.2. The text presented was prepared using an ordinary editor, and was simply typed in without any particular attention to line endings, or any sort of 'formatting'. The 'formatting' will be TEX's concern, not ours. The only concession to the 'logical' structure of the text has been to divide the text into paragraphs, by leaving a blank line at the end of each paragraph.

Before going through the details of running TEX now, examine the input and output. From a brief glance of the input to Figure 2.1, it appears that we had to do very little in order to turn a text entered at the keyboard into something which looks fairly presentable. Although TEX is a markup language, there is actually very little visible markup in this example: in fact, a great deal has been done for us by default. TEX has a 'default' set of descriptions built into it, which specify things like:

▷ the typeface to be used and its size,
▷ the height and width of the mass of text on the page,
▷ the gap between individual lines,
▷ the gap between each paragraph,
▷ the indentation on the first line of each paragraph,
▷ the style of page numbering to be used (Roman numerals or Arabic), and
▷ where the page number should be placed (if you choose to have one at all),

just to mention a few of the straightforward and obvious ones. These are all defaults, and may therefore be changed – you can control them all. In fact, these are not even part of TeX. They are part of a default style, available to TeX on a special file usually termed `plain`; `plain` may be considered a 'style-sheet'. We may alter or add to this `plain` style.

Plain typesetting

Perhaps the first thing that we may notice is just how ordinary the typeset text in Figure 2.2 looks. It almost looks like any other printed page. This is rather comforting, since it is exactly what we are aiming for. The typeface is just that – a 'type' face, recognizably similar to that used in printed documents.

The text is divided up into paragraphs. How did TeX 'know' to paragraph? TeX has a number of ways of signifying paragraphs – one of them is by leaving an entirely blank line. This text uses such a blank line to indicate a paragraph break. The first line of every paragraph is indented by a fixed amount. This is a fairly standard convention. *Typewritten* text tends not to be indented, but there is often an extra line inserted between paragraphs just to separate them out. These typewriter conventions are not really appropriate with typeset material, so TeX substitutes new (appropriate) conventions. You may notice that there is a shade more space between paragraphs than between lines within paragraphs. Typeset material has more 'fine' control over the position of text than typewritten.

While the 'original' text was entered with no regard to aligning the right margin, TeX has also taken care to justify the text, so that all lines (with the exception of the first and last in a paragraph) are of the same length, and they all line up on their left and right margins.

Ligatures

But there is nothing very much out of the ordinary here, until we start to look more closely. TeX is a typesetting system, and has built into it the expectations and requirements of genuine typsetting. One feature which often distinguishes typesetting is the use of ligatures. Ligatures are recognized 'runnings together' of letters, to form a new symbol. The most common examples are fi, ffi, fl, ffl, and ff. This is not simply a 'very close' duo or trio of

I stuffed a shirt or two into my old carpet-bag, tucked
it under my arm, and started for Cape Horn and the
Pacific. Quitting the good city of old Manhatto, I duly
arrived in New Bedford. It was on a Saturday night in
December. Much was I disappointed upon learning that the
little packet for Nantucket had already sailed, and that
no way of reaching that place would offer, till the
following Monday.

As most young candidates for the pains and penalties of
whaling stop at this same New Bedford, thence to embark on
their voyage, it may as well be related that I, for one,
had no idea of so doing. For my mind was made up to sail
in no other than a Nantucket craft, because there was a
fine boisterous something about everything connected with
that famous old island, which amazingly pleased me.
Besides though New Bedford has of late been gradually
monopolizing the business of whaling, and though in this
matter poor old Nantucket is now much behind her, yet
Nantucket was her great original -- the Tyre of this
Carthage; -- the place where the first dead American
whale was stranded. Where else but from Nantucket did
those aboriginal whalemen, the Red-Men, first sally out in
canoes to give chase to the Leviathan? And where but from
Nantucket, too, did that first adventurous little sloop
put forth, partly laden with imported cobblestones -- so
goes the story -- to throw at the whales, in order to
discover when they were nigh enough to risk a harpoon from
the bowsprit?

Now having a night, a day, and still another
night following before me in New Bedford, ere I could
embark for my destined port, it became a matter of
concernment where I was to eat and sleep meanwhile. It was
a very dubious-looking, nay, a very dark and dismal
night, bitingly cold and cheerless. I knew no-one in the
place. With anxious grapnels I had sounded my pocket, and
only brought up a few pieces of silver, -- ''So, wherever
you go, Ishmael,'' said I to myself, as I stood in the
middle of a dreary street shouldering my bag, and
comparing the gloom towards the north with the darkness
towards the south -- ''wherever in your wisdom you may
conclude to lodge for the night, my dear Ishmael, be sure
to inquire the price, and don't be too particular.''

Figure 2.1
Source (part)

individual letters, but a complete new symbol. Historically, there have been other ligatured letters. It was not uncommon to ligature c and t together up to the early 19th century. Other languages expect other ligatures too – German, for example, has a ch ligature. Scandinavian languages usually have an fj ligature. Since this letter combination is vanishingly rare in English, few English or American typefaces will have this particular ligature. Ligatures are not present in all typefaces. But even within a single typeface, different realizations may have different conventions. The 'generic' Times family (a very commonly used typeface) normally has ligatures, but *The Times* itself seems to have dispensed with their use. Within the immediate world of personal typesetting and 'desktop publishing' some typefaces which 'should' support ligatures may not. It is a key question whether you would have noticed the lack of these features before they were pointed out. If you did not, just how important were they in the first place? Does this really look any different and more difficult to read?

Kerning

Another feature of much typesetting is the use of kerning. Kerning refers to the closing up of the gap between letters in a word to give them the appearance of a more regular placement. In particular, letters which have strong diagonal elements, like A, K, V, W, X, and Y, may require kerning when placed next to some other letters. 'AWE' may look awfully ugly unless the gap between the A and the W is closed up to give AWE. Of course the effect is not limited to juxtapositions of capital letters, although the use of diagonals for lower case is less prevalent (k, v, w, x, y). To obtain a 'pleasing' appearance when one of a number of lower-case letters follows a capital T, we ought to kern. Did you notice an unsightly gap in the first word of the previous sentence? Compare 'To' and 'To'. The presence and extent of kerning depends upon the typefaces being used. Kerning is not supported in all fonts. In particular, you would probably not want kerning in a font which was supposed to have the appearance of typewriter characters.

Where did the information necessary for ligatures and kerning come from? Each font which TEX uses has an associated 'TEX font metric' (or `tfm`) file which contains information on the dimensions of characters in that font; it also includes details of how particular letter pairs should be kerned and which character combinations are to be ligatured.

I stuffed a shirt or two into my old carpet-bag, tucked it under my arm, and started for Cape Horn and the Pacific. Quitting the good city of old Manhatto, I duly arrived in New Bedford. It was on a Saturday night in December. Much as I disappointed upon learning that the little packet for Nantucket had already sailed, and that no way of reaching that place would offer, till the following Monday.

As most young candidates for the pains and penalties of whaling stop at this same New Bedford, thence to embark on their voyage, it may as well be related that I, for one, had no idea of so doing. For my mind was made up to sail in no other than a Nantucket craft, because there was a fine boisterous something about everything connected with that famous old island, which amazingly pleased me. Besides though New Bedford has of late been gradually monopolizing the business of whaling, and though in this matter poor old Nantucket is now much behind her, yet Nantucket was her great original — the Tyre of this Carthage; — the place where the first dead American whale was stranded. Where else but from Nantucket did those aboriginal whalemen, the Red-Men, first sally out in canoes to give chase to the Leviathan? And where but from Nantucket, too, did that first adventurous little sloop put forth, partly laden with imported cobblestones — so goes the story — to throw at the whales, in order to discover when they were nigh enough to risk a harpoon from the bowsprit?

Now having a night, a day, and still another night following before me in New Bedford, ere I could embark for my destined port, it became a matter of concernment where I was to eat and sleep meanwhile. It was a very dubious-looking, nay, a very dark and dismal night, bitingly cold and cheerless. I knew no-one in the place. With anxious grapnels I had sounded my pocket, and only brought up a few pieces of silver, "So, wherever you go, Ishmael," said I to myself, as I stood in the middle of a dreary street shouldering my bag, and comparing the gloom towards the north with the darkness towards the south — "wherever in your wisdom you may conclude to lodge for the night, my dear Ishmael, be sure to inquire the price, and don't be too particular."

Moving on, I at last came to a dim sort of light not far from the docks, and heard a forlorn creaking in the air; and looking up, saw a swinging sign over the door with a white painting upon it, faintly representing a tall straight jet of misty spray, and these words underneath — 'The Spouter-Inn: — Peter Coffin.'

"Coffin? — Spouter? — Rather ominous in that particular connexion," thought I. "But it is a common name in Nantucket, they say, and I suppose this Peter is an emigrant from there." As the light looked so dim, and the place, for the time, looked quiet enough, and the dilapidated little wooden house itself looked as if it might have been carted here from the ruins of some burnt district, and as the swinging sign had a poverty-stricken sort of creak to it, I thought that here was the very spot for cheap lodgings, and the best pea coffee.

It was a queer sort of place — a gable-ended old house, one side palsied as it were, and leaning over sadly. It stood on a sharp bleak corner, where that tempestuous wind Euroclydon kept up a worse howling than it ever did about poor Paul's tossed craft. Euroclydon, nevertheless, is a mighty pleasant zephyr to any one in-doors, with his feet on the hob quietly toasting for bed. "In judging of that tempestuous wind called Euroclydon," says an old writer — of whose works I possess the only copy extant — "it maketh a marvellous difference, whether thou lookest out at it from a glass window where the frost is all on the outside, or whether thou observest it from that sashless window, where the frost is on both sides, and of which the wight Death is the only glazier." True enough, thought I, as this passage occurred to my mind — old black-letter, thou reasonest well. Yes, these eyes are windows, and this body of mine is the house. What a pity they don't stop up the chinks and crannies though, and thrust in a little lint here and there. But it's too late to make any improvements now. The universe is finished; the copestone is on, and the chips were carted off a million years ago. Poor Lazarus there, chattering his teeth against the curbstone for his pillow, and shaking off his tatters with his shiverings, he might plug up both ears with rags, and put a corn-cob into his mouth, and yet that would not keep out the tempestuous Euroclydon. What a fine frosty night; how Orion glitters; what northern lights! Let them talk of their oriental summer climes of everlasting conservatories; give me the privilege of making my own summer with my own coals.

But what thinks Lazarus? Can he warm his blue hands by holding them up to the grand northern lights? Would not Lazarus rather be in Sumatra than here? Would he not far rather lay him down lengthwise along the line of the equator; yea, ye gods! go down to the fiery pit itself, in order to keep out this frost?

But no more of this blubbering now, we are going a-whaling, and there is plenty of that yet to come. Let us scrape this ice from our frosted feet, and see what sort of place this 'Spouter' may be.

1

Figure 2.2

After T_EX
(reduced in
size)

Individually, the effects of ligaturing and kerning may seem very slight and of limited significance. Taken cumulatively, over an entire page, or a book, they do contribute to the feel and texture of the text. The printed page is more than just the meaning of the words. The patterning and presentation can help to influence our interpretation, perhaps at rather subtle levels.

"Quotes"

There are other symbols used in typesetting (but not in type-writing) which TₑX can supply. Quotation marks (that is, double inverted commas) come in open and close varieties in many type-faces. Usually the 'open quote' looks like a miniaturized 66, while the 'close quote' is like a 99. TₑX employs the quote (also known as *apostrophe* and *prime*) and grave. Unfortunately, some characters like the grave do not have standardized positions, and their location may differ from keyboard to keyboard. On some keyboards, especially those with 'national' characters, the grave is nowhere to be found, but is accessible through the 'alternate' characters. But in order to overcome these areas of potential confusion and keyboard inadequacies, TₑX does provide a way of accessing these and other apparently absent symbols, which we will encounter later. The keyboard provides you with only a single left or right quote mark at a time: TₑX *ligatures* two successive quote marks, whether they be grave or 'quote', to form a single 'double' quote mark. Thus, to form a double open quote mark on output, type two graves – ' '; and to form the corresponding double close quote, type two quotes – ' '. The double quote symbol on your keyboard will probably not translate into the correct symbol on your type-set output. Most likely it will be treated as a 'close double quote' symbol, but this transformation is nowhere defined in TₑX (except in the typewriter font, where no distinction is made between open and close quotes, and all ligatures are disabled anyway).

Dash

One other feature to note is the dash symbol. In fact, dashes come in lots of forms. Formally we identify the following: the hyphen, the en-dash, the em-dash, and the minus sign (Figure 2.3). In most typestyles these will be different characters.

A *hyphen* is fairly obvious, and is conveyed to TₑX as a - symbol. Hyphens are commonly used when a word has to be broken

Name	TEX	Typeset	Example
hyphen	-	-	hy-phen
en-dash	--	–	1–7
em-dash	---	—	Knuth—the archiTEXt
minus	-	–	$x - y$

Figure 2.3
Dash

up between lines. Note that, should this happen, TEX normally determines the hyphenation point, and actually inserts the hyphen itself. If you explicitly type a hyphen – as in 'pin-prick' – TEX will honour it. But there are two sorts of hyphen. One is used to indicate that a word has been divided in some way, usually at a line boundary, but the 'link-hyphen' is used in words like 'half-baked' or 'single-engined' to indicate that the words are to be linked in some way, not divided. Any word which contains such a 'link-hyphen' will be permitted to break there, but will not be given any other hyphens by TEX, no matter how long that word may be.

The text given here will not have many hyphens inserted by TEX's hyphenation algorithm, for reasons which become more obvious later. You should only include deliberate hyphens in your input text, ones which you wish to see in the typeset version. If you are using a word processor as the source for TEX input, make sure that it does not do any hyphenation for you.

An *en-dash* is a longer symbol (historically the length of an N in the current font, or, more correctly, half the length of an em-dash), and is therefore conveyed to TEX as --; an en-dash is usually employed to convey the idea of a numerical range, for example 1–10.

The *em-dash* is even longer, and is given to TEX as ---. The em-dash is punctuation in text. An em-dash, as its name suggests, has something to do with an M. Traditionally, an em was the width of an M-squared: imagine the bounding *square* of an M in any chosen font. (Why an M? Simple, it is the largest letter in any particular font.) The length of that bounding square would be the length of an em (in that font). In fact, a piece of type of those dimensions was termed a 'quad'. Which leads us into a rather circular definition for a quad. But the length of both a quad and an em are about the same as an M. More important, in TEX they have the property of being font related.

In this book, the en-dash is used for punctuation in text. It also differs from Knuth's usage by having space on either side. This has some interesting repercussions which will be noted later. The em-dash *should* be nowhere to be found (except for this chapter).

Lastly, the *minus* is a mathematical symbol which has to be given in maths mode as $-$. The whole topic of mathematical setting will be addressed later.

The typeset text also has page numbers at the foot. You will discover that you have great control over the layout and content of whatever is printed both at the head and foot of a page.

If we measure the dimensions of the text on the page, it should turn out to occupy an area 6.5 inches by 8.9 inches. These dimensions, set up in `plain`, are suitable for the US Letter page size (275 mm × 215 mm; or 10.8 in × 8.46 in): these are sufficiently close to A4 (297 mm × 210 mm; or 11.7 in × 8.27 in) for now. Later we will want to change them to something better. Naturally, margins are left around the text, and the text is usually centred within the (US Letter) page. The position of the text on output is not actually TEX's concern. It has no way of knowing what output medium is likely to be selected. If you recall the device independent nature of TEX, this ignorance is clearly deliberate, and the responsibility of appropriate positioning on the page is that of the program which handles the printing of the page.

It would not be true to say that there was no explicit TEX instruction in the input text. Right at the end is the command `\end`. This is a command to instruct TEX that it is to terminate processing. Without this command, TEX will sit quietly, expecting further text (or instructions). All TEX commands are introduced by the 'backslash' character. Fortunately, it is a character which is seldom encountered in normal text.

Leaping into the dark

We now have to consider how to run TEX on the system you have available. Since TEX is available on a very wide range of systems, all that can be offered here is a broad outline of the likely routeway.

Almost inevitably, there will be a system command called `TEX` which will run the program. If you are using a *wimp* – window, icon, mouse, and pull-down menu – system, like a Macintosh or an Atari, then this command may be replaced by a menu selection. Assume that we have a file `EXAMPLE` which contains text which we wish to process with TEX. The majority of computer systems expect file names to have an 'extension' which in some way identifies the type of file. If your system requires these file name extensions, the appropriate one for a TEX file is `.TEX`. The 'correct' name for our input file is probably `EXAMPLE.TEX`. You can use either upper- or lower-case letters, the operating system *probably* won't mind. TEX itself is rather more fussy, but we are not yet using TEX.

In order to start things happening, we should be able to issue a command (or make a menu selection) like
TEX EXAMPLE
This starts the TEX processor off, and provides sufficient information to have it use the contents of the file EXAMPLE.TEX. Because you have not provided a file name extension, TEX is smart enough to assume that the extension ought to be .TEX. If you were to provide the extension explicitly, then the default extension .TEX would be overridden by whatever you had typed at this point. This operation creates the .dvi or *device independent* file:

example.tex

TEX

example.dvi

Unfortunately, the .dvi file is not immediately useful to us. It is not 'human-readable', although it does contain masses of useful information. We need some way of viewing the output, either in a preview form, on a screen, or on hard copy from a matrix or laser printer. How you do this is highly dependent on your particular system. But it is not necessary to have 'typeset' output in order to learn something useful. As you are running TEX some information will have flashed up on the screen before you. A transcript, an even more extensive version of what is appearing on the screen, will be written to a log file. If your system supports file name extensions it will probably be given the extension .log or .list and its name will be whatever was the first file to be input to TEX. This is often a useful source of additional information. The log file obtained from running EXAMPLE.TEX through TEX is given here:
Textures 1.4 (preloaded format=plain 91.6.24)
                                        1 MAR 1992 15:21
(example [1]
Output written on example (1 page, 6699 bytes).
There is not a great deal of information here, but then not a great deal untoward happened. The [1] shows the page number of the pages being set, and is a useful indication of what TEX is doing. Other log files can contain more information, some of it useful.

However, let's be a little more honest and admit that typographically we should not be entirely satisfied with the appearance of our text as set by the default plain. The lines are rather too long for the size of type that we are using. The usual recommended line length for this size of type would be somewhere between 3 and 4.5 inches (treat this recommendation as a guide, not a command). The range is due to the fact that type size is not the only variable at work here. Why then are we using 6.5 inches for the line length? If you are using either a matrix printer or a laser printer as your output device, you will be able to work out why. Most paper available in an office environment is A4 size (or the similar US Letter size). Why should that be so? Because of the legacy of typewriting: using a conventional typewriter, with an elite or pica 'typeface', constant character widths, and healthy margins, these are good paper sizes; and not unnaturally, the manufacturers of office equipment perpetuated this size when they manufactured photocopiers, laser printers, and all the other paraphernalia that we take for granted in a conventionally equipped office. This only 'explains' the line width, it does not account for the type size which TEX selects by default. TEX's type size default is appropriate for books, especially scientific books.

Figure 2.4 indicates some recommendations made by a number of typographers, document designers, and hacks. It requires just a bit of interpretation, since almost every suggestion uses different units. Words and letters are easy enough to interpret, but does 'characters' imply 'all characters, including blanks'? It certainly does for Lamport, but may not for Miles. Nevertheless, the general consensus is about 10 words, or 60–65 letters/characters, however we interpret that. The word count rather suggests 'words in English', so the letter/character count is perhaps a more general one, although there may well be stylistic differences between some national printing conventions. Note how difficult it is to come up with rules in this context.

Measurement

Before we can contemplate changing our line width, we must know what units TEX can understand. In fact, TEX is quite flexible, and can cope with a variety of measurement systems, like printer's points, picas, didôt points, millimetres and centimetres, as well as inches. Curiously, there are two sorts of printer's points in TEX. One of them is termed a 'big point'. In fact it is not very much bigger at all, as the conversion table (Figure 2.5) shows. TEX's is the real and true printer's point, but the 'big point' is the one adopted by a fair number of computer terminal manufacturers,

Guru	Measure
Stanley Morison	10–12 words
Karl Treebus	10–12 words, 60–70 letters
John Miles	60–65 characters
Leslie Lamport	≤ 75 characters
Linotype	7–10 words, 50–65 letters
Alison Black	60–70 letters

Figure 2.4
Suggested line
widths

who make screens which give a resolution of '72 dots to the inch'.
The distortion introduced is not likely to be very noticeable.

You may use whichever of the dimensions you like, and you do
not have to stick to any one preferred system. But, although real
printers in the UK use picas and points together – 'two picas and
four points' – TeX will insist that you use only one measurement
system for any one measurement.

TeX uses the conversions as *exact* ratios. Any value preceding
one of these dimensions may be specified as either a whole (integer)
number, or one with a decimal point. Since TeX does not support
mixtures of dimensions, the 'two picas and four points' would only
be acceptable as 2.3333333 pc or 28 pt. The 'scaled point' is something new, and something specific to TeX. The scaled point is the
really fundamental, or 'atomic', dimension. Every measurement
is converted to scaled points *inside* TeX. Scaled points may take
only integer values. This helps ensure that every version of TeX
everywhere produces the same results, since every one works in
the same base units.

Abbreviation	Name	Exact conversion
pt	point	
pc	pica	$1\,pc = 12\,pt$
in	inch	$1\,in = 72.27\,pt$
bp	big point	$72\,bp = 1\,in$
cm	centimeter	$1\,in = 2.54\,cm$
mm	millimeter	$10\,mm = 1\,cm$
dd	didôt point	$1157\,dd = 1238\,pt$
cc	cicero	$1\,cc = 12\,dd$
sp	scaled point	$65536\,sp = 2^{16}\,sp = 1\,pt$
em	width of a quad	
ex	height of 'x'	

Figure 2.5
Printing
dimensions
understood by
TeX

The printer's point makes some sort of sense as a base unit,
since all the fonts are described only in terms of their 'point' size.

But outside that particular area, any other 'size' can be described in any of the above dimensions. If you do not include a dimension, TₑX will often assume points are meant; it is safer to give the dimension.

The structure of TₑX commands

The one explicit TₑX command already used – \end – provides a clue to the form of the commands we will use to control the horizontal extent of the text. TₑX has literally hundreds of special 'commands', which are all of a similar form – a backslash followed by one or more characters. In very general terms, the commands tend to have some sort of mnemonic quality. After all, \end was fairly explicit. In any system which employs mnemonic commands there is a tension between explanation and brevity. While it is very comforting to the beginner to have a command which is self-explanatory (and therefore rather long-winded), the more experienced user tends to prefer something which takes less time to type in. To a large extent TₑX has managed to accommodate this by employing a small number of regular abbreviations; almost every command which has to do with 'horizontal' will start with an h (and 'vertical' with a v). The longer commands are reserved for things which will in general be found only once within the text. Thus the commands you tend to use frequently are short (and because you use them frequently you tend to remember them), while infrequently used commands are longer, and more self-explanatory.

Professional typesetting systems tend to take the brevity of commands to extremes, insisting that a single letter will be sufficient for a command. This tends to make such systems rather intimidating for the novice, but they are not systems used by novices. Further, those who use them are often paid by the keystroke. Short commands imply less keystroking (and perhaps higher productivity).

The page size

The command used by TₑX to control the line length (or width) is \hsize, that is to say, 'horizontal size'. There is a corresponding \vsize for the vertical extent of the text on the page. Both of the sizing commands require more information; they require a number and a dimension:

```
\hsize=6.5in
\vsize=8.9in
```

The equals sign is entirely optional; its inclusion often helps to make things clearer. Any TeX command which sets up a general size characteristic for the document, where some 'size' is followed by a number and a dimension, may also include an equals sign. The dimension is *always* given as an abbreviation, *never* as its longer, explicit form. Note also that all this dialogue is in lower case. TeX is 'case sensitive', and will discriminate between commands in upper and lower case: \hsize is different from \Hsize and \HSIZE.

These two commands were presented on consecutive lines. We could have written them both on the same line:

```
\hsize=6.5in\vsize=8.9in
```

but this is a little less easy to read. The choice is yours – it is largely a stylistic one. From TeX's viewpoint there is no difference.

TeX has a large number of predefined commands. If your command is not recognized, it will tell you, and you have a slim chance to correct the input interactively.

Fundamental commands

So far we have described three specific commands, two of which allow us some control over layout. Besides the page dimensions, TeX needs to have information about the fonts we wish to use, the distance between lines, the distance between paragraphs, the indentation on the first line of a paragraph, and so on. Within the plain description, this is set up by commands which have been specified in a form like:

```
\baselineskip=12pt
\parskip=20pt
\parindent=15pt
```

These are not necessarily the actual values and dimensions which appear in plain, they are simply examples of the commands which control certain key features.

The vertical distance between character baselines is termed \baselineskip by TeX. It is easiest to view baselines in the context of characters like a, b, and c – those without descenders. Descenders are found on letters like g, j, p, q, and y; except in a few typefaces upper-case letters very rarely have descenders

(Q and J are the common exceptions); on the other hand, the height of a lower-case letter with an 'ascender' and the height of an upper-case letter are usually (but not always) the same. The baseline is then simply the base of the character. The 'baseline skip' should normally be greater than the font size. A common recommendation is that the baseline skip should be about 20% greater than the type size. Since we shall tend to work with 10 point fonts to begin with, a good value for \baselineskip is about 12 points. A typesetter might describe such an arrangement as '10 on 12' or 10/12: that is to say, a 10 point typeface on baselines which are 12 points apart. In fact, the typesetter would be more inclined to describe the typeset material as having 'two points of leading', where the leading is the extra space in addition to the notional minimum between lines – in this case, two points. Sometimes you need more flexibility in where the baselines are, but we will discuss this later. For the time being we will be rather inflexible.

Where do these commands go? Since they describe a characteristic of the formatting which is intended to apply to all of the text, they should be placed at the beginning of the text. T_EX reads these commands first, they override the default values built into T_EX, and formatting proceeds appropriately. There is no reason why commands need not be placed elsewhere within the text. Note that since T_EX handles a paragraph at a time, it adopts whichever of the paragraph-relevant commands was last encountered for that and any following paragraphs. In other words, even if we place \baselineskip=20pt right in the middle of a paragraph, expecting that the lines before the command will take the default baseline and those after will have the new value, we will be sadly disappointed.

Paragraphs

The other two commands refer to paragraphs. While individual lines have some identity in a typeset work, paragraphs represent some sort of 'logical entity' from the viewpoint of meaning.

The distance between the end of one paragraph and the beginning of the next is the 'paragraph skip' or \parskip. If this value is set to zero, the distance between paragraphs will simply be the same as that between lines of text within a paragraph.

The first line of any paragraph is generally indented. The amount of indentation is termed the \parindent. Indentation

Typeface style	Font name	Command
Computer Modern Roman	cmr10	\rm
Computer Modern Bold Extended Roman	cmbx10	\bf
Computer Modern Slanted Roman	cmsl10	\sl
Computer Modern Text Italic	cmti10	\it
Computer Modern Typewriter	cmtt10	\tt

Figure 2.6
Basic fonts

is sometimes written 'indention', but that is pedantry.

In general terms, books have a paragraph skip of 0 point, and a paragraph indentation of perhaps 20 or 30 points. (It is perhaps better to express this as 2 or 3 ems since the em is a 'context-sensitive' measure. Remember too the corresponding 'ex' for vertical measure – the height of the letter x.) Although these are good values for books, they may not be appropriate for articles, memos, letters, etc. A rather fuzzy rule sometimes used in typesetting is to indent lines of up to 3 inches by 1 em, and for every additional inch or part of an inch, to increase the indent by half an em. Again, this is only to be considered a guide.

Earlier the blank line was described as a way of indicating the end of a paragraph. This is an implicit piece of markup. There is another explicit command – \par. As soon as this is encountered a paragraph will be terminated.

Fonts

TEX is at its very best with a few fonts: these fonts form the Computer Modern family. At present we will concentrate on a subset of this font family: CM Roman, CM Text Italic, CM Bold Extended Roman, CM Slanted Roman, CM Typewriter, and, in addition, the CM Math Symbol and CM Math Extension fonts – they are sufficient for our immediate needs. These TEX fonts are often available at a wide variety of sizes, but right now we will stick with a small range of sizes, based on 10 point.

In passing, note that 'Modern' of 'Computer Modern' does not imply 'contemporary', or even recent. The first typefaces describing themselves as 'Modern' were introduced towards the end of the 18th century. Computer Modern itself is a reasonably faithful emulation of Monotype Modern 8A, and many typographers would consider it a little old-fashioned by contemporary standards.

TEX is unable to handle the extremely long and descriptive names that we have used, and has to employ a shortened form to refer to the font: the translation of the five fundamental 10 point

'text' fonts outlined above is given in Figure 2.6. The mnemonics
\rm, \it, and so on are relatively meaningful.

These are all 10 point fonts. What does that mean? One way to
create typefaces is with reference to a 'design size'. Or put another
way, this particular font was designed to be seen at a particular
size. Had the designer been concerned to have the typeface used at
a different size, she or he would have designed another face, more
suited to that particular size. This is a somewhat idealized viewpoint. At a practical level, designers sometimes create typefaces
which may be 'the same' over a range of sizes, designing perhaps
four or five subtly different designs to cover a typical range from
4 pt to 72 pt or bigger. The real purist would argue that even two
faces 1 point different in size ought to be designed differently. But
life is too short. Some typefaces are merely magnified over their
entire range. This is probably an oversimplification, but for many
reasons it is a solution popular with the manufacturers of typesetting equipment. T_EX adopts both solutions, as we shall see later.

Why bother giving the two names? After all, Computer Modern
Roman is reasonably unambiguous. The answer is twofold. Firstly,
'Computer Modern Roman' is a 'type style'; that is to say, it is
simply one of a range of styles in the general typeface 'Computer
Modern'. It does not describe the size that we will use. A 'font'
is a particular realization of a type style, at a particular size. We
could therefore talk of 'Computer Modern Roman at 10 point'
to describe a font. Secondly, from a computer's viewpoint it is
more convenient to call the font cmr10, rather than the longer,
descriptive, human-readable form. In the end we have to admit
that T_EX is occasionally suborned by the realities of computing.
In fact, the short name is a sort of file name. This helps explain
the brevity, especially when we realize that on many operating
systems, file names are severely limited in length (perhaps to as
few as eight characters).

plain T_EX sets up a connecting link for these five basic fonts,
so that the commands \rm, \it, \bf, \sl, and \tt will produce
the following effects:

\rm   the quick brown fox comes to the aid of the party
\it   *the quick brown fox comes to the aid of the party*
\bf   **the quick brown fox comes to the aid of the party**
\sl   *the quick brown fox comes to the aid of the party*
\tt   `the quick brown fox comes to the aid of the party`

To those interested in typography in general, the slanted font
is really one of the few new developments in typographic design.

Appendix A gives examples of the fonts which form the default Computer Modern family.

By default `plain` TEX assumes you will be starting your document with `\rm`. Thus if you make no conscious decision, you will be in Computer Modern Roman at 10 point. This is a reasonably good all-purpose font, very suitable for technical documentation, where the information content of the typeface itself must be low, in order that it does not detract from the material itself – that is, where the medium should not interfere with the message. For emphasis you can use *slant* and **bold**. Do not use underlining on a laser printer or typesetter. It does not look right. (Like all rules, this <u>may</u> be broken.) It is very tempting to use lots of different fonts (and sizes, when you learn how to) in the same piece of work. Unless you are preparing advertising material, where the function is to arrest the eye and confuse the mind, you will probably find that 'less is best'. In general, the function of a change in type style is to emphasize, or perhaps to separate, classes of text (for example, spoken word, implied stress). If you employ too many changes, the whole notion of emphasis or separation tends to fall apart, and you are left with a patchwork of cute typefaces. Used sparingly, a change in font can have great effect, at a rather subtle level. Remember too that typefaces tend to be designed in 'families', where there is some sort of common theme between them – a family relationship. Gaily swapping from family to family can lead to a cacophonous jumble. In the end, the responsibility is yours. You may want a cacophonous and slightly off-key presentation. This is unusual in scholarly work, but can be entirely appropriate in other areas.

Groups

TEX has a very powerful feature which allows it to 'group' material which is, in some sense, to be treated as a unit. The left and right brace – { and } – form a *transparent* set of brackets, which are useful in a myriad of circumstances. Braces may be used in TEX script itself, where chunks of text are braced. The braces themselves will not appear in output, but their effects might. For example

```
A {\bf bold} example is needed now
```
would have the effect of setting the word 'bold' in the bold font:

A **bold** example is needed now

while the remainder would be in whatever was the current font. Equally, we could have said

`and here an even \bf bolder \rm example is needed`

where we 'flag' the font changes. However, this has the effect of putting us into roman type after bold, which might not be the correct effect. To take a specific example, we might be including a quotation within our text. Commonly, quotations are presented in italics. If we are in a quotation and using `\bf` for emphasis, then we have to remember to change back to the current font, in this case `\it`. Why not let TEX remember the current font by using grouping? Why should you have to retain all this extra information? Similarly, it is not unknown to decide to change some of the conventions used for presentation – to decide that quotes really ought to be in `\sl` instead. Now we have to go through the entire document changing every `\it` which occurs within a quote to `\sl`. This need not be the same as changing every `\it` to `\sl`, a relatively trivial task with a text editor.

Grouping can be carried on to any depth (that is, braces within braces within braces. . .) with the only provision that they must be balanced. Actually TEX will supply extra closing braces under some circumstances, but this is hardly to be encouraged.

The notion of a braced group is pervasive within TEX. Without the braces, and the concept underlying them, TEX would have far less power.

Do it yourself 3

The handful of commands which were introduced in the last chapter were introduced with the idea that we can now re-run the `EXAMPLE.TEX` file, changing the various parameters. We can generate more white space between lines by increasing the value associated with the baseline skip, put more white space between paragraphs, change the font we are using; but more useful at this stage would be to alter the page dimensions. Changing the page width in particular will most quickly generate interesting, educational, results.

An A4 page has a width somewhere in the region of 600 points (over 8 inches), but making the `\hsize` larger does not do anything very interesting. We shall make the page narrower, as if we were creating columns for a newspaper.

The object of this particular exercise (running some text through TEX) is to note that things start to happen when you squeeze TEX's page width by altering the value of `\hsize`. If nothing had happened, I would just have squeezed harder. Figure 3.1 shows the first page with a much more slender column, produced by adding the command `\hsize=180pt` (that is, two and a half inches), at the very beginning of the input file.

The way that a file may be run through TEX has already been outlined but it will be tackled in a bit more detail here, since there are several useful alternatives. Assuming that the file is named `EXAMPLE.TEX` we can say

`TEX EXAMPLE`

with or without the extension. TEX knows enough to know that if no extension is given, it should use a `.tex` one.

A second alternative is to start TEX going, without mentioning the file you wish to process:

`TEX`

where TEX will give some header line and then provide a 'double-asterisk' prompt. This is fairly unique and indicates a very special situation. It is T_EX's way of asking for a file to process. It is the only time it is ever going to do this. Then supply an appropriate file name:

```
TEX 3.14 preloaded format
**EXAMPLE
```

If the file had all the commands in that you wanted, this would be quite an acceptable approach, but there is no real reason why any commands which you have inserted should live in the same file as the 'text'. In fact, there are probably excellent reasons for separating the two as far as possible. Although the ** expects a file name, there are other things that can be done here, and there are other ways to input a file when T_EX is running. Let's assume a fairly crude situation, where we type in the commands, as T_EX is running. This is crude because we tend to forget them (who reads the log file?). In general, we can type any command at the prompt, but the recommended command here is a 'do nothing', \relax (this provides another clue to the geographic location of T_EX's origins). Basically the \relax says that we are not going to provide a file name right away. So then we could type any commands:

```
**\relax
*\baselineskip12pt
*\hsize4in
```

Each time the <return> key is depressed to enter a command, T_EX responds with a single-asterisk prompt. This is the usual one we expect to see. How do we tell T_EX to read a file? The \input command will do this:

```
\input example
```

This is a very flexible approach, since we could have placed all the commands in another file, say `command.tex`, and then said

```
**command
*\input example
```

or even

```
**\relax
*\input command
*\input example
```

Equally, the file `command.tex` might end with the command

```
\input example
```

There is something more. What will the name of the `.dvi` file be? In general, it will take the name of the first file read in, unless commands other than \input have been processed. So the pre-

I stuffed a shirt or two into my old carpet-bag, tucked it under my arm, and started for Cape Horn and the Pacific. Quitting the good city of old Manhatto, I duly arrived in New Bedford. It was on a Saturday night in December. Much was I disappointed upon learning that the little packet for Nantucket had already sailed, and that no way of reaching that place would offer, till the following Monday.

As most young candidates for the pains■ and penalties of whaling stop at this same New Bedford, thence to embark on their voyage, it may as well be related that I, for one, had no idea of so doing. For my mind was made up to sail in no other than a Nantucket craft, because there was a fine boisterous something about every-thing connected with that famous old is-land, which amazingly pleased me. Be-sides though New Bedford has of late been gradually monopolizing the business of whal-■ ing, and though in this matter poor old Nantucket is now much behind her, yet Nantucket was her great original – the Tyre of this Carthage; – the place where the first dead American whale was stranded.■ Where else but from Nantucket did those aboriginal whalemen, the Red-Men, first sally out in canoes to give chase to the Leviathan? And where but from Nan-tucket, too, did that first adventurous lit-tle sloop put forth, partly laden with im-ported cobblestones – so goes the story – to throw at the whales, in order to dis-cover when they were nigh enough to risk a harpoon from the bowsprit?

Figure 3.1
Narrow column

vious examples will create either `EXAMPLE.DVI` or `COMMAND.DVI`.
When we started off with
```
**\relax
*\baselineskip12pt
*\hsize4in
```
TeX will have had to choose a name itself. The name chosen in
such a situation will be `texput.dvi` (texput is derived by analogy
to input and output).

Back to the formatting

To explain what is going on when TeX is formatting, we have to
reveal a little more about the way in which TeX works. TeX works
with boxes. The fundamental paradigm is that of boxes and glue.
If we go right back to basics and start to assemble a page of text
we can gain some insight into many aspects of TeX, and the way
it sees the world. In some respects, although we are using an electronic system, the approach is very like that which a traditional
hot metal typesetter would use. We start with individual characters (or glyphs): the components of the fonts (the 26 soldiers of
lead with which Beatrice Warde believed you could conquer the
world, or in TeX's more realistic case, 256 characters).

What does TeX actually know about these characters? Not very
much. It 'knows' three basic quantities: the width, height, and
depth. Where does this information come from – the TeX font
metric, or `tfm` files. The width of the character is fairly obvious,
but why is there a height and depth? Notionally, every character
'sits' on the baseline. An adequate definition of baseline is difficult
to establish, although we appear to have an intuitive feel for it. If
we can agree that there is a baseline, then the height of a character
is the height above the baseline, while its depth is the depth below
it. In general terms, capital letters have no depth, and are usually
all of the same height. The letters with descenders (for example,
g, j, p, q, y) have both height and depth. But TeX knows nothing
about the contents (well, not very much): its interest is purely
geometric. Thus we could throw away the information on content
and just look at the form, and how it is handled.

When TeX starts to handle a word like

Type

what it sees are the components:

T̲y̲p̲e̲

or rather:

Once it has actually assembled them into a word, what it sees next is one single 'word box'

It is this word box which is then joined together with other word boxes to create the line. The size of characters is determined rigidly. Therefore the size of a word is determined rigidly. There is a rigid, fixed space between letters (characters). Letterspacing, where the spacing between letters in a word can be altered, post-dates the Monotype system and really is a photosetting invention; it is not easily obtainable in TeX.

Of course, in true Knuthian (or perhaps Chthonic) style, we haven't quite told the whole truth. There are at least two other things going on which will affect the word: the first is kerning. Certain letter combinations 'look' better if they are adjusted to be a little closer. Traditionally, each piece of type was a rectangle. Thus there was no possibility of adjustment. However, especially as *italic* type became more widely used, it became common to adjust the shape of the letters in order to close up some groups of letters. In the example above, the 'T' and the 'y' are closer together – they have been kerned. Once I put the boxes around them, this implicit kerning does not apply. There is an important distinction to be made in TeX between the combination Ty and the combination {T}{y} or T{}y. The grouping forces these characters to be treated separately. Unfortunately, the kerning amounts are not too easy to get hold of. They are found in the tfm files, which we shall glance at later.

Besides assembling the boxes of a set of characters into a larger box (a word), TeX has to assemble these into a line. If we think of the assembly work in terms of a paste up, some of Knuth's ter-minology (which spills over into command names) becomes more straightforward. Between successive word boxes we can allow a certain flexibility – white space is not absolute – which we can use in order to spread out the word boxes in a line to form a line box. The white space is not a box, it is 'glue' which has the capability of expanding or shrinking (within some predefined limits) to achieve some optimum results. This is one area of TeX where you do not really have a lot of close control. Your choice of font has already implicitly defined the glue which is allowed between words. Some fonts have greater glueyness than others. However, if you really must play around with interword glue, you will find a way.

White space between words has a 'natural' width, but this can be permitted to expand by some factor, or shrink by some factor (not necessarily the same factor). The object of the exercise is to end up with a 'masterpiece of the publishing art'. This is the glue of TeX, but as Knuth points out somewhere, a better metaphor would be a spring, but the notion of glue seems to have caught on.

What happens next? Although we have focused on lines, TeX is not really interested in lines at all. It is mostly interested in paragraphs. But to create a paragraph we normally have to divide the text into line-length chunks. To do so, TeX determines 'feasible' breakpoints. This is a multiple pass procedure, and on the first pass TeX ignores hyphenation. If we wanted to have a paragraph with no hyphenation at all, one way to achieve this aim is to set the value of \pretolerance to a high figure (say 10,000). This is a 'badness' value. What is going on is TeX attempting to create a paragraph which contains lines, each of which has badness below a certain figure. On the first pass, the badness is compared to the \pretolerance figure. Making it very high ensures that no further pass takes place, since the criterion is met. Otherwise, on the next pass, when discretionary hyphens are inserted, the reference value is \tolerance. The default value for \pretolerance is 100, and for \tolerance is 200. Note that these values are, in a sense, application specific. The wider the 'measure', the lower these tolerances may be. If we are setting to a rather narrow measure, then we should increase them somewhat. There is a tendency to use lines of too great a measure.

Naturally, you cannot always accommodate words and allowed white space on the line. The line may be still too long or too short. By default, TeX justifies text – that is, the left and right margins occur at the same vertical position on each line. When TeX hyphenates, it calls on a powerful, if conservative, in-built hyphenation algorithm. TeX is believed to find 90% of known hyphenations correctly (in American English). Unfortunately, as you squeeze lines down, the glue associated with interword space becomes insufficient, and however much you hyphenate, you can end up with 'overfull boxes' – that is, boxes (lines) which are too big for the line width that you specified with \hsize.

Each font has associated with it certain \fontdimen values; among these are the interword space (the ideal space between words), the interword stretch (the extra amount which may be put between words on any one line), and the interword shrink (the amount by which the interword gap may shrink). In `cmr10` these are 3.33 pt, 1.67 pt, and 1.11 pt respectively. Later we will examine how these may be changed. The interword gaps are made equal between all the words in a line; furthermore, TeX tries to make adjacent lines have similar interword gaps. If the badness of a line is 12 or less, TeX considers it to be 'decent'. How does TeX evaluate the badness? It looks to see how much it must stretch or shrink in order to be of the desired length. The available stretch or shrink will depend on the number of words in the line (which is why `\tolerance` is related to the measure). To take an example: if the line has (say) seven words, the total shrinkability will be 6.67 points, and the maximum stretchability 10 points. If the glue is then to be shrunk by 4 points to get the words on the line, TeX will compute a badness of $100 \times (4/6.67)^3 \approx 21$. On the other hand, if it had to stretch the glue by 4 points the badness computed would have been $100 \times (4/10)^3 \approx 6$. If the glue has to stretch, the line is 'loose', and if it shrinks, 'tight'. A line with a badness of over 100 (that is, where it exceeds the combined interword stretch) is 'very loose'. TeX will not allow the gaps between words to be shrunk below the minimum value. When TeX is unable to put the words on the line successfully it will complain of 'overfull' or 'underfull' boxes. By far the most common are 'overfull' boxes.

By default, whenever an overfull box is encountered, TeX does two things: first, it issues a message in the log file, similar to `Overfull \hbox (0.41714pt too wide) in paragraph at lines 18--26 []\tenrm The object of this particu-lar exer-cise (run-ning some text through` which identifies the amount of the excess and also echoes the line on which the problem was found, indicating the potential hyphenation points; second, on output, TeX places a 'black blob' in the right-hand margin so that we can identify the line where that overfull box occurred. The stridency ensures that we are encouraged to do something about the problem.

The object of this exercise has been to create 'overfull boxes', to illustrate the problems which often occur, and more important, to indicate that there are always solutions made more straightforward by some understanding of what is going on. In addition it is useful to become familiar with the sorts of messages which TeX will present to you. To begin with, these messages seem peremptory and intimidating.

Becoming flexible

To every problem there is at least one solution. TₑX has several possible solutions to the 'overfull box' problem.

Hyphenation

We could force extra hyphenation – TₑX does not know all words. You can hyphenate words yourself as they occur, by inserting a special command which indicates a *potential* or *discretionary* hyphenation. For example, in `Tyr\-rhenian` the `\-` indicates a discretionary hyphenation. Note that this command is not followed by a space. As a general rule, any TₑX command made up of a control character (that is, a `\`) and a symbol (that is, a non-alphanumeric) should not have a space after it. Declaring each potential hyphenation is tedious, and one alternative is to declare the hyphenations as:

`\hyphenation{Tyr-rhenian manu-script manu-scripts}`

That is, simply a list of hyphenated words, separated by spaces. This has a global effect, since what happens here is that these words are added (temporarily) to TₑX's 'exception dictionary'. As noted earlier, TₑX hyphenates by algorithm, but there is a small dictionary of exceptions. It is therefore a more hybrid approach than it at first appears. There is usually a limit of 307 to the number of exceptions which can be placed in this dictionary.

Note that TₑX will not realize that `manu-scripts` is merely a regularly formed plural of `manuscript`. Similarly, this mechanism can know nothing about any other regularly formed inflections. On the other hand, the standard hyphenation can cope with many inflections. As noted earlier, explicitly declaring hyphenation points will not help words which already contain hyphens. While 'pricking' by itself can be hyphenated to 'prick-ing', 'pinpricking' is not hyphenated to 'pin-prick-ing'. If we were to say

`\hyphenation{pin-prick-ing}`

we could easily end up with 'pinpricking'. In this case we would have to use `pin-prick\-ing` throughout the document.

There are some problems with hyphenation in foreign languages, but which fortunately do not affect English: sometimes the spelling changes around the hyphen. For example, in German, 'Schiffahrt' is hyphenated to 'Schiff-fahrt'. To tackle this in TₑX we can say

`Schi\discretionary{ff-}{f}{ff}ahrt`

This looks a bit formidable. What does it mean? The three groups

of characters following the command \discretionary are treated
as follows: if there is no break, just use the third set – in this case,
the word typeset is Schiffahrt: if there is a break, then put the
first set of characters before the break, and the second set after –
Schiff-fahrt. The discretionary hyphen \- works like
\discretionary{-}{}{}
If a break ocurrs, put a hyphen at the end of the text before the
break, but nothing after it. If there is no break, the discretionary
hyphen does not appear.

We have to admit that until very recently TEX handled hyphenation in accented words very badly. Since some of these versions
of TEX may still be around, it is worth pointing out that words
would be hyphenated up to an accent, but not after it. Basically,
TEX realized at that point that it was a 'foreign' word, and that
therefore the in-built 'American/English' hyphenation would be
inappropriate. Therefore do nothing. Fortunately TEX3, unveiled
in 1989, has the potential to handle accented words correctly. But
if they are 'foreign' words, they may still be hyphenated wrongly.
It is possible to load other hyphenation schemes which use the
standard algorithm, but which have been trained to hyphenate
particular languages. Even in English, TEX has a tendency to
hyphenate words after the second letter: this is unconventional,
although apparently acceptable in American English. A pair of
new commands, \lefthyphenmin and \righthyphenmin, control
the length of the smallest 'fragment' of words at the beginning
and end of the word. For English, these should be set to 3 and 2
respectively, although the default is 2.

In order to find out what hyphenation points TEX will identify,
you can type
\showhyphens{oxymoron}
at the * prompt, and TEX will repond with a few lines of output,
which will include the key line:
[] \tenrm oxy-moron
which is 'oxymoron' hyphenated the way that TEX would do it,
if pressed. Using \showhyphens adds nothing to the .dvi file.
Although TEX has done some processing, it has generated no print-
able output.

Tolerance, tolerance

We could change the value of the \tolerance command; \tol-
erance takes a numeric argument, and is a kind of 'accept worse'

instruction. 'Accept worse' here only means accept worse gaps between words. As noted above, TEX is hard at work looking at the quality of each line. By default, the parameter which it uses to determine whether it has found 'acceptable' breakpoints is \tol-erance, which plain gives a value of 200. Recall that this selection of breakpoints is normally a two-pass procedure, where the first time round TEX does no hyphenation at all and uses the \pre-tolerance command (set by default to 100). It is really only as line measure is reduced that TEX finds the need to hyphenate at all. With long lines there is generally enough flexibility to permit the interword gaps to be within the limits, and the second pass may not even be needed. But work with narrow measure will require that the defaults are changed to a larger value. It might even be worth ignoring the first pass altogether, disabling it by \pretolerance=-1. TEX3 introduced a new feature to counteract one unfortunate by-product of TEX's selection of breakpoints. Under some circumstances TEX would prefer to have one truly awful line rather than three or four moderately awful lines. If the new command, \emergencystretch, is positive, TEX will perform another pass and will incorporate this extra stretchability. Now it should end up with several moderately bad lines instead.

This avoids the question of the actual set of breakpoints that TEX chooses for a paragraph. TEX determines a number of possible routes which all satisfy the basic requirements in some way, and then selects the one with fewest penalty points. Features like hyphens automatically incur penalties or demerits. Hyphens on two consecutive lines incur even more penalties. A hyphen on the last full line of a paragraph is similarly frowned upon. These are taken with the badness values for each of the possible lines, with the notion that TEX selects the least bad solution. Chapter 20 delves into the way TEX breaks up lines and constructs paragraphs in far more detail.

Raggedness

Or you could let the right-hand margin be a bit more ragged. Note that we are not necessarily talking here of 'ragged-right' text setting. TEX uses the command \raggedright to allow the right margin to be ragged, or non-justified (German uses the rather delightful term 'butterfly-setting' to describe ragged-right). It takes as much work in TEX to set a ragged margin as to justify. TEX will also be hard at work making sure that the interword gaps are acceptable, and will be hyphenating where it feels hyphenation is needed. You do not save time or money.

Some current thinking argues that a ragged margin is more 'friendly'. The reasoning goes: if it is justified, it must be computer set, and hence 'unfriendly' – therefore use the computer to roughen it up again! What do we have in mind here? You can set a command \hfuzz which permits lines to project into the margin by a specified amount. The default value for \hfuzz set in `plain` is a miserly 0.1 pt. In justified text you may be able to get away with \hfuzz=1pt or thereabouts. Perhaps on high-quality typesetting, where the output medium is a high-resolution typesetter, the smaller value would be used. On a 300 dpi laser printer, 1 pt is only about 4 dots, and is extremely unlikely to be picked up. Recall too that the right-hand margin is made up of letters whose major characteristic is that they are not made up of straight lines. Noticing the irregularity could be a real challenge, but to help you, this paragraph has been set with an \hfuzz value of 1 pt.

If you use both \raggedright and \hfuzz, you could set \hfuzz to a much larger value and it would be very difficult to notice, since there would be no 'standard' length to use as a prototype.

Cheating!

Sometimes you are prepared to live with overfull boxes, but not with the black blob. You can redefine the blob, or to give it its correct name, the \overfullrule, to be a blob of no width:
\overfullrule=0pt
TEX will still report its overfull boxes, and will also typeset this blob, which, having no width, will be invisible. While we might cavil at the philosophical implications, it does make the output look a bit better. Sadly there are times when the devil drives and this must be done. LATEX does it all the time. It is surprising how often books set with LATEX can be found with overfull horizontal boxes. It is obvious that the warnings that TEX issues are not enough. The overfull rule must be there as well before people will pay attention. The default setting for the width of this blob is 5 pt.

When all else fails

Last, but not least, rewrite the text. This is Knuth's suggestion. In fact it isn't so absurd as it seems. He almost suggests that if TEX cannot set your text properly, then there could be something amiss with your text. Of course, it is not always possible to rewrite the text. If you were TEXing someone else's work, they may not be pleased by your editorial hatchet work, far less the implication that they should rewrite.

Underfull boxes too

You might also find an 'underfull box' from time to time. Most often this is an underfull \vbox. Essentially what is happening here is that you have set the vertical page size to some value which cannot be divided exactly by the distance between baselines. If we were using the default page height (8.9 in or 643.203 pt) together with a \baselineskip=12pt and a \parskip=0pt we would find that we had an underfull \vbox. TEX wants to place '53 and a bit' lines on the page. It is the 'bit' of a line which is creating the 'underfull' box. You have told TEX to create a particular page size, it has failed to carry out your instructions to the letter, and it tells you. In general it is not too harmful, and a simple \raggedbottom, analogous to \raggedright, will cure it. There is also a \vfuzz which could be used.

But both underfull and overfull boxes should not be ignored entirely. There will be a good reason for both, and if you really require something of the highest quality, you should try to resolve the underlying problem which led to them.

TEX is really an interactive program. Purists might claim that since output does not appear immediately, this is a rash claim. However, if you really wanted, you could type all your TEX at the keyboard, whilst the system was running. This is hardly efficient. Some mainframe implementations of TEX require a lot of memory, and this can either prohibit interactive use, or make interaction slow. If you do have to run in batch mode, you obviously cannot correct errors as TEX is running. TEX still provides a 'log' file, which will help to pinpoint errors. Frankly, anyone who has used an interactive TEX would never want to use it in batch, unless they had a really enormous file to process. The discussion which follows assumes that you will be running TEX interactively.

Errors

Almost inevitably, you will make mistakes on input, and will encounter TEX's error processing capability. It is possible to correct some errors interactively. If you should successfully correct the input in this way, you must also remember to correct the original (assuming you might just need to re-run sometime). The most common errors are probably typing errors, where either a command is mis-spelled, or perhaps a space is missed out.

When you encounter an error, TEX will respond with a message like:

```
! Undefined control sequence.
1.1  Oh dear, I {\itknew
                        } this would happen!
?
```

TEX is trying hard to indicate where the error lies, principally by breaking the line to indicate just where it has foundered. In the example above, it is the \itknew which has caused the problem (should be \it knew). TEX has correctly pointed out that this is an undefined control sequence (that is, command), one it has never been taught.

When an error is encountered and you are presented with the ? prompt you have a number of alternatives. You may

▷ type ? – TEX gives a summary of the following options:
```
Type <return> to proceed, S to scroll future error
                                        messages,
R to run without stopping, Q to run quietly,
I to insert something, E to edit your file,
1 or ... or 9 to ignore the next 1 to 9 tokens of
                                        input,
H for help, X to quit.
```

▷ type <return> – just prod the **return** key if you have one. Some computers (especially IBM pcs) rename this **enter**. TEX proceeds as best it can, until it encounters another error.

▷ type X or x – TEX stops (eXits); any pages which have already been completed will not be lost, but the current one will certainly be lost; the previous one might be as well.

▷ type E or e – this stands for Edit, and should drop you into an editor. Not all systems have this linking of TEX and system editors. The best way to find out if it does work on your system is to try it. If it does work you would find yourself editing the erroneous file, at about the right line.

▷ type I or i – you may now type text to be Inserted at the current place in input. At first this seems intimidating, but with some practice it does become a viable route. Its major drawback is that you tend to forget these spontaneous corrections. In the earlier example, the following dialogue could have occurred:

```
? i\it knew
```
and TEX would have been well satisfied with the new command. Note that we would also supply the 'knew' part, since TEX thought that that was part of the undefined command. Merely typing i\it would have resulted in a line where the 'knew' was omitted.

▷ type a number between 1 and 99 – TEX deletes this number of characters and commands from input, then asks for more information. Again, taking the last example:
```
? 1
1.1  Oh dear, I {\itknew}
                         this would happen!
? i}
```
Typing the 1 removes the next character, the }. TEX repeats the line, noting where it has now read up to. Since there is an 'open' brace, we should insert a closing brace to balance things up. Note that the offending command was automatically discarded.

TEX sees a command as a single item *and* also a character as a single item – otherwise termed tokens.

▷ type H – TEX gives some sort of help. The best message you get here, besides the useful ones, is the one which says:
```
Sorry, I already gave what help I could...
Maybe you should try asking a human?
An error might have occurred before I noticed any
                                         problems.
''If all else fails, read the instructions.''
```

▷ type S – this is like typing **return** (or **enter**) for every subsequent error message. The error messages are logged, but you have no chance of interaction. The 'S' is an abbreviation for \scrollmode, a TEX command you could use to enter this condition directly.

▷ type R – this is like S only worse; under no circumstances stop. This time, 'R' is a shorthand for \nonstopmode.

▷ type Q – even worse; TEX suppresses all output to the terminal (goes a lot faster, subjectively), but perhaps not the best route unless you are very confident that you know what you are doing, which obviously you don't, else you would not have made a mistake in the first place. This state may also be entered by the command \batchmode.

⇒*Exercise 3.1:*   You may note that the summary says you can delete 9 tokens of input, while the fuller description says you can delete up to 99. Which is correct?   ⇐

While you are in this error mode, the prompt is ?. There is obviously a temptation just to type **return** and let TeX surge ahead to report on any other errors. Unfortunately the corrections TeX may have made in order to do something apparently sensible may lead to other mistakes later on. When I do not feel up to mental gymnastics I much prefer to leave TeX (by typing X) and correct the error, then return to TeX. Obviously this is potentially expensive with a large file, but with the ease of input through \input, a suitable strategy is to assemble a succession of files, correcting them one at a time, and then run them together through TeX. There are other advantages to be accrued from this style of working.

There is another class of mistake which may be made, and from which recovery is sometimes difficult. If you have \input thesis in the text of the file you are processing, and TeX is unable to find that file thesis.tex, it will ask you to provide another file name. The usual reason for TeX not finding a particular file is not really that it does not exist, but rather that you have put it in another directory, or on another drive. If you can provide the 'full' name of the file, for example,

a:\tex\thesis\thesis

(if you were using MS-DOS), or whatever was appropriate to your particular environment, then you would be able to input the correct file. Unfortunately, panic often sets in, and the full name is difficult to remember. What do you do? How do you stop TeX, find the file, and start again? There is no universal answer to this. Simply hitting the **enter** or **return** key will probably not help. The machine will merely repeat the question. (Eventually TeX would give up, but only after a long time.) Switching the computer off is a little drastic. Most computer systems have a way of exiting from an executing process (like TeX), and it will probably have something to do with a **ctrl** key combination. You really ought to find out which ones. A more elegant alternative is to have a **null** file available which you can use at this time. This **null** file can be empty, or just contain \relax (very apt right now!). Whatever it contains, it satisfies TeX's current problem. Many computer systems will have a **null.tex** file which is universally available. If whoever implemented TeX on the system you use was particularly thoughtful, they may have named it **nul.tex**, or **nultex.tex**, and a few other similar things as well.

It would be at least honest to admit that TeX's error messages are sometimes (often) a little cryptic. I often have the feeling that TeX thinks I am a lot smarter than I am, providing me with information which is decidedly unhelpful, but earnest. It is in such situations that one suspects that TeX is a true expert system – one that only experts can understand. But experts don't make mistakes..., do they?

If you are particularly interested in monitoring the progress of your input file, you can make TeX divulge much more information. There are tracing commands which will report on things like hyphenation, and lots lots more. You might like to try `\tracingall=1` and `\tracingcommands=1`. The most feared error message which apparently indicates some major problem is

`!TeX capacity exceeded, sorry`

and will suggest:

`If you really absolutely need more capacity,`
`you can ask a wizard to enlarge me.`

This is usually something of a red herring, since normally there is a less spectacular reason for this, like an excessively long paragraph, or you forgot to close a brace. It could just be that you have done something legitimate, but TeX has been unable to cope. Unlikely, but knowing that it is possible, you will be able to find a way.

While TeX is bug free, it does have some limitations. Software is *never* bug free, but at the time of writing there were only a couple of known bugs, neither of which were serious (honest). The wide distribution of TeX does help to ensure that bugs are quickly weeded out.

One of the peculiarities of TeX is that a page is not actually set, as such, until it is complete. In fact, it often does not get set then. Line boxes are built, in their turn, into paragraph boxes. The paragraphs are assembled into pages, but TeX seeks to minimize widows and orphans. A widowed line is one at the end of a paragraph which finds itself on a separate page from the rest of its paragraph. They are also known as 'club' lines. In keeping with the 'widow' metaphor are 'orphan' lines. These are the first lines of paragraphs, living on a page separate from the remainder of the text in that paragraph. TeX in fact looks ahead a little to decide where to break a page. The result of all this is that a page is not finalized until some way into the next page. If an error occurs, you may lose information up to about a page and a half ago. Therefore you will not be able to see your output up to the error which made TeX collapse.

⇒*Exercise 3.2:*   What happens if you leave two blank lines? Or type `\par\par`?   ⇐

⇒*Exercise 3.3:*   Why does TeX require `\end` or `\bye` to tell it that we have finished? Why does the detection of the end of the file not signify the end of input? ⇐

⇒*Exercise 3.4:* How would you get ouput which looked like this --- (that is, successive hyphens)? ⇐

⇒*Exercise 3.5:* Perhaps you don't like ligatures. Can you suggest a way of making the standard TEX Computer Modern Roman font ignore ligatures? ⇐

⇒*Exercise 3.6:* Suppose that you have a quote within a quote – ' "Starboard", he cried.' How do you propose to set this? ⇐

⇒*Exercise 3.7:* There is no complement to \raggedright. Once it has been switched on, you cannot say \noraggedright or \justify. Assuming you did want to set a part of your document ragged-right, how would you restore justification? ⇐

⇒*Exercise 3.8:* Since the backslash character is not available by merely typing \, what do you guess you will have to do to obtain a backslash? ⇐

⇒*Exercise 3.9:* Attempt to change the characteristics of a paragraph in the middle of a paragraph; for example, change the baseline skip half way through. ⇐

Beginning mathematics 4

In many respects this is where TeX gets to be lots more fun. There is something extraordinarily satisfying about being able to set mathematical formulae. TeX permits this both within the text (*text* style) and displayed on lines by themselves (*display* style). The same expression can be given in text or display style, and there will be a few stylistic changes, which TeX takes care of automatically.

All mathematical formulae are enclosed in special delimiters – the dollar symbol, $. A few examples soon convey most of the ideas and conventions behind this:

`$x = y + z - 10 $`

will result in $x = y + z - 10$, with TeX setting the alphabetic characters in italics, and coping quite gamely with the other symbols, the $=$, $+$, and $-$. Note that here we have a true minus sign (which looks different from en-dash, em-dash, and the hyphen). TeX also takes care of all the spacing. It matters not one whit whether you type

`$x=y+z-10$`

or even

`$ x= y +z - 1   0$`

TeX will produce the same thing, and generally correctly: $x = y + z - 10$.

$\Rightarrow$*Exercise 4.1:*   Although these few examples look rather trivial, they help demonstrate the ease with which TeX handles simple mathematical expressions, and in particular, how good they look, with no input of skill on your part. You are left to guess how to input (and) to TeX. Typeset the following:

Show that the volume V is given by $V = l(a - 2b)(a + 2b)$.

Common factors: $ab + ac = a(b + c)$.

$s = kP$, where k is a constant.

If $y = kx$, and $y = 15$ when $x = 6$, find the constant k.

$\Leftarrow$

		α \alpha		β \beta		
		γ \gamma		δ \delta		
ε \varepsilon		ϵ \epsilon		ζ \zeta		
		η \eta		θ \theta		ϑ \vartheta
		ι \iota		κ \kappa		
		λ \lambda		μ \mu		
		ν \nu		ξ \xi		
		o o		π \pi		ϖ \varpi
ϱ \varrho		ρ \rho		σ \sigma		ς \varsigma
		τ \tau		υ \upsilon		
φ \varphi		ϕ \phi		χ \chi		
		ψ \psi		ω \omega		

Figure 4.1
Lower-case
Greek symbols

The examples given above are of the text style of mathematics, where the expression is embedded within the text, and may be broken at line ends (according to some inbuilt rules on where such breaks are acceptable). The text mathematics are surrounded by single $ signs. Display style is handled almost identically, but is 'signalled' by *double* $ signs before and after the expression. Thus
`$$x = y +z - 10$$`
would produce the same expression as before, but it would be *displayed*. That is, it would be centred over the page, and a certain amount of space would be left after text which precedes it, and before the text that follows it. Provided no extra blank lines are inserted between the text and the displayed mathematics, the text and maths are treated as part of the same paragraph, so no annoying indentation of text occurs after the display.

⇒*Exercise 4.2:* When 'double dollars', $$, are used to surround a mathematical expression instead of single dollars, TEX handles the typesetting a little differently. You can take some of the last examples and recast them slightly (take out the punctuation which follows the 'closing' double dollars; it won't look right):

Show that the volume V is given by
$$V = l(a - 2b)(a + 2b)$$
Common factors:
$$ab + ac = a(b + c)$$

⇐

There are a host of commands which are defined for use in maths. In particular, you may access the Greek alphabet. Note that this is not a Greek font as such, in the sense that you would not use it in order to set Greek text. It is best considered as just another set of symbols. Within maths (that is, within the $ or $$

Γ	\Gamma	Γ	\mit\Gamma	Δ	\Delta	Δ	\mit\Delta
Θ	\Theta	Θ	\mit\Theta	Λ	\Lambda	Λ	\mit\Lambda
Ξ	\Xi	Ξ	\mit\Xi	Π	\Pi	Π	\mit\Pi
Σ	\Sigma	Σ	\mit\Sigma	Υ	\Upsilon	Υ	\mit\Upsilon
Φ	\Phi	Φ	\mit\Phi	Ψ	\Psi	Ψ	\mit\Psi
Ω	\Omega	Ω	\mit\Omega				

Figure 4.2
Upper-case
Greek symbols

'environment'), the general form of access is much as you might anticipate: a Greek α is obtained by \alpha, a γ by \gamma – the 'English' name for the letter, preceded by the backslash (Figure 4.1). To obtain upper-case Greek, use \Gamma and so on. Since some upper-case Greek letters have the same form as their Roman equivalents, there are no entries for these overlaps (Figure 4.2). For example, the upper-case Greek α is A. Similarly, there is no lower-case omicron, although it has been included in the figure for completeness. A few Greek symbols are frequently encountered in a variant or alternate form. It would be uncommon to find someone using (say) both φ and ϕ in the same paper, but TeX gives both forms and leaves the decision up to you.

There is an extension to the upper-case Greek fonts which may also be useful. You can obtain 'italic' Greek (an oxymoron if ever there was one) by $\mit\Lambda$ and so on. Note that upper-case Greek is 'upright', while lower-case is 'slanted' or 'italic'. On the other hand, there is no way to obtain 'upright' lower-case Greek symbols.

⇒*Exercise 4.3:* It might be concluded that $\mit\sigma$ would be a tautology, and therefore lead to odd results. Provide some evidence. ⇐

⇒*Exercise 4.4:* Why 'upper case'? And why is lower-case Greek not upright like 'normal' upper-case Greek? ⇐

⇒*Exercise 4.5:* The Greek symbols, just like all other mathematical symbols, must occur in 'maths mode', that is within either single or double dollar signs. Since it is not uncommon to forget to include the dollar signs, or even to forget to terminate them at the end of a maths expression, it is useful to become accustomed to the sort of error message which TeX will produce under these circumstances, and what, if anything, you can do to put TeX back on the rails. Try the following example:

When \alpha=0, the dispersive stress is greatest.

This example may be difficult to get out of since TeX will assume that you forgot a $, insert it *itself*, and continue. When you then wish to enter \end to terminate the exercise, you will still be in maths, and TeX just won't let you exit. One solution is to type $ at the * prompt (which therefore 'balances' the $ which TeX inserted, and restores you to the correct mode, where \end or \bye will work).

Now try this:

`In the case of x+y-4x=0, the longest arc is given by:`

which has different mistakes, although TeX apparently does not detect them. What should it be?   ⇐

⇒*Exercise 4.6:*   The Greek symbols are not really for typesetting Greek text. But you can. How would you typeset $\tau\epsilon\chi\nu\eta$? What does it mean?   ⇐

Ups and downs

One of the things which mathematicians do is to use subscripts and superscripts. These are so fundamental that TeX makes them very easy. We employ two keyboard symbols to trigger these events: the carat or circumflex ^ to signal that the next character (or group of characters) is to be superscripted, while the underline symbol _ is used for subscripts. The underline or underscore or low bar symbol is different from all the other dashes, hyphens, and minuses we have met so far. In the remote chance that your keyboard does not have these symbols, TeX will allow \sp (superscript) and \sb (subscript) to be substituted.

Let us try this out:

`$10x^3 - 3x^2 + 4x - 2 = 0$`

or

`$10x\sp3 - 3x\sp2 + 4x - 2 = 0$`

You will find it easier if you space out your formulae into 'logical' groupings, just letting TeX take care of the spacing. Jamming all the symbols together leads to problems. The result of this example should be: $10x^3 - 3x^2 + 4x - 2 = 0$

When we start handling sub- and superscripts it becomes obvious that it may be necessary to have more than one symbol which is sub- or superscripted. In other words, we need to produce something like n^{31} or τ_{xy}, or even $c_{1,1}$. The 'commands' ^ and _ take the very next symbol or group of symbols, and make them into sub- or superscripts. Therefore, to subscript the xy, first turn it into a group by placing braces around it: {xy}. TeX is then happy to take this and produce the subscripted pair of symbols. This is just another application of the grouping feature. It may be interesting to note in passing that `$n\sp3$` is exactly equivalent to `$n^3$`. The \sp is followed by a non-alphabetic character, and therefore there is no ambiguity, or possible confusion with a command. On the other hand, m^h could not be written `$m\spm$`, although it could be written `$m^n$`.

Putting the expressions between single dollar signs employs *text* style: that is, these are formulae which appear within the text. We are really considering the situation like

```
The surface is $y=h_s(x)$, the bed is $y=h_b(x)$;
the slopes,  if small, are $\alpha=-dh_s/dx$,
$\beta=-dh_b/dx$. If $\alpha$, $\beta$ are small,
```

which yields*:

> The surface is $y = h_s(x)$, the bed is $y = h_b(x)$; the slopes, if small, are $\alpha = -dh_s/dx$, $\beta = -dh_b/dx$. If α, β are small,

As an appropriate aside, we should note that if TEX has to divide a text style equation over two lines, it will do so according to a set of rules which favours breaking after a relation like $=$, or an operator like $+$. Breaking after a relation is slightly preferred. Just as normal text may have potential hyphenation points introduced, there is a similar 'discretionary $\times$' in maths. Since it is conventional for ab to mean $a \times b$, while all the other operators are given explicitly, TEX may be helped by the insertion of a discretionary multiplication sign, `\*`: `$a\*b$`.

It may also be worth noting that all the punctuation has been placed outside the text style mathematics. This does ensure that TEX understands that it is punctuation, and not some mathematical operator, which it would treat in a slightly different way. Although TEX is an extremely efficient mechanism for typesetting both text and mathematics, it assumes that mathematics does not normally contain text, or textual items, like punctuation.

$\Rightarrow$*Exercise 4.7:*   There is one other reason that the punctuation is 'outside'. Take the last example and place the punctuation inside the dollar signs. Examine the output very carefully. You will note a difference in the style of the punctuation. It will be more difficult to note TEX's unwillingness to break a line at such punctuation. $\Leftarrow$

Had we been required to set any mathematics in *display*, we would have used double dollar signs. This can be illustrated by continuing the last example :

```
If $\alpha$, $\beta$ are small, the equation can be
transformed into this coordinate system to give the
approximate relation $$\tau_b=\rho gh\alpha+2G-T$$
where $h=h_s-h_b$, the ice thickness,
```

If we look at how this is set:

---

* The text is narrower here to make it easier to detect where such examples start and end. Normally the typeset version would take up the whole width of the text.

If α, β are small, the equation can be transformed into this coordinate system to give the approximate relation

$$\tau_b = \rho g h \alpha + 2G - T$$

where $h = h_s - h_b$, the ice thickness,

we notice that a displayed equation is centred within its current page width, and that a certain amount of space is left above and below the displayed equation. The displayed equation is part of the paragraph in which it occurs. Introducing the display does not terminate one paragraph and begin another. Had you left a blank line before and after the display, then it would be treated as a paragraph on its own. Whatever follows will also be treated as a new paragraph, by virtue of the blank line which precedes it. When an equation is written down in TEX form, leave no blank lines within the scope of the dollars or double dollars. If you do leave blank lines, TEX will assume that you have made an error and will try to help. It will get in a dreadful muddle.

$\Rightarrow$*Exercise 4.8:*   It is best to encounter errors under controlled circumstances. Introduce a blank line in the middle of a displayed equation and see what TEX makes of it. You might be able to interact your way out of trouble. $\Leftarrow$

The amount of space left above and below a displayed equation will vary, depending on the length of the line of text which immediately precedes or follows it.

Deeper and deeper

You can sub- or superscript as deeply as you wish; TEX will reduce the size of the first level (by default to 7 point), but any further sub- or superscripting will be at 5 point by default, however deeply you do it. These reductions could be changed to some other value.
`$a^{b^{c^{d^e}}}$`
gives an expression where c, d, and e are all the same point size (5 pt). (An aside is appropriate here. If this expression, $a^{b^{c^{d^e}}}$, appears in text, TEX will by default insert a little extra space between the lines so that the higher superscripts do not 'interfere' with the previous line.) They are all superscripted, but just do not get any smaller. Do note that the sequence
`$a^b^c^d^e$`
is illegal. TEX will complain

```
! Double superscript.
<recently read> ^
1.3 $a^b^
          c^d^e $
```

but it will still go on and typeset things 'correctly', assuming that what you meant was a^{bcde}. If you meant `$a^{bcde}$` or `$a^{b^{c^{d^e}}}$` you should say so. Note too that when you 'simultaneously' sub- and superscript, for example x_n^2, the sub- and superscripts will be lined up (at their left-hand edge). We could therefore have written that as `$x^2_n$`, and obtained the same result: x_n^2.

A set of examples is given below, which account for many situations.

`x^2`	x^2	`x_2`	x_2
`2^x`	2^x	`x^2y^2`	x^2y^2
`x ^ 2y ^ 2`	x^2y^2	`x_2y_2`	x_2y_2
`x_2y^2`	x_2y^2	`_2x^2`	$_2x^2$
`{}_2x^2`	$_2x^2$	`x^{2y}`	x^{2y}
`x^{2^y}`	x^{2^y}	`x_{2^y}`	x_{2^y}
`x_{2_y^2}`	$x_{2_y^2}$	`x_{2_y^2}^{3_z^3}`	$x_{2_y^2}^{3_z^3}$

$\Rightarrow$*Exercise 4.9:* Can you see how the following are different? And how to express them in TeX?

$$(((a^4)^3)^2)^1 \qquad (((a^4)^3)^2)^1$$

$\Leftarrow$

Before absorbing TeX's handling of sub- and superscripts as 'a good thing', look at the following:

$$a_2^2 \qquad a_2 \qquad a^2$$

or even

$$a_1 a_2^2 c^4$$

Although it is possible to see the reasoning behind placing sub- and superscripts differently, depending on context, it does tend to make 'mixed' expressions untidy. There is a simple, if inelegant, solution, where 'null' superscripts are introduced: for example
`$a_1^{} a_2^2 c^4$`
Introducing a superscript on the first term forces its subscript to be lower, bringing it in line with the others. There is a better way, addressed in Chapter 18.

⇒*Exercise 4.10:*   Although by now we have absorbed TEX's basic mathematical typesetting, Greek symbols, and sub- and superscripts, it is still difficult to find any useful mathematics to set which does not seem trivial. Nevertheless, the following displayed equations may provide a little experience:

$$h_0 + \epsilon = h + p = h_0 + h_1 + p$$
$$(m + 1)h_1/h_0 + m\alpha_1/\alpha_0 = 0$$
$$h^{m+1}\alpha^m = h_0^{m+1}\alpha_0^m$$
$$\tau^2 = \tau_{xy}^2 + \tau_{zx}^2$$
$$\lambda = A\tau^{n-1}m = \rho$$
$$eM_\omega/PM_a = 0.623\rho e/P$$

⇐

⇒*Exercise 4.11:*   These examples in the previous exercise are rather 'abstract', since the real tasks come when mathematical expressions are interspersed in text and display. The following short specimen comes a little closer to the real world:

> The number of atoms of a radioactive element at time t years can be found from the original number present at time zero by the relationship
> $$P_t = P_0 e^{-\lambda t}$$
> where P_t is the number of atoms at time t, P_0 is the original number of atoms of the parent nuclide, and e is 2.7183.

⇐

If there are problems with mathematics so far, they are usually problems of vocabulary. Even those with a scientific background may be confused by some Greek symbols. The ϖ looks very like an ω, and may easily be confused with, say, $\bar{\omega}$. Similarly ν, υ, v, and u might be confused at first. Equally, some symbols are not generally used and it may be difficult to remember the 'English' for ν or η. For someone 'translating' a manuscript, this can be a nightmare. It therefore gives TEX the appearance of awkwardness, since it seems to suggest that you have to know what an alpha looks like before you can use it. Many first-class technical typists recognize letters by their shapes and can remember where they are on the keyboard, traditionally accessing them through some combination of keystrokes. To someone familiar with TEX, typing *control-shift-a* to obtain α on output seems even more perverse than does typing \alpha to the TEX naive. Both approaches might just have their place. I confess that once I understood that \alpha gave α, I could guess how I obtained ξ. That seems like an advantage to me.

More simple operators

Square roots can be expressed quite simply by the `\sqrt` command:
`$\sqrt2$`
produces a 2 with a square root symbol around it – $\sqrt{2}$.

Note again how a TEX command works. A command is made up of a backslash followed by *either* any number of alphabetic characters, *or else* a single non-alphabetic character. Thus `$\sqrt2$` is the command `\sqrt` followed by the numeral 2, while `$\sqrtx$` is a new (undefined) command. On the other hand `\2` could be a command, since it consists of the `\` followed by a single non-alphabetic character; `\A4` could not be a command – although it could be the command `\A` followed by a 4. There is therefore no confusion with `$\sqrt4$` or `$\sqrt\alpha$`, but to obtain $\sqrt{x}$ you must type `$\sqrt x$` or `$\sqrt{x}$`. If more than one symbol is to appear under the bar of the root, it must be grouped. For example, $\sqrt{4ac}$ has to have the term within braces: `$\sqrt{4ac}$`. When the term has a sub- or superscript, TEX still takes the 'next term', before applying the sub/superscript: in other words, in the case of `$\sqrt b^2$`, TEX square-roots *before* placing the exponent. If we mean $\sqrt{b^2}$, we must say `$\sqrt{b^2}$`.

The bar over the square-rooted expression will be extended if required: thus
`$\sqrt{b^2-4ac}$`
will have the bar over the whole of the *grouped* expression – $\sqrt{b^2 - 4ac}$.

⇒*Exercise 4.12:* TEX would be quite happy with `$\sqrt4ac$`. What does it produce? What about `$\sqrt16c^4$`? ⇐

Both `\overline` and `\underline` work with individual and grouped symbols. (Another name for 'overline' is *vinculum*, which sounds a bit more specialized, and may convey the notion of grouping.) Thus:
`$\overline \alpha + \underline\gamma^2$`
should do just what it says: $\overline{\alpha} + \underline{\gamma}^2$.

We can combine these (with grouping) to form things like:
`$\overline{\underline{\sqrt{xy}}}$`
or
`$\sqrt{\underline{\underline{xy}}}$`
or even
`$\overline{\sqrt{\underline{xy}}}$`
to obtain $\overline{\sqrt{xy}}$, $\sqrt{\underline{\underline{xy}}}$, and $\overline{\sqrt{\underline{xy}}}$.

\hat a	$\hat{a}$
\check a	$\check{a}$
\tilde a	$\tilde{a}$
\acute a	$\acute{a}$
\grave a	$\grave{a}$
\dot a	$\dot{a}$
\ddot a	$\ddot{a}$
\breve a	$\breve{a}$
\bar a	$\bar{a}$
\vec a	$\vec{a}$

Figure 4.3
Accents
available in
maths

⇒*Exercise 4.13:* Demonstrate the minimum grouping which is actually required for $\sqrt{\bar{x}}$. ⇐

In order to get nth roots, you can use the

$\root n\of a$

which would produce $\sqrt[n]{a}$. It might appear that grouping was needed to obtain something like $^{n-1}\!\!\sqrt{a}$, but here the 'structure' provided by the \root and \of implies that whatever ocurrs between them must be the 'root' term. So all we need type is $\root n-1\of a$. It is interesting to note that typing \of in any other circumstance will lead to trouble.

⇒*Exercise 4.14:* What would $\root {n-1\of b^2}$ produce? ⇐

Mâthémåtìcāl acçents

Mathematicians often like to put modifiers over symbols (so do other people, but we shall give them honorary mathematical status for just now). As we shall see later, TₑX supports some accents in its 'normal', non-mathematical mode. In maths, it also supports quite a wide range of accents (Figure 4.3).

These are genuinely mathematical accents; you cannot use them in 'normal' text – TₑX will complain loudly. Treat them as a type of symbol. After all, the whole of mathematics appears to use some symbols which may look identical, but which have different meanings depending on context. It is partly this which makes setting mathematics appear rather tricky in the first place. Unlike normal accents, which almost always modify a single letter, a mathematical accent may apply to parts of a whole formula, as well as a single symbol – but beware, the accent appears centred over the whole group, whether a single character, or many. Thus $\vec{a+b}$ gives us $\vec{a+b}$. Perhaps we really meant $\vec{a} + \vec{b}$.

Exclude \overline and \underline from this. Although $\bar{x}$ and $\overline{x}$ look rather alike, they are obtained differently. As the previous section illustrated, an overline or underline will stretch over its own group so that if we had written $\bar{xy}$ – $\bar{xy}$ – it would have been clearly differentiated from $\overline{xy}$ – $\overline{xy}$.

Similarly, there are two other 'grouping' accents, \widehat and \widetilde, which grow to accommodate whatever is below them – within limits. The hat or tilde grows with the expression, up to a maximum size: for example, $\widetilde{abc}$.

⇒*Exercise 4.15:* Examine the differences between $\tilde x$ and $\widetilde x$, and also see how both the \widetilde and \widehat accents behave as their 'group' gets larger. ⇐

Mathematical accents have some interesting properties. They may be stacked one above another. This provides us with the capability of writing something like:

$$\bar{\bar{W}}_I = \bar{\bar{W}}_T + \bar{\bar{W}}_R + \bar{\bar{W}}_L$$

But a small confession has to be made here. Often when accents are stacked one on top of another, they appear to be misplaced, either too far to the right or left. There seems no straightforward way of guessing what is likely to be the extent of the problem. The adjustment is trial and error by use of a command \skew. The command is followed by a number which in some way specifies the adjustment. The last example
$$\bar{\dot W}_I=
    \bar{\dot W}_T+\bar{\dot W}_R+\bar{\dot W}_L$$
looks fine, but to obtain

$$\bar{\bar{\dot X}}_I = \bar{\bar{\dot X}}_T + \bar{\bar{\dot X}}_R + \bar{\bar{\dot X}}_L$$

we would require
$$\skew3\bar{\dot X}_I=\skew3\bar{\dot X}_T+
    \skew3\bar{\dot X}_R+\skew3\bar{\dot X}_L$$
Hardly very elegant, but if it helps discourage the use of multiple accents, it cannot be all bad.

The extra height the accent contributes to a symbol is not taken into account for superscripts. An expression like

$$\dot{\epsilon}^2 = A^2\tau^6$$

looks quite satisfactory.

\aleph	ℵ	\prime	′	\forall	∀
\hbar	ℏ	\emptyset	∅	\exists	∃
\imath	ı	\nabla	∇	\neg *or* \lnot	¬
\jmath	ȷ	\surd	√	\flat	♭
\ell	ℓ	\top	⊤	\natural	♮
\wp	℘	\bot	⊥	\sharp	♯
\Re	ℜ		*or* \vert	│	\clubsuit	♣
\Im	ℑ	| *or* \Vert	‖	\diamondsuit	◇
\partial	∂	\triangle	△	\heartsuit	♡
\infty	∞	\backslash	\	\spadesuit	♠
\angle	∠

Figure 4.4
Some of the
many symbols
available

The collection of mathematical accents may be insufficient. Provided that the required symbols occur somewhere, it can be possible to add new accents, for example you might need to be able to write

$$\overline{X \overset{\circ}{\ominus} B} = \dot{B} \ominus \overline{B}$$

where the mathematical accent ° means 'open'. This turns out to be fairly straightforward and will be covered later. On the other hand, $\ddot{x}$ is much more tedious in `plain`, although its construction will also be examined later.

We have many ways of doing this...

The language of mathematics is a very rich one, and the vocabulary expects a very wide range of symbols and operators, much larger than that encountered in normal text. TeX allows access to many symbols: Figure 4.4 gives some useful new symbols, with their commands. There are yet more, but exposure to the rich diet of TeX might lead to indigestion.

While we might query the inclusion of ♭ and ♡ in the mathematical symbols, especially when useful chemical symbols are not present in the default fonts, we must allow Knuth some indulgences. After all, without him, we would have none of this. On the other hand, '...infinite string $♯^\infty τ♯^\infty$ ...' occurs in a well-known book on image processing.

Do note, however, that \angle will not get smaller when used as a sub- or superscript – $\angle a$ and $c^{\angle a}$ both have the same sized $\angle$ (why would you want to do this anyway?). The ℘ symbol is Weierstrass p, and ℏ is also known as 'Planck's constant over 2π'. The ℵ is the only Hebrew letter available in TeX's standard character set. The 'dotless' $\imath$ and $\jmath$ help to make accents on these symbols 'look' better: certainly $\hat{\imath} + \hat{\jmath}$ looks a little strange. The expression $i + j$ will probably always appear ambiguous. Is it `$i+j$` or `$\dot\imath+\dot\jmath$`?

Prime

The normal use of prime is as a superscript. The character you should obtain by `$\prime$` is a rather large, non-superscript symbol. To use it in its normal way, it is superscripted in the form `$x^\prime$`. Similarly, you can use the right quote mark: thus `$x^\prime$` and `$x'$` are equivalent and give x'. In a sense TEX's shorthand for the prime is even more powerful, since `$x''$` is accepted to give x'', a much more agreeable outcome than `$x^{\prime\prime}$`. You will find that even `$x''^2$` works. Unfortunately, though, the almost 'equivalent' `$x^2''$` gives a message about `Double superscript`. One of the reasons that \prime does not come ready superscripted is that that would limit its capabilities, and under certain circumstances lead to strange spacing. For example, `$x\prime_2$` might yield x'_2 or even x'^2 instead of x'_2. And it becomes possible, for example, to obtain $x_/$, should you ever need to. But there is no 'shorthand' for that.

$\Rightarrow$*Exercise 4.16:* Since one way to acquire confidence in using a new vocabulary is to use it, set the following:

$$DT/Dt - k\partial^2 T = H/\rho c$$
$$u = A'\tau_b^m$$
$$\vec{OA'} = k\vec{OA'}$$
$$\angle COQ = \theta$$

This only begins to scrape the surface. $\Leftarrow$

Above and beyond

We place items 'over' other items with the command \over. This is intended for fractions, so it also places a line between the items;
`$a \over b$`
produces the fraction $\frac{a}{b}$. Although available in text style, it is really much better in display style, where it produces

$$\frac{a}{b}$$

It is important to note that \over has the peculiarity that it applies to everything in the formula, so that

```
$$a+b+c+d \over \sqrt{x^2 - y_1} +a$$
```
will place the a+b+c+d over \sqrt{x^2 - y_1} +a:

$$\frac{a+b+c+d}{\sqrt{x^2 - y_1} + a}$$

In order to achieve fine control, use braces to group:
```
$$a + {b\over c}  +d  $$
$$a +   b \over {c +d} $$
$${a + b \over c} +d  $$
```
and so on. It is possible to get very confused with \over. It is infuriatingly easy to end up with an expression like:

$$x = \frac{-b + \sqrt{b^2 - 2a}}{4ac}$$

It seems inconsistent that an operator like \sqrt refers only to the next character or group, while \over applies to the whole of the formula preceding and following, unless modified by grouping. As with sub- and superscripts,
```
$$a \over b \over c$$
```
is illegal, although
```
$${a \over b} \over c$$
```
is acceptable, and produces

$$\frac{\frac{a}{b}}{c}$$

in display. The first group is in smaller type, with a thinner fraction line.

⇒*Exercise 4.17:*   This opens a wide range of new possibilities. Try to typeset the following:

$$\frac{\partial \zeta}{\partial t} = -\frac{\partial M}{\partial x} - \frac{\partial N}{\partial y}$$

$$\psi_M = \frac{a}{r_1} e^{-i\kappa r_1}$$

$$\sqrt{\frac{\kappa}{2z_1}}(x - x_0) = \sqrt{\frac{\lambda}{2z_1}}(x - x_0)$$

$$\frac{\partial \Im}{\partial s} = \pi s$$

$$C_d = a_1 Re^{-1} + a_2 Re^{-\frac{1}{2}} + a_3$$

⇐

Variations on this theme

There are a number of variants of \over, namely: \above, \atop, \choose, \brack, and \brace.

The thickness of the fraction line is controlled in \above so that
$$x \above 1pt y$$
places a fraction bar of thickness 1 pt between x and y:

$$\frac{x}{y}$$

The bar between the groups is omitted with \atop, so that
$$x \atop y$$
gives

$$x \atop y$$

The command \choose has similarities to \over: for example,
$$a\choose b$$ gives

$$\binom{a}{b}$$

Since this is *very* similar to \over, it also requires the same sort of grouping when used in more complex situations. Note that this is not an easy way of writing simple vectors. For that we would use something altogether different which will be covered in the next chapter. Because two things look alike does not necessarily imply that they will use the same command. The \choose command's colleagues, \brack and \brace, work in the same way, but give square bracketed or braced results. The underlying command which allows these to be created is called \atopwithdelims. The reference to \atop gives a clue. The construction uses the \atop structure, but expects to be told which two delimiters are to be used. The two delimiters may be chosen from any of the delimiters recognized by TEX (and considered in Chapter 8), and of course, need not be 'paired' in any particular way (provided there are two of them). Writing
$$a\atopwithdelims()b$$
is equivalent to $$a\choose b$$, but rather long-winded. There are also two other constructs, \overwithdelims and \abovewith-delims. This latter requires that the thickness of the line introduced is specified, just like \above.

Continuing mathematics   5

More uses of sub- and superscripts

The conventions described in the previous chapter for sub- and superscripting may also be used for some of TEX's 'large operators'. Perhaps the two key operators are \sum for summation, and \int for integral sign. Note that \Sigma and \sum are different (they may look *similar*, but they behave differently): when placed side by side – Σ and $\sum$ – the difference is quite apparent. In order to place the limits on \sum and \int simply subscript and/or superscript. TEX correctly understands that these special operators must have their sub/superscripts placed below/above the symbol. Like 'normal' sub- and superscripts, there is no ordering implied: the top limit can precede or follow the bottom limit, although it usually makes mores sense to put the lower limit first: 'the summation *from* $i = 1$ *to* n; the integral *from* $-\infty$ *to* 0'. For example:

```
$$ S = \sum_{r=1}^7S_r $$
```

will produce

$$ S = \sum_{r=1}^{7} S_r $$

and

```
$$ \int_{V_l}^{V_g} P(V,T) dV = 0 $$
```

gives

$$ \int_{V_l}^{V_g} P(V,T)dV = 0 $$

In text style, though, these two equations will look a little different: $S = \sum_{r=1}^{7} S_r$ and $\int_{V_l}^{V_g} P(V,T)dV = 0$. There is one obvious difference to the way that TEX treats these two operators in display and text styles. One places the limits above and below, while the other places them to the right. These defaults follow the mathematical convention. It is possible to override them with two modifiers, \limits and \nolimits. Where the limits are placed above and below corresponds to the case of \limits; where they are to the right corresponds to \nolimits. In order to instruct TₑX that a summation should be in the \nolimits form, use \sum\nolimits:

```
$$ S = \sum\nolimits^7_{r=1}S_r $$
```

and similarly, to put \int into the \limits form:

```
$$ \int\limits_{V_l}^{V_g} P(V,T) dV = 0 $$
```

This will give

$$ S = \sum\nolimits_{r=1}^{7} S_r $$

and

$$ \int\limits_{V_l}^{V_g} P(V,T)dV = 0 $$

There are a number of these large operators (Figure 5.1), all of which behave in a similar way, with the use of the sub- and superscript conventions to handle the limits.

⇒*Exercise 5.1:*   Demonstrate what differences occur when the large operators are used in text style and display style.   ⇐

⇒*Exercise 5.2:*   It is not immediately clear which of the large operators default to the \limits and \nolimits form. Investigate both text and display versions.   ⇐

⇒*Exercise 5.3:*   Turn the following into a suitable TₑX form:

$$ \overline{\eta^2} = \frac{1}{2} \sum_{k=0}^{\infty} \sum_{\theta=0}^{2\pi} a_n^2 $$

⇐

A confession

TₑX does not always get it right. Especially when dealing with integrals, TₑX often needs a bit of help. Most equations with integral signs in them also have a d-something term or two. If we look at an equation containing an integral like

$$ I = \int_C \frac{4\,dz}{2z^2 + 5iz - 2} = \int_C \frac{2\,dz}{(z + 2i)(z + \frac{1}{2}i)} $$

we notice that the dz term has a little extra space before it. This is a fairly typical convention, which helps to emphasize that the dx is a single concept, not the two variables d and x. TₑX is simply

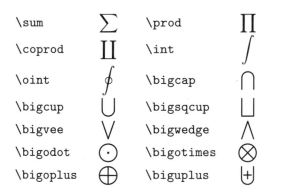

\sum	$\sum$	\prod	$\prod$
\coprod	$\coprod$	\int	$\int$
\oint	$\oint$	\bigcap	$\bigcap$
\bigcup	$\bigcup$	\bigsqcup	$\bigsqcup$
\bigvee	$\bigvee$	\bigwedge	$\bigwedge$
\bigodot	$\bigodot$	\bigotimes	$\bigotimes$
\bigoplus	$\bigoplus$	\biguplus	$\biguplus$

Figure 5.1
The large
operators

not smart enough to anticipate this difference, and to help it we must introduce a 'thin space'. This is defined in maths mode to be \,. The last example was therefore obtained by 4\,dz and 2\,dz in the numerators.

On the other hand, double integral (or triple) integrals often seem too far apart, especially if they are given without their limits. The reason for this is not too obscure. There are no implicit kerns in maths. The integral signs have a strong diagonal element to them, and since TEX is butting together rectangular boxes 'containing' the symbols, there seems to be too much space between them. In the expression

$$E_i(y') = \iint A(s)e^{isy}\sigma(y - y')dy\,ds$$

the two integrals have been drawn together by inserting 'negative thin space' between them. This quantity is the same distance as \, but removes space. In fact, in this case we use two such quantities. The command is \!, so the integrals have been expressed as
\int\!\!\int
⇒*Exercise 5.4:*   Reproduce that last example.   ⇐

Even when multiple integrals are used which each have limits associated with them, the inclusion of negative thin space seems necessary. So when an integral has limits, and whether it uses the \limits or \nolimits form, the negative thin space is required.
⇒*Exercise 5.5:*   Express the following integral equation in both the \limits and \nolimits form, with suitable adjustment of negative thin space.

$$\overline{\nu^2} = \int_0^\infty \int_0^{2\pi} E(k,\theta)dk\,d\theta$$

⇐

Other operators

TeX also has an extensive suite of ordinary (and extraordinary) operators which are used in equations. Before presenting them all, it is useful to try to establish some order, which helps in the understanding of how TeX treats these operators. The first group can be described as binary or dyadic operators since they are normally preceded and followed by other symbols, for example $x + y$, $a \times b$, $n \div m$, or $\alpha - \beta$. Obviously some of these might also exist on their own as monadic (or unary) operators: $x = -1$.

Many people would be happy to make a distinction here, and so too does TeX. It makes its difference in terms of spacing. The spacing around the minus is different in the expressions `$x=a-b$` and `$ x=-y $`.

⇒*Exercise 5.6:*   Illustrate the difference in spacing between monadic and dyadic operators by examining the way TeX handles a simple expression like `-4-2\pi i`   ⇐

TeX recognizes no less than 32 'primitive' operators (Figure 5.2), in addition to the operators already available from the keyboard: $+$, $-$, $/$, and $*$. There are also facilities to define your own if you wish. Once defined as a binary operator, TeX will apply the rules for binary operations. There appears to be no difference in the way that TeX handles $*$ and `\ast` in maths. Most of the operators are 'reasonably' familiar, or at least their names follow without too much difficulty, but `\wr` may be slightly more unusual. Its 'full name' is 'wreath product'. Some of them are also used in normal text. The † and ‡ are accessible 'normally' as `\dag` and `\ddag`. It is not unusual to require •, ·, or even ⋆, but these have no non-mathematical alternative description and to use them in text you would have to include the `$` symbols around them:

`to require $\bullet$, $\cdot$, or even $\star$, but`

As we have noted above, binary operators normally have extra space around them. At the moment it is sufficient to say that if the operator is not being used in a binary way, TeX is 'smart' enough to treat it as a simple symbol (most times). Thus H^{2+}, f^*, or even $g^\circ \mapsto g^*$ will use the 'operators' as simple symbols, leaving no extra space.

⇒*Exercise 5.7:*   Your enlarged vocabulary now permits the following expressions to be expressed in TeX form:

$$X \ominus \check{B} = X \cap X_{-h}$$

$$X \ominus B = \bigcup_i X_i \ominus B$$

\pm	$\pm$	\mp	$\mp$
\div	$\div$	\times	$\times$
\ast	$*$	\setminus	$\setminus$
\star	$\star$	\diamond	$\diamond$
\bullet	$\bullet$	\cdot	$\cdot$
\cup	$\cup$	\cap	$\cap$
\sqcup	$\sqcup$	\sqcap	$\sqcap$
\triangleleft	$\triangleleft$	\triangleright	$\triangleright$
\bigtriangleup	$\bigtriangleup$	\bigtriangledown	$\bigtriangledown$
\wr	$\wr$	\bigcirc	$\bigcirc$
\vee *or* \lor	$\vee$	\wedge *or* \land	$\wedge$
\oplus	$\oplus$	\ominus	$\ominus$
\otimes	$\otimes$	\oslash	$\oslash$
\amalg	$\amalg$	\uplus	$\uplus$
\circ	$\circ$	\odot	$\odot$
\dagger	$\dagger$	\ddagger	$\ddagger$

Figure 5.2
Binary
operators

$$\int_{-B/2}^{B/2} R''(y,y')\varphi''(y')dy' = \gamma''\varphi''(y)$$

$$\vec{f}^{(1)} = \vec{f}^{(0)} - \frac{(\vec{w}_1 \cdot \vec{f}^{(0)} - p_1)}{\vec{w}_1 \cdot \vec{w}_1}\vec{w}_1$$

$$((A \vee \neg B \vee C \neg D) \wedge (\neg E \vee \neg F))$$

as well as permitting you the luxury of being able to write $6°$ Centigrade or 9.46×10^{12} kilometres per year. But how? $\Leftarrow$

Relations

As the Figure 5.3 shows, there are lots of relations in the family of TEX. A fairly common mistake is to assume that $>$ and $<$ are obtained by \gt and \lt. Unfortunately this is permitting intuition to carry you away, and although $\leq$ may be obtained from the two commands, \le and \leq, the same privilege was not extended to $>$ and $<$. On the other hand, few people would expect $=$ to be accessed by \eq.

If you look back to Figure 4.4 which shows some of the many symbols available, you will note that | and ‖ appear there, under the 'names' | or \vert and \| or \Vert. Why then do they also appear in Figure 5.3 under the names of \mid and \parallel? In case the answer is not obvious, consider the different functions the same symbol is performing. On the one hand they may be simple symbols, while on the other they are treated as binary operators. The context should determine whether $a|b$ is somehow

=	$=$	<	$<$	>	$>$
\leq *or* \le	$\leq$	\geq *or* \ge	$\geq$	\equiv	$\equiv$
\prec	$\prec$	\succ	$\succ$	\sim	$\sim$
\preceq	$\preceq$	\succeq	$\succeq$	\simeq	$\simeq$
\ll	$\ll$	\gg	$\gg$	\asymp	$\asymp$
\subset	$\subset$	\supset	$\supset$	\approx	$\approx$
\subseteq	$\subseteq$	\supseteq	$\supseteq$	\cong	$\cong$
\sqsubseteq	$\sqsubseteq$	\sqsupseteq	$\sqsupseteq$	\bowtie	$\bowtie$
\in	$\in$	\ni *or* \owns	$\ni$	\notin	$\notin$
\vdash	$\vdash$	\dashv	$\dashv$	\models	$\models$
\smile	$\smile$	\mid	$\mid$	\doteq	$\doteq$
\frown	$\frown$	\parallel	$\parallel$	\perp	$\perp$
\colon *or* :	$:$	\neq *or* \ne	$\neq$	\propto	$\propto$

Figure 5.3
Relations

three symbols, or the | is an operator, in which case it should look like $a \mid b$. In manuscript form it is seldom clear which is intended.

The colon is also present in the table as a relation. When used in maths, it will be treated as a relation, and not as punctuation. To obtain a colon as punctuation, you *have to* use \colon. This is not quite as perverse as it sounds, since : tends to be used as a relation, while the other 'punctuation' – comma, semi-colon, and full point – tends to be used more conventionally. But if you are accustomed to writing $a := a + 1$, you may find having to type \colon= an irritation.

⇒*Exercise 5.8:*   Here, '|' means 'projection onto'; therefore it is an operator:

$$\frac{1}{\pi} U(X) = \frac{1}{2\pi} \int_0^{2\pi} L(X \mid \Delta_\alpha)\, d\alpha$$

Turn it into TₑX.   ⇐

If you ever require a negated version of one of these relations, like $\not\smile$, or more likely, $\neq$, then you precede the relation by \not – \not\smile or \not\equiv. The positioning is not always perfect, notably with \in, and there is another version \notin which looks better.

There is a minor danger lurking within \neq. If the 'truth' be told, it is really an abbreviation for \not=. This is hardly a surprise, but should we ever require to use the expression $x^{\neq}$ we have to be careful to write it as $x^{\neq}$, and not as $x^\neq$. What TₑX sees in the latter case is $x^\not=$, and what you see is $x \neq$!

⇒*Exercise 5.9:*   Compare $\notin$ with $\notin$ and decide which 'not in' looks better. Which is which?   ⇐

⇒*Exercise 5.10:*   A handful of equations to set:

$$\tau_1/\tau_0 \approx 0.5p/h_0$$

$$h/L \gg \partial h/\partial x$$

$$\frac{\Delta}{t} \geq \sqrt{2gh}$$

$$\nabla^2 f(i,j) \equiv \delta_x{}^2 f(i,j) + \delta_y{}^2 f(i,j)$$

$$Q \in N(P) \iff P \in N(Q)$$

⇐

If the vast array of relations is not sufficient for you, there are also lots of arrows. Both \Longleftrightarrow and \iff give the same symbol, but \iff has extra space around it: $a \Longleftrightarrow b$ and $a \iff b$.

⇒*Exercise 5.11:*   Again, this opens up all sorts of new possibilities:

$$(W \ominus \check{B}) \cap (W \ominus \check{B})_{-h} \neq \emptyset \Leftrightarrow B \cup B_h \subset W$$

$$Y \subset X \Rightarrow \psi_\lambda(Y) \subset \varphi_\lambda(X)$$

$$X \to x_1 \rightleftharpoons x_2$$

$$2HCO_3{}^- \longrightarrow H_2O + CO_2 \uparrow + CO_3{}^{2-}$$

This last example demonstrates TeX's weakness at handling chemical equations through maths.   ⇐

As if this was not enough, you can place symbols over left and right arrows with the aid of the \buildrel command. For example, $a\overset{\mathrm{def}}{\to}b$ is obtained by

$a{\buildrel \rm def \over \rightarrow}b$

Note in particular that \over has nothing to do with fractions here. The braces are not really necessary; they simply make the construction more obvious. Shortly we will uncover a way of creating commands which will make the use of these constructs less awkward and more intuitive. This construction will also work with =. For example, $x\overset{\triangle}{=}y$ is obtained from

$x{\buildrel \triangle\over=}y$

⇒*Exercise 5.12:*   The \buildrel works with the various relations, but does not work easily with the negated relations. Although this is hardly likely to be a very critical restriction, verify it, and then see if there is a reasonably straightforward way around the problem.   ⇐

Simple arrows (Figure 5.4) may be used in a manner similar to \overline. Both \overrightarrow and \overleftarrow will place an arrow above an expression, extending the shaft to span the expression: for example, $\overrightarrow{a+b}$ is obtained from

$\overrightarrow{a+b}$

Text and display modes

This section is needed in order to explain some aspects of sizing in very particular situations, chiefly associated with \over and its variants. Most of it can be safely ignored most of the time, but if things do appear a little strange this section may help provide an explanation. You may have observed that TEX handles the same information slightly differently, depending on whether you are in text style (between single dollars), or in display style (between double dollars). Sometimes these differences are rather subtle. A very obvious example would be something like
`$${A\over B}\over{A-{B\over C}}$$`
which turns out like

$$\frac{\frac{A}{B}}{A-\frac{B}{C}}$$

when we might really have wanted something like

$$\frac{\frac{A}{B}}{A-\frac{B}{C}}$$

Formally we recognize the following styles in maths mode: *text* style, *display* style, *script* style, and *scriptscript* style. There are corresponding commands which force the conventions associated with each of these styles, and therefore allow you to override what TEX thinks it wants to do. The first two styles, \textstyle and \displaystyle, are those which are 'triggered' by \$ or \$\$ respectively. Whenever an expression within single \$ symbols is encountered, TEX defaults to 'text style' maths. Substituting the double \$\$ symbols would mean the expression was set in 'display style'. Usually these look much the same, so that
`setting $e^{i\pi}$ and $$e^{i\pi}$$ will be identically set.`
setting $e^{i\pi}$ and

$$e^{i\pi}$$

will be identically set. 'Script' style encompasses first-level sub- and superscripts. In the previous example, the $i\pi$ part is set in 'script style'. This style is also accessible through \script- style. Logically then, 'scriptscript' style applies to nth-order sub- and superscripts, where $n > 1$, which are themselves applied to sub- or superscripts. As implied earlier, there is no concept of 'scriptscriptscript style'!

`\leftarrow` *or* `\gets`	←	`\longleftarrow`	⟵
`\Leftarrow`	⇐	`\Longleftarrow`	⟸
`\rightarrow` *or* `\to`	→	`\longrightarrow`	⟶
`\Rightarrow`	⇒	`\Longrightarrow`	⟹
`\leftrightarrow`	↔	`\longleftrightarrow`	⟷
`\Leftrightarrow`	⇔	`\Longleftrightarrow` *or* `\iff`	⟺
`\uparrow`	↑	`\Uparrow`	⇑
`\downarrow`	↓	`\Downarrow`	⇓
`\updownarrow`	↕	`\Updownarrow`	⇕
`\mapsto`	↦	`\longmapsto`	⟼
`\hookleftarrow`	↩	`\hookrightarrow`	↪
`\leftharpoonup`	↼	`\rightharpoonup`	⇀
`\leftharpoondown`	↽	`\rightharpoondown`	⇁
`\rightleftharpoons`	⇌		
`\nearrow`	↗	`\searrow`	↘
`\swarrow`	↙	`\nwarrow`	↖

Figure 5.4
Arrows

This is all very straightforward up to now, and introduces nothing exceptional. However, there are variant styles where the *exponents* are not raised quite so much. These may be termed the 'cramped' styles.

How can we illustrate these differences easily? The use of the `\sqrt` always changes an exponent to the 'cramped' style. Therefore we should be able to gauge the difference by comparing the a^n in an expression like
`a^n\sqrt{a^n}`
The differences are not great – $a^n\sqrt{a^n}$, but you may be able to observe that the exponent is a little lower in the case of the `\sqrt{a^n}`. This effect also applies to `\overline`.

Note that the effect is confined to exponents. Therefore subscripts are totally unaffected, although superscripts of subscripts could be. This is not quite true. All subscripts are rendered in a 'cramped' style. There is no such thing as an 'uncramped' subscript. Why bother having such a category then? Probably for the following reason: once a symbol has become 'cramped' all its sub- or superscripts also become cramped. This was probably obvious in the case of a super-superscript like $\overline{a^{n^m}}$, but it is slightly less obvious that the m in a_{n^m} is also cramped.

You might suppose that the height of an exponent is equivalent in all the uncramped styles. It is not. Again the differences are not large. We can compare display and text style:

$$a^m a^m$$

the second a^m has been forced to be treated as if it were in text style.

The 'trend' continues through script and scriptscript styles, although it becomes more difficult to demonstrate. By using the \textstyle, \scriptstyle, and \scriptscriptstyle commands, it is possible to show what is happening:

```
$$
{\textstyle a^m}
{\displaystyle a^m}
{\scriptstyle{\displaystyle a}^{\scriptstyle m}}
{\scriptscriptstyle{\displaystyle a}^{\scriptstyle m}}
$$
```

There is an extra pair of braces around each subexpression, just to emphasize their apartness:

$$a^m a^m a^m a^m$$

It is in circumstances like these that criticism of long commands becomes prevalent.

What are the effects in 'cramped' styles?

```
$$
{\textstyle a^m\sqrt{a^m}}
{\displaystyle a^m\sqrt{a^m}}
{\scriptstyle  {\displaystyle a}^{\scriptstyle m}
\sqrt{{\displaystyle a}^{\scriptstyle m}}}
{\scriptscriptstyle {\displaystyle a}^{\scriptstyle m}
\sqrt{{\displaystyle a}^{\scriptstyle m}}}
$$
```

gives

$$a^m \sqrt{a^m} a^m \sqrt{a^m} a^m \sqrt{a^m} a^m \sqrt{a^m}$$

where the finesse of the positioning becomes (barely) noticeable.

Similar effects are obtained when dealing with subscripts, but are perhaps even less observable.

Leaving sub- and superscripts, the differences in style are more apparent when we use fractions: the key example is one like $a\over b$ or $$a\over b$$. The denominator will always be cramped. Theoretically it is possible for the numerator to be cramped, but illustrating this is especially obscure. If any of the styles adopted for a start out as cramped, then the corresponding b will also be cramped (Figure 5.5).

One interesting interaction which might not have been anticipated is that in the expression $$a\over b$$, we are originally

Original style	a	b	Example
display	text	cramped text	$\frac{a}{b}$
text	script	cramped script	$\frac{a}{b}$
script, scriptscript	scriptscript	cramped scriptscript	$\frac{a}{b}, \frac{a}{b}$

Figure 5.5
Mathematical
styles

in display style, so the numerator and denominator are this time rendered in text style.

What this all implies

Naturally, the reason all this information has been presented is so that you can interfere with TEX's 'natural' manipulations in order to control the output more correctly. The commands already met will allow this. There is, however, no way to force the 'cramped' styles – TEX does that itself.

Under what circumstances might you wish to control the sizes yourself (or put another way, when do TEX's own rules go wrong?). Fortunately, this interference is seldom required. You will, however, know instantly once you see the output – a little late perhaps, but the alternative is to retain all this information about changing styles as you go along (no easy task). Perhaps the most frequent use for manipulating styles may be with the \over family, when several are used together:

```
$$a \over {b+c \over{d+e+f \over{g+h+i+j}}} $$
```

According to the style rules this will look decidedly odd:

$$
\frac{a}{\frac{b+c}{\frac{d+e+f}{g+h+i+j}}}
$$

the top line is in display style, the second in cramped script style, the third in cramped scriptscript style, the fourth also in cramped scriptscript style. It would seem more reasonable to make all four lines the same style:

$$
\frac{a}{\frac{b+c}{\frac{d+e+f}{g+h+i+j}}}
$$

as with

```
$$a \over \displaystyle{b+c \over \displaystyle{d+e+f
    \over \displaystyle{g+h+i+j}}} $$
```

You might even prefer something like:

$$\cfrac{a}{\cfrac{b+c}{\cfrac{d+e+f}{g+h+i+j}}}$$

which is obtained from

```
$$a \above2pt   \displaystyle{b+c
    \above1.5pt\displaystyle{d+e+f
    \above1pt   \displaystyle{g+h+i+j}}} $$
```

But even these examples are rather arcane. These are not forms which are commonly used. It is noticeable that with the \above form there appears to be a rather unexpected change into 'uncramped' style.

A slightly more relevant example crops up with the use of large operators:

$$\sum_{\substack{i \ne j \\ j=1}}^{\substack{i=n \\ j=n}} X_{ij}$$

obtained from

```
$$ \sum_{i \ne j \atop j=1}^{i=n \atop j=n} X_{ij} $$
```

The subscript (in this case, a limit) on the summation is in cramped script style, but since this itself is composed of two components (a \atop b), the two elements a and b will be in cramped scriptscript style. 'Cramped' style because they are sub-scripts – consider $a^{b \over c}$ where clearly the b \over c part would be broken down to scriptscript style and cramped scriptscript style. This 'cramped' aside is relatively unimportant here. What is important is the shift to scripscript style. In the summation, the limits are in scriptscript style and smaller than they would have been if we had only single sets of limits. Thus a better (more readable) solution when dealing with multiple limits on large operators in general is:

```
$$ \sum_{\scriptstyle i \ne j \atop \scriptstyle j=1}^
{\scriptstyle i=n \atop \scriptstyle j=n} X_{ij} $$
```

to give us

$\Rightarrow$*Exercise 5.13:* You should now be able to set

$$\frac{\frac{A}{B}}{A - \frac{B}{C}}$$

'correctly'. Do so. $\Leftarrow$

This seems like a lot of work, and it comes as a great relief to acknowledge that most times TEX gets it right and we do not have to worry. But at least the tools are there, should you find you need them.

$\Rightarrow$*Exercise 5.14:* The examples have tended to concentrate on displayed forms. To redress the balance slightly, set the following short extracts:

The expected cost, $c(i|\vec{z})$, is given by $\sum_j p(j|\vec{z})\lambda(i|j)$; if both $\lambda(i|i) = 0$ and the $\lambda(i|j)$'s are equal when $j \neq i$, minimizing the expected cost is equivalent to minimizing $\sum_{j \neq i} p(j|\vec{z})$.

The Laplacian $\partial^2 f/\partial x^2 + \partial^2 f/\partial y^2$ is an orientation-invariant derivative operator.

The responses of $\sqrt{\Delta_+{}^2 + \Delta_-{}^2}$ are $h\sqrt{2}$, $h\sqrt{2}$, h, and h.

$\Leftarrow$

$\Rightarrow$*Exercise 5.15:* And lastly, as a passing-out exercise, return to displayed equations and typeset the following equations. There are one or two snags or deliberate catches, just to ensure that you examine the output fairly closely. As has been pointed out, TEX sometimes needs a little help with its spacing. Some of these examples are remarkably tedious to type in, but worthwhile nonetheless!

$$G_\rho = \dot{F}_\rho = \bigcup_{\epsilon > 0} F_{\rho+\epsilon} = \bigcup_{\epsilon > 0} G_{\rho+\epsilon}$$

$$d(X_i, X) \to 0 \Rightarrow W_k^{(n)}(X_i) \to W_k^{(n)}(Y), \forall n, k$$

$$\gamma_z(h) = \frac{(\gamma * K)_h - (\gamma * K)_0}{A^2(Z)}$$

$$C^*(k) = \frac{\sum_{\lambda=1}^g A(Z_\lambda) \cdot C_\lambda^*(k)}{\sum_{\lambda=1}^g A(Z_\lambda)}$$

$$\frac{\partial}{\partial t} \int_{-h}^\zeta \rho U_\alpha \, dz = \frac{-\partial}{\partial x_\beta} \int_{-h}^\zeta (\rho u_\alpha u_\beta + p\delta_{\alpha\beta}) \, dz + (p)_{z=-h} \frac{\partial h}{\partial x_\alpha}$$

$$r^2 = \frac{\int_{-\infty}^\infty w(x)c^2(x) \, dx}{\int_{-\infty}^\infty c^2(x) \, dx}$$

$$\iint fg \le \sqrt{\iiint f^2 \iint g^2}$$

$$p(1)p(z|1) + p(2)p(z|2)$$

$$p(h|r) = \sum_z q(z|r)q(z + h|r)$$

$$\frac{e^{-m'/2}}{\sqrt{2\pi}\,\sigma_1{}^{m'}} \cdot \frac{e^{-m''/2}}{\sqrt{2\pi}\,\sigma_1{}^{m''}} = \frac{e^{-m/2}}{\sqrt{2\pi}^m \sigma_1{}^{m'}\sigma_2{}^{m''}}$$

$$f_\delta(x, y) \equiv f(x, y) - f(x + \delta x, y + \delta y)$$

$$\exists j : k < j \leq N : X_k > 0 \wedge X_j > 0 \wedge \neg(\exists i : k < i < j : X_i > 0)$$

$$\Leftarrow$$

More words
6

Even the most erudite and involved mathematical treatise needs the glue of words to hold the pieces together. Despite the incredible ease and simplicity with which TₑX can handle equations, as we have already discovered, it also handles non-technical material in a straightforward and direct way. Unfortunately, the rules for 'normal' text are less rigid. Why unfortunately? The greater the amount of choice, the greater the amount of disagreement. We can generally agree when equations 'look wrong', but deciding when text 'looks right' is rather more tricky. The general approach adopted here is to concentrate on the plainer aspects, assuming that the content is the important component, and that the presentation should be as bland and anonymous as possible. At the extreme, we hope the presentation will be invisible. If we are very fortunate, it may even contribute subtly to the message. But, before the heavyweight material, something carefree.

Trivial pursuits

It is time for something frivolous. One of the nice features of TₑX (although of marginal real use in English) is its excellent support of diacritical marks and foreign letters. Naturally there is an ulterior motive for introducing these now.

First the special letters. TₑX recognizes commands for the ligatures Œ, Æ, œ, and æ (used in Latin, Old English, and modern French, among others). It also recognizes the German 'ß' or 'essthet' symbol. It will handle the Å, å, Ø and ø of some Scandinavian languages, although the Icelandic 'th' letters (eth and thorn) are ignored. And lastly, it copes with the Polish suppressed-L, L and ł.

How do we get these into our text? As usual, TₑX does something with a special command. The commands are given in Figure 6.1.

To begin with, each time you use one of these defined commands, leave a space before the next character. Thus to write

Œdipus in TEX, you actual write \OE dipus. This helps to distinguish \OE dipus from \OEdipus, which TEX would assume was a new (probably undefined) command. Notice that any extra spaces between \OE and dipus are ignored, as far as forming the output is concerned, but are essential for the syntax. Since all extra spaces are ignored, leaving a few extra, or even typing
```
\OE
dipus
```
will not leave a space between the ligature and the text which follows when the passage is set. This gobbling up of extra blanks is a normal feature of TEX. We could also group the command, in which case it should not be followed by a space; for example, {\OE}dipus is an acceptable solution. Notice that the end of line was just another space to TEX.

⇒*Exercise 6.1:* What effect would the following have: {\OE }dipus, \OE{}dipus, \OE {dipus}, \O{E}dipus, {\OE} dipus?   ⇐

What implication does this have for commands at the end of words? Consider trying to write:
```
the Schlo\ss of the Rhine valley
```
The word Schloß would appear as we require, but the spaces which follow would be ignored on output. The space after a command is used to separate out the command so that TEX can recognize it. Multiple spaces are treated as a single space. Thus the next word would begin immediately after the ß. This is generally not what we want. In order to solve this problem, a new command, \␣], that is the backslash followed by a space, introduces what is called a 'control space'. This ␣ symbol does not occur on the keyboard: it is just a way of indicating that there really is a space. If there is ever any particular requirement to indicate 'spaces', they will be shown this way.

What we probably wanted was
```
the Schlo\ss\ of the Rhine valley
```
Earlier it was suggested that a command containing alphabetic characters should be followed by a space, in order to let TEX know where the command ends. If you look at this more closely, you will realize that there are other ways to signify the end of a command. One of them was illustrated with the {\OE}dipus sequence. There the } was able to indicate the end of the command. Actually, in that case, \OE{}dipus would have had the same effect. The sequence {} looks odd, and seems to mean nothing, but from time to time, even nothing has its uses. Another alternative is shown with the Schlo\ss\␣ sequence. The occurrence of a \ 'obviously'

\ss	gives the German ß
\OE	gives the Œ ligature
\oe	gives the œ ligature
\AE	gives the Æ ligature
\ae	gives the æ ligature
\O	gives the letter Ø
\o	gives the letter ø
\AA	gives the letter Å
\aa	gives the letter å
\L	gives the letter Ł
\l	gives the letter ł

Figure 6.1
'National'
letters

begins a new command, and therefore indicates the end of the previous one.

⇒*Exercise 6.2:*   There is a very real difference between \OE dipus and \OE{}dipus or even {\OE}dipus. What will happen to the implicit kerning?   ⇐

Since we are in the realm of national letters, we may also mention two more ligatures. At least, as far as TEX is concerned, they are ligatures. In Spanish, sentences which are questioning or exclamatory begin with inverted question or exclamation marks. This is rather a nice convention, since when read aloud such sentences are usually given different intonation. In English you usually find out too late! In order to obtain ¿ and ¡ TEX uses the ligature mechanism, but what we type are ?' and !'. In normal circumstances this should never present an ambiguity. It is difficult to see the circumstances in which ? or ! would be followed by a single open quote, except by mistake.

TEX also has lots of diacriticals (Knuth refers to them as accents, but some are not: diacriticals include all the accents, but also the cedilla and dieresis/umlaut). The list is given in Figure 6.2. By and large, the commands are fairly logically named. The diacriticals fall into two main categories: those which are generated by an alphabetic character, namely

\v \u \H \b \t \c \d

and those which are controlled by a non-alphabetic character –

\. \^ \` \' \= \" \~

To reiterate, one of TEX's important rules is that after a command consisting of a non-alphabetic character, no space is required (in fact any space left in such cases is treated as space, and is not eaten). Thus we may type \'eclat for éclat, but to type façade properly, we will need to type fa\c cade or fa\c{c}ade. It is common (but not always correct) to see a space left after almost all commands. In general terms, a command made up of a backslash and a single non-alphabetic character should not be followed by a space, or that space will be accepted by TEX as a real 'to be printed' space. For example, the command `\&` gives the ampersand, &: If we write

`Had we World enough, \& time`

the space after the `\&` is respected. But accents are not 'normal' non-alphabetic commands. Accenting a space is meaningless. TEX looks for a character to modify.

You may wonder why Knuth bothered to make the cedilla a diacritical divorced from the c itself (that is, why didn't `\c` give the c and the cedilla together?). Languages like Turkish, Lithuanian, Latvian, Romanian, and Navajo use cedillas under other letters.

In order to get diacriticals over i and j, you really ought to take the dot off first. As Figure 6.2 indicates, TEX supports a dotless i and j, provided by `\i` and `\j`. These allow you to do things like î (from `\^\i`), or even ĳ (from `\t\i\j`), should you ever find a reason to do so.

The general rule with all these sequences is – diacritical first, then letter. At first this sounds counter-intuitive, after all, we say 'e-acute', or 'o-circumflex'.

None of these accents is really 'fundamental' to TEX, in the sense that they are all created in much the same way, a way that is accessible. You can create your own superior diacriticals with the `\accent` command, should `plain` TEX be unable to provide you with the marks you need. In essence, the 'accent' is superimposed over the character which follows, and is centred; it is raised or lowered as appropriate (essential to accommodate capital letters). Note that this applies only to the 'superiors', the accents placed over a character. The cedilla and other 'inferior' diacriticals require quite different manœuvring.

There should be only a single character following a diacritical – that is, a group will not be accented: `r\^{o}le` is acceptable, as is `r\^{ole}`, but TEX merely modifies the next following character, o. A font change may follow a diacritical: something like `r\^{\it o}le` would work (although `r{\it\^o}le` might make more sense), but `r\^\it ole` would end up by accenting a space.

The tie accent is clearly an exception, since it expects to handle two characters, but strangely, the second one may be a space.

Command	Name	Example
\`	grave	\`e gives è
\'	acute or aigu	\'e gives é
\^	circumflex or hat	\^o gives ô
\v	inverted circumflex (háček accent)	\v z gives ž
\u	breve	\u g gives ğ
\=	macron, long vowel	\=u gives ū
\"	umlaut or dieresis	\"u gives ü
\H	Hungarian umlaut	\H u gives ű
\~	tilde	\~n gives ñ
\.	dot accent	\.z gives ż
\t	tie	\t oo gives o͡o
\c	cedilla	\c c gives ç
\d	dot under	\d u gives ụ
\b	bar under	\b a gives a̱

and although not diacritics, we should mention

\i	dotless i	\i gives ı
\j	dotless j	\j gives ȷ

Figure 6.2
Diacriticals and
their use

Speaking in tongues

However, it is still not especially clear why you would ever want to
create your own \accent sequences. You may, because Knuth was
not exhaustive in his handling of diacriticals, even for European
languages. The Swedish Å is a letter; it is not an A with an accent.
Earlier versions of TeX merely treated it as an A with an accent.
In order to rectify this glaring anomaly, Knuth allowed the circle
accent to disappear. Unfortunately, Czech uses the circle as an
accent. For reasons that baffle me, I set some Czech in TeX and
came across this problem. In order to create ů I had to type
\accent23u
This is unbearably clumsy. TeX does have a better way which we
shall uncover shortly.

Perhaps it might be appropriate to come a little cleaner about
baseline skip at this point: \baselineskip is a rather rigid structure, and when we have characters with diacriticals, it is possible
that successive lines could run into one another. This is considered undesirable. In order to solve this problem, there is another
command, \lineskip, which adds a certain amount of space (as
specified) between lines to prevent this occurring. The default
setting for \lineskip in plain TeX is 1 point. Normally, this is
not likely to be needed. If we are using a 10 point font, we would

expect to set it with 11 or 12 point baselines. From time to time
it may be desirable to use 10 on 10 (for a telephone directory,
or somewhere where space was at a premium). That is to say, a
10 point font on 10 point baselines. Here the letters might run
into one another. On the other hand, when the extra space is
included, the irregular density of the lines obtained through the
extra line skip tends to look rather unpleasant. Really the decision is between having a few letters run into one another, or the
density of lines on the page being irregular. An example of the
application of \lineskip was seen earlier in Chapter 4: $a^{b^{c^{d^e}}}$.

You will be pleased to know that diacriticals work on upper and
lower case alike. T_EX *will* hyphenate words which contain diacriticals and the letters which are accessed through commands.
But it will only hyphenate up to the first diacritical or command.
Since these tend to be foreign words, do not be surprised if the
hyphenated words contain embarrassing blunders.

You will also find that trying to get two diacriticals on a single
character is difficult – in fact, T_EX is very reluctant to let you do
this. But you could find a way if you really wanted. If you were
Vietnamese, it would be essential: you would want to be able to
write things like Mǎg.

Diacriticals are available with almost all fonts, although the
typewriter font contains one or two surprises. However, you might
note that even with manipulation of existing T_EX characters, as
with ů, there are some missing diacriticals. I started looking at
some Polish, and, assuming that because ł was there, all necessary symbols would be present for Polish, I was disappointed to
find that the 'hook' or 'ogonek' symbol ('little tail' – rather like a
cedilla in reverse) was missing. Doubtless there are others.

Typing in these command is tedious, especially if you have
a keyboard already equipped with accented characters. Knuth
suggests a strategy where T_EX accepts certain combinations of
characters as ligatures: for example, typing 'eclat, the 'e combination would be recognized as a character pair and produce é.
It is not immediately clear whether every **AE** combination should
produce Æ, or how this would accommodate cedillas or breves.
The simple examples above do not require any changes to T_EX,
but can be achieved by altering the T_EX font metric files (**tfm**
files). It would reduce the transportability of T_EX. But real help
is at hand. T_EX3 has much better support of diacritical marks,
and it will eventually remove the hyphenation problem.

⇒*Exercise 6.3:*   Typeset the following:
Zde se všemožně snaží mě předuvit, abych zůstal ještě několik měsíců a napsal ještě jednu operu. Hayır! İş öyle değil. Büyüğü küçüğüne takilmayı pek severdi. Ce fût d'ores et déjà une idée dégénérée et ambigüe. ¡Γειό σου!

⇐

⇒*Exercise 6.4:*   How will you ensure that foreign words are hyphenated correctly?

⇐

Although the diacriticals do work in exactly the same way with almost all the fonts, there is an exception, the typewriter font. In any case, the typewriter font is a little special. It is a 'mono-space' font. That is to say, each character has the same width. The ligatures fi, fl, ff, ffi, ffl are not required, nor are the em-dash and en-dash. Similarly the opening and closing double quotes (again accessed by the ligature mechanism in all the other fonts) are not present. In typewriter font, the keyboard's double-quote character can be used for opening and closing quotes. Lastly, it turns out that the long Hungarian umlaut ("), the dot accent, and the Polish silent l are not available.

Naturally, having removed these characters, some others are substituted. In particular, we gain {, }, <, >, ↑, and ↓. The font table in Appendix A will show how the font was rearranged.

Making it larger

Sometimes a document benefits from being printed in a larger font size, or maybe just enlarging the title or other key elements would provide better emphasis. There are several ways to achieve this. Taking the simplest first, we can increase the size of the *entire* document, including the fonts, through the use of the \magnification command. To do this, we can place a command like
\magnification=\magstep1
right at the beginning of our document. This command has to be in operation before anything substantial happens, or TEX will complain. Put it first. There may only be one \magnification command in any one document. If TEX encounters more than one, it will complain. Thus we cannot use this technique to change the characteristics of the document 'dynamically'.

There are various predefined 'steps' of magnification (Figure 6.3). These are named \magsteps, and range from \magstephalf, through \magstep1, to \magstep5 (and sometimes beyond). The larger magnifications are not always supported in all fonts for every installation. All of these magnification steps are based on powers of 1.2. The smallest, \magstephalf, takes the 'base' size and enlarges it by $\sqrt{1.2}$. For \magstep1, the magnification is 1.2^1, and so on.

This gives us some flexibility. If we are using a 'normal' 10 point font, then the effect of using \magstep1 or \magstep5 is fairly obvious (an 'effective' size of 12 points or 24.88 points respectively). Since Computer Modern Roman includes a 17 point design size, it would also mean that the largest font easily available would be 17×2.488 points, that is about 42 points.

The action of \magnification is not restricted to any one font, or indeed, any one dimension. It is universal. Everything in the document is magnified. If you had a \parskip of say 10 points, at \magstep1 the actual *measured* paragraph skip would be 12 points – that is, 10×1.2. Similarly, an \hsize of 6 inches would become 7.2 inches. Obviously the paper in the laser printer or typesetter does not magically stretch because TeX has magnified its text.

We can prevent particular dimensions from being magnified by specifying them as *true* measurements. An \hsize of exactly 6.25 inches (as measured) could be obtained, no matter what \magnification had been selected, by saying

\hsize=6.25truein or \hsize=6.25 true in

This is very useful for setting the \hsize and \vsize so that they accurately reflect the area available on your printer, separate from any \magnification you may have selected. If you are using international A4 paper size, you may find it useful to specify

\hsize=6.25truein
\vsize=8.9truein

TeX then adopts a printed page size of 6.25×8.9 inches. Intuitively you might expect that plain TeX sets up these values as true dimensions. You would be wrong. There is some sort of TeX magic going on in there, where despite these default dimensions being set up in 'ordinary' inches, they come out in 'true' inches. We shall look into this later.

If the line length remains constant when you use \magnification, you will probably find an increase in the number of 'overfull boxes', since the larger the font, the fewer words can be fitted on the line, and hence fewer interword spaces; therefore there is less scope for stretch and shrink.

⇒*Exercise 6.5:*   Repeat one of the previous exercises which involves some text and try some of the levels of magnification. It could be wise to reset \hsize and \vsize if you go much above \magstep2.   ⇐

	Magnification factor	'Scale'
\magstep0	1.2^0 or 1.0	1000
\magstephalf	$1.2^{\frac{1}{2}}$ or 1.095	1095
\magstep1	1.2^1 or 1.2	1200
\magstep2	1.2^2 or 1.44	1440
\magstep3	1.2^3 or 1.728	1728
\magstep4	1.2^4 or 2.074	2074
\magstep5	1.2^5 or 2.488	2488

Figure 6.3
The 'standard' magnifications

$\Rightarrow$*Exercise 6.6:*   Use the \magnification command at the beginning of a document. Within the document, issue another \magnification command. How does TEX react to this error? $\Leftarrow$

More fonts

So far we have met the standard upright roman font (cmr10), plus *text italic* (cmti10), **bold extended** (cmbx10), *slanted roman* (cmsl10), and `typewriter type` (cmtt10). These are all at 10 point, as their names suggest. A very basic, or minimal, implementation of TEX could make do with just 16 fonts. This minimum subset is given in Chapter 18. It comprises the fonts mentioned earlier, plus some maths symbol fonts (which we don't yet need). But notice also that some fonts are provided at 5 and 7 point sizes as well. These are chiefly fonts intended for use in mathematics, as well as, or instead of, text.

Many more fonts are available in a full implementation of TEX – there are actually over 70. Some of these 70 are the same typeface at different design sizes, so the true number of 'different' styles is somewhat less. There are facilities for CAPS AND SMALL CAPS, sans serif, a genuine 'designer' font, and even *unslanted italic*, or the truly bizarre. There is no use pretending that these are essential; the gratuitous use of a multitude of fonts serves to confuse, not delight. Nevertheless, they can be useful in moderation.

But how do we use them? They are not all there by default. Each one needs to be separately named and assigned. This is done through the \font command:

\font\myfont=cmr8
\font\sans=cmss8

which would assign the name \myfont to the font which TEX knows as 'cmr8' – Computer Modern Roman at 8 points. \sans would be Computer Modern Sans Serif at 8 point. Note that it might not be a good idea to use \ss for 'sans serif', especially if you planned to talk about a few Schloß. We cannot name fonts directly as `cmr8` or `cmss8`. Nor can we have names like `\cmr8` or `\cmss8`. We must use this 'pointing' technique.

These new names can be used in the following manner
```
Here's {\myfont some eightpoint} text and some
    {\sans sans serif}.
```
This would produce:

> Here's some eightpoint text and some sans serif.

Individual fonts can be scaled in `\magsteps`. This gives greater ranges to the point sizes we may employ, and also to the range of point sizes which can be used in a single document. Somewhere in `plain`, the sequence `\bf` is set up to give a boldface font. There is a statement like
```
\font\bf=cmbx10
```
We might reasonably want to use a bold font for titles too, but at a larger size. We can say
```
\font\bigbf=cmbx10 scaled\magstep2
```
in order to obtain a bold font at 14.4 points. The same base font can therefore be used at different magnifications, within the same document. If you also had `\magnification` in play, the result would be cumulative. The combination
```
\magnification=\magstep1
\font\bigbf=cmbx10 scaled\magstep2
```
would result in `\bigbf` being used at 17.28 points – that is, `\magstep1` plus `\magstep2`. It may not be immediately obvious, but `\magstephalf` must be used with caution. Take the previous example, and imagine that it had read
```
\magnification=\magstephalf
\font\bigbf=cmbx10 scaled\magstep2
```
The `\bigbf` font would now be at $10 \times 1.2^{2.5}$ (or 15.77) points. Curiously, it is not T_EX which would complain, although things would probably not work out quite as you expect.

⇒*Exercise 6.7:*   Sans serif style is not available by default. There are no convenient names set up for its use. Given that three of the sans serif Computer Modern fonts are `cmss10` (CM Sans Serif), `cmssi10` (CM Sans Serif Italic), and `cmssbx10` (CM Sans Serif Bold Extended), set the following piece of text:

> In very general terms, type should seek to be unobtrusive. It should never **dominate** the text. At some *subtle* levels it may manage to influence the reader.

⇐

Another (small) confession

When an 'upright' and a sloping font occur side by side, there often appears to be insufficient space between them. This is particularly noticeable when, for example, a tall sloping character like an l or a d is followed by an upright b or k: 'one *bad* knee, and one *good* knee'. The distance measured along the baseline is probably fine, but the letters still feel too close together. Unfortunately, to avoid this problem, you have to intervene. The intervention is in the form of the 'italic correction'. This is rather inaccurately named, since it is not confined to the italic font, or the slanting fonts, but is present in *all* fonts. Although it is present, it may be zero. The correction adds an extra amount of space (if appropriate). This is another of the pieces of information which lives in the `tfm` file. The italic correction may therefore be different for every character in a font. The command to insert the correction is \/. In the example, the preferred expression would have been

`one {\sl bad\/} knee, and one {\sl good\/} knee`

which will now give a slight adjustment, which, it must be agreed, does look a little nicer: 'one *bad* knee, and one *good* knee'. Does it matter? That is for you to decide.

The italic correction may also be necessary when one of the bold fonts is used. This may seem a little contrived, but ' "**Off**", they shouted', really ought to have the italic correction inserted after the word in bold. Trying to create a rule set for the application of the correction is fraught with exceptions. The 'best' solution seems to be: to be aware, to be vigilant, and to look at the output. The time and effort spent in anticipating problems like these could be better spent in reading the output (you might even find a typo too). But with experience you will begin to anticipate the 'problems'.

Plumbing

Let's go a little deeper: an alternative approach to scaling a font to (say) \magstep1 is to say

`\font\new=cmbx10 scaled 1200`

The use of \magstep1 is only a shorthand, more convenient, way of saying 1200. Referring back to Figure 6.3, note that \magstep1 is equivalent to a magnification factor of 1.2. Since TeX prefers to work with integer values, it uses this value multiplied by 1000. Therefore \magstep5 is equivalent to scaling by a TeX factor of 2488. TₑX is oblivious of whether there really is a font which is scaled in this way. All it cares about is whether it can find a `tfm` file for the font mentioned. It is the same `tfm` file which is used whatever the scaling factor. The `tfm` file determines the characteristics of each letter in a given font. The scaling is a purely linear transformation. The problem will arise when the `dvi` file is presented to an output driver. If the fonts at a particular scaled size are not present, what will happen? I wish I knew. It all depends. Some drivers are better than others. Some will substitute 'intelligently' (and tell you). Some may substitute blank space for 'missing' or 'unobtainable' characters. All drivers *should* tell you if they are substituting. Some drivers will even scale up an existing font to the requested size. This is rarely entirely satisfactory (at least, not with bit mapped fonts).

⇒*Exercise 6.8:*   By experiment, find out how the drivers available to you handle 'missing' fonts.   ⇐

⇒*Exercise 6.9:*   If you encounter the problem of 'substitute' fonts, whose responsibility is it? Is it TₑX's, Knuth's, whoever wrote your driver, or do you bear any responsibility?   ⇐

True triumphs

You can prevent the automatic magnification of fonts by using **true** dimension again. Defining

```
\font\larger=cmr10 at 14.40truept
\font\sc=cmcsc10 at 10.95truept
```

would ensure that `\larger` would always print at 14.4 points irrespective of any global magnification superimposed by a `\magnification` command. Similarly, `\sc` would always be at 10.95 points.

⇒*Exercise 6.10:*   What happens when you try to set up a font at `\magstep6`?   ⇐

Is there a solution to the 'missing' font problem? There is, but it is not particularly direct or foolproof. METAFONT allows the creation of suitable fonts. There is no real reason why you should not generate your own fonts at the sizes you want. After all, the METAFONT descriptions are widely available. There is at least one full TₑX implementation on the Amiga whose driver multi-tasks METAFONT to generate particular sizes if it does not 'have them in stock'. Similarly, the driver supplied with the NeXT implementation generates all its fonts as required, slowly building up an extensive set. Of course, generating your own means that the portability of your document may be a little compromised.

If you look at the list of standard TEX fonts, you will note that there are several versions of, for example, Computer Modern Roman. It comes in the following varieties: cmr5, cmr6, cmr7, cmr8, cmr9, cmr10, cmr12, cmr17. Obviously if I want a 12 point font all I have to do is magnify the 10 point font by \magstep1. Why go to the bother of having all these extra fonts?

The main reason revolves around the concept of the design size. Going back to the tfm files, you may recall that a font has a 'design' size. This is the size at which it was meant to be read. In the (good) old days, every letter in every size was 'different'. It was not just scaled up or down geometrically, but there were subtle non-linear changes as we went up the scale from a 6 pt to a 24 pt character. Since each piece of type was a separate hand-crafted artefact, there were likely to be differences. Photosetting rather killed this idea, since in photosetting there is often just one master shape, from which all sizes are generated. In some cases there may be three or four 'masters', each applicable to a particular range.

Knuth emulated the traditional technique of providing several different design sizes for a given style. Terminology becomes difficult here. Computer Modern is a typeface, and as such encompasses everything from CM Roman to the awful CM Funny Font. The whole assembly is a 'family' (despite Knuth using the 'family' concept in another context within TEX). An individual realization, like cmr10 is a font; so is cmr9, or cmr17. How then do we describe all the different design sizes of cmr? Despite this attention to design size, he also provided the scaled fonts (it turns out that this is awfully easy to do once you have the correct META-FONT description). The advantage of the scaled fonts is that the tfm information is identical for all the \magsteps of (say) cmr10. The tfms are not the same for cmr5, cmr6, cmr7..., nor are they simple geometric increases.

In fact there is a slight flaw with \magsteps, if they are to be used to generate larger fonts. The interletter spacing increases too much and the same letter combinations may appear to have an overgenerous amount of white space between them. Thus the use of, say, cmr17 rather than cmr10 scaled \magstep3 (\magstep3 is a factor of 1728) should give 'better' spacing between letters, although cmr10's letter spacing should be satisfactory.

What difference does it make, you ask? Look at the following:

the quick brown fox jumps to the aid of
the party

the quick brown fox jumps to the aid of the
party
the quick brown fox jumps to the aid of the party
the quick brown fox jumps to the aid of the party
the quick brown fox jumps to the aid of the party
the quick brown fox jumps to the aid of the party

These six examples are nominally about the same 'size', approximately 12 points. They were obtained by scaling particular design sizes of the CM Roman to the following particular sizes.

```
\font\five=cmr5    at 12.44  truept   %'true'\magstep5
\font\six=cmr6     at 12.44  truept   %'true'\magstep4
\font\seven=cmr7   at 12.09  truept   %'true'\magstep3
\font\eight=cmr8   at 11.52  truept   %'true'\magstep2
\font\ten=cmr10    at 12     truept   %'true'\magstep1
\font\twelve=cmr12 at 12     truept   %'true'\magstep0
```

They should illustrate that not only do the characteristics of the individual letterforms change, but also the spacing grows to give a rather odd appearance. This is the first time that the % symbol has appeared. It can be considered to signal a comment. The %, and anything following it on the same line, is ignored. Thus, if any material is to be ignored by TₑX, it can still be included in the text to be processed.

⇒*Exercise 6.11:*   Take a ruler to examine whether the change in length above is approximately linear. In other words, allow for the fact that we don't quite manage to get to 12 pt each time. There is about 1 pt difference between the smallest and the largest of those nominal 12 fonts.   ⇐

⇒*Exercise 6.12:*   Similarly, look at the length of the same piece of text but set with the same font at different \magstep values. The increase in length should be linear. Is it? How readable are the different sizes?   ⇐

Recall that TₑX has a \baselineskip command which sets the distance between successive baselines. If you use a different font size you should change the \baselineskip appropriately. There are few hard and fast rules in typography, but in general the distance between baselines is usually about 1.2 times the font size.

⇒*Exercise 6.13:*   To emphasize that using two fonts at the same apparent size but based on different design sizes yields different results, take a chunk of text from one of the earlier exercises and set it with cmr12 and cmr10 scaled\magstep1.   ⇐

Although it may seem that the optimal solution is to use fonts at their design size, there are some good reasons for using \magnification to scale an entire document. For drafting, where revision is likely to take place, and where the drafts will be printed on a low-resolution device like a 300 dpi laser printer, a scaled document is likely to be easier to read, while at the same time it retains the line and page breaks of the final 'true' size document. If the end product is to be presented on an A4 or similar size page, slipping a \magstephalf or \magstep1 at the beginning does make it so much easier to read. I prefer \magstep1, and no doubt as I get older I will begin to prefer \magstep2. Rearranging all the necessary bits of plain to ensure that a true 12 pt is the principal size used requires a fair amount of effort. To be honest, it would require a dedicated typographer to be too critical of the difference between cmr10 magnified to \magstep1 and cmr12.

The adoption of the magnification approach allows the finished document to be printed at a higher apparent resolution. If a basic 10 pt document is printed on a 300 dpi laser printer, but at \magstep2, it may then be reduced photographically back to the 10 pt type size that was originally intended. This would have the effect of emulating a resolution of 432 dpi.

One other application of magnification is in the preparation of overhead transparencies. The whole notion of design size rather falls apart when we are planning to project the characters on to a screen. We seldom have any idea of the size at which the image will be presented.

In defence of Computer Modern

From time to time there is some criticism of the Computer Modern family. Many would like to have other fonts available to TEX. There is really no problem here. It is possible to use TEX with any font, *provided* the tfm files can be made available. There are many examples of TEX used to typeset using either the Adobe POST-SCRIPT fonts, or the Bitstream outline fonts. Often the screen preview is poorer, or non-existent, since the fonts are not available in an appropriate form for the screen. When it comes to setting mathematics, few other typefaces have the richness required. It is not uncommon to see Computer Modern mixed with some other typeface, with CM handling the maths, and the other typeface handling the text.

Computer Modern is a reasonable, unobtrusive typeface. It is well suited to scientific and technical documentation. Its collection of special characters is unrivalled among the widely available contemporary digital typefaces.

Commands 7

A great many of TEX's mysteries are bound up in commands. Alternative terms are 'macros', 'control sequences', or 'definitions': although Knuth refers to them as macros, unless you are familiar with computer science jargon, there is no advantage in this usage. The 300 or so fundamental TEX commands are the building blocks which can be assembled quite easily (and all too readily) into rather arcane powerful commands. It is easy to be overwhelmed by the apparent simplicity and sheer power of commands. It is this feature of TEX which gives it the appearance of a programming language, rather than a simple set of commands. One of the first places we might look to see working commands could be `plain.tex` which is the record of all that plain TEX knows about, and is what *The TEXbook* discusses. However, there is a problem here for the would-be TEXnician or TEXpert. The commands provided in `plain.tex` and in *The TEXbook* are *developed* commands which are efficient, often using cute aspects of the language to achieve their effects. There is also an additional, but lesser, problem in that the definition given in *The TEXbook* may not be identical to the one in `plain.tex`

> ...because the actual macros have been 'optimized' with respect to memory space and running time. Unoptimized versions of the macros are easier for humans to understand...; `plain.tex` contains equivalent constructions that work better on a machine.

Knuth does document them, but you end up having to read large chunks of *The TEXbook* in order to do something which seems pretty straightforward. It sometimes feels as if Knuth's approach is like that of an automobile manufacturer who demands that users of their car should be able to take it to pieces and reassemble it from scratch – a point of view often encountered in the computing world. This is of course unfair to Knuth.

It is possible to write very convoluted and obscure *code* which can only be understood with great difficulty. Since very few people can ever manage to do this correctly first time, and some errors (also known as 'bugs' or 'features') may be present, fully understanding the implications of a command may be fraught with problems. The problems may be compounded by the fact that TEX is, to a large extent, an interpreted language: an error in a command will not be detected until that command is used. Syntactic errors are usually picked up pretty quickly, but detection of errors in the use of a command may require the use of that command in a variety of circumstances.

A command is tautologically something which has been defined somewhere using a `\def` command. There are one or two other devious routes which may be taken to create commands. If a command has not been defined in some way, you will get the Undefined control sequence message which we all come to know and love. You can actually have TEX tell you what it thinks a given command means, by using the `\show` command, at the * prompt:

`\show\anycommand`

will tell you what TEX thinks `\anycommand` is. It will start to 'expand' it into 'simpler' components. In this case, the response will be

```
*\show\anycommand
(show
> \anycommand=undefined.
l.1 \show\anycommand
?
```

Note that we end up with the ? prompt, not the *. TEX therefore expects some sort of 'error correction' response. This is inapplicable here, and the chances are you just want to enter return.

⇒*Exercise 7.1:*   Use the `\show` mechanism on some of the commands which have already been encountered. Some of the expansion will seem unintelligible at present, but some should be interpretable.   ⇐

Some commands do not expand. These are TEX's primitive commands (the ones marked with an asterisk in the index of *The TEXbook*). They are not really commands, since they have never been defined, but rather are the atoms from which everything else is built. If you use `\show` on them they will respond by saying that they are themselves: for example, `\show\hsize` will provide the enlightening information that

```
> \hsize=\hsize.
```

Essentially this is saying that it can be broken down no further.

⇒*Exercise 7.2:* There are 312 TEX atoms: that is, primitive, indivisible commands. What does this indicate about the complexity of text as opposed to something natural like the universe, which just might be explicable in terms of quarks, leptons, and a couple of bosons? ⇐

TEX, or rather `plainTEX`, has its own set of commands built into it. Other TEX-based 'packages', like LATEX or $\mathcal{AMS}$-TEX, will also have their own commands. Some commands in `plain`, LATEX, and $\mathcal{AMS}$-TEX may have the same name, but they need not necessarily have the same function. Beware. Fortunately, we are only looking at `plain` TEX. But do not assume that everything that is present in `plain` may be applied to any other package without some careful thought or attention.

In a very broad and generalized way, the use of the primitive commands is rather like using traditional typographic markup where every movement is specified rather minutely. Creating commands should distance us from this detailed approach and allow us to concentrate on broader concepts. Naturally the writer of commands will have to try to bridge the conceptual gaps between the detailed setting of type and the needs of documents. That this is a complex task is confirmed by the length of time it took Lamport to create LATEX, or Spivak $\mathcal{AMS}$-TEX and $\text{L}\mathcal{AMS}$-TEX. Very few other TEX-based packages have achieved such wide currency. The problems are anything but trivial. But don't let that stop us.

The very simplest commands are just 'substitution' commands:
`\def\me{Malcolm}`
so that whenever I employ the command `\me`, TEX expands it to Malcolm. Straightforward, but let us first note that the substitution part is enclosed in braces. The braces are an integral part of the syntax.

What does this really mean? As far as TEX is concerned, every character which is presented to it falls into one of 16 different categories. These are termed the `\catcode`s. All 256 characters which you might type from the keyboard fall into one of these categories. The default `plain` format sets up the transformations. There is nothing *fixed* or immutable about the transformations. We could choose to change the escape character, ignored characters, or any other of these 16 categories.

The category code table (Figure 7.1) requires some explanation, chiefly because it refers to some concepts we have yet to meet. It should be obvious by now that there is a lot of translation going on between what is entered from the keyboard, and what comes out of TEX. The NUL, DEL, and `return` are simply keyboard entries which TEX intercepts and deals with, just as \ss is a string of entries which is output as a single character. As mentioned above, 256 characters can be entered from the keyboard (some, like NUL, DEL, and return have no physical representation on the screen); in any one font, up to 256 characters may be output. There need not be a one to one correspondence.

⇒*Exercise 7.3:*   Again \show can be employed with the characters in the \catcode table. Try it with #, &, and {; also see what \show responds with a single letter. Note that \show{ yields something useful, but that \showA does not. By now you should know why.   ⇐

At this point, the important concept is that the open brace has category code 1, for beginning of group; and the close brace has category code 2, for end of group. If we set other symbols to have these category codes, they could be used too. This is not just a whim. There is some relevance here. In Scandinavia, the { and } keys on the keyboard are replaced by something odd like å and ø. Although this still works, it does look awkward, and has none of the feeling of 'grouping'; one alternative is to give [and] the appropriate category codes for opening and closing a group. The \ is missing too, but since that too has a category code (of 0 this time), there are ways around that problem too. For example, to reassign the [and] to have the characteristics usually adopted by { and } we may write

\catcode'\[=1

\catcode'\]=2

The syntax of the \catcode command is explained later (in Chapter 18) but essentially it is setting the characters [and] to category codes 1 and 2 respectively. The '\ part of the \catcode is a robust way of specifying the character to be \catcoded. To be consistent, the category codes of { and } should be reset to 12 (for 'other'). Perhaps the most commonly found occurrence of resetting the category code is to reassign @ to the code for 'letter', and back again to 'other', so that it can be used as part of a command name. Provided this is hidden in commands which are never used explicitly, TEX is happy with this manœuvre.

TEX permits you to redefine any of its commands. It will not check to see if a command already has a meaning. TEX assumes you know what you are doing. This 'dynamic' redefinition of commands is a mixed blessing. Equally, there are some built-in commands which you rarely see, and whose accidental redefinition can lead to problems. Among these are the apparently innocuous \big, \radical, and \body.

Category	Description	Default
0	escape character	\
1	opening of a group	{
2	closing of a group	}
3	math 'shift'	$
4	alignment tab	&
5	end of line	carriage return
6	parameter	#
7	superscript	^
8	subscript	_
9	ignored character	NUL
10	space	␣
11	letter	A. . .z *and* a. . .z
12	other character	everything else
13	active character	~
14	comment character	%
15	invalid character	DEL

Figure 7.1
Category codes
employed by
default

Many of the simplest commands involve font changes. Consider, for example, the 'currency sign' command, where Knuth, in a short-sighted moment, placed both the dollar sign and the pounds sterling sign in the same position in different fonts. He recommends or provides \it\$ as a mechanism to obtain £. Ignoring any criticism of this fundamental error (a far better font to use is cmu), we need a convenient command: in LATEX, Lamport provides one he calls \pounds, but I prefer \quid:

`\def\quid{\it\$}`

is an inadequate definition. The enclosing braces are not part of the command at all. They are part of the definition of the command – the syntax. Their role here is not that of grouping operators, but as the delimiters for the replacement or substitute text. On replacement TEX 'sees' only the \it\$. This has the distressing result that all that follows it is also turned into italics.

In other words, when we write

`At a mere \quid1.99, it was indeed a gift.`

TEX expands the \quid to \it\$, with the result that we obtain

At a mere *£1.99, it was indeed a gift.*

Hardly what we wanted. The solution of course is to define \quid as

`\def\quid{{\it\$}}`

Now it is {\it\$} which is the substitute text. All is well.

This is an important lesson in the creation of your own commands. The outer 'shell' of braces is stripped away and does not contribute to any grouping.

Practically anything may be part of the substitute text, including, as the previous example shows, other commands.

⇒*Exercise 7.4:*   In a previous chapter, we noted that it was possible to use the \circ command to create a 'degree' symbol: °. It is very tedious to have to type this out as $^\circ$ every time 'degree' is needed. More important, it is not very intuitive. We could define a command \degree which would take care of all the details so that in future what we type is 60\degree.

Write your own \degree command. Be sure to test it. Does it work in normal text or in mathematics?   ⇐

⇒*Exercise 7.5:*   In physics, we may require to talk about various particles like negative and positive pions, denoted by π^-, π^+, tau-neutrinos, denoted by $\bar{\nu}_\tau$, muon-neutrinos, $\bar{\nu}_\mu$, and positive kaons, K^+, among others. Rather than having to keep bobbing in and out of mathematical mode, create some meaningful commands to simplify writing about these particles. Try to make them charming rather than strange.   ⇐

More power

To extend the power of commands, it is convenient to introduce two other attributes of T_EX which begin to give it the appearance of a 'normal' programming language. These are arithmetic and conditionals. If you do not like the idea of T_EX having aspects of a programming language, it is unlikely that you will ever try to use these commands, although you could just treat these as ways which can be used to manipulate text and to control page make-up. Some people are distracted by the idea of 'programming' text; others revel in it. To some extent, it just depends on the way you look at things.

The different branches of arithmetic

T_EX can do a fair amount of arithmetic. There is one notable drawback though. T_EX only does integer arithmetic. One of the reasons for this stems from T_EX's ambition to be portable. Knuth actually included all the necessary routines in T_EX to do arithmetic. He took nothing for granted, and one consequence was that T_EX keeps delivering the same results, no matter what machine it is run on. If he had tried to employ real arithmetic, the task would have been greater (but not insurmountable).

There are two main 'quantities' which can be used arithmetically: 'dimensions' and 'counters'. (Later we will see that there are two other quantities which may also be used in similar ways.) TeX has a number of \dimen registers and \count registers. Counters are obviously integer, but 'dimensions' need a bit more explanation, since they apparently come in 'real' amounts. Well, they do and they don't. TeX does not really work in points, or inches, or any other 'accessible' unit. It works in 'scaled points', of which there are 2^{16} to the point. That's pretty small (way down in the wavelength of x-rays: 100 sp is about the wavelength of yellow light). All dimensions are automatically translated to scaled points (or sp). The effect of this is that we can get close to real arithmetic. Another practical effect is that accumulated errors usually don't accumulate to very much: nothing visible anyway.

We have already met two dimension registers, \hsize and \vsize. They are an integral part of TeX, as the earlier experiment with \show\hsize demonstrated. There are also 256 dimension and counter registers which may be used, numbered from 0 to 255, in true computing style. Ultimately, TeX knows these as \count0 through to \count255, and \dimen0 to \dimen255, but there is a way to give a counter or a dimension a more meaningful name, through the \newcount and \newdimen commands:

\newcount\exnum

\newdimen\wordlength

would let TeX assign a new counter, giving it the name \exnum and a new dimension, named \wordlength. In passing, it will assign the value 0 to the counter, and a dimension of 0 pt to the dimension. There is no way of 'un-assigning' a register, except by having the original \newcount or \newdimen appear within a group. Outside the group such assignments will be undefined.

Assigning a value to a register is very straightforward:

\count0=10

\count11 2

\exnum10

\exnum=\count10

\dimen1=\hsize

\wordlength=10.76pt

will all assign a value. Note that the = sign is optional, although it does make a good deal of sense as a separator. In general the = sign is unnecessary in TeX commands. When it can help to make the intention a little clearer, in a potentially ambiguous or obscure situation, include it.

The use of \newcount and \newdimen are useful for other reasons. TeX itself uses various registers. For example, the page number is held in \count0. By using \newcount (or the other \new commands) TeX handles the choice of the appropriate register and ensures that an already chosen register is not used, since it assigns the first available one.

Similarly, the registers which hold dimensions are \dimen0 through to \dimen255. TeX assigns them through the use of \newdimen. Note that when a dimension register is given a value, it is either the value of an existing dimension register, or it is a value which has its units inluded.

⇒*Exercise 7.6:*   Try assigning a dimension register to a value which does not have its units expressed: for example, \dimen0=10. What does TeX do?   ⇐

⇒*Exercise 7.7:*   Now consider the case where an assignment like \dimen0=10 was followed immediately by text such as spoil, Ptarmigan, or insensitive. What does TeX do now? Why?   ⇐

When registers are assigned through the use of \newcount or \newdimen, a record will normally appear in the log file.

The simplest operator is one to accumulate, or \advance:

```
\advance\count1 by 1
\advance\count2 by-\count1
\advance\dimen1 \by\hsize
```

We may even add \hsize to \count1. Note that there is no explicit subtraction.

In order to obtain some feeling for what TeX is doing here, we can use the \showthe command to obtain the current value of any of these registers. This is seldom needed in a normal TeX run, but when you are developing a command, it sometimes provides useful feedback. Use of \showthe is rather similar to the \show command, since it interrupts TeX's normal flow of control and appears to invoke the error handling part of TeX. Each \showthe will print out something on the screen and require that you press return at the * prompt in order to tell TeX to continue.

⇒*Exercise 7.8:*   Using \showthe, find out what happens to the value of \count1 when you set it equal to \hsize.   ⇐

It is also possible to multiply and divide:

```
\divide\count1 by 2
\multiply\dimen1 by\count1
\divide\dimen2 by\dimen0
```

The values held in the \count registers should be in the range $-2\,147\,483\,647$ to $+2\,147\,483\,647$ (or, $-2^{29} - 1$ to $2^{29} - 1$). The dimensions should not exceed 2^{30} sp. This is just over $5\,1/2$ metres. It does imply that TEX was not designed to do bill boards.

To take a specific example, we can have TEX calculate the number of hours since midnight. First we must know that there is a basic command \time which 'contains' the number of minutes which have elapsed since midnight. (This is actually 'frozen' once TEX starts to execute, so any plans to use it to calculate how long it takes to set a particular document are dashed.) Let's do the job properly, by letting TEX assign the register:

```
\newcount\hours
\hours=\time
\divide\hours by 60
```

The counter register \hours now contains the number of full hours which have elapsed since midnight. The question that we should raise is 'what do we do with it now?' Simply saying \hours will not result in the value of the register being printed out. We probably only see

```
! Missing number, treated as zero.
<to be read again>
```

What is TEX trying to say? It expects a reference to \hours, or any other register to be followed by some assignment into that register. If nothing suitable follows (and it is possible to envisage situations where something suitable might follow, unintentionally), TEX complains. Had we typed \hours 0 TEX would have been happy, assuming that the value 0 was to be assigned to \hours.

In order to turn the register value into something which will be typeset, it is quoted as a \number. Therefore \number\hours will appear in the output as 15 (or whatever is the appropriate time picked up from the computer's clock).

Before we can incorporate something like this in a command, there is one further peculiarity that must be addressed. It is not possible to have a \newcount statement within the body of a command or definition. In other words,

```
\def\clock{\newcount\hours
\hours=\time \divide\hours by 60\number\hours}
```

will generate an error. This time, it is fairly understandable:

```
Runaway definition?
->
! Forbidden control sequence found while scanning
definition of \time.
```

although the reference to a runaway definition is difficult to follow. Nevertheless, what follows the notification about a forbidden 'control sequence' is meaningful, once we realize that some things may not appear in a definition. The allocation of registers is one of those things. This is rather sad. The strategy therefore has to be either to allocate the register before the command, or to use a 'scratch' register:

```
\def\clock{\count255=\time
    \divide\count255 by 60\number\count255}
```

Here we use `\count255` as a convenient register and use it in the calculations. This rather loses some of the advantages of being able to assign names to registers, but at least permits the command to be written. It still does not work properly. Since it is tedious to have to go through the TeX→dvi→preview→edit and back to TeX cycle again and again, we can circumvent this a little by having TeX show the value of `\count255`.

```
\showthe\count255
```

gives the value calculated. Sadly, the value calculated is unlikely to be anything other than zero.

⇒*Exercise 7.9:*   Create this particular command, run it, and verify that the value it generates is indeed zero.   ⇐

Why? The problem revolves around the

```
\divide\count255 by 60\number\count255
```

statement. TeX dutifully divides `\count255` *not* by 60 as we wished, but by 60`\number``\count255`, which is what we asked. This turns out to be a number somewhere between 601 and 601440, according to `\showthe``\count255`. The 60 is easy to understand, but where does the 1–1440 part come from? It is simply the value in the `\count255` register, expressed as a number. In this context TeX sees it as part of a number, and not as part of the output to be created. There are a number of 'solutions'. The best one is to insert a new command between the 60 and `\number`. A suitable command is `\relax`. This is a do-nothing command, but it serves the function of ensuring that TeX knows where the number used in the division should end:

```
\divide\count255 by 60\relax\number\count255
```

Another alternative is to leave a space instead:

```
\divide\count255 by 60 \number\count255
```

In general, the use of `\relax` is preferred, since it is sometimes possible to 'lose' a space. Here it is unlikely, but in more complex commands, such things are always possible.

That last example merely calculated the hour since midnight. It is not much more work to separate out the minutes past the hour as well:

```
\newcount\minleft
\newcount\milhour
\milhour=\time
\divide\milhour by60
\minleft=\milhour
\multiply\minleft by-60
\advance\minleft by\time
```

(the prefix `mil` is just to indicate 'military' time, since this is a 24 hour clock). We now have two registers, `\milhour` containing the hours, and `\minleft`, the minutes past the hour. When we come to display these, say as

```
\number\milhour:\number\minleft
```

they may look like 8:20 or 16:6 or 20:20. We would probably prefer the middle example to look like 16:06, and perhaps even the first one to be 08:20, but we have no mechanism, as yet, to take these exceptions into account, nor to have TEX vary the way that `\number` works. In order to do this we introduce a new range of TEX manipulations.

Conditionals

Conditionals allow us to adopt one route rather than another: they are 'branching' commands. The commands which allow control of the branches all start with an `\if` prefix. This command describes some condition, like a statement, which can be either *true* or *false*. TEX supports a number of these `\if` primitives, but it also allows you to create your own, through the `\newif`. Although `\newif` has the appearance of `\newcount` it works in a very different way, which will be examined later.

Any of the `\if` conditionals must be terminated by a `\fi`. There are several `\if`s, from a simple `\if` to `\ifnum`, `\ifodd`, `\ifdim`, and a few more. But all end just with the `\fi`. There is one other important related command, the `\else`. This permits structures like

```
\ifhtesti do this when the test is
true
            \else do this when the test is false
\fi
```

There need be no text associated with 'true', in which case it could as easily be written

```
\if... \else  false text \fi
```

and if the 'false' text can be omitted, the `\else` can be omitted too:

```
\if... 	true text \fi
```

Therefore the sequence `\else\fi` need never be seen. The ellipsis must be understood to expand to contain the appropriate form of the `\if` (for example, `\ifnum`), together with the appropriate test.

One of the simplest forms is `\ifnum`, which allows the value of a number (for example, a `\count` register, to be tested). A concrete example might be

```
\ifnum\time<720 before noon\else after noon\fi
```

It is important to appreciate that

```
\if\time<720 before noon\else after noon\fi
```

will not work correctly, although it will not generate an error. The 'simple' `\if` simply examines the character codes of the next two tokens. If they agree, then the true text is followed, otherwise the false. In this case, TₑX is testing `\time` against `<`; their character codes are different, and therefore it is always 'after noon'.

In this simple example the 'before noon' is used when the value of `\time` is less than 720 (12 o'clock). Otherwise the text following the `\else` is used.

More formally we can describe this test as

```
\ifnum number_one  relation  number_two
```

where `number_one` and `number_two` are integers. The `\ifnum` compares two integer values. The *relation* may only be $<$, $>$, or $=$. The use of the `=` as part of the syntax of the conditional is one of the very few places in TₑX where an equals sign is essential and may not be omitted with impunity. The other case is with `\ifdimifdim*/ifdim`, which has the same sort of structure, but tests two dimensions. These are not constrained to be integer, but of course must have their (abbreviated) units present:

```
\ifdim  dimension_one  relation  dimension_two
```

Again the *relation* may only be $<$, $>$, or $=$.

There is a simple condition to test whether an integer is odd:

```
\ifodd  number
```

The condition is true when the integer is odd, false when even. (Note that there is no `\ifeven` command.) This turns out to be very useful when building pages, since it provides a way of ensuring that the page number of a book always appears on the outermost margin – that is, not next to the spine, where it is difficult to find.

There are many more, but they refer to concepts and commands we have yet to meet. To put some more flesh on this, return to the last example: instead of printing out

```
\number\milhour:\number\minleft
```

we can test the value of the `\minleft` register: if it is below 10, we output an extra 0:

```
\number\milhour:\ifnum\minleft<10 0\fi
                           \relax\number\minleft
```

The `\relax` is probably not required, but it is always nice to have one in: perhaps an example of 'safe TeX'.

⇒*Exercise 7.10:*   This code would be a lot happier encapsulated in a command, where it really belongs. Handling a leading zero when the `\milhour` is less than 10 has not been considered. Do so.   ⇐

⇒*Exercise 7.11:*   As a peaceful sort, I would much rather see 3:54 p.m. than 15:54. How would I do that?   ⇐

Another well-known example of the use of an `\if` is the `\today` command in *The TeXbook*. To be able to use this we need first to be introduced to another conditional, the `\ifcase`, and an associated command, `\or`: the `\ifcase` is followed by a number; this number is tested to find out whether it is 0, 1, 2..., If it is 0, the text following the test is used; if it is 1, the text following the first `\or` is used; if it is 2, the text following the second `\or` is used, and so on until we run out of `\or`s. If the test just terminates with a `\fi`, any value outside the range will cause no text between the `\ifcase` and the `\fi` to be used, but if there is an `\else`, that piece of text will be used. This is a useful way of ensuring that any extreme or unexpected values are accounted for.

The `\today` command may be written as

```
\def\today{\ifcase\month\or
    January\or   February\or    March\or     April\or
    May\or          June\or     July\or     August\or
    September\or  October\or  November\or  December\fi
\space\number\day, \number\year}
```

Note that TeX has built-in commands which allow us to determine the year, the month, and the day within the month, as well as the one we have already met to help indicate the time. The only truly new command here is `\space`. It is just a way of ensuring that a 'normal' space occurs after the month, but before the day. The first part may look strange: `\ifcase\month\or` until we realize that the `\month` is never zero, and therefore there need be no text to account for zero.

⇒*Exercise 7.12:*   This form of the date is language dependent, since we chose the English names for the months. A more general form of the date might be to present it as numbers, like 1/1/90. Ignore the fact that this can be ambiguous (which is first, the month or the day?; in North America it is the month, while in Britain it is usually the day) and create another version of the command to generate dates of this form.   ⇐

This opens up all sorts of convenient manipulations. Knuth is still writing *The Art of Computer Programming*. One of the volumes is dedicated to non-numerical algorithms. One of the non-numerical algorithms is the calculation of the date on which Easter Sunday falls. This is of some significance, since it is possible that arithmetic survived in Europe through the Middle Ages because of the need to calculate this date. It is not difficult to program this algorithm to have it calculate the correct dates, like this:

> In 1992, Easter Sunday fell on April 19. In the year 2000, it will fall on April 23.

With these capabilities, it is a small step to find out the day of the week (Thursday), or even the phase of the moon (waxing gibbous), for today, June 11, 1992.

⇒*Exercise 7.13:*   Modify the \today command so that it gives 1st, 2nd, 3rd, 4th, etc., *or* write something which gives the correct astrological house for a given date. You may even be able to automate horoscopes! ⇐

Less and less

Although every command is preceded by a \, it is possible to make a single character behave as if it were a command. These are termed 'active' characters, and have category code 13. The most likely active character that you will find is the ~ for a 'tie' space. Somewhere in the bowels of **plain** TEX you will uncover a statement like

`\def~{\penalty10000\ }`

which basically says 'a space but don't you dare break it'. And somewhere else, the ~ has been made active. The command \active is available in case you forget that the catcode of an active character is 13:

`\catcode'\~=\active`

There are some circumstances in TEX where the space and even the end of line are made active. TEX, as has been hinted already has a scheme of penalties and demerits which it employs when it builds and breaks lines. Penalties will be examined a little more closely in Chapter 21. Associating a large penalty immediately before the space ensures that the line does not break at that space (or rather, that it is exceptionally unlikely that it will   a penalty of 10,000 is regarded as being infinite for all practical purposes).

⇒*Exercise 7.14:*   In French books (and in many older English books) a colon was preceded by some white space too. It was not placed immediately after the word. It is possible to define the colon to be active and have it insert some unbreakable space between it and the word – after all, you wouldn't want the colon starting a line, would you?   ⇐

Although these simple substitution commands may seem pretty trivial, that does not stop them being very useful. True, a decent text editor could do all this work for you, but who wants to see things like `\penalty10000\` lurking about in their text?

More maths

8

This chapter draws together some more of TeX's wide range of facilities for mathematics, filling in some of the features which provide the flexibility needed to support a very diverse area of technical typesetting. Some of these features help to lay the groundwork for an understanding of the way that TeX really does work. Such an understanding may not be necessary for the vast majority of tasks to which we put TeX, but may give us the confidence to believe that we can handle the exceptional or novel situations too.

Lots of delimiters

One of TeX's pleasing attributes is its selection of brackets and delimiters: as you will already have guessed, the left and right braces used for grouping require the special commands if they are to be included in the text, rather than used as 'ghost' grouping characters. This provides the clue for other delimiters. We can use angle braces, ceilings, floors, square brackets (and even slashes); they are all given in Figure 8.1.

(	(	)	)
[	\lbrack *or* [	]	\rbrack *or*]
{	\lbrace *or* \{	}	\rbrace *or* \}
⟨	\langle	⟩	\rangle
⌈	\lceil	⌉	\rceil
⌊	\lfloor	⌋	\rfloor
/	/	\	\backslash
|	\vert *or* |	‖	\Vert *or* \\|
↑	\uparrow	↓	\downarrow
⇑	\Uparrow	⇓	\Downarrow
↕	\updownarrow	⇕	\Updownarrow

Figure 8.1
Delimiters

These all give delimiters/brackets which are suitable for 'normal' simple equations.

There are two ways to use big delimiters. You can let TEX do all the work, or you can stay in control.

Do it yourself

A series of big delimitersis defined by the prefixes –

```
\bigr    \Bigr    \biggr    \Biggr
\bigl    \Bigl    \biggl    \Biggl
\bigm    \Bigm    \biggm    \Biggm
```

This is a set of four increasingly large parentheses. These prefixes are made up of two parts: a 'size' component, big, Big, bigg, and Bigg, in that order from smallest to largest, and a 'positional' indicator, l, r, and m, which distinguishes left, right, and middle. The 'middle' category is not really a parenthesis or delimiter at all, but it has a similar structure, and is therefore included here. It is in fact treated as a relation by TEX, and extra space will be placed around it when it occurs in an equation.

To use these delimiters we specify the prefix and the delimiter: `\bigl(` or `\Biggr\rbrace` or even `\biggl\rbrack` It is necessary to be able to declare that an apparent 'right' or closing delimiter is used as an opening delimiter because some people have to be able to write things like

$$]m, n[$$

TEX does not even require that these delimiters are balanced. They are just another sort of symbol. They allow us to write:
`$$ \Biggl\langle \biggl\lceil \Bigl\lbrace \bigl( (x)`
`   \bigr) \Bigr\rbrace \biggr\rfloor \Biggr\rangle $$`
for

$$\Big\langle \Big[\big\{ ((x)) \big\} \Big] \Big\rangle$$

In this case we specify the sizes. All `\bigg` delimiters are essentially the same size, so that we know in advance that any big delimiter fits inside a Big one, and so on. Note too that the 'normal' delimiter, without the prefix, is a smaller size again.

Let TEX do it for you

Just by saying
`$$\left\lbrace ... `*lots of formula*` ... \right\rbrace$$`

TEX will place the brace delimiters where you specify. It calcu-
lates the size required with reference to the size of the enclosed
expression. This therefore appears to be quite a good strategy.
You can use *any* of the delimiters outlined above, so that
\left\lceil ... \right\rceil
\left/ ... \right\backslash
\left| ... \right\|
are all acceptable. You should note that TEX expects that for
every \left delimiter there should be a \right delimiter. Note
again that the delimiters need not be identical, so that \left(can
be paired with \right\rangle. However, this does leave a minor
problem. From time to time you do not actually want the other
half of the pair. This does seem unusual, since it is vanishingly rare
to see an equation which contains a 'lone' unbalanced delimiter.
This becomes most critical if we have to spread an equation over
more than one line, a topic which is covered in the next chapter.
When the problem does arise it is necessary to force the pairing
by using, \right., or \left. as appropriate. The '.' itself does
not appear in the typeset equation. It is simply a polite fiction,
since the command \left or \right expects to be followed either
by a delimiter itself, or the dot.

A plausible example might be
$${a+b\over2} \left/ {c-d\over3} \right.$$
to obtain

$$\frac{a+b}{2} \left/ \frac{c-d}{3} \right.$$

In fact, I should be more honest here. Although you just might do
this if you were not sure how big the extent to which the terms
might grow, you would be much more likely to use one of the \big,
\Big, \bigg, and \Bigg family we have met already. Without the
l, r, or m suffix, these can also be used as simple symbols:
$${a+b\over2} \bigg/ {c-d\over3}$$
The question that might arise could be 'should it not be \biggm
that is being used here?' Careful examination of the results will
indicate that the version given here is 'tighter' with greater overlap
on the 'delimiter', in this case used as an operator. In fact, there
is really something quite interesting going on here. The 'opening'
delimiters are defined with the help of a command \mathopen;
the 'closing' delimiters use \mathclose, and the 'middle' is given
the description \mathrel (for relation). It is in this way that the
relative spacing within the equation is determined. If, however,

we were to look at the way `\bigg` itself works, we would find no reference to any of these, so it is used just as a simple symbol.

Caveat: there are some points to be made about these features. The 'automatic' sizing only works with some of the delimiters. Some delimiters are constructed from 'primitives' which can be assembled to give as a large a construct as desired. Parentheses, bráces, floors, ceilings, square brackets, and the vertical bars and arrows, all fall into this category. On the other hand some delimiters are merely available in a range of sizes, and cannot exist outside that range. These are the delimiters which have a major 'diagonal' component, like the slashes and the angle brackets.

$\Rightarrow$*Exercise 8.1:*   Experiment to see how large `\backslash` or `\langle` and `\rangle` may become. $\Leftarrow$

A pleasing feature of `\right` delimiter and `\left` delimiter is that they are grouping operators too: this helps to explain why you have to balance all your `\left` and `\right` delimiters. You will have noted from the example above that it is not actually necessary to balance `\left\lceil` with `\right\rceil`. All that is needed is a balance of `\left` and `\right` – of course you would not write something like

```
$$\left\lbrace x {a+b\over c \right\rbrace }$$
```

would you? You can also write `\right\lbrace`; TEX is very broad-minded.

Sometimes automatic sizing is not what you want, although the example below is rather forced:

$$||x| + |y||$$

and was obtained from

```
$$ \left\vert    \left\vert x \right\vert
 + \left\vert y \right\vert    \right\vert $$
```

$\Rightarrow$*Exercise 8.2:*   How would we have obtained what we really wanted?
$$\left|\,|x| + |y|\,\right|$$
For once, the answer is not 'group.' $\Leftarrow$

And sometimes the parentheses might be a little too large: this happens mainly in the case of enclosed summations. By way of illustration, look at

$$\left(\sum_{k=1}^{n} A_k \right)$$

The obvious way to set it is
$$\left(\sum_{k=1}^n A_k \right)$$
Then look at

$$\left(\sum_{k=1}^{n} A_k \right)$$

and note that the parentheses are a little smaller, and that the equation looks a little neater.

⇒*Exercise 8.3:*   Try to emulate that last 'refined' equation.   ⇐

Although not directly relevant here, you may be pleasantly surprised to note that TEX allows its square root symbol to grow as the expression inside 'grows'. Therefore the expression
$$\sqrt{a+\sqrt{b+\sqrt{c+\sqrt{d+\sqrt{e\sqrt f}}}}}$$
should really look quite good:

$$\sqrt{a+\sqrt{b+\sqrt{c+\sqrt{d+\sqrt{e\sqrt f}}}}}$$

Other operators

Some operations do not have a 'special' symbol, but instead are represented in mathematics by special phrases – sin, cos, log, ln, and so on. It is conventional to distinguish these from symbols by leaving them in roman style. If $\sin \alpha$ was simply written as sin\alpha, then the result would not be pleasant: $sin\alpha$. In order to avoid problems like this, TEX has a large number of these operators (or functions?) defined in **plain** and listed in Figure 8.2. Most of them are self-explanatory.

These commands are used in a quite straightforward manner. They also behave in a quite straightforward manner. For example,
$$a^{\sin\alpha}+b^{\cos\beta}$$
will provide superscripts which are properly 'diminished'. Do note that although the commands appear to put the alphabetic part into roman/upright form, these are genuine, ordinary, TEX commands. Using \limsup or \liminf would have dispelled this idea, since they give $\lim \sup$ and $\lim \inf$, where the 'lim' is separated from the rest of the operator by a small amount of space. Simply saying \sgn and expecting TEX to divine that you wish a new maths command 'sgn' is expecting too much. There are ways to define new mathematical operators, should you need to extend TEX's repertoire.

Looking into `plain` T_EX's definitions, we can find
`\def\cos{\mathop{\rm cos}\nolimits}`
This gives us the clues we might need to create our own 'extra'
commands, like 'sgn', or 'Log', or any other which might be
required for particular esoteric branches of physics, maths, engineering.... There is one new command, `\mathop`, in the definition,
and one old one, `\nolimits`, although this is used in a rather different circumstance. Taking the familiar one first, `\nolimits` is
indicating that this particular mathematical operator is one which
does not take limits. A moment's reflection suggests that something like max is an operator which could take limits, just like `\sum`
and `\int`. The second part of the table, from `\max` onwards, is
made up of these pseudo-'large operators'. You would also specify
the limits in a similar way to `\int` and `\sum`.
`$$\lim_{n\to\infty}$$`
gives

$$\lim_{n\to\infty}$$

Of course, on the other hand,
`$\lim_{n\to\infty}$`
gives $\lim_{n\to\infty}$.

The other part of the definition uses `\mathop`. This indicates
that the command (or operator) will be treated as a mathematical
operator, just like the `\sum` and `\int`: the spacing associated with
all these operators will be the same. Essentially this is needed to
distinguish a 'large' operator from a binary operator, or a relation,
or any other of the classes of mathematical character. There are
in fact commands `\mathbin`, `\mathrel`, and so on which can be
used in order to force T_EX to handle things in particular ways.

Perhaps the `\bmod` and `\pmod` need further explanation. They
generate the text 'mod'. The prefix refers to whether they are
to be used in a 'binary' or in a 'parenthesized' way. The binary
form, `m\bmod n` will have the same characteristics of any other
binary operator: $m \bmod n$. The parenthesized form, `m\pmod n`,
looks similar, but it also provides the parentheses: $m \pmod n$.
⇒*Exercise 8.4:*   Transform the following equations into T_EX form:

$$W_0 = \lim_{R\to 0} \pi R^2 q_0$$

$$\frac{h}{L_0} = \frac{h}{L} \tanh \frac{2\pi h}{L}$$

$$\frac{v}{u} = -\tanh k(h+y) \cot kx$$

\sin	\arcsin	\csc	\sinh	\ker
\cos	\arccos	\sec	\cosh	\arg
\tan	\arctan	\cot	\tanh	\coth
\log	\lg	\ln	\exp	\dim
\deg	\hom	\pmod	\bmod	
\max	\min	\inf	\liminf	\Pr
\det	\lim	\sup	\limsup	\gcd

Figure 8.2
Operators

$$p_{ij}^{(r+1)} = \min_{h=1}^{n} \left[\max_{k=1}^{m} c(i,j;h,k) p_{hk}^{(r)} \right]$$

$$\text{minimize} \{ \hat{\vec{f}}^{t} [C]^{t} [C] \hat{\vec{f}} \}$$

$$\lim_{x \to 0} \ln(1+x) = x$$

$$M = \log_{10} \frac{A}{A_0}$$

⇐

⇒*Exercise 8.5:* How do we write

$$\lim_{n \to \infty}$$

and what would \lim_{n\to\infty} have given? ⇐

There are two other commands, \overbrace and \underbrace, which are rather similar to operators which take sub- or super-scripts, except that the ordering is rather more crucial:

$$\underbrace{\overbrace{a+b+c}^1+$$
    \overbrace{a^2+b^2+c^2}^2}_{a\ne b\ne c}$$

This composite example may illustrate what is going on:

$$\underbrace{\overbrace{a+b+c}^{1}+\overbrace{a^2+b^2+c^2}^{2}}_{a\neq b\neq c}$$

The main points to note are that when using \overbrace, the 'superscripted' expression which follows is the one associated with the brace, even if a subscripted expression should intervene:

$$\overbrace{a+b}_n^1$$

yields

$$\overbrace{a+b}^{1}_{n}$$

and a similar situation applies to \underbrace. The other point is that while an expression which is (say) underbraced may have other components which are overbraced, the different bracing cannot overlap. Of course, the braces may be nested:

$$
\overbrace{\underbrace{a+b}_{1}+c}^{2}
$$

⇒*Exercise 8.6:*   Tackle the following equation:

$$
B = \underbrace{\left(\frac{1}{k}B\right) \oplus \left(\frac{1}{k}B\right) \oplus \ldots \oplus \left(\frac{1}{k}B\right)}_{k \text{ times}} = \left(\frac{1}{k}B\right)^{\oplus k}
$$

⇐

More boxes

You will have noticed that text like sin and cos is treated differently from variables like x and y. They appear in roman rather than italic font. Very often we require part of a formula to contain text which would look best in roman font – thus removing all potential ambiguities. For example, we might want something like

$$
\log(\text{amplitude}) = -(2H+1)\log(\text{order})
$$

There are a couple of ways this can be achieved. We can use \hbox (examined in detail in Chapter 9), or we can use \rm. Thus
`$$\log(\hbox{amplitude}) = -(2H+1)\log(\hbox{order})$$`
and
`$$\log(\rm amplitude) = -(2H+1)\log(\rm order)$$`
are equivalent, in this instance. *But* \hbox uses the *current* font. This has two important side effects. Firstly, it restricts its size to the current size (probably 10 point), making it unsuitable for sub- or superscripts, and secondly, the current font might not be roman. Some mathematicians put their lemmas in slant or italic. Thus within a block which used \sl, the display maths use of \hbox would turn out to be in slant too:

$$
\log(\mathit{amplitude}) = -(2H+1)\log(\mathit{order})
$$

On the other hand, \rm will turn out suitably sub- or superscripted. Note that you do not have to switch off the effect of \rm within a set of $ or $$ signs. It is switched off automatically when these delimiters are encountered. On the other hand, you probably don't want the scope of the \rm to be in operation for the whole equation – or everything will be in 'normal' text.

⇒*Exercise 8.7:*   Suggest how the following were obtained:

$$a_{\text{red}} + a_{\text{green}} + a_{\text{blue}} = a_{\text{white}}$$
$$\text{colour} \propto b_{\text{intensity}}, b_{\text{spectra}}, b_{\text{hue}}$$

Note the irregularity in the baselines.   ⇐

Sometimes you are happy to accept subscripted words in italics. You will already have noticed that an easy way to get italics in ordinary text is just to slip the odd character between $ symbols, for example Figure 1(a). Purists will shudder – mainly at the thought of using this easy italicization, realizing that there is a command \mathsurround which allows us to put extra space around equations in text. \mathsurround normally has a value of 0 pt. If we change it to \mathsurround=2pt, Figure 1(a) will find itself with more space between the parentheses and the a.

⇒*Exercise 8.8:*   Change the value of \mathsurround to see what effect it has. How noticeable is it?   ⇐

What would happen to the following phrase in an equation?
```
$$u_{ex} = u_{maximum Airy wave}(1-F)$$
```
Do try it, just to convince yourself that the answer is 'nothing nice'.

$$u_{ex} = u_{maximum Airy wave}(1 - F)$$

The subscripted 'ex' looks acceptable, but the 'maximum Airy wave' is dreadful. TEX (rightly) assumes that this is merely a string of symbols, ignores spaces, and regurgitates the phrase without regard to meaning. Assuming that we really do want the phrase in italics, what we might have meant (?) was
```
$$u_{\it maximum Airy wave}$$
```
which gives a series of error messages, along the lines '\script-font 4 is undefined'. On the other hand, although
```
$$u_{\hbox{\it maximum Airy wave}}$$
```
works, it still does not give us quite what we wanted:

$$u_{maximum\ Airy\ wave}$$

Let us assume that the problem lies mainly with the choice of font, and that a Roman font would do quite nicely. This time,
```
$$u_{\rm maximum Airy wave}$$
```
gives

$$u_{\text{maximum Airy wave}}$$

But again, there is a problem of spacing: there are important aspects of inserting text into formulae. Single words are usually fine, but when we want several words, TEX in maths mode has no means of knowing that they are separate words. Remember that TEX is deciding all the spacing within these equations, and the spaces we leave will be ignored (disregarding those which are necessary for syntax – to separate out commands). Therefore `u_{maximum Airy wave}` is just a string of letters to appear in italic typeface. The spaces will be ignored. Whenever we require spaces to be left, we must indicate so, with the use of the control space `\⊔`. We may be prepared to accept

`$$u_{maximum\ Airy\ wave}$$`

which gives

$$u_{maximum\ Airy\ wave}$$

The second point to make is that the 'extra' typefaces available here (`\it`, `\sl`, and `\tt`) are only available at 10 point. They will not work as 'diminished' sub- and superscripts. We must either put up with this restriction, or use `\rm`, which is still available at 10, 7, and 5 point.

Besides having the capability of dropping into italics through `\it`, whilst in maths, we have 'maths italic', `\mit`. Why bother having both? Actually they are different fonts. This is most easily demonstrated by comparing *different* and $different$. The first of these is `\it`, the second is `\mit`. The maths italic is slightly larger, and does not support ligatures. This enables us to be able to write $fl = f \times l$ rather than $\mathit{fl} = f \times l$. This of course illustrates one of the weaknesses of an approach like `u_{maximum\ Airy\ wave}`, since in the event that one of those subscripted words contained a ligature, no ligature will actually appear. But why should we want a maths italic font at all, since we default to it every time we enter maths mode? It is really there to enable us to italicize the upper-case Greek symbols.

⇒*Exercise 8.9:*   Experiment to find the difference between `\mit\Omega` and `\Omega`.   ⇐

A minor restriction is the inability to use mathematical accents in this font: for example, `\mit\hat\Delta` will not produce the desired results, but gives $\hat{\mathit{\Delta}}$ instead of $\hat{\Delta}$. The desired result was obtained by `\hat{\mit\Delta}`. Although fairly obvious here, the correct ordering could be less easy to discern in a more involved equation.

⇒*Exercise 8.10:*   In what way(s) would `u_{\mit maximum\ Airy\ wave}` or `u_{maximum\ Airy\ wave}` have produced a different result from `u_{\it maximum\ Airy\ wave}`?   ⇐

Other voices

From time to time it is necessary to embolden symbols. This can be done through the use of \bf. Do note that emboldening (like \rm) affects only A to Z, a to z, 0 to 9, and \Gamma to \Omega. The mathematical accents may also be emboldened or romanized. What this means is that delimiters, lower-case Greek, operators, and so on are not affected. Emboldening is sometimes used to indicate vectors.

There is one more variation: you may employ 'calligraphic' letters through the command \cal. These apply only to upper-case A to Z, and give you access to $\mathcal{A}$ through to $\mathcal{Z}$. Applying this sequence to other letters, like lower case or Greek, will give interesting results, but probably not the ones you wanted.

$\Rightarrow$*Exercise 8.11:*   Do you suppose \bf and \cal can be subscripts? Either work it out from first principles, or experiment. $\Leftarrow$

From time to time, other fonts are used in mathematics and physics, notably Fraktur and Blackboard Bold. Knuth mentions both of these in *The TEXbook*, but they are not part of plain TEX. If you really cannot live without them, you could obtain $\mathcal{AMS}$-TEX, where they are available. Actually, if you do have $\mathcal{AMS}$-TEX, your friendly TEXpert will be able to make them available for you.

$\Rightarrow$*Exercise 8.12:*   The following equations use some of the font changes outlined above. Turn them into TEX:

$$B \equiv B' \iff B \overset{\mathcal{I}}{\equiv} B'$$

$$\mathbf{f}(N+1) = \rho\mathbf{f}(N) + \mathbf{v}(N+1)$$

$$\mathcal{Q}[f] = 1 \text{ if } \sum_{\mathcal{I}} a_i \mathcal{P}_i[f] \geq t$$

Since setting display equations gives us a distorted view of the universe, also set this text:

Let $\mathcal{O}$ be an operation that takes pictures into pictures. We say that the property $\mathcal{P}$ is *invariant* under $\mathcal{O}$ if $\mathcal{P}[\mathcal{O}[f]] = \mathcal{P}[f]$ for all f.

$\Leftarrow$

Numbers

We now have vast power and lots of tools to exploit that power. There is much more fine detail to TEX's mathematical control, but it is probably overwhelming to be exposed to it all at present. There is one important area still outstanding: numbered equations. To obtain numbers associated with equations, the commands \eqno or \leqno may be used. They must be placed at the

end of the equation:
`$$\eta = x^2 + y^2 - r^2 \eqno(4)$$`
to yield:

$$\eta = x^2 + y^2 - r^2 \qquad\qquad (4)$$

while `\leqno` places the equation number on the left.
`$$\eta = x^2 + y^2 - r^2 \leqno(4)$$`
to give:

$$(4) \qquad\qquad\qquad \eta = x^2 + y^2 - r^2$$

It must be emphasised that although the equation number appears on the left when it is typeset, it is actually written as the last part of the equation. Left-numbered equations are relatively rare.

Since TEX is able to advance counters, it would be relatively simple to arrange that each time an equation was numbered, it had its number incremented. This sounds plausibly attractive, but recall that the probable reason for numbering an equation is to be able to refer to it elsewhere (why else would you bother?). If this is the case, then if you deleted an existing equation, or inserted another one, you would also have to seek out the point at which you refer to the equation, and attend to that. Since you would not know the number of the equation until it had been through TEX at least once, the problems start to mount up. We need some way of cross-referencing. It is possible to devise such a scheme, but it is complex to do from scratch. LATEX has a cross-referencing scheme like this. Spivak has some interesting comments to make. He considers that equation numbering is not really necessary, since authors tend to locate the equation and its textual reference very close together.

⇒*Exercise 8.13:*   Since the equation number occurs at the far left or right, what will happen if we have a rather long equation which extends almost to the margin? Where will the number be placed?   ⇐

⇒*Exercise 8.14:*   What happens to text placed within `\eqno`?   ⇐

Spaces and dots

Ellipses are handled quite well in maths mode, but we identify several different varieties, depending in part on whether we employ 'centre dots' or 'low dots'. The fundamental commands are: `\ldots` and `\cdots` where the prefix `l` or `c` differentiates 'low' or 'centre'.

At this point it is useful to return to the notion of space, which we touched on briefly before. TEX allows you a fair amount of

Command	Description	Equivalent	Size (and glue)
\,	a thin space	\thinmuskip	3 mu
\>	medium space	\medmuskip	4 mu plus 2 mu minus 4 mu
\;	thick space	\thickmuskip	5 mu plus 5 mu
\!	negative thin space	−\thinmuskip	−3 mu
\enspace	an en space		0.5 em
\quad	a quad space		1 em
\qquad	two quad spaces		2 em

Figure 8.3
Mathematical spaces

control of the space you introduce into formulae. Notice that this discussion is aimed at maths mode. The control space we used is available in both modes, but most of the others are not. TEX frequently uses the \quad. This turns out to have been defined already: a quad is about the width of a capital M (an em-dash is usually one quad wide); one quad in 10 point type is usually about 10 points wide. You will also find a \qquad which is just two quads. The mu is a 'mathematical unit', and Knuth assigned 18 mu to 1 em. The em is a font-related measure, and the \quad is defined in terms of an em. The em is related to the upright Roman font which TEX uses when it starts a maths expression. Therefore a \quad is the same size in text, display, script and scriptscript styles. TEX has a number of shorthand forms for introducing spaces into formulae. These are given in Figure 8.3.

This implies that the mathematical spaces will adjust, according to where and how we use them – for example, in sub- and superscripts. The figure also gives the 'ideal' width, with its glue – the stretch and shrink components. Note that \quad, \qquad, and \enspace have no stretch and shrink associated with them. They may be used in any mode. Using the others in text will lead to an error where TEX thinks it is in maths mode, and tries to correct by inserting its own $.

Since there are so many of these spaces, some notion of their applicability might be useful. Starting with the simplest case, of a fixed space, both \quad (and \qquad) may be useful in the following situation:

$$F_n = F_{n-1} + F_{n-2}, \qquad n\ge2$$

The space after the comma would normally be a \qquad. We shall see some other situations later, in laying out tables, where \quads can be very useful.

The thin space ($\,$) has three main areas of use: the first is before the dx, dy, or dwhatever in formulae with calculus. For example,

$$dx\,dy = r\,dr\,d\theta$$

is obtained from `$$dx\,dy = r\, dr\,d\theta$$`. Without the refinement it would have appeared as

$$dxdy = rdrd\theta$$

Note that some texts have a tendency to put the 'd' of dx into roman type:
$$\mathrm{d}x\,\mathrm{d}y = r\,\mathrm{d}r\,\mathrm{d}\theta$$

Secondly, it may be used after square roots which come 'too close' to the symbol which follows:

$$O(1/\sqrt{n}) \text{ and } \sqrt{x}2$$

look better as
$$O(1/\sqrt{n}\,) \text{ and } \sqrt{x}\,2$$

The adjustment was achieved by including some thin space:
`$$O(1/\sqrt n\,)\sqrt  x\,2$$`
And lastly the thin space can be applied after a factorial symbol, when the ! is followed by a letter, number, or left delimiter –

$$\frac{(2n)!}{n!\,(n+1)!}$$

Without the negative thin space after the first factorial, this would look like
$$\frac{(2n)!}{n!(n+1)!}$$

You might reasonably ask why TₑX does not do this itself, so that an exclamation mark maps to `!\,` in all cases. Basically the answer lies with the counter-example `(a!+b!)/n` where a ! followed by a right parenthesis (or a relation) does not require extra space.

Negative thin space ($\!$) is needed in two main situations: firstly, when dealing with multiple integral signs:

$$\int\!\int dx\,dy$$

which look a little spaced out, and we might require
$$\int\!\!\int dx\,,dy$$
to give

$$\iint dx\,dy$$

or even more negative thin space to bring the integrals even closer together. This is one of the times that display and text styles are not truly equivalent. Try multiple integrals in both modes to find out what you feel is required. In a second case, you might consider using negative thin space in a situation like $\Gamma_2\Delta^2$, which is written `\Gamma_{\!2}\Delta^{\!2}`. Without the negative thin space this is $\Gamma_2\Delta^2$.

Often space seems needed with the solidus as well: m^n/n^m could usefully be closed up a little to become m^n/n^m. Most times TeX gets its spacing correct, but there are situations where a helping hand is appreciated.

The other two mathematical spaces, `\;` and `\>`, seem hardly ever to be used. The first of these, the thick space, is used once in `plain`, in the definition of `\iff`:
`\def\iff{\;\Longleftrightarrow\;}`

Back to dots

In general, `\cdots` is used between signs inside a formula – `x_1 = \cdots = x_n = 0` which would give us $x_1 = \cdots = x_n = 0$. But we might need extra help for `$y_1 + y_2 + \cdots\,$`. where the dots immediately precede a full stop in a sentence: 'The equation: $y_1 + y_2 + \cdots$.'

The low dots, `\ldots`, leave no space before or after. Knuth suggests that three low dots *followed by* a thin space should be used before a comma:
`The vector $(x_1, \ldots\, , x_n)$`
for 'The vector $(x_1, \ldots, x_n)$'; on the other hand, does 'The vector $(x_1, \ldots, x_n)$' really look so bad?

Thin space before and after `\ldots` would be employed when there is no surrounding operator sign,
`$x_1 x_2 \,\ldots\, x_n$`
'$x_1 x_2 \ldots x_n$' but on the other hand $x^1 x^2 \ldots x^n$ does not require a thin space after the 2 (because there is some space there already after the second x):
`$x^1 x^2 \ldots\, x^n$`

⇒*Exercise 8.15:*   Tackle the following:

The predicates of χ_S are Boolean functions of the Boolean variables $P_1, \ldots, P_N$. For example, the predicate "$|S| = 1$" ("there is only one 1 in χ_S") corresponds to the function

$$\bigvee_{i=1}^{N} (\bar{P}_1 \wedge \cdots \wedge \bar{P}_{i-1} \wedge P_i \wedge \bar{P}_{i+1} \wedge \cdots \wedge \bar{P}_N)$$

where the overbars denote logical negation.

and

In this chapter, Σ denotes a picture; subsets of Σ are denoted by $S, T, \ldots$, and points by $P, Q, \ldots$.

⇐

Confused, or just perplexed? These features may all be useful, but often you see the need for them only when you realize that a formula does not look quite right. The key problem is that mathematics has so many exceptions that any set of rules will break down somewhere. TEX's rules are simple, and we have ways of overriding them.

Punctuation

This has brought us back to the general area of punctuation. Punctuation in maths has some peculiarities. Comma and semi-colon are treated as genuine punctuation, and extra space is inserted after them. If a colon is intended as punctuation, it should be written \colon. This allows a construct like $x := 0$ to be written as `$x:=0$` – a case where the colon is not punctuation at all. What would `$x\colon=$` have given us? Since a comma attracts extra space, and since TEX decides on all its own spacing in maths mode, irrespective of where you placed spaces (or omitted them), writing `$123,456$` would give us $123, 456$ rather than $123{,}456$. How do we get the latter effect? By bracing the comma: `$123{,}456$`.

⇒*Exercise 8.16:*   Reproduce the following three extracts:

The condition $B_x^2 \subset X^c$ is always fulfilled, and the eroded set Y is the locus of the points x, such that B_x is included in X:

$$Y = \{x : B_x \subset X\}$$

and

Finally, let $S_n(K_0; K_1, \ldots, K_n)$ denote the probability that X misses the compact set K_0, but hits the other compact sets $K_1, \ldots, K_n$.

and finally,

$$\Lambda(x) = \text{Sup}\{\lambda : x \in \psi_\lambda(x)\}$$

⇐

Boxing 9

To explain how TEX handles boxes we can first return briefly to some of the ideas introduced very briefly in Chapter 3. There the boxes considered were those which were associated with individual letters which were themselves assembled into a larger box – the line. The horizontal lines are then stacked together into a vertical list of boxes.

Let's go back to the simplest cases. There are two fundamental sorts of boxes: horizontal and vertical. When TEX is creating a line of text, it is creating a horizontal box. When it assembles several paragraphs into a page, it is creating a vertical box. Explicity, we can create our own horizontal and vertical boxes. For example,

`\hbox{Oh brother, not hamsters again.}`

will place the component letters and words into a horizontal box. The interword gaps will be the constant value referred to in Chapter 3, without any stretch or shrink. This is the 'natural' width. The width of such a box can be determined and made visible. Obviously TEX knows the width, but it can be made to divulge its secrets. A straightforward approach is to make use of the box registers (very similar to the other registers already met):

`\setbox0\hbox{Oh brother, not hamsters again.}`

'sets' the contents of the horizontal box into a box register. TEX has 256 such box registers, which may each be accessed explicitly by referring to their numbers: `\box0` to `\box255`. In very general terms it is recommended that you refer only to the first 10 boxes by number. Many of the others have already assigned functions. The last box, `\box255`, is an interesting one: it is where TEX puts the built-up page. Do not interfere with it (yet). While the first 10 boxes are regarded as 'scratch' boxes, available for general use, you can also access others indirectly if you need, since TEX permits you to assign them dynamically, just like the other registers:

`\newbox\hamster`

makes TEX choose a box register (the first free one), which may then be used. Thus the example may be made slightly more general:

```
\newbox\hamster
\setbox\hamster\hbox{Oh brother, not hamsters again.}
```

We shall see later that it is not always possible to assign boxes in this dynamic way.

Once a box has been allocated, information about its contents is accessible. A variation of the `\show` command, `\showbox`, may be used:

```
\showbox\hamster
```

will produce

```
> \box16=
\hbox(6.94444+1.94444)x125.13916
.\tenrm O
.\tenrm h
.\glue 3.33333 plus 1.66666 minus 1.11111
.\tenrm n
.\tenrm o
.etc.
```

What does this mean? Since we asked T_EX to assign the box, we discover that it has allocated `box16` to the task. The contents of this `box16` are a horizontal box whose height is 6.94444 pt, depth is 1.94444 pt, and whose width is 125.13916 pt. All the succeeding lines are preceded by a . which indicates that they are *inside* a box. If we had a box within a box, there would be two dots, and so on. The extract finishes with an `etc.`, saying that there is more to come, but it has been suppressed. T_EX has two 'tracing' parameters which control the depth and breadth of the boxes on which it reports: these are `\showboxbreadth` and `\showboxdepth`. The 'breadth' referred to is the maximum number of items shown per level; by default it is 5: the 'depth' is the deepest level to go to; by default this is 3. If we wanted more information we could reset these parameters. There is always a danger of being overwhelmed by this information.

There are other ways of finding out the height, depth, and width of a box. The primitive commands `\ht`, `\dp`, and `\wd` will allow manipulation of the height, depth, and width respectively of a particular box. In order to have them printed out at the terminal, the command `\showthe` may be used:

```
\showthe\wd\hamster
\showthe\dp\hamster
\showthe\ht\hamster
```

In this particular case, the result would have been

```
> 125.13916pt.
l.4 \showthe\wd\hamster
?
> 1.94444pt.
l.5 \showthe\dp\hamster
?
> 6.94444pt.
l.6 \showthe\ht\hamster
```

where for some deeply fathomable reason, the dimension precedes the echo of the command. As usual with the `\show` commands, we are invoking the error recovery part of TEX, and must respond correctly to the `?` prompt. In this case, answering correctly is straightforward: just `return`.

If we can find out the values, we can start to do things with them. We can test them against other values; we can even reset them, and fool TEX into believing they have totally different characteristics. But we'll look at that later.

In Chapter 3, we noted the presence of kerns between many letter pairs, and made the comment that it is not obvious what values the kerns have. We are now in a position to investigate this a little further. First, let's store 'Type' in a box: `\setbox0\hbox{Type}`. Instead of allocating a new box, I've just borrowed `box0`. Since there are only four elements (tokens) in the word, `\showbox0` will provide the information we want – the width of the box. If we now look at the width of `\setbox0\hbox{T{}y{}p{}e}` through `\showbox` we'll see the cumulative effect of any kerns.

```
\hbox(6.83331+1.94444)x22.50005
.\tenrm T
.\kern-0.27779
.\tenrm y
.\tenrm p
.\kern0.27779
.\tenrm e
```

Perhaps the first thing to notice is that there are two kerns, one negative, one positive: the font designer decided to close up the letter combination 'Ty' by a small amount, but also to separate 'pe' by a little bit extra too. The 'normal' expectation of a kern is to bring letters closer together, but obviously there is no real reason why other refinements need not be practised. Since these two kerns are equal in magnitude but opposite in sign, the second example, where null boxes (the {}) are introduced between each letter pair in order to force each letter to be treated independently,

turns out to have exactly the same length. However, it is still worth
comparing the look of the two words:

$$\text{Type} \qquad \text{Type}$$

and trying to decide to what extent you perceive these little subtleties. Since the individual kerns amount to little more than 1%
of the total width of the word, they may be tricky to discern. On
a 300 dpi laser printer, the amount by which the letters are kerned
is approximately equivalent to one dot.

One of TEX's deficiencies is the way in which it handles accented
characters. If an explicit accent is placed on a character which
would have been kerned, the kern is thrown away. This does lead
to some slight irregularities in words with accents. Although it is
well known that TEX abandons hyphenation on finding the first
explicitly accented character, it is not so widely appreciated that
the interletter spacing is also affected. If you have access to the
256 character set, together with the Extended Computer Modern
typeface, you may find it possible to enter é as a single character,
rather than \'e. In this case, the kerning should be 'correct'. In
order to distinguish between é and \'e, they are termed implicit
and explicit here.

⇒*Exercise 9.1:*   Demonstrate the difference made by typesetting 'ver-
itable' rather than 'véritable'. Can you type 'véritable' without having to
use \'? How does your TEX handle it: and your driver?   ⇐

The strategy used so far simply uses horizontal boxes at their
'natural' width. The width may be manipulated fairly directly
with the aid of two 'alternative' keywords: to and spread. Examples are

`\hbox spread 10pt{Make my day}`

and

`\hbox to \hsize{Bring me my Arrows of desire:}`

⇒*Exercise 9.2:*   Find out what it means to spread the box: what actually spreads?   ⇐

We have only looked at horizontal boxes in order to find out a bit
more about the way that TEX sees them. There are many other
things we can do with boxes. Once something has been placed
inside a box its contents can still be used. There are a number of
ways of obtaining the contents of a box. Taking the \hamster box,
we can \copy it, or merely quote it as a \box. In the first case it
is indeed a copy which is obtained, and the contents of \hamster
remain intact; in the second case the box becomes empty (or void)
once it is used. There are further possibilities: we may \unhbox
or \unhcopy the horizontal box. These last possibilities make the

contents available and allow us to reset the interword glue, for example (which none of the others would).

Let's examine some of these:

```
\newbox\callaghan
\newbox\blake
\setbox\callaghan\hbox spread 10pt{Make my day}
\setbox\blake\hbox to 0.5\hsize{Bring me my Arrows of
desire:}
```

Taking `\box\blake` gives 'Bring me my Arrows of desire:' – suitably taking up half the `\hsize`, but trying to `\box\blake` for a subsequent time yields an empty box, and we see nothing. On the other hand, `\copy\callaghan` gives 'Make my day', and copying `\callaghan` again will still give 'Make my day'. Had we used the other forms, `\unhcopy\callaghan` would have resulted in 'Make my day' while `\unhbox\blake` gives 'Bring me my Arrows of desire:'. Again, `\callaghan` could have been reused, but `\blake` would be empty.

When the contents of the box are to remain as they were boxed, the `\copy` or `\box` are preferred; the `\unh-` forms are not encountered frequently, but it is useful to know that we can re-examine the contents of boxes. If the contents are not required again, then it is best to surrender the box register by using `\box` rather than `\copy`. After all, there are only 256 registers. Right now it may seem unlikely that they would all be used, but any finite limit is likely to be exceeded eventually. One of the lessons of computing is that whatever space is available will be inadequate. Although we have not yet covered grouping explicitly, it turns out that boxes may have local application too. This means that

```
\setbox0\hbox{Cath}
{\setbox0\hbox{Pandora}}
\box0
```

will yield Cath. You may use the `\newbox` within a group too, with the anticipated results that the new box will have no meaning outside the group. One place you may not use `\newbox` is within the definition of a command.

Moving boxes

We may also move boxes around. In particular, they may easily be `\raise`d or `\lower`ed. Perhaps one of the first things you learn about TeX, after the session on pronunciation, where your keyboard becomes slightly moist, is how to create the logo. It is

worth looking at this here
```
\def\TeX{T\kern-0.1667em
          \lower0.7ex\hbox{E}\kern-0.125emX}
```
since it helps remind us how to raise or lower boxes. Before anything can be raised or lowered it must be boxed. Since lowering is just negative raising, I've always wondered why we have two commands: in other words, this definition is equivalent to
```
\def\TeX{T\kern-0.1667em
          \raise-0.7ex\hbox{E}\kern-0.125emX}
```
There are two other things to look at here. One is the use of \kern to move the boxes in a horizontal sense. There are other ways to achieve this, but this is economical.

The other thing to note is the use of the em and the ex as the units of measurement. This makes a lot of sense here, since these are measures related to the current font. In fact, they are one of the many \fontdimen values that were mentioned earlier in Chapter 3. Since T_EX may be set in a variety of fonts (or sizes), it would be unwise to fix the values irrevocably. Note, though, that the L^AT_EX logo is rather less general – but is not part of plain T_EX anyway. A common (but not the only) definition for L^AT_EX is
```
\def\LaTeX{{\rm L\kern-.36em
      \raise.3ex\hbox{\sc a}\kern-.15em
      T\kern-.1667em\lower.7ex\hbox{E}\kern-.125emX}}
```
This locks the logo into the current \rm, but more important, uses \sc for the raised 'small capital' A. This is a reference to the Computer Modern Caps and Small Caps font, a rather restricted font which is only available in one form: cmcsc10. We are assuming that somewhere the font has been set up, since it is not available by default:
```
\font\sc cmcsc10
```
There is no slanted or italic version of this font. Thus it is fairly easy to say T_EX, but considerably more difficult to say L^AT_EX.

Although it is not apparent, the use of the explicit \kern removes any implicit kerns. This is sometimes a source of some confusion, since from time to time it is obvious that some letter pairs need adjustment. Unless you look very carefully and first establish what kerns are already present, simply inserting a \kern may not be sufficient. Recall the 'Type' example. In the particular font used, there was a negative kern of -0.27779 pt between the T and the y. Had we written T\kern-0.2pt y it would not have brought the two letters as close together as writing nothing at all.

⇒*Exercise 9.3:* Estimate and then confirm the difference in length between `Type` and `T\kern-0.2pt ype`? ⇐

⇒*Exercise 9.4:* Just for amusement, create the following: D_EK. ⇐

Most of what has already been said about horizontal boxes is more or less true about vertical ones. In general terms, horizontal boxes are placed in vertical boxes, but those vertical boxes may themselves be placed in other boxes. A working rule is to place horizontal boxes within vertical boxes within horizontal boxes..., but there are many situations where this rule need not apply. In particular, we can easily place lots of horizontal boxes within other horizontal boxes.

The vertical box analogues of `\raise` and `\lower` are the 'move' commands, `\moveright` and `\moveleft`. There is no analogue of `\kern`, because a kern responds to the mode that TEX is in.

It may be helpful to glance at TEX's notion of 'modes' here. There are six 'modes', two of which concern maths, and which we shall ignore here. Of the remaining four modes, two are relevant to horizontal manœuvres, and two to vertical.

The two horizontal modes are 'horizontal' and 'restricted horizontal'. Horizontal is the mode in which TEX creates paragraphs, where it is building a horizontal list: restricted horizontal is similar, but there is no line breaking: for example, when material is put in an `\hbox`.

The vertical modes are 'vertical' and 'internal vertical'. Vertical is the mode in which TEX starts out, and is the one where it creates pages (from the so-called 'main vertical list'); internal vertical mode is the one where we are inside a vertical box.

TEX automatically switches from vertical to horizontal mode when it encounters the first token of a new paragraph. Such a token would normally be a character. The commands `\indent` or `\noindent` will also automatically switch to horizontal mode. If the first token were merely an `\hbox` TEX would not realize that it should switch to horizontal mode (after all, we can stack `\hbox`es within `\vbox`es). How can we force TEX to do what we want? In the slightly unusual situation that the first token in a paragraph was a horizontal box, TEX would be in vertical mode when it encountered the box, would put it on a line by itself, and then tackle the rest of the paragraph as if it started anew after the box. Probably not what was intended. This rather forced example

```
\copy\hamster\ is the caption of one of my
favourite Far Side cartoons.
```

gives

Oh brother, not hamsters again.

is the caption of one of my favourite Far Side cartoons.

⇒*Exercise 9.5:*   There are lots of ways to get out of the last problem. Ideas? Comments?   ⇐

Although the obvious solution is to start with \indent or \noindent, TEX has a command \leavevmode which does just that, and works nicely in such a situation. Of course, who would ever start a paragraph with a box? But what if that box was hidden in a command? This is where the well-written command would have a \leavevmode to ensure that the catastrophe outlined here would never occur.

⇒*Exercise 9.6:*   Demonstrate that a text which began

```
\hbox{A title}
\hbox{A subtitle}
```

would respond differently to one which started

```
\leavevmode   or   \noindent
\hbox{A title}
\hbox{A subtitle}
```

                                                                        ⇐

Vertical hold

There are two main ways of creating vertical boxes: through the \vbox and the \vtop. The difference lies in where each of these considers its 'reference' point to be. Every box has height and depth. In the simple case of the \hbox the baseline is the reference point from which the height and depth are measured. A \vbox generally has lots of height and only a little depth. The depth is determined by the nature of the last box (the last line). If, for example, it contains a character which has a descender, its depth will be positive. It may sometimes be zero. In the case of a \vtop the box probably has a small height but great depth. Here, the reference point is still the baseline, but of the first box (normally the first line). The point is that when these boxes are placed on the page, they are located according to their reference points.

To take a more concrete example: \vbox{one} sets 'one' in a vertical box. What are its dimensions? In order to find this out it is easiest to place it into a box and then check its height and depth through \showthe:

```
\setbox0\vbox{one}
\showthe\ht0
\showthe\dp0
```

Here this will yield 4.30554 pt for \ht0 and 0.0 pt for \dp0. Since there are no descenders, which would extend below the baseline, there is 'no' depth. On the other hand

```
\setbox0\vbox{eight}
\showthe\ht0
\showthe\dp0
```

with the letter 'g' should have some depth. And this time `\dp0` is 1.94444 pt while the height is different too, at 6.94444 pt. The difference in heights is explained by 'one' having no ascenders either, so that the height should be close to the x-height of the characters in the font. The ascenders in 'eight' ensure that it must have greater height.

⇒ *Exercise 9.7:*   If the box containing 'one' is stacked on top of the box containing 'eight', what will the height and depth of the resulting box be? Place the two vertical boxes containing 'one' and 'eight' into another vertical box. Examine its height and depth for confirmation. ⇐

Examining the height and depths of boxes which have been created with `\vtop` will reveal exactly the same characteristics. This is hardly surprising, since the first and last boxes are the same here. If we widen the situation to something more general, where there is more than one (horizontal) box making up the vertical box, then the position of the reference point will change. For example,

```
\setbox0\vbox{Of all the strange things that Alice saw
in her journey Through The Looking-Glass, this was the
one that she always remembered most clearly.}
\setbox1\vtop{Of all the strange things that Alice saw
in her journey Through The Looking-Glass, this was the
one that she always remembered most clearly.}
\showthe\ht0\showthe\ht1
\showthe\dp0\showthe\dp1
```

will provide a way of looking at the different positions of the reference point for two vertical boxes which contain the same text. The value of `\hsize` was reduced to guarantee a few lines, so that there is normal line breaking, and the first and last boxes are definitely different.

⇒ *Exercise 9.8:*   What do you expect the values of the height and depth of those two vertical boxes to be (roughly). Confirm your expectation. ⇐

With an `\hsize` of 267 pt and `\parindent` of 9 pt, the text is set like

> Of all the strange things that Alice saw in her journey
> Through The Looking-Glass, this was the one that she always
> remembered most clearly.

There is little very exceptional to note: the text is indented; the lines in the paragraph break normally. This serves to emphasize that text in a \vbox is set in the normal way for paragraphs. Although not apparent here, the text will *not* break across pages. This chunk of text is treated as a single indivisible unit. This is sometimes a useful attribute when it is necessary to force a material to be treated as a single unit.

Again it is possible to see the influence of TₑX's different modes (for this example the \hsize has been deliberately reduced – you will soon see why):

```
\hsize251pt
hello
\vbox{Of all the strange things that Alice saw in her
journey Through The Looking-Glass, this was the one
that she always remembered most clearly.}
goodbye
```

appears to do something a little odd.

> Of all the strange things that Alice saw in her journey
> Through The Looking-Glass, this was the one that she
> hello always remembered most clearly.

goodbye

When TₑX encounters the \vbox it is in horizontal mode. It sets the sentence quite normally, but places it to the right of the 'hello'. It also aligns the bottom of the box containing the \vboxed material with the bottom of the box containing 'hello'. The 'goodbye' is still part of the paragraph beginning 'hello', so it is not indented. At first it seems very odd that the \vboxed material appears to start before the 'hello', but this is all to do with how the \vbox works. Of course, this really serves to illustrate that you would not normally put a \vbox in the middle of text.

The size of material in a \vbox can be controlled in several ways. The vertical extent is normally the box's 'natural' extent. To alter this we may say

```
\vbox to 100pt{....}
```

or

```
\vbox spread 10pt{....}
```

in a similar way to an \hbox. To see how TₑX interprets such manipulations, \showbox can help:

```
\setbox\alice\vbox{Of all the strange things that
Alice saw in her journey Through The Looking-Glass...}
\showbox\alice
\setbox\longalice\vbox to 400pt{Of all the strange
things that  Alice saw in her journey
Through The Looking-Glass...}
\showbox\longalice
\setbox\spreadalice\vbox spread 10pt{Of all the strange
things that Alice saw in her journey
Through The Looking-Glass...}
\showbox\spreadalice
```
The key lines are these:
```
\vbox(90.94444+1.94444)x469.75499   for  \alice
\vbox(400.0+1.94444)x469.75499      for  \longalice
\vbox(100.94444+1.94444)x469.75499  for  \spreadalice
```
which demonstrates that TEX has done exactly what was asked, extending the height of the box to 400 pt, or increasing it by an extra 10 pt. Note that the box still has some depth in addition to the height, so that when we say \vbox to 400pt we are saying that the height is 400 pt. We make no comment about the depth. Where does the additional space go? In the case of \hbox to 200pt or \hbox spread 10pt, TEX puts glue between the words, in fact allowing the box to be 'underfull' if necessary. Does the same sort of thing happen here? The short answer is no, but let's look at the reasons for this.

In a simple approach, we might assume that if we ask a vertical box to be spread beyond its natural vertical extent that white space would be added between lines. This is only partly true. The glue between lines is controlled by the \baselineskip (because it is a \skip it can have glue associated with it). By default, the \baselineskip has no glue associated with it. Therefore all that happens is that the extra white space is added at the end, after the last of the text. The easiest way to demonstrate this is by taking the boxes created above and
```
\hrule
\box\longalice
\hrule
\box\spreadalice
\hrule
```
The \hrules are horizontal lines (rules) which extend across the whole page and separate each box. In this way we can easily see where one box ends and another begins.

If we make things more flexible and change the baseline glue, for example to

`\baselineskip12pt plus 1pt`

being careful to insert this command before the boxes are 'set', that is before the `\setbox` command, and look at the output again, we will see that this time the text is spread out vertically, in the sense that there is much more white space between lines. Because this example adds 1 pt of glue to the skip, you might have supposed that what TₑX would do is just allow the baseline skip to increase up as far as 13 pt. But it is clear that the increase is much more than this. How can this be so? Most of the reason lies in the fact that we are forcing TₑX to do something a little odd. In setting 'normal' text, we would rarely specify the actual dimensions to be 'filled'. And again, normally we add glue at the end of the text, which has the effect of overcoming the glue between the lines. One other unusual aspect of this example has been that it is only one paragraph long. Paragraphs are separated by `\parskip` – yet another sort of glue, and this could modify the distribution of the white space.

⇒*Exercise 9.9:*   Using some suitable chunk of text, place it in a vertical box; then alter the size of the box; modify the baseline characteristics; lastly, divide the text into more than one paragraph.   ⇐

It should come as no real surprise that the baseline skip cannot be altered through a paragraph. It is not possible to set a single paragraph with varying distances between the baselines of successive lines. It is certainly possible to set successive paragraphs with different values of `\baselineskip`, but the value remains constant within the paragraph unit. Similarly, the value used is the one in operation at the end of the paragraph. As a result, it is perfectly feasible to place the `\baselineskip` at the end of a paragraph (although this does look a little odd in the marked up text). And if there are multiple values, the last one is the one used. This also helps to emphasize the 'non-*wysiwyg*' nature of TₑX. Until it reaches the end of the paragraph, it can do nothing.

The width of the vertical box is controlled by the current `\hsize`. It is not immediately obvious that to create 'narrower' boxes, we change the `\hsize`. This sounds odd. After all, we do not want the 'real' `\hsize` to change. This is another case for grouping. If we write

`\setbox\alice\vbox{\hsize3in`
`Of all the strange things that Alice saw in her...}`

the horizontal extent of the text will be set up for the duration of

Of all the strange things that Alice saw in her journey Through The Looking-Glass, this was the one that she always remembered most clearly. Years afterwards she could bring the whole scene back again, as if it had been only yesterday – the mild blue eyes and kindly smile of the Knight – the setting sun gleaming through his hair, and shining on his armour in a blaze of light that quite dazzled her – the horse quietly moving about, with the reins hanging loose on his neck, cropping the grass at her feet – and the black shadows of the forest behind – all this she took in like a picture, as, with one hand shading her eyes, she leant against a tree, watching the strange pair, and listening, in a half-dream, to the melancholy music of the song.

"But the tune *isn't* his own invention," she said to herself: "it's '*I give thee all, I can no more.*'"

Figure 9.1
Two boxes side by side

the box, and will not change anything outside its group. We may even become more subtle and say

```
\setbox\alice\vbox{\hsize0.3\hsize
Of all the strange things that Alice saw in her...}
```

where we let the horizontal extent be controlled as some proportion of the 'external' horizontal width.

Let's demonstrate lining up two \vboxes. Two vertical boxes have been set up already, \alice and \song:

```
\newbox\alice
\setbox\alice\vbox{\tolerance2000\hsize0.6\hsize
\noindent  Of all the strange things that Alice saw in
her journey ...}
\newbox\song
\setbox\song\vbox{\pretolerance10000\hsize0.3\hsize
\noindent``But the tune {\sl isn't\/} his own
...}
```

These two may be set side by side by enclosing them in an \hbox

```
\hbox{\copy\alice\qquad\copy\song}
```

The \qquad is only there to keep them apart (Figure 9.1).

⇒*Exercise 9.10:*   What *might* happen if the two boxes were not enclosed in a horizontal box?   ⇐

Since we have two made up-boxes, it is worth having a look at their height and depth through the mechanism of \showbox:

```
*\showbox\alice
> \box16=
\vbox(138.94444+1.94444)x281.85585   followed by more
*\showbox\song
> \box17=
\vbox(42.94444+0.0)x140.92792   followed by more
```

Examining the dimensions of these boxes, we may be relieved to note that one is twice the width of the other, but that one has no depth. It also presents a problem, as the example shows. The \song box has no descenders in its last line. Because the reference point is the baseline in both cases, the two boxes nevertheless have their respective lines aligned (because they were both set with the same distance between baselines).

⇒*Exercise 9.11:* Repeat the last example, but instead of using a \vbox, use a \vtop.   ⇐

⇒*Exercise 9.12:* It is also a reinforcing exercise once you have placed these bits of text into boxes to start to use some of the other pieces of information you have lying about. Let's assume you want a piece of text to occupy exactly *n* lines. Outline how you might do that. Assume that the text is all in a single paragraph.   ⇐

There is another point to be drawn from the last example. In addition to the control of the \hsize, the \tolerance and \pretolerance have been adjusted temporarily. When 'narrow measure' is being used, there is less scope for the interword glue. Increasing the \tolerance helps here. The \pretolerance is set to the high value to switch off hyphenation. When TEX processes a paragraph it will generally make at least two passes. On the first pass it assesses the badness of the paragraph without allowing for any hyphenation. It will accept this paragraph if the badness calculated is less than or equal to the \pretolerance value. Otherwise it goes on to a second pass, where it hyphenates and now uses \tolerance in its assessment of the suitability of various breakpoints. In general, within TEX, a value of 10,000 is taken as equivalent to 'infinity'. Or equally, in the calculation of 'badness', any value over 10,000 is reset to 10,000.

When these vertical boxes are constructed, it is straightforward to employ glue too. This really only makes sense when you \vbox to or \vtop spread. But glue deserves some further discussion. The glue which has been discussed most up to now is the sort that is fairly implicit, and over which we have little control. Explicit glue comes in several packages, but the most common are with skips and with fills. The skip primitives are \hskip and \vskip. These can be employed to provide particular vertical and horizontal movements:

\hskip 1 in

\vskip 300 sp

but in most cases this is primitive in the extreme.

But note that we have already met a mechanism for moving text around – the \kern. It is perhaps worth noting why \kern does exist when it appears to do the same job as \hskip. A \kern might be slightly more economical. How do we demonstrate this? If we return to the definition of TEX, and replace the \kerns by \hskips, we could look at the difference in the amount of TEX's memory which is consumed. If we set the \tracingstats parameter to 3, TEX will report on the amount of memory that is used (among other things). The key line is one which looks like

5773 words of memory out of 65536

It turns out that both

\def\TeX{T\kern-0.1667em
        \lower0.7ex\hbox{E}\kern-0.125emX}

and

\def\TeX{T\hskip-0.1667em
        \lower0.7ex\hbox{E}\hskip-0.125emX}

occupy the same amount of memory. Of course, one form might be more 'efficient' than the other: a skip may have glue associated with it. Therefore whenever TEX sees \hskip3pt it anticipates that the dimension may be followed by a plus or a minus. It therefore has to check what the next letter (or perhaps group of letters) really is. A kern on the other hand is just a kern, so no further scanning is needed. There is one important difference. An explicit kern will not be a breakpoint. On the other hand, a line break is permitted at an \hskip.

This might suggest that we could therefore

\def\TeX{\hbox{T\hskip-0.1667em
        \lower0.7ex\hbox{E}\hskip-0.125emX}}

in order to ensure that TEX was never broken at the end of a line. What then happens when a paragraph begins with TEX? Do we really have to go on to say

\def\TeX{\leavevmode\hbox{T\hskip-0.1667em
        \lower0.7ex\hbox{E}\hskip-0.125emX}}

in order to avoid the use of the \hskip? This also turns out to use four more words of memory!

There are two more points we can make about the difference in
the use of \kerns and some sort of skip: firstly, the various skips
are more flexible, since they may have glue associated with them;
secondly, \kerns work in both horizontal and vertical mode – if we
are already in vertical mode, a \kern will provide vertical motion.
A last point might be that in some circumstances it feels more
natural to employ a kern, or a skip: in other words, we use the
form which most nearly equates to how we perceive the operation.

It always depresses me when I see an explicit \vskip. I much
prefer them hidden away somewhere where they do not detract
from the form and structure of the document. This 'hiding' is
exactly what commands are for. No-one should ever have to type
an \hskip or \vskip in plain text except in the most peculiar
circumstances.

⇒*Exercise 9.13:*   What does \hskip1inch do?   ⇐

The 'better', or more acceptable, forms of vertical skips are
tucked away in \smallskip, \medskip, and \bigskip. The exact
amount of vertical movement is not critical here, although it is
explored in Chapter 12. Their construction is worth looking at
more closely, since they have some glue associated with them.
They are all very similar, so it is enough to look at one. The
definition in plain is:

\def\smallskip{\vskip\smallskipamount}

which merely obliges us to look further to:

\newskip\smallskipamount
\smallskipamount=3pt plus1pt minus1pt

There are several useful points to be made here. Firstly, just as
boxes may be allocated dynamically, so too may skips be allocated. And there are 'equivalent' commands like \skip0. The
amount of a skip has glue associated with it in the form of a plus
and a minus amount. It is valuable to appreciate the syntax being
employed here. There are only a few words in T_EX's vocabulary
which are not case dependent. Dimensions (like pt, in, dd) may
be expressed in upper, lower, or mixed case, as might file names,
font names (sometimes), and so too plus and minus. The plus
must precede the minus. Of course, the keywords are only 'valid'
in context. Elsewhere they will indeed print out as 'plus 3pt', or
whatever. In the unlikely event that I was to say

\vskip 1in

Plus-fours are seldom seen, except on the golf course.

T_EX would be rather upset.

⇒*Exercise 9.14:*   What message would that example generate? And how should we solve the problem best? If the skip had been hidden in another command somewhere it could have been more difficult to spot. But we'll discuss 'safe TeX' and its relation to commands elsewhere. ⇐

Skips which have glue associated with them are useful when building pages. Remember what TeX is trying to do. It has a fixed size \vsize into which it is attempting to place n lines, each with a \baselineskip of some figure. If

$$n \times \text{\textbackslash baselineskip} \neq \text{\textbackslash vsize}$$

we will have a problem. The problem isn't too difficult to solve, since TeX's page-building facilities have some other parameters to play with. But that is a simplistic account. One way to help TeX is to let the inter paragraph skip, \parskip, have sufficient glue that it can cope without distress. By default, \parskip is all positive glue – 0pt plus1pt. You might ask why it does not have a more generous figure, or alternatively why the \baselineskip figure does not have glue associated with it.

⇒*Exercise 9.15:* Why do you think the glue is so stingy in the case of \parskip, or non-existent in the case of \baselineskip? One way to test your conclusion is to try modifying these skips empirically on a couple of paragraphs. ⇐

The asymmetry of glue is always interesting, and does make the spring analogy much more appealing that that of glue, since springs may behave differently on compression and expansion from their 'natural' size. But we seem to be stuck to glue.

We do not always know how much glue is applicable. There are situations where all we know is that we need to add glue. TeX has a couple of fills which can be used in such situations. A fill is an amount of glue (it may be positive or negative) which will expand or contract as required. A fill is a sort of a unit. There are in fact three different levels of fill. They are referred to as fil, fill, and filll. The last of these is seldom seen. In general we are most familiar with \hfil, \hfill, \vfil, and \vfill. Although they are actually fundamental TeX commands, their *equivalences* are given here:

\vfil	*approximates*	\vskip 0pt plus 1fil
\vfill	*approximates*	\vskip 0pt plus 1fill
\hfil	*approximates*	\hskip 0pt plus 1fil
\hfill	*approximates*	\hskip 0pt plus 1fill

Note that they are all positive amounts of glue fill. There are two other commands, \hss and \vss, which are equivalent to

\vss	*approximates*	\vskip 0pt plus 1fil minus 1fil
\hss	*approximates*	\hskip 0pt plus 1fil minus 1fil

These last two have negative and positive glue. This provides the opportunity for two boxes to overlap, if, say, \hss were placed between them.

Given this possibility of negative glue, there are a further two commands:

\vfilneg   *approximates*   \vskip 0pt minus 1fil
\hfilneg   *approximates*   \hskip 0pt minus 1fil

Besides placing the curious negative glue between boxes, these last two will also cancel out a \vfil or an \hfil, as appropriate.

Since both `fil` and `fill` may be given quantities, we have to establish their interrelationship. Basically, any amount of `fill` exceeds any amount of `fil`. You simply cannot accumulate sufficient `fil` to have any effect whatsoever on the smallest possible amount of `fill`. For example,

$$0.000001\,\mathtt{fill} > 100000\,\mathtt{fil}$$

Let's look at this more closely. A possible strategy to centre a piece of text across the page runs like this:

\hbox to\hsize{\hss A piece of text \hss}

This is the essence of the \centerline command, to be introduced in the next chapter. Knowing how it works, we can subvert it:

\centerline{\hfill Title}

will mean that the material is not centred at all, but instead is pushed to the right of the page.

One of the interesting features of the `fil`s is that it is possible to 'float' material proportionally. For example, we might want twice as much white space on the right as the left:

\hbox to\hsize{\hfil Two Thirds\hfil\hfil}

Similarly, I often find that if I am preparing something which takes up less than one side of a page, I don't really want to centre it vertically, but positioning it so that there is some glue at the top but more at the bottom, gives a pleasing appearance.

⇒*Exercise 9.16:*   Arrange some text to be floated within a page so that there are two units of glue at the top and three at the bottom. Now imagine you have two 'blocks' of information on a page. Arrange the material so that the glue at the top and between the blocks is the same, and that below is twice as much.   ⇐

⇒*Exercise 9.17:*   This is a shade more difficult. Outline how you might arrange two blocks of text so that they fit side by side on the page. The width of the blocks will not be equal, but their vertical extent will be the same. There is a trivial solution to this too.   ⇐

Lapping

One of the more interesting box manipulations is involved in manipulating a box so that TEX assumes it has no width. This allows a sort of 'back spacing' to be created. There are two such commands, called `\llap` and `\rlap`. The first, `\llap`, is properly back spaced, while the second, `\rlap`, is a sort of mirror image. The result of writing `Y\llap{=}` is to give us a crude approximation to the symbol for 'yen'. The reason that it is not a very good approximation is because the widths of both Y and = are not exactly equal. An almost equivalent rendition of `Y\llap{=}` is `\rlap{Y}=`. These actually look slightly different, as you might expect from lapping the = over a Y, as opposed to a Y over an =. How do these two commands work? There are a number of ways in which they could be created, but the actual definition of `\llap` is
`\def\llap#1{\hbox to0pt{\hss#1}}`
In other words, create a box of no width, preceding the argument by glue which has both stretch and shrink. That places the text of the argument to the left, and so gives a back-spacing effect. Transposing to
`\def\rlap#1{\hbox to0pt{#1\hss}}`
pushes the text to the right, but it takes 'no space', so that whatever follows starts at the same place as the text. As an example, it could be possible to place a symbol to the left of the text in a paragraph:
`\leavevmode\llap{$\Rightarrow$\indent}`
When placed at the beginning of a paragraph, this will position the ⇒ in the margin.

⇒*Exercise 9.18:*   Modify this set of commands to place an arrow in the right margin.   ⇐

When the `\everypar` command is uncovered, a route will appear where every paragraph can begin with such a symbol (or perhaps more usefully, with a paragraph number).

Commands#1   **10**

Commands (definition or macro) start to get much more interesting when they have parameters. The basic form of the definition
of a command with parameters is something like

`\def\one#1{#1}`

where the first `#1` says that there is to be one single parameter.
The repetition of `#1` within the braces merely tells TEX how you
want the parameter (or argument) to be treated. Having defined
`\one`, we can use it by saying `\one{argument}`. All this does is
to place `argument` into the text at this point. In this instance the
command is dull and rather pointless, so let's have a look at a more
interesting single-parameter command. TEX has a small clutch of
commands for placing text on lines: `\centerline`, `\leftline`,
and `\rightline`. They all have the same fundamental structure
which is shown *approximately* by

`\centerline#1{\hbox to\hsize{\hss#1\hss}}`

The argument is placed in a horizontal box the width of the page
and the globs of glue on either side 'push' it to the middle of that
box.

Using a command like this we have to understand what TEX
thinks the `#1` means. If we say

`\centerline Me`

TEX will pick up the next 'token', which in this instance is the
'M' It will not centre 'Me'. It will centre 'M' and then come back
for the 'e' as part of the normal typesetting. To ensure that it
takes the whole group we have to enclose the argument in braces:
`\centerline{Me}`. This should all be so obvious as to be second
nature, but it is worth clarifying just in case you are becoming
overintuitive.

⇒*Exercise 10.1:*   The other two commands, `\leftline`, and `\right-`
`line` are fairly self-descriptive. What do you think they do? Now compare
your ideas with what `\show` tells you about them.   ⇐

Although this last group of examples have one parameter, and
have used it once, we could ignore the parameter completely:

```
\def\ignore#1{}
```
or repeat the argument again and again:
```
\def\again#1{{\it #1}, {\bf #1}, {\sl #1}, {\tt #1}}
```
⇒*Exercise 10.2:*   I could have named the last command `\repeat`, but I thought better of it. Why?   ⇐

When there is more than one parameter, the pattern is a simple extension:
```
\def\lots#1#2#3#4{....}
```
so that each parameter is numbered sequentially, up to the total number. Since the pattern is so straightforward, you might wonder why you don't just have some way to say 'four parameters' or something similar. There is a reason. Note that there may be no more than nine parameters. Oddly, although all the boxes and skips and so on (and even the `\ifcase`) all start at zero, command parameters start at one. This restriction to nine is seldom irksome, and if it is, there are always ways to get round it.

⇒*Exercise 10.3:*   Why do you think there is a restriction to nine parameters in a command?   ⇐

In the expansion, the parameters may appear in any order you like, and, as we have already seen, they may appear as frequently as you want, or not at all. There are some restrictions on the replacement text. For example, it must not have any unbalanced braces. Apart from that, almost anything goes.

I looked through lots of my files to find examples of commands with parameters and found that I seldom seem to use commands with more than one or two arguments. Since I usually feel that real examples have a shade more validity than artificially constructed ones this does hamper a demonstration of how involved commands work. Nevertheless, let's make a simple example:
```
\def\rightleft#1#2{\hbox to\hsize{#1\hfill#2}}
```
which is just a way of taking the first argument and left justifying it, and the second argument and right justifying it. There is nothing really exciting about this, but it still deserves some further examination. Spaces are often a problem in commands: consider the following
```
\rightleft{ word }{ another word }
```
Just what does it produce? The streetwise will realize that all the argument goes in, spaccs and all. This is one instance where TeX does not ignore spaces. But equally, if one of the arguments was `{      word   }`, TeX would only 'see' a single space on either side. One space means something, but multiple spaces are elided into one. To show what happens:

```
\rightleft{ word }{ another word }
\rightleft{word}{another word}
```

word   another word

word   another word

There are times where this can be very trying. For example,

`\def\title#1{\centerline{\inch#1}\vskip10ex\noindent}`

This apparently harmless command to provide a title has a fatal flaw. The flaw is that when it is used, the implicit 'carriage control' at the end of the line is treated as a space and is pre-pended to the no-indented line. If there was normal indentation the problem would still be there, but it would be a bit less visible. The 'crude' solution of

`\def\title#1{\centerline{\inch#1}\vskip10ex\noindent}`
`\title{A Beginning}`
`\noindent`

is hardly satisfactory. The 'real' answer is

`\def\title#1{\centerline{\inch#1}\vskip10ex`
                    `\noindent\ignorespaces}`

which effectively 'removes' the spaces. But this does help to emphasize how difficult it can be to see spaces. Often when we create commands which go over several lines it is a safety measure to end each line with a % symbol to ensure that no spurious spaces/end of lines are incorporated in the expanded text. Of course this is unnecessary where the line ends in a command with no argument, since the spaces are effectively gobbled up.

⇒*Exercise 10.4:*   Provide another example. When else are spaces gobbled up in this way?   ⇐

Besides being careful with spaces in the body of the command, we have to be careful too in the parameter part, since

`\def\title#1 {...`

means something rather different to the previous definition. Here, the space really is important. The commands described up to now are]'undelimited'. Or rather, there is another class of commands which is described as being 'delimited'. Instead of placing the arguments in braces when we use them,

`\title{A longer title this time}`

we say in the actual definition how we expect the arguments of the command to be broken up. Returning to the 'new' definition of `\title`

`\def\title#1 {...`

the space which follows the #1 is a delimiter. It tells TₑX that the argument will be everything up to the first space. Thus

```
\title Sesquipedalian
```
will turn the whole of 'Sesquipedalian' into a title, while
```
\title Aardvarks are seldom harmful
```
only turns 'Aardvarks' into the title. The remainder of the text is new material, presumably to be handled as normal text here. Of course there are endless variations on this. And there are endless discussions on the wisdom of delimited commands. The major problem revolves around the need for the delimiters to match exactly. For example
```
\def\title#1\par{\centerline{\inch#1}\vskip10ex
                            \noindent\ignorespaces}
```
is a reasonable definition, where the title text is delimited by either a blank line or a \par statement. This is a rather interesting case, since if we forget to put the blank line in (so easy to do), the whole of the following paragraph becomes the title.

A simplified version of this could be
```
\def\simple#1\par{{\bf #1}}
```
The emboldening is just to enable us to identify the extent of the action. Consider the following case:
```
\simple The first line
```

```
A second paragraph
```
The blank line (identical here to a \par) delimits the argument. In fact we could demonstrate the equivalence by writing this definition as
```
\def\simple#1
```

```
{{\bf #1}\par}
```
with a blank line explicitly in the definition. What actually happens when we use either of these commands? We find the following behaviour (again, this has been deliberately narrowed):

The first line A second paragraph

Why is there no paragraph break? Simply because the blank line is a delimiter, not a real command. To ensure that a new paragraph begins, we must include such a command as part of the definition of the command:
```
\def\simple#1\par{{\bf #1}\par}
```
One delimited command has already been introduced:
```
$\root n-1 \of m$
```
uses the \of as a separator. It has no other function.

There are a couple of similar \par delimited commands in plain TₑX, namely \beginsection and \proclaim. The full commands are given on page 355 of *The TEXbook*. Although the body of the command contains some 'new' features, it is the delimiting template which is really of interest:

`\def\beginsection#1\par{...`

`\def\proclaim #1. #2\par{...`

The first is used to begin sections, where the title of the section is the argument, and as discussed earlier, it is delimited by a blank line or a \par command. The second of these is worth considering in more detail. The definition has two arguments which are delimited by .␣ and \par. An example of its use might be

`\proclaim Theorem 1. The stirrup pump will not`
`extinguish the fires of hell\par`

⇒*Exercise 10.5:*　　In order to gain some experience in the use of delimited commands, state what you expect, and then verify what happens, when you: leave two spaces between `\proclaim` and the first argument; leave *no* space between `\proclaim` and the first argument; leave *two* or more spaces between the first delimiter (the dot) and the second argument; leave *no* spaces between the first delimiter (the dot) and the second argument; omit the dot or the \par.　　　　　⇐

It is also important to realize that the . which is used as part of the delimiter has nothing to do with the bold full point which appears in the typeset version. The `\proclaim` definition itself contains a full point. In this case there is the world of difference between 1.␣ and 1.1␣. While they both look like numbers to be used in the `\proclaim`, only the first one is syntactically correct and will yield the sort of results we probably want.

Of course, even when the parameters are delimited, you can still put braces around them. Indeed you may need to. Imagine in the last example that you wanted to say

`\proclaim (after T. S. Eliot). The stirrup pump`
`will not extinguish the fires of hell\par`

The T.␣ will delimit the first argument of `\proclaim` with the rather odd result that **(after T.** will appear in bold. In order to have the correct part taken as the first argument, write

`\proclaim {(after T. S. Eliot)}. The stirrup pump`
`will not extinguish the fires of hell\par`

or even

`\proclaim (after {T. S.} Eliot). The stirrup pump`
`will not extinguish the fires of hell\par`

The delimiters must still appear at the 'outer' level.

Again note that the \par is merely a delimiter. No paragraph will actually be begun. Normally the command expansion text would take care of this. This does mean we can have the apparently odd situation of an undefined command which does not cripple TEX:

`\def\title#1\closetitle{..`

where `\closetitle` is merely a delimiter and not a command.

Partly because of the potential problems of 'runaway arguments', where TEX never finds the closing delimiters, there are some built-in safety measures. Normally TEX will complain when it thinks the argument includes a paragraph break, and will give the 'runaway argument' message. There is a way around this. There is a class of `\long` definitions which may indeed contain paragraph breaks:

`\long\def\theorem{...`

would allow the parameters passed through to this command to contain more than one paragraph. Of course there is a reason for this constraint. TEX has to read all of the argument into memory before it does something with it.

Another convenient example might be

```
\long\def\Boxit#1#2{\vbox{\hrule\hbox{\vrule\kern3pt
   \vbox{\kern3pt\vbox{\hsize#1\noindent\strut#2}%
   \kern3pt}\kern3pt\vrule}\hrule}}
```

(mainly borrowed from Knuth, page 331), where the first argument is the width of the text in the box; the frame is 3 pt 'outside' the text, hence the reference to `\kern`s of 3 pt, and the `\strut` is a new command which will be examined later in Chapter 15, but is used here to ensure that the vertical spacing is 'correct'. This would enable us to have something like Figure 10.1.

Many commands contain other commands. Normally this is not a real problem, but a few have been deliberately locked so that they cannot appear within other commands. There are two notable examples of these restricted use, or `\outer`, commands: the first is `\bye`, and the other is the command which allows `\newdimen`, `\newbox`, and other similar facilities to be set up.

⇒*Exercise 10.6:*   Try placing `\bye` within the body of a definition and see what happens.   ⇐

I have difficulty in seeing the strategy for limiting `\newdimen` and `\newbox` by creating them with `\outer`, since it seems a little overconservative. There are many situations where it would be particularly useful to be able to use `\newbox` or `\newdimen` or `\newcount` in the definition of a command.

It is wise to remind ourselves of the purpose of commands, by quoting from Knuth:

"The name of the song is called '*Haddocks' Eyes.*'"

"Oh, that's the name of the song, is it?" Alice said, trying to feel interested.

"No, you don't understand," the Knight said, looking a little vexed. "That's what the song is *called*. The name really *is* '*The Aged Aged Man.*'"

"Then I ought to have said 'That's what the *song* is called'?" Alice corrected herself.

"No, you oughtn't: that's quite another thing! The *song* is called '*Ways and Means*': but that's only what it's *called*, you know!

"Well, what *is* the song, then?" said Alice, who was by this time completely bewildered.

"I was coming to that," the Knight said. "The song really *is* '*A-sitting On A Gate*': and the tune's my own invention."

"But the tune *isn't* his own invention," she said to herself: "it's '*I give thee all, I can no more.*'"

Figure 10.1
Meta-names

TₑX is intended to support higher level languages for composition in which all of the control sequences that a user actually types are commands rather than TₑX primitives. The ideal is to be able to describe important classes of documents in terms of their components, without mentioning actual fonts or point sizes or details of spacing: a single style-independent document can then be set in many different styles.

⇒*Exercise 10.7:*   What will this do? `\def\eatme#1*{}`   ⇐

⇒*Exercise 10.8:*   Write a command where `\<word>` will result in ⟨word⟩.   ⇐

⇒*Exercise 10.9:*   Perhaps one of the commonest sources of misunderstanding with new TₑX users is the distinction to be made between `{\it italicize me}` and `\it{italicize me}`. Because it is so fundamentally obvious, old TₑX hands find the question mind-bafflingly difficult to answer. Devise a convincing explanation. Please.   ⇐

⇒*Exercise 10.10:*   Devise a command which *emphasizes*, so that it gives a different font depending on the context. In an upright font it will use a sloping font (or perhaps a bolder font). In a sloping or bold font it will choose something else to be appropriate. Are you going to worry about the italic correction?   ⇐

Most of the useful commands which are encountered either do something awfully easy but convenient, or do things which are individually quite involved, but taken together encapsulate a single idea. Usually such commands combine several different

components of TEX. The following demonstrates the conjunction
of some things we have already encountered, and some we have
not. Non-trivial examples which merely build on what we have
covered so far are so difficult to find. At least the next examples
have the merit of apparently having serious intent.

The effect that is to be achieved at the beginning of a new section is a section number, followed by the section 'title' crammed
into a rather narrow width, and then the first paragraph of the
section; the following paragraph should not be indented at the left
margin. An example is shown in Figure 10.2.

As usual, there are many possible solutions. This is only one:

```
\def\sectionhead#1#2#3\par{{%
  \setbox0=\hbox{{\bf#1}\hskip0.5em}
    \advance \hsize by -\wd0
  \setbox1=\vtop{\raggedright\hsize 3pc\noindent #2}
    \advance \hsize by -\wd1
  \setbox2=\vtop{\noindent #3}
    \hbox{\box0  \box1  \box2}
    \bigskip\noindent}}
```

What are the main points? Firstly that it is a delimited command.
Delimiting with the \par seems reasonable for a case like this. The
paragraph break is an integral part of the problem. The calculation
of the widths of the individual components is fairly straightforward, and helps to account for the double braces which open the
command. Without the second brace, the value of \hsize would
decrease each time we use this command. Embarrassing. The reason for stuffing everything into boxes is that we do not necessarily
know the width of the first box. Provided we have no more than
nine sections, we could set the width of that box to be static.

How do we use it? Like this:

```
\sectionhead{I.}{First section}
Twas brillig and the slithy toves did gyre and gimble
in the wabe: all mimsy were the borogoves, and the mome
raths outgrabe.

Beware the Jabberwock, my son!
The jaws that bite, the claws that catch!
Beware the Jubjub bird, and shun the
frumious Bandersnatch!
```

⇒*Exercise 10.11:*   Solve the problem a different way.   ⇐

I. First   'Twas brillig and the slithy toves Did gyre and gimble
   section in the wabe: All mimsy were the borogoves, And the
           mome raths outgrab.

"Beware the Jabberwock, my son! The jaws that bite, the claws
that catch! Beware the Jubjub bird, and shun the frumious Ban-   **Figure 10.2**
dersnatch!"   A section head

More command subtleties

There are a variety of ways to create commands. The one description given so far is to use \def. There are variations to \def,
and there are also slightly different ways to create commands.
As usual, examples help to illustrate what is implied here. If the
command \let is used to 'equivalence' two other commands, a
new command may be created very cheaply:

\let\command\centerline

gives a new command, \command, which not only has all the
attributes of an existing command, \centerline, but really is the
same as the existing command. Inside TEX it 'points' to the same
token list. However, should we redefine the original command
\centerline, while the redefinition will affect \centerline, it
will not affect \command. Why would we want to do something
quite so bizarre? The following example might help answer that
question:

\let\endpara\par
\def\par{\endpara\vskip2pt\hrule\vskip2pt}

would ensure that every paragraph ended with a horizontal rule.
Actually there is a better way to do this with \everypar. Nevertheless it does demonstrate that we can redefine primitive commands, without incurring the expense of recursion. Imagine

\def\par{\par\vskip2pt\hrule\vskip2pt}

⇒*Exercise 10.12:*   From time to time it is possible inadvertently to
create a recursive definition like the last one. When it is used it just loops
around and around, usually until TEX runs out of one of its varieties of
stack space. If you don't know what that means, it does not really matter.
This can be frustrating. It is wise to find out whether there is some way of
breaking into TEX when such an event occurs, or whether you just have
to be patient. Do so.   ⇐

   The \let command is even more powerful, since new commands
can apparently be introduced. Almost any token can be used:

\let\\=\cr
\let\hash #

But it would be naive to assume that \hash could take the place of # when that symbol was used to indicate the parameters in a \def, but on the other hand (jumping ahead slightly) it *could* be used in an alignment. The commonest use of \let is in the temporary reassignment of a command.

An 'ordinary' definition can be given certain additional powers through suffixes: the suffixes \global, \outer, and \long can be placed before \def. We have looked at the last two of these briefly already.

The \long prefix is used to say that a command argument may be more than one paragraph long. Remember that an argument which contains more than one paragraph will likely be a very *long* one. This could fill up lots of TEX's memory. The structure of a \long\def does not allow us to distinguish between first argument, which might be allowed to be more than one paragraph long, and another, which should not be more than one paragraph. It's all or nothing.

The \outer prefix prevents a command from becoming part of another one. As we commented earlier, it does seem overused.

⇒*Exercise 10.13:*   Look through the plain TEX commands to see which are defined as \outer. You may have to work around things to see what they really do (or don't). Are you foolhardy enough to redefine some of these without the restrictions?   ⇐

There are still a few 'special' forms of \def to consider. These are \edef and \xdef. Since the latter turns out to be merely \global\edef, we can more or less ignore it now. What is an \edef? It is an 'expanded definition'. When TEX reads the commands of the definition part of a command, it stores them in memory. It does not interpret them. It does not even bother to find out whether any commands inside your definition actually exist. It thinks you know what you are doing. Once the command is used, it is expanded, and all the parts are interpreted. They are given their current meaning.

The \edef variant allows you to fix the meaning of a command at definition time. All the commands and commands used in the defining text are expanded immediately. Therefore there may be no undefined command in the text:

\def\test{\information}
\def\information{Old}

will work when you come to use \test, but

\edef\test{\information}
\def\information{Old}

will not, because \information has not been defined by the time it is required to be expanded in \test.

If the command definition contains a command which should not be expanded, but should be interpreted later, it is possible to inhibit the expansion with \noexpand:

\def\information{Old}
\edef\test{\information\ -- \noexpand\information}
\def\information{New}

gives the rather interesting result that \information yields New, while \test generates Old – New.

There are one or two other special conditions where something like a command is defined. The \every... commands allow you to set up a series of one or more commands which are executed whenever a particular situation occurs. The commands are \everypar, \everycr, \everymath, \everydisplay, \everyhbox, and \everyvbox. There is also an \everyjob, but since this may only be used in INITEX, it will not be considered further. INITEX is not a production version of TeX, but one used to set up, for example plain.

Each one of these \every commands has the same sort of meaning. In the case of \everypar, whenever a new paragraph is encountered, the text specified is processed:

\everypar={\bigskip}

There are far better ways to do this, through \parskip, but this illustrates the way that \everypar could be used to insert extra space every time a blank line or \par was encountered.

More usefully, we could force the first word of every paragraph to be set in a different style:

\def\start#1 {{\sc #1}}
\everypar{\start}

Provided that \sc had been set up to do something (for example, to turn on the 'caps and small caps' font, every paragraph would find its first word in that style.

⇒*Exercise 10.14:* Repeat the last example so that the first letter of a paragraph is given in a different font. ⇐

Local and global

The most obvious and common use of grouping is to localize some change, for example a font change. Putting \it in braces makes the command effect only the text up to the next closing brace: {\it...}. This is because the assignments made by the expansion of \it are *local* to the *group* formed by this pair of braces. This is the default case: assignments apply only within the group in which they are made, and at the end of the group everything is restored to the 'original' state.

Here *everything* means the values of all the parameters and variables, the meanings of all the commands, plus many of the other things which control TEX's current activities. Naturally *everything* has exceptions. There are few things which are intrinsically not local, and changes to these, even inside a group, will have a *global* effect. Some of the common commands and assignments with a global effect are

```
\magnification1000
\hyphenation{command, para-meter}
\batchmode
```

There is some plausible reason why it does not make much sense to see these as temporary changes.

All command definitions, \let assignments, and register assignments are local to their group unless they are prefixed by \global. As it suggests, this has the effect of a global assignment, and overrides any grouping. A shorthand for \global\def is \gdef:

```
\global\count0=1
\global\baselineskip 12pt plus 1pt
\gdef\title{Global}
\global\let\next\relax
\global\long\def\section#1/#2{\leftline{\sl#1}\par
                \noindent#2\medskip}
```

Some flavour of the potential use of \global can be found from:

```
\count0=1
{\advance \count0 by 2\relax \number\count0}
\number\count0
{\global\advance \count0 by 3}
\number\count0
```

The first grouped \advance increments \count0 by 2, but this increment is 'lost' when we revert back out of the group. The second time that \count0 is typeset, it has the value that it had originally. In the next case, where it is incremented globally, the change survives the group.

⇒*Exercise 10.15:*   Consider the following assignments:

```
\count1=2
{\count0=1 \advance\count0 by\count1}
{\global\advance\count0 by\count1}
```

What value will \count0 have now?   ⇐

In a sense, font assignments are global. Although
`{\font\fib=cmfib10}`
will result in `\fib` being undefined (since the setting up of the
font is grouped), the font metric information will have been loaded
and will be more readily available in future.

Groups

Although the most obvious way to create a new group is with
braces, this is by no means the only way. There are 'implicit'
groups. These are confined to some aspects of maths, boxes, and
alignments. Alignments crop up in the next chapter, but will be
included here for the sake of completeness. As soon as you enter
text or display maths you are in an intrinsic or implicit group. In
a sense then, `$` and `$$` are grouping symbols. Any extra definitions will be local. Within maths, groups are also formed between
`\left` and `\right` items. Not only do these create parentheses,
they enclose TEX groups. The material inside a box (`\hbox`, `\vbox`,
or `\vtop`) is in a group: there is perhaps an unexpected repercus-
sion here that, in displayed maths, there is a hidden `\hbox` in
an `\eqno` or `\leqno` so that any text between these commands
and the `$$` is typeset in a horizontal box. Thus anything in there
is grouped. Each entry of an alignment (as we'll soon see, this
means within the `&`s) is a group (and so too is the alignment
itself). Material in a `\noalign` is also in an implicit group.

Of these, perhaps the boxed material is the one which can cause
some confusion. Until you realize what `\centerline` really means,
`\centerline{\sl This text}`
does not seem all that different in use from
`\def\quid{\it\$}`
`\quid32.00`
The `\centerline` has an implicit group (an `\hbox`) which ensures
that the `\sl` is 'confined'. The definition of `\quid` should of course
have an extra pair of 'insulating' braces.

Groups can be nested as deep as you like, although presumably TEX will run out of space eventually, since each new layer of
grouping requires that some information is stored.

Alternatives – almost

There are two commands which may be used to open and close
a group: `\begingroup` and `\endgroup`. They can be used in any

case where braces will do, provided the braces are being used to group. They will not work for

```
\def\quid\begingroup\it\$\endgroup
```

or to enclose a box. In those contexts the braces are used as delimiters and have a definite syntactic requirement. A \begingroup may only be terminated by a \endgroup. It should not be necessary to say that you cannot write something like

```
\begingroup
{....
\endgroup
...}
```

Groups cannot overlap. They may be like Russian dolls and sit inside one another, but they cannot overlap.

Although braces may be thought of chiefly in their role of creating groups where 'local' or confined actions take place which have no longer lasting effect, braces do have other uses, some of which have been addressed already. For example, braces will be found as part of a command definition, marking the beginning and end. Similarly, there will always be braces after box-creating commands like \hbox and \vbox. Again the braces are marking the beginning and end of something which forms an implicit group. They indicate a group, but they are not the 'cause' of the group. In these cases the braces are not used merely to indicate a group. They therefore *must not* be replaced by \begingroup \endgroup pairs.

On the other hand, there are two commands \bgroup and \egroup which may be used in place of { and } in most, but not all, contexts. Their definitions are

```
\let\bgroup {
\let\egroup }
```

They may be used wherever braces form a group, including an implicit group. They may not be used to replace the braces which begin and end the arguments of a command. It is instructive to see what TeX would make of this:

```
\def\one\bgroup x\egroup
```

Seeing it written down like this, and remembering about delimited commands, it comes as no real surprise that TeX generates a message like

```
Runaway definition?
\bgroup x\egroup
```

since it assumes that the \bgroup x\egroup is just part of the template of the command.

⇒*Exercise 10.16:*   If the last example was more realistic and had a few definitions:
```
\def\one\bgroup x\egroup
\def\two{y}
```
would the error message be the same?   ⇐

    A case where **\bgroup** and **\egroup** are not exactly equivalent to { and } is when they surround the argument of a command.

    It is possible to write
```
\centerline\bgroup Centred information\egroup
```
but rather unexpected things happen. The command **\center-line** absorbs **\bgroup** as its argument, so that what TEX sees, after expanding **\centerline**, is
```
\hbox to\hsize{\hss \bgroup
                 \hss }Centred information\egroup
```
which is 'equivalent' to
```
\hbox to\hsize{\hss {\hss }Centred information}
```
    Outside the restrictions of delimiters of replacement text in a command and delimiters of a command's arguments, the only other context where { and } must be used is with a token string (discussed briefly at the end of this chapter). The grouping of **\bgroup** with } is normally quite satisfactory, as is { and **\egroup**. Although they may be paired with { and } they may not be paired with **\begingroup** and **\endgroup**. The following is therefore legal
```
\setbox0\hbox
        \bgroup
           \begingroup \bf This {%
                        \it is \egroup
           \endgroup legal, but difficult to read
        }
```
and somewhat obscure to follow; while
```
\setbox0\hbox
        \begingroup
           \bgroup\bf This {%
                        \it is \egroup
           \endgroup illegal, and difficult to read
        \egroup
```
is not only difficult to follow, but also syntactically incorrect.

    These commands do have some quite far-reaching advantages. It becomes possible to have a command with an 'unbalanced' group. Of course, if the balancing part does not follow later, TEX may well complain. If the **\it** and similar commands present a

problem, they could be augmented by a \beginit \endit pair,
where the definitions would look something like
```
\def\beginit{\begingroup\it}
\def\endit{\endgroup}
```
In a similar way
```
\def\beginminipage#1{\hbox to\hsize
  \bgroup\hss\vbox\bgroup\hsize#1\relax}
\def\endminipage{\egroup\hss\egroup}
```
would create a 'centred mini-page' command pair which takes a
single argument which defines the width of the mini-page. Note
that the text of the material to be typeset is not passed as an
argument, just the width. In this way all the contents of the mini-
page need not be held as an argument. This also means that we
do not have to worry about making the command \long.

⇒*Exercise 10.17:*   The \beginminipage 'environment' might be modified by boxing the material (see page 156). Combine the two commands
to create a 'boxed mini-page'. Retaining the centring reduces your future
flexibility. How would you place two boxed mini-pages together across a
page?   ⇐

Other ways

There are a few other ways in which commands may be created.
Token strings are used a little, and have properties which make
them look rather like commands. Token strings occupy registers
just like counters, dimensions, and skips. There are therefore up
to 256 of them. The 'fundamental' command is \toks; thus
```
\toks0={Walrus}
```
has the effect of storing the text Walrus in the token string. In
fact, the string may be any string and can include other commands if needed. As usual, the = is not obligatory. To use the
token string, we do not say \toks0, since if we did, T_EX would
be expecting some suitable string: instead, we precede \toks0 by
\the. To make it disgorge its contents:
```
\the\toks0
```
Rather than use the form where each string is numbered, we can
use
```
\newtoks\oyster
\oyster{Carpenter}
\the\oyster
```
in a manner equivalent to the other registers. A token string
therefore looks rather like a command without parameters. The

question is bound to arise, why? If the two are similar, and if in fact it is necessary always to precede a token string by \the in order to use it, making it less 'friendly', why bother? This is not an easy question to answer. Primarily, token strings are already with us. When we used \everypar, for example, what was happening was that a token string was being set up. The syntax is identical:

\everypar={\hrule}

The explicit use of \toks0 or \newtoks merely makes accessible what is already there. On the other hand, it is possible to do some rather powerful things with token strings – much too powerful for a primer.

One of the commonest uses of token strings is in setting up headlines and footlines. These are the extra information which typically lies outside the normal text boundaries, which may, for example, contain the chapter title (or current section title), page number, and a variety of other information. Two token strings are available for this use, \headline and \footline. These will be examined a little more closely in a later chapter.

Token strings are sufficiently similar to commands that they require the use of braces around the 'replacement text'. Trying to use \bgroup and \egroup will generate errors.

Commands which violate the rules

The last way of setting up a command which will be presented here is through \csname. This is just a little odd, especially since it allows us to violate one of the rules about command names which was set up earlier. Taking a simple case first:

\def\join#1#2{\csname#1#2\endcsname}

will take two arguments, and join them together as a single, named command. For example, \join{centre}{line} would be equivalent to \centerline, and \join{}{line} would be equivalent to \line. To use this command we can say

\join{left}{line}{the frumious bandersnatch}

This seems a little long winded, and in this instance, perhaps

\def\join#1{\csname#1line\endcsname}

would have the advantage of being briefer, and also demonstrating that almost anything may appear between the \csname and \endcsname.

The \csname \endcsname pair are not exactly equivalent to the backslash form of a command: for example, it would be possible to have the following

```
\def\bizarre#1{\def\csname*&!\endcsname{#1}}
\bizarre{It's full of stars}
\csname*&!\endcsname
```
in order to make this odd sequence of characters equivalent to the piece of text. But look at it more closely. It merely appears to work. The 'enclosed' definition
```
\def\csname*&!\endcsname{#1}
```
actually redefines \csname and treats *&!\endcsname as the delimiters of the command. Should we come to use \csname again it will not work as we expect.

The problem is that the commands are expanded in the wrong order. We need some way of having T_EX ignore the \def until the \csname and \endcsname have been dealt with (expanded). The relevant command is \expandafter. It allows the expansion (or use) of a command to be delayed until the following one has been processed. To take a simple example, for the purposes of illustration,
```
\def\word{{Alpha}{Omega}}
\def\choose#1#2{#1}
```
If we simply say \choose\word, the command may complain that it cannot find a second argument (or maybe the next token will mysteriously disappear). On the other hand
```
\expandafter\choose\word
```
forces \word to be expanded, leaving two arguments, {Alpha} and {Omega}. T_EX therefore prints out the first of these.

One area where these new commands can come in useful is in setting up keys for labels used in cross-referencing. Broadly, the theory is this: we may choose a label, for example \label{aardvark}. The label will contain the page number, or a section number, or perhaps an equation number
```
\def\label#1{\def\csname#1\endcsname{\the\secno}}
```
and when we come to use the label aardvark, there will be the section number. From what was said earlier, this last definition is wrong, since what it is doing is redefining \csname. We have to find some way of delaying the use of \def until \csname and \endcsname are expanded. This time, one \expandafter will not do, and we need three in order to force the delay to be quite long enough (as a rule, \expandafters occur in odd numbers):
```
\def\label#1{\expandafter\expandafter\expandafter
            \def\csname#1\endcsname{\the\secno}}
```
The other half of this problem is how we use the label in a reasonably 'friendly' way. No-one wants to type in

```
\csname aardvark\endcsname
```
in order to expand the label to find the section number. Writing
\aardvark is acceptable, but is not quite what we want. The likely
solution is to define another command
```
\def\ref#1{\csname#1\endcsname}
```
where the new command \ref{aardvark} simply expands to give
the section number where aardvark (or whatever) was last used.

These are likely to be features which are found embedded within
other commands. They will seldom see the light of day. There are
many other commands and structures like this. Some will be seen
briefly later.

Tidying up

In previous chapters, extra accents in both text and mathematics have been introduced. How can we supplement the basic set of
accents? Consider the use of accents in text. The example of Chapter 6 was ů. To write a command to place the circle accent is fairly
sraightforward, once it is known that \accent23 provides the
appropriate accent. The \accent is a command which assists TEX
in placing the symbol correctly. A suitable definition might be:
```
\def\u#1{{\accent23 #1}}
```
where \u u will provide a suitable accent. The main problem
is in deciding an appropriate name for the new command, and
remembering to leave a space between 23 and #1 in the definition.

The mathematical example of Chapter 4 is slighly different,
since it does not require a definition with a parameter. The \math-
accent command itself is enough. This helps to re-emphasize the
difference between accents in text and maths. The main mys-
tery is how to select the accent itself. To do this easily we need
information provided in Chapters 18 and 19:
```
\def\open{\mathaccent"7017}
```
Firstly, accept that the " indicates a hexadecimal value. The
number is most easily read as 7, 0, 17. The 7 indicates that the
symbol is from the 'variable family' class, a category whose subtlety is great; the 0 indicates the symbol is in font family 0 (usually
\rm); and the 17 (actually "17) gives its position in the font table.
Eventually this allows us to write $\open u$ for ů.

Matrix manipulations 11

So far we have merely looked at fairly simple equations which can conveniently be written either in the text, or in a one-line display. We have not considered more 'two-dimensional' structures, like matrices. It is probably fair to say that large equations, which go over more than one line, as well as matrices (or tables) are unlikely to be found in *text* rather than *display*. Almost all of the following discussion therefore assumes implicitly that we are talking about displayed equations and formulae.

There are two special 'elements' to setting aligned expressions (which is the way TeX treats matrices), which can be introduced at once – the special symbol &, which can be treated as a sort of *tab* character, and the command \cr, which can be thought of as 'carriage return', that is, end of this particular line. Perhaps 'complete row' would be a better expansion of the acronym, since it really has nothing to do with carriages or returns. Do note that \cr only works in this way within an alignment. Placing it within your text will seldom achieve anything positive, and may generate a dubious error message.

Setting a matrix is rather straightforward:

```
$$T=\left\lbrack \matrix{
    1    &    0    & 0 \cr
    0    &    1    & 0 \cr
\delta x & \delta y & 0 \cr}
    \right\rbrack
$$
```

This helps to illustrate the use of the & and \cr. The basic operator at this point is the \matrix. The extra commands merely place large square brackets around the matrix. You may use any of the convenient delimiters given earlier. Knuth has a tendency to concentrate on the use of 'round' brackets, but I tend to find square brackets more natural. That expression would yield:

$$T = \begin{bmatrix} 1 & 0 & 0 \\ 0 & 1 & 0 \\ \delta x & \delta y & 0 \end{bmatrix}$$

which also illustrates that the `T=` part is 'balanced' or centred vertically with respect to the matrix.

Really, what more can be said about matrices? You might need to put dots into the matrix, to obtain something like:

$$B = \begin{vmatrix} a_{11} & a_{12} & \ldots & a_{1n} \\ a_{21} & a_{22} & \ldots & a_{2n} \\ \vdots & \vdots & \ddots & \vdots \\ a_{n1} & a_{n2} & \ldots & a_{nn} \end{vmatrix}$$

This presents few problems, once the new control sequences `\ddots` for *diagonal dots* and `\vdots` for *vertical dots* are introduced:

```
$$B=\left\vert \matrix{
 a_{11} & a_{12} & \ldots & a_{1n} \cr
 a_{21} & a_{22} & \ldots & a_{2n} \cr
 \vdots & \vdots & \ddots & \vdots \cr
 a_{n1} & a_{n2} & \ldots & a_{nn} \cr}
\right\vert
$$
```

⇒*Exercise 11.1:*   Turn this small example into TEX form:

$$A = -C \begin{vmatrix} z_0 - f & y_0 \\ c & b \end{vmatrix} \bigg/ \begin{vmatrix} x_0 & y_0 \\ a & b \end{vmatrix} \tag{20}$$

⇐

If you always use matrices with the same sort of delimiter, and that delimiter is a parenthesis, things can be yet simpler. The command `\pmatrix` allows you to omit the `\left(` and `\right)` which may otherwise be required. But it is straightforward to devise other control sequences which automatically use square brackets, braces, or whatever delimiter is required.

The definition of `\pmatrix` is simply

```
\def\pmatrix#1{\left( \matrix{#1} right)}
```

so that it is trivially easy to incorporate your own definitions.

One of the features of the way TEX handles matrices is that it 'centres' the components around some imaginary horizontal axis. Therefore

$$\begin{pmatrix} a & b & c \\ d & e & f \end{pmatrix} \times \begin{pmatrix} i & j \\ k & l \\ m & n \end{pmatrix}$$

is obtained from:
```
$$\pmatrix{
  a & b & c \cr
  d & e & f \cr}
    \times
  \pmatrix{
  i & j \cr
  k & l \cr
  m & n \cr}
$$
```
It is possible to modify this 'centering' action, but it is not a convenient thing to do. If we were to look into the definition of \matrix, we would note a command \vcenter. This command is similar to \vbox and \vtop, but may only be used in maths mode. It is the command which is used for the vertical centering. This vertical centering will also apply to an equation number included in the expression, whether through \eqno or \leqno.

It is perhaps worth pointing out that when I lay out matrices, I tend to be rather longwinded. The last example could have been written:
```
$$\pmatrix{a&b&c\cr d&e&f\cr}
  \times
  \pmatrix{i&j\cr k&l\cr m&n\cr}$$
```
which is a little terse, and rather difficult to comprehend. It is easy to omit the odd & or \cr inadvertently, and a certain amount of confusion ensues. No real penalty is incurred by laying things out fairly clearly. The benefits are largely social. Very often expressions need to be edited, either to be corrected, or simply because they are reusable as a sort of 'template'. It is during editing that the benefits of clear laying out become evident.

Naturally, one-dimensional matrices (vectors) are just as simple. For example:

$$\left\lceil \matrix{a\cr b\cr c} \right\rfloor$$

is expressed as
```
$$\left\lceil \matrix{a\cr b\cr c\cr} \right\rfloor $$
```
A row vector can be written in the same way:
```
$${\cal C} = [\matrix{R&G&B\cr}]$$
```
but since a very plausible alternative could be obtained from
```
$${\cal C} = [R\quad G\quad B]$$
```

it is worth discussing why one might be preferred to the other. The form which uses \matrix emphasizes that what is being dealt with *is* some sort of matrix. The formal relationship of the other representation is not clear. There may be no advantage here from the point of view of someone reading the typeset version, where the subtleties embedded in the markup are not available, but if we are prepared to adopt the idea that there exist 'views' of documents, where the typeset version represents but one aspect among several, then the encoded version has some value, and may possibly be required as reference to clarify the author's intention. In finding examples to be incorporated in this book I have often been unsure of the original author's intention (as modified by the typesetter), and would have been grateful for the clarification that access to TEX commands could have granted me. On the other hand, some authors, on the basis of 'minimizing keystrokes', would prefer the second form of the expression (perhaps to the extent somewhere of abbreviating the \quad to a shorter form if it were to be used frequently). I do not favour terseness at the expense of comprehension. But many do. A last point is that the \matrix form will adopt the same spacing as other examples of \matrix, while placing \quad between each element is just a guess. To see how good a guess it is, here are the two expressions, typeset:

$$\mathcal{C} = [R \quad G \quad B]$$

$$\mathcal{C} = [R \quad G \quad B]$$

⇒*Exercise 11.2:*   Which of these expressions is the vector?   ⇐

It may not be obvious, but the entries within a matrix are centred in their columns. If we wish to manipulate this, we can insert horizontal fill, \hfill, in any entry to right or left justify it within a given column. Thus we can have

```
$$\left\lbrace \matrix{
   c_0\hfill    & \ldots & c_n     \hfill    \cr
   c_1\hfill    & \ldots & c_{n+1}\hfill    \cr
   \vdots\hfill & \ddots & \vdots\hfill    \cr
   c_n\hfill    & \ldots & c_{2n}\hfill    \cr}
\right\rbrace
$$
```

to give us

$$\left\{ \matrix{ c_0 & \ldots & c_n \cr c_1 & \ldots & c_{n+1} \cr \vdots & \ddots & \vdots \cr c_n & \ldots & c_{2n} } \right\}$$

Note that a simple \hfil is insufficient here. Its use would have no effect whatsoever. Without the \hfill, the matrix would have looked like

$$\left\{ \begin{array}{ccc} c_0 & \cdots & c_n \\ c_1 & \cdots & c_{n+1} \\ \vdots & \ddots & \vdots \\ c_n & \cdots & c_{2n} \end{array} \right\}$$

⇒*Exercise 11.3:* Which of these two solutions is more 'attractive'? With the \hfill, the \vdots in the first and last columns seem too far to the left. Suggest a 'better' way of setting this matrix. Add an equation number to the expression. ⇐

⇒*Exercise 11.4:* If it seems a little far-fetched that it might be an advantage to manipulate the way the elements of a matrix are handled, consider the following:

$$\mathbf{f} = \begin{bmatrix} f_e(0) \\ f_e(1) \\ \vdots \\ f_e(M-1) \end{bmatrix}$$

where arranging that the $M - 1$ term does not dominate the expression, but just concludes 'naturally', requires a certain amount of forethought. Can you reproduce the form here? Compare it with a simple, or naive approach. Is it worth the effort? ⇐

There is another alternative when dealing with a *bordered matrix* of the form

$$S' = \begin{matrix} & \begin{matrix} 4 & 5 & 6 & 7 & 8 \end{matrix} \\ \begin{matrix} 4 \\ 5 \\ 6 \\ 7 \\ 8 \end{matrix} & \begin{pmatrix} 1 & 1 & 0 & 0 & 0 \\ 1 & 1 & 1 & 0 & 0 \\ 0 & 1 & 1 & 1 & 0 \\ 0 & 0 & 1 & 1 & 0 \\ 0 & 0 & 0 & 0 & 1 \end{pmatrix} \end{matrix}$$

This is obtained from

```
$$S' = \bordermatrix{
     & 4 & 5 & 6 & 7 & 8 \cr
   4 & 1 & 1 & 0 & 0 & 0 \cr
   5 & 1 & 1 & 1 & 0 & 0 \cr
   6 & 0 & 1 & 1 & 1 & 0 \cr
   7 & 0 & 0 & 1 & 1 & 0 \cr
   8 & 0 & 0 & 0 & 0 & 1 \cr}
$$
```

The contents of the matrix are not too important. The critical parts are the 'surrounding bits':

$$
S' = \begin{array}{c}
 \\
4 \\ 5 \\ 6 \\ 7 \\ 8
\end{array}
\begin{array}{ccccc}
4 & 5 & 6 & 7 & 8 \\
\left(\begin{array}{ccccc}
 & & & & \\
 & & & & \\
 & & & & \\
 & & & & \\
 & & & &
\end{array}\right)
\end{array}
$$

The top border is given by the sequence `& 4 & 5 & 6 & 7 & 8 \cr`. We start with the `&`. This merely has the effect of using a blank as the first entry in the row; or, looking at it another way, omitting the very first entry. Similarly, we could omit any entry from any matrix, simply by putting nothing between the `&` markers. And should we wish to write something like

$$
\left\langle \begin{array}{ccc}
a & & \\
 & b & \\
 & & c
\end{array} \right\rangle
$$

we do it with an expression like
```
$$\left\langle
    \matrix{a \cr & b\cr & & c\cr} \right\rangle$$
```
The `\cr` terminates the row, and therefore all of the entries in a given line need not be complete.

A matrix may of course appear within a matrix:

$$
[C] = \begin{bmatrix}
1 & & & & & & & & \\
-2 & 1 & & & & & & & \\
1 & -2 & 1 & & & & & & \\
 & 1 & -2 & & & & & & \\
 & & 1 & & & & & & \\
 & & & \ddots & & & & & \\
 & & & & 1 & & & \\
 & & & & -2 & 1 & & \\
 & & & & 1 & -2 & 1 \\
 & & & & & 1 & -2 \\
 & & & & & & 1
\end{bmatrix}
$$

was obtained from

```
$$\def\one{\matrix{%
  \hfill 1\cr
  \hfill-2&\hfill 1 \cr
  \hfill 1&\hfill-2&\hfill 1\cr
        &\hfill 1&\hfill-2\cr
        &        &\hfill 1\cr}}
[C]=\left[\matrix{\one&&\cr
                  &\ddots\cr
                  &&\one\cr}\right]
$$
```

This opens up all sorts of possibilities.

⇒*Exercise 11.5:*   It is difficult to see how there may be any real problems with matrices. To demonstrate your prowess, you might like to set something like this:

$$[\mathbf{R}\quad \mathbf{G}\quad \mathbf{B}]\begin{bmatrix} 2/\sqrt{6} & -1/\sqrt{6} & -1/\sqrt{6} \\ 0 & 1/\sqrt{2} & -1/\sqrt{2} \\ 1/\sqrt{3} & 1/\sqrt{3} & 1/\sqrt{3} \end{bmatrix} = [\,M_1 \quad M_2 \quad M_3\,]$$

Really the major question is how to make sure the columns are centred (in the case of the first one) and right justified, (in the case of the others). The rest is simple manipulation. Do be careful with the square brackets round the vectors though. Note that they do not seem centred with respect to the capital letters.   ⇐

Aligning the column vectors so that they are either centred, left justified, or right justified is not always sufficient control. Consider the following example:

$$\begin{bmatrix} s_x\cos\theta & s_x\sin\theta & 0 \\ -s_y\sin\theta & s_y\cos\theta & 0 \\ -x_0 s_x\cos\theta + y_1 s_y\sin\theta + x_1 & -x_0 s_x\sin\theta - y_1 s_y\cos\theta + y_1 & 1 \end{bmatrix}$$

While it is fine to centre the columns, we really do want the first two entries in the first column to appear right justified with respect to one another. How did we achieve this? TEX allows us to \phantom a character, or string of characters. All the spacing associated with these *phantom* characters is computed and employed, but the characters themselves never appear. In the case above, a phantom minus was included before the first entry:

`\phantom{-}s_x\cos\theta & s_x\sin\theta & 0 \cr`

We might have argued for a similar inclusion of phantoms for the first two entries in the second column too, so that their relationship with the bottom entry was the same in both columns.

⇒*Exercise 11.6:*   Another example:

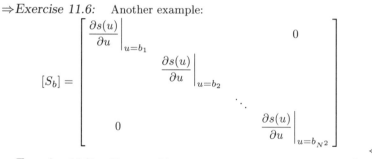

$$[S_b] = \begin{bmatrix} \left.\dfrac{\partial s(u)}{\partial u}\right|_{u=b_1} & & & & 0 \\ & \left.\dfrac{\partial s(u)}{\partial u}\right|_{u=b_2} & & & \\ & & \ddots & & \\ 0 & & & & \left.\dfrac{\partial s(u)}{\partial u}\right|_{u=b_{N2}} \end{bmatrix}$$

⇐

⇒*Exercise 11.7:*   How would you get text into a matrix entry? For example

$$\left\|\begin{matrix} \text{small} & \text{smaller} & \text{smallest} \\ \text{sum} & \text{summer} & \text{summit} \end{matrix}\right\|$$

⇐

Having introduced the issue of text in alignments, there is a special control sequence `\cases` which incorporates text in a fairly simple way. To obtain an expression like

$$G(\omega) = \begin{cases} T, & |\omega| < 2\pi f_c \\ 0, & \text{otherwise} \end{cases}$$

we simply type
```
$$G(\omega)=\cases{
   T,&$\vert\omega\vert<2\pi f_c$\cr
   0,&otherwise\cr}$$
```
The part between the & and the `\cr` is assumed to be handled as text, so that it is necessary to take special action to turn any entry there back into mathematical style. Should this need to have an equation number assigned to it, just add an `\eqno` before the terminating `$$`.

⇒*Exercise 11.8:*   How would we therefore obtain the following?

$$h_l(y) = \int_{-1/2n}^{1/2n} n^2 dx = \begin{cases} n & \text{for } |y| \le 1/2n \\ 0 & \text{otherwise} \end{cases}$$

214

⇐

The interesting features of `\cases` are the inclusion of the { symbol automatically and the fact that the second 'argument' in the list is automatically placed into text. By experimenting to find out whether this was done by `\hbox` or `\rm` in the command which powers this construct, you could create your own version.

⇒*Exercise 11.9:*   Suggest how this is created:

$$|x| = \begin{cases} x, & \text{if } x \ge 0; \\ -x, & \text{otherwise.} \end{cases}$$

⇐

$\Rightarrow$*Exercise 11.10:* Similarly, how is

$$z' = \begin{cases} \dfrac{z_K - z_1}{b - a}(z - a) + z_1 & \text{for } a \leq z \leq b \\ z_1 & \text{for } z < a \\ z_K & \text{for } z > b \end{cases}$$

to be obtained? $\Leftarrow$

Spaced out

From time to time it appears that TeX does not get its vertical spacing quite right in constructs like \matrix and \cases. There are a number of strategies that can be employed to 'improve' spacing. In aligned entries like \matrix and \cases, it is possible to open out entries just a little, by putting some extra white space between the lines: one way to do this is by the use of \noalign. A \noalign may occur after any \cr and will open up the rows by an amount which may be specified, for example:

\noalign{\vskip2pt}

The \vskip should be for a legitimate amount – for example, 2pt (in this case, the maths unit mu is not a legal amount, although we *seem* to be in maths). Applying this to one of the previous examples,

$$z' = \begin{cases} \dfrac{z_K - z_1}{b - a}(z - a) + z_1 & \text{for } a \leq z \leq b \\ z_1 & \text{for } z < a \\ z_K & \text{for } z > b \end{cases}$$

is obtained by including a \noalign{\vskip3pt}:

```
$$z'=\cases{\displaystyle
  {z_K-z_1\over b-a}(z-a)+z_1&for $a\le z\le b$\cr
  z_1&for $z<a$\cr
  \noalign{\vskip3pt}
  z_K&for $z>b$\cr}
$$
```

This spaces out the second and third lines of the \cases construct. The value was found just by guesswork. By no great coincidence, TeX has a useful 'general' value which is also appropriate. This is the \jot. TeX quantifies this 'small amount' as 3 points. We could therefore have written

\noalign{\vskip1\jot}

In the case where a \vskip is used, we need to know approximately how much extra space we require. Again this is something which is best done after you have seen the first draft, or after you have looked at the equation on the screen (or even on the page). This perhaps helps to emphasize the convenience of completing equations in small batches, so that they are correct before you assemble them into the complete work. There are few things more frustrating than 'errors' on the last page of your manuscript, which often means running the whole thing through TₑX again. On the other hand, errors on page 1 can be worse. After they are corrected the whole structure of the document may change. Best not to make mistakes.... This is hardly a paean to 'structured' documentation: if you have to look at the equation before you can decide whether it is typeset correctly, you might almost as well use a direct manipulation system. Fortunately TₑX provides enough examples where everything works just fine.

Another strategy is through the use of phantoms. We have already met the 'ordinary' \phantom, which has all the characteristics of the contained material, but just does not appear on the page. Its height, width, and depth are just the same as the original construct. It should also have the same properties, so that, for example, binary operators work correctly. There are two other varieties of phantoms, the \vphantom and the \hphantom. The \vphantom is *vertical* phantom, which implants the height and depth of some construct, without its width. In other words, an invisible, vanishingly thin character (or group of characters). The \hphantom is a *horizontal* phantom with zero height and depth but its 'true' width. These are sufficiently general that they are not restricted to maths. You can use them in ordinary text too (should you need them).

To try to illustrate the use of the \vphantom take the following example:

$$P = \begin{bmatrix} 1 & 0 \\ \dfrac{1}{d} & 1 \end{bmatrix}$$

If we just adopt the straightforward approach of
```
$$P=\left[\matrix{
  1&0\cr
  \displaystyle{1\over d}&1\cr}\right]
$$
```
the two rows will appear rather too close together. The solution adopted here was to say

```
$$\def\pover{\vphantom{\displaystyle{1\over d}}}
  P=\left[\matrix{
  \pover1&0\cr
  \displaystyle{1\over d}&1\cr}\right]
$$
```

The definition of a local command here is not essential: it merely makes the contents of the matrix look a little tidier. It might have seemed simpler to write

```
\everycr{\vphantom{\displaystyle{1\over d}}}
```

instead. This elegant solution does not work. Why not? If we were to unravel the definition of `\matrix`, we would eventually find that `\everycr` is used, and therefore replaces the one we thought that we were using.

There is a useful command, `\mathstrut`, which is defined in terms of a `\vphantom` left parenthesis. In general terms, a parenthesis (left or right) is the highest and deepest 'normal' character in TeX. So this sometimes is useful as a way of ensuring that lines are a guaranteed distance apart.

An additional command which is sometimes used in this context is `\smash`. This may be used with a formula, but unlike a phantom command, the formula appears, and TeX treats its height and depth as zero.

These 'adjustments' may be required from time to time. Knuth notes (*The TeXbook*, page 327) in a similar context that 'such refinements usually can't be anticipated until you see the first proofs'.

$\Rightarrow$*Exercise 11.11:* As an example, typeset the following:

$$\begin{pmatrix} Q_{02} \\ \eta_{02} \end{pmatrix} = \begin{pmatrix} -1 & -\dfrac{1}{Z_3^*} \\ 0 & 1 \end{pmatrix} \begin{pmatrix} Q_{01} \\ \eta_{01} \end{pmatrix}$$

$\Leftarrow$

Back to equations

There is still one class of equations we need to handle: those which are too long to go over a single line, or which for structural reasons, we wish to present in parts. For example,

$$a_{\text{tot}} = a_1 + a_2 + a_3 + \cdots + a_n$$

$$= \sum_{i=1}^{n} a_n$$

is best written over two lines, although we could squeeze it into one. These 'aligned' equations have many uses, and in fact they merely require us to employ the skills which have already been acquired. First, though, we need to know that there is a new command `\eqalign`. Do note that it is spelled `\eqalign` and not `\equalign`. It means *equation alignment*, not *equal alignment*, if that helps. This is perhaps a good case for

`\let\equalign=\eqalign`

just for practical spelling reasons. Most of the rest of it you should be able to work out for yourself. Both `&` and `\cr` are used again. The `&` is the pivot, which indicates the position at which 'elements' are aligned. The `\cr` merely signals the end of an entry, as you would anticipate. Here is a complete example:

```
$$\eqalign{
   m(n)&=2m(n-1)+2^{n-1}\cr
   a(n)&=2a(n-1)+2^{n}\cr}
$$
```

which gives us

$$m(n) = 2m(n-1) + 2^{n-1}$$
$$a(n) = 2a(n-1) + 2^{n}$$

The `&=` ensures that the equations are aligned about the equals sign. This is probably correct for many examples, but you need not use this convention if you do not wish.

⇒*Exercise 11.12:*   The following two examples can be handled with `\eqalign` and a little imagination:

$$H(j,k) = 0, \quad j = 1, 2, \ldots, 8$$
$$H(257 - j, 257 - k) = 0, \quad k = 17, 18, \ldots, 256$$

$$(221)$$

and

$$\mathbf{f}_1 = (f_{11}, f_{12}, \ldots, f_{1m}),$$
$$\mathbf{f}_2 = (f_{21}, f_{22}, \ldots, f_{2m}),$$
$$\vdots$$
$$\mathbf{f}_M = (f_{M1}, f_{M2}, \ldots, f_{Mm}).$$

$$(9.84)$$

⇐

A long equation might have to be broken so that it continues over more than one line:

$$\sigma^2(x,y) = \frac{1}{(2X+1)(2Y+1)} \sum_{m=-X}^{X} \sum_{m=-Y}^{Y} \Big\{ [\bar{g}(x+m, y+n)$$
$$- w(x+m, y+n)p(x+m, y+n)]$$
$$- \big[\bar{g}(x,y) - \overline{w(x,y)p(x,y)}\big] \Big\}^2$$

There is a lot here, but most of it is padding: the nub is the
```
$$\eqalign{\sigma^2
   &={1\over(          \cr
   &\quad-w(
   &\qquad-\Bigl[     \cr}$$
```
which introduces little that is new. The main question is what to
put on the second and third lines, after the &. Basically we must
push the equations over to the right somehow. We do not want it
to start immediately under the equals sign. In the example above,
I chose to indent it by a \quad and a then a \qquad. For the
record, the complete form was
```
$$\eqalign{\sigma^2(x,y)
   &={1\over(2X+1)(2Y+1)}\sum_{m=-X}^X\sum_{m=-Y}^Y
        \Bigl\{\bigl[\bar g(x+m,y+n)\cr
   &\quad-w(x+m,y+n)p(x+m,y+n)\bigr]\cr
   &\qquad-\Bigl[\bar g(x,y)-
          \overline{w(x,y)p(x,y)}\Bigr]\Bigr\}^2\cr}$$
```
Looking carefully, note the way in which the various delimiters
are handled. Focusing only on the delimiters which are not just
the simple symbols, the delimiters are
```
$$\eqalign{
   &=      \Bigl\{\bigl[   \cr
   &       \bigr]
   &       \Bigl[    \Bigr]\Bigr\}    \cr}
$$
```
Why cannot we simply use \left and \right and let TEX do the
work? This is one situation where these commands will not work
correctly. Within an aligned line, the parentheses created with
\left and \right must balance. If we adopt the simple solution
and balance each \left parenthesis with a \right. we may still
not get the result we desire. Since these variable size delimiters
take their size from what is contained, they have no 'memory',
and there is therefore no guarantee that the subsequent line, where
the parenthesis terminates, will adopt the same size as its opening
partner. That is
```
$$\eqalign{
   &=      \left\{\left[   \right.\right.\cr
   &\left.     \right]
   &\left.\left[   \right]\right\}   \cr}
$$
```
may easily result in uneven delimiters.

$\Rightarrow$*Exercise 11.13:*   Try this example using \left and \right. $\Leftarrow$

There is another form which would have been useful in this last case. The basic structure is given in

```
$$\displaylines{\sigma^2(x,y)
  ={1\over(2X+1)(2Y+1)}
  \sum_{m=-X}^X\sum_{m=-Y}^Y
          \Bigl\{\bigl[\bar g(x+m,y+n)\hfill\cr
  \hfill-w(x+m,y+n)p(x+m,y+n)\bigr]\hfill\cr
  \hfill-\Bigl[\bar g(x,y)-\overline{w(x,y)p(x,y)}
                      \Bigr]\Bigr\}^2\cr}$$
```

which yields

$$
\sigma^2(x,y) = \frac{1}{(2X+1)(2Y+1)} \sum_{m=-X}^{X} \sum_{m=-Y}^{Y} \left\{ \left[\bar{g}(x+m,y+n) \right. \right.
$$
$$
-w(x+m,y+n)p(x+m,y+n) \Big]
$$
$$
- \left[\bar{g}(x,y) - \overline{w(x,y)p(x,y)} \right] \right\}^2
$$

This form is not quite correct, on three counts. The first two are related. This equation has its first line hard left, and its last hard right – up against their respective margins. This is perhaps a little excessive, and it would be better to start and end with some space. So let us start and finish with a \quad. The third point is a bit more subtle, and goes back to the discussion of operators. The second and third lines begin with a minus sign. Anything before is just space. They will not be treated as a binary operators, but just as unary operators (and therefore will not have enough space associated with them). To force them to be binary operators, we could merely include a null box {} (or \null. So the equation could read

```
$$\displaylines{\sigma^2(x,y)
  ={1\over(2X+1)(2Y+1)}
  \sum_{m=-X}^X\sum_{m=-Y}^Y
          \Bigl\{\bigl[\bar g(x+m,y+n)\hfill\cr
  \hfill\null-w(x+m,y+n)p(x+m,y+n)\bigr]\hfill\cr
  \hfill\null-\Bigl[\bar g(x,y)-\overline{w(x,y)p(x,y)}
                      \Bigr]\Bigr\}^2\cr}$$
```

to give

$$
\sigma^2(x,y) = \frac{1}{(2X+1)(2Y+1)} \sum_{m=-X}^{X} \sum_{m=-Y}^{Y} \left\{ \left[\bar{g}(x+m,y+n) \right. \right.
$$
$$
- w(x+m,y+n)p(x+m,y+n) \Big]
$$
$$
- \left[\bar{g}(x,y) - \overline{w(x,y)p(x,y)} \right] \right\}^2
$$

The differences are not great, but are nonetheless important, if we are concerned with 'quality' typesetting. Once you become attuned to these sorts of distinctions, many textbooks become distressingly sloppy in appearance.

$\Rightarrow$*Exercise 11.14:* That last example uses `\hfill`. What happens if we merely use `\hfil`? Also, examine what happens when we have a measure of only 4 inches. The way we handle such an equation is partly a function of the physical attributes of the output medium. $\Leftarrow$

$\Rightarrow$*Exercise 11.15:* This example raises some of the issues explored above (and one or two others):

$$-D\left\{u\frac{\partial}{\partial x}\left[\frac{\omega}{D}\right]+v\frac{\partial}{\partial y}\left[\frac{\omega}{D}\right]\right\}=\underbrace{\frac{\partial}{\partial y}\left[\frac{R_x}{\rho D}\right]-\frac{\partial}{\partial x}\left[\frac{R_y}{\rho D}\right]}$$

$$\underbrace{\phantom{-D\left\{u\frac{\partial}{\partial x}\left[\frac{\omega}{D}\right]\right\}}}_{\text{non-linear term}}\qquad\underbrace{\phantom{\frac{\partial}{\partial y}\left[\frac{R_x}{\rho D}\right]}}_{\text{frictional term}}$$

$$+-\underbrace{\frac{\partial}{\partial y}\left\{\frac{1}{\rho D}\left[\frac{\partial}{\partial x}S_{xx}+\frac{\partial}{\partial y}S_{xy}\right]\right\}+\frac{\partial}{\partial x}\left\{\frac{1}{\rho D}\left[\frac{\partial}{\partial x}S_{xy}+\frac{\partial}{\partial y}S_{yy}\right]\right\}}_{\text{forcing term}}$$

Reproduce it using two different approaches. $\Leftarrow$

$\Rightarrow$*Exercise 11.16:* The `\displaylines` may also be useful when the equation is on a single line, but the information of its range would give a line which is far too long:

$$\int_{-\infty}^{\infty}\int_{-\infty}^{\infty}m(\alpha-x,\beta-y)R_{gg}(x,y)dx\,dy=R_{fg}(\alpha,\beta),$$

$$-\infty<\alpha<\infty,\ -\infty<\beta<\infty\ (33)$$

An alternative to using `\displaylines` is to enclose the range of α and β and the equation number as an `\eqno`. Try this too, noting the differences in the setting. $\Leftarrow$

Back to the real stuff: there are only a couple of other things we should know about. We need to get equation numbers attached to our formulae. There is a refinement `\eqalignno` which takes care of this:

$$x=y+z \qquad\qquad 2a$$
$$x^2=y^2+z^2 \qquad\qquad (2b)$$

This is obtained from
`$$\eqalignno{x&=y+z & 2a\cr x^2&=y^2+z^2 & (2b)\cr}$$`
A further refinement is `\leqalignno`, which places the numbers at the left. Like `\leqno`, the TeX still has the equation number at end of the equation, but positions it on the left.

Equation numbers may be included with `\displaylines`, but only by a little manipulation, forcing the number to the right (or left) with \hfill. Consider the following example:

$$a = b \tag{1}$$

$$a + b + c = 0$$
$$a^2 + b^2 + c^2 = 1 \tag{2}$$

This makes at least two points: firstly, you do not have to number every line, and secondly, that left to its own devices, \display-lines centres the entry:

```
$$\displaylines{\hfill a=b \hfill (1)\cr
    a+b+c = 0 \cr
    \hfill a^2+b^2+c^2 = 1 \hfill (2) \cr}$$
```

Why did we not use \eqno here? If you do, you get one of the most amazing error messages obtainable from T_EX:

```
! You can't use '\eqno' in math mode.
```

This is obviously not really what T_EX means. You would hardly expect to use \eqno outside maths mode. Just don't use \eqno in this situation, but give the equation number as above. This seems a bit unsatisfactory, but revolves around the definition of (at least) \displaylines.

Another point which might be overlooked from that last example is that the second two lines are an example of serendipity. They appear to be aligned on the equals sign. This is mere chance, brought about by the equation number. There are at least two ways that this might be tackled. Using a phantom on the line which does not have an equation number seems satisfactory, at first glance:

$$a = b \tag{1}$$

$$a + b + c = 0$$
$$a^2 + b^2 + c^2 = 1 \tag{2}$$

where the second line is

```
    a+b+c = 0 \phantom{(1)}\cr
```

but if we think about this a bit more carefully, we realize that the equations are centred over the remaining space, rather than over the whole line. We may prefer to centre the equation 'absolutely', rather than in this relative way. One way to handle this is to use an \llap:

```
$$\displaylines{
   a=b\cr
   \hfill a=b \hfill \llap{(1)}\cr
   a+b+c = 0 \cr
   \hfill a^2+b^2+c^2 = 1 \hfill \llap{(2)} \cr}$$
```

This command effectively 'overlaps' the equation numbers. In essence, the material is set in a box of width zero. There is obviously a question here: where is the material actually typeset? With \llap, the material is set to the left, while with another command, \rlap, it would be set to the right.

Spaced out again

Earlier, we looked at ways of spacing out material vertically in the commands \matrix and \cases. In commands like \displaylines, \eqalign, and \eqalignno, the same approaches can apply: \noalign and the \mathstrut (or other phantoms) can provide extra space at any particular place. But with these particular commands, there is another choice. Should you ever require more space between lines, you can \openup by some specified amount. The \openup command applies to all the lines within a single alignment. The commands \displaylines, \eqalign, \eqalignno, and \leqalignno all have \openup1\jot in their preamble, to give an *extra* 'jot' of space between lines. As mentioned earlier, a \jot is defined to be 3 points. You could as easily have written \openup3pt, but somehow there is a rather nice feeling to giving it a 'jot'. Of course you could equally \openup-2pt for one of these commands to obtain an *overall* 1 point extra between each of the lines. In other words, when we use \openup, the effects are cumulative. Why does this not work with \matrix and \cases? If we look closely at the definitions of both of these commands, we will see that they contain a \normalbaselines command. Looking also at the way that \openup is defined, we can begin to make sense of this. With \openup, the 'normal' line spacing commands \baselineskip, \lineskip, and \lineskiplimit are all incremented (\advanced) by the amount specified in the \openup. Whenever \normalbaselines is invoked, we return to the 'default'default interline skip.

Having said this, it is quite possible to make a temporary redefinition of \normalbaselines so that it will not come into play in \matrix. Taking an earlier exercise, we could have written

```
$$\let\normalbaselines\relax
   \openup2\jot
   P=\left[\matrix{
   1&0\cr
   \displaystyle{1\over d}&1\cr}\right]
$$
```

This spaces out the matrix in a similar way. But there is an important consequence, since any other matrices would be similarly 'stretched'. On the other hand, it is easy to group or localize the action. The value of 2\jot was just an educated guess.

In general \openup might be preferred when applicable, but \noalign can have its uses, since it permits us to separate some equations with text and write something like:

```
$$\displaylines{\hfill a=b \hfill \llap{(1)}\cr
  \noalign{\hbox{but remember}}
  a+b+c = 0 \cr
  \hfill a^2+b^2+c^2 = 1 \hfill \llap{(2)}\cr}$$
```

which would give us

$$a = b \tag{1}$$

but remember

$$a + b + c = 0$$
$$a^2 + b^2 + c^2 = 1 \tag{2}$$

In truth, this facility is probably needed only very rarely. But sometimes it is necessary to 'force' part of a mathematical argument to be treated as a unit: that is, to prevent any page breaks. This might be a situation where it would be necessary to structure the equations so that they were in a single block of displayed mathematics. For the sake of an example, consider the following:

... Similarly,

$$K_1 \subset K_2 \oplus B(\rho_1 + \rho_2)$$

Thus $\rho_3 \leq \rho_1 + \rho_2$.

where it would be distressing to have to turn the page to read 'Thus $\rho_3 \leq \rho_1 + \rho_2$.'

⇒*Exercise 11.17:*   The following two examples help to synthesize many of the points made so far:

$$\frac{1}{2}[g(x - 1, y + 1) + g(x + 1, y + 1) + g(x - 1, y)$$
$$+ g(x + 1, y) + g(x - 1, y - 1) + g(x + 1, y - 1)]$$
$$- [g(x, y + 1) + g(x, y) + g(x, y - 1)]$$

at (x, y).

$$K(y) = (2\pi)^{1/2} e^{-y^2/2}, \tag{6.11a}$$
$$K(y) = [\pi(1 + y^2)]^{-1}, \tag{6.11b}$$

and

$$K(y) = \begin{cases} 1 - |y|, & |y| \leq 1, \\ 0, & |y| > 1. \end{cases} \qquad (6.11c)$$

$\Leftarrow$

Adjusting delimiters

If we look back at some of the examples where delimiters are used, we may notice that the vertical extent of the delimiters is not quite as great as that of the material they surround. For example, Exercises 11.5, and 11.11, and the 'phantom' example on page 180, do appear to have a slight shortfall. Part of the reason for this shortfall is that it is considered 'best not to cover the formula completely' (Knuth, p.152). In the examples considered here, lengthening the delimiters around the notional axis of the formula would lead to symmetric lengthening above and below the axis, and perhaps the criticism that we are surrounding some empty space. Still, if you really want to ensure that the formula is completely surrounded, and nothing protrudes above or below, there is a way to do it. There are two commands available: this in itself presents a slight problem, since their interaction is not immediately apparent. Assume that the maximum of the height or depth of the formula, M, is $2\max(\text{height}, \text{depth})$. The size of the delimiter chosen is then $M \times \backslash\text{delimiterfactor}/1000$, *or* $M - \backslash\text{delimitershortfall}$. The default value for $\backslash\text{delimiterfactor}$ is 901, and for $\backslash\text{delimiter-shortfall}$ is 5 pt. In general terms therefore, the delimiters are likely to be up to 10% or 5 pt shorter, whichever is the greater.

$\Rightarrow$*Exercise 11.18:*   Taking one of those three examples, and with some experimentation of the values controlling the delimiter size, can you adjust the size of the delimiters in a satisfactory way? Are there any knock-on effects? Check the way that this appears to be handled by publishers who set their maths in a different style (for example, Pergamon). Do they adopt the same sort of approach? $\Leftarrow$

Pages 12

Although a great deal of TeX has been presented already, only a very small amount has been directed towards the handling of fairly ordinary text. Even the most esoteric mathematics usually requires the 'glue' of words to hold it together. In this chapter, some of the tools and techniques available will be discussed. Text looks deceptively simple. It is probably considerably more difficult to format text than mathematics. The range of possibilities for text is so much greater. Examination of a couple of non-technical books will probably yield more variation in typesetting than comparable technical (especially mathematical) books.

Some basics

Some of the very basic ideas have already been introduced. The basic unit is the paragraph. In general, each paragraph is begun with an indent. In TeX, this indent is controlled by the `\parindent` dimension. A great many books use no indentation at the beginning of a chapter or section. In order to turn off the indent, the command `\noindent` may be used. Equally, to 'force' an indent of the value of `\parindent`, the command `\indent` may be used. In Chapter 10, a command was introduced which could be used to handle a title and to provide for the situation where no indentation was required on the first paragraph.

Paragraphs may be separated by a different amount of space than that which separates lines. Lines are separated by `\baselineskip`, while paragraphs may be separated by `\parskip`. Both of these may have glue amounts associated with them. Under normal conditions, TeX attempts to make each page of text exactly the same length. As has been pointed out in Chapter 9, unless there is some glue available, this may not always be possible, with the complaint that there may be an `overfull vbox`. There are several routeways out of this dilemma. We may permit some glue to be associated with the `\parskip`: this is not guaranteed to work, since there may be very few paragraphs on the individual pages, and therefore only a few places in which the extra space needed may be distributed. The option of allowing glue to be associated with the `\baselineskip` is rather unsatisfactory for documents which are supposed to be set to a high standard, since the change in 'density' is remarkably easy to discern. There is a `\vfuzz` command, just like `\hfuzz`, which could give some flexibility in the page 'depth'. A further option is to allow TeX some flexibility in the page size by using `\raggedbottom`, a sort of philanthropic approach. This is broadly analogous to `\raggedright`. In both these last cases, the restriction to make each page exactly the same depth has been compromised. In the case of `\vfuzz`, the text on the page may be slightly greater, while in the case of `\raggedbottom`, it may be slightly less. In both cases, the first line of text on the page is in exactly the same place. The bottom line on the page is the one that exhibits the variability.

There is one other important place where some flexibility may be permitted, and where it will be hardly noticeable. When we have displayed equations, the distance between the text and the following display is controlled by one of two commands: `\abovedisplayskip` and `\abovedisplayshortskip`. Basically, the 'short' skip is used when the preceding line is itself 'short', and the equation is 'short': in other words, when the distribution of 'horizontal' white space would make the vertical white space between the text and the equation appear too great. The mechanics of this is not too crucial here; the important fact is that there is a skip, with its associated glue, which may give some added flexibility. Since there is a skip between the text and the display material, there is naturally a corresponding skip between the display and the succeeding text. This skip is termed `\belowdisplayskip`. There is also a `\belowdisplayshortskip`, although it is far more difficult in practice to see the sorts of circumstances where it is likely to be used.

There are other `skips` which are explicit alternatives to the inter-paragraph gaps driven by `\parskip`. They are 'equivalent' to the following:

`\smallskip`	$\equiv$	`\vskip 3pt plus 1pt minus 1pt`
`\medskip`	$\equiv$	`\vskip 6pt plus 2pt minus 2pt`
`\bigskip`	$\equiv$	`\vskip 12pt plus 4pt minus 4pt`

This may rekindle the question 'why the plus and minus parts?' These simply give TeX a little extra scope when it is building its pages, in areas where the glue (remember glue?) need not be rigid.

The definition of these skips is not the simple and direct one that you might expect:

`\def\smallskip{\vskip 3pt plus 1pt minus 1pt}`

Instead, the small skip is set indirectly through reference to another skip quantity, `\smallskipamount`:

`\newskip\smallskipamount`
`\smallskipamount 3pt plus 1pt minus 1pt`
`\def\smallskip{\vskip\smallskipamount}`

and similarly for the medium and big skips. Why did Knuth bother to do this? He suggests in *The TEXbook* that this will permit greater flexibility when using fonts other than the 'default' 10 pt sizes.

Text indentation

Since we are still discussing text here, it is worth noting one further common requirement: hanging indentation. (Sometimes indentation is written indention, mainly on the argument that indentation is something that happens to your car, while indention happens to text: dictionaries are reluctant to support this distinction.) TEX supports hanging indentation in a number of ways. The very simplest way is to `\hang`. This leads to the entire paragraph being indented by the amount of `\parindent`. The very first line will have the same amount of indentation as the remainder of the paragraph, so that by default the left margin of the entire hanging paragraph will line up: the `\parindent` does not accumulate in this case. If you really do want the paragraph to start with an indentation, then it must be explicit. This introduces a rather unexpected effect: `\hang\indent` does not lead to the first line being indented. In fact, if we simplify further and look at the effect of `\indent` at the beginning of any paragraph, it will be found to have no apparent effect at all. Normally this passes unnoticed. In the case of a paragraph which starts with a `\hang`, it would be necessary to repeat the `\indent` to achieve the indentation we expect.

⇒*Exercise 12.1:*   What effect would `\hang\noindent` have?   ⇐

Note that these commands work on the following paragraph. To be a little more accurate, they work on the paragraph of which they are part. It would be possible to terminate a paragraph with `\hang`, and the command would still apply to the paragraph. From the point of view of understanding what is going on, such an approach is not helpful. Of course, the next paragraph follows the 'normal' setting for `\parindent`.

The amount of hanging indentation is controlled by a command \hangindent. This defaults to 0 pt, but could be reset:

\hangindent=20pt

would have the effect of indenting the left margin by 20 pt until the end of the current paragraph. To indent the right margin,

\hangindent=-20pt

Any existing \parindent will be included: that is to say,

\parindent=10pt   \hangindent=20pt

will lead to the first line being indented by 30 points, and the rest of the paragraph by 20 points. Similarly, the \parindent still works when the hanging indentation is negative, and the right margin is indented. If you did not wish the normal first-line indentation, you should switch it off with \noindent. There is yet more subtlety to \hangindent. Hanging indentation is switched on for, or after, a given number of lines have been output, using the \hangafter command. Thus

\hangindent=20pt\hangafter=3

means this hanging indentation of 20 points only applies after the first three lines of the paragraph have been output – from line 4 onwards. If \hangafter-3 had been used, the hanging indentation would be used on the first three lines. Even within a hanging indent, normal paragraph indentation as controlled by \parindent will apply.

⇒*Exercise 12.2:*   These ideas begin to take on some meaning once they are used. Take some of the text that was used earlier and experiment with these new commands. If you wanted to repeat the same sort of structure on each paragraph in turn, it would be possible to use \everypar.   ⇐

⇒*Exercise 12.3:*   These 'hanging' commands may be useful for bibliographies or glossaries, where the first line of each 'paragraph' is to be the full line width, with no indentation, but the rest of the block is to be indented, so that each entry stands out clearly. For example:

Zahir: beings or things possessing the property of being unforgettable;
          in Arabic, 'notorious' or 'visible'. See Borges, *The Zahir.*

Demonstrate how this might be done.   ⇐

Note too that \hangafter may also take a negative argument:

\hangindent=2em\hangafter=-4

would have the effect of indenting only the first four lines by 2 ems; the remainder of the paragraph would have no indentation.

⇒*Exercise 12.4:*   A practical application of this last feature might be found in a 'dropped capital', where the first character in a paragraph is presented in a larger size. If, for example, the chosen font for the dropped capital took up the same depth as two normal lines, we could

`\hangafter-2`, provided we had some way of extracting the first character and placing it at the beginning of the line, where the gap had been left for it. This is not too difficult, although it requires some thought, and a bit of experimentation. Like most things in TEX, it's all done with boxes. Sketch a likely solution.   ⇐

Only the last `\hangindent` encountered is used: therefore
`\hangindent=2em\hangindent=-2em`
as a technique for indenting left and right margins at the same time will not work. How then do we indent both margins simultaneously? Provided we wish to indent both margins by the amount of the current paragraph indentation, this is simple:
`{\narrower ..... text ...`
`\smallskip}`
There are a few things to watch out for here. Firstly, if you do not wish to use the currently operating indentation set up by `\parindent`, you can use the bracing or grouping to set up a new temporary indentation:
`{\parindent=40pt\narrower ..... text ...`
`\smallskip}`
Secondly, the paragraph *must* end before ending the group; the inserted `\smallskip` is one of several ways other than `\par` or leaving a blank line to end a paragraph. Alternatively, `\medskip`, `\bigskip`, or an explicit `\vskip` amount would be suitable.

Thirdly, you must finish the last paragraph before using `\narrower`. What this means is that you cannot
lots and lots of text.
`{\narrower .... lots more text ....`
`\smallskip}`
and expect that the *lots more text* will be in a paragraph all on its own. The text 'before' will be included as part of the same narrowed paragraph, and the whole new (longer) paragraph will be narrowed/indented. One way of viewing this is that the definition of `\narrower` does not begin with a `\par` or other indication that a new paragraph is beginning.

In this discussion `\narrower` is used within a group. This is not obligatory, *but* if `\narrower` is not grouped, it will be difficult to switch the indentations off, and return to 'normal'. Moreover, the effects of `\narrower` are cumulative: a section of narrowed text could contain paragraphs which were themselves `\narrower`. A `\hangindent` may occur within a section of narrowed text. The apparent complexity of `\narrower` comes as a result of Knuth ensuring that the various methods of indentation may be mixed.

How does \narrower work? Its definition looks very simple:
```
\def\narrower{\advance\leftskip by\parindent
    \advance\rightskip by\parindent}
```
It is probably possible to guess what \leftskip and \rightskip
are. They are clearly glue amounts, since they are skips: they are
the amounts of glue placed at the left and right ends of lines in
a paragraph. Normally they default to 0 pt, but when \narrower
is used, they place an amount of glue equivalent to the current
\parindent value at the ends of every line, making them that
much narrower.

Having seen the definition, it is fairly easy to see how to modify
it so that different effects may be obtained. One of my minor criti-
cisms of plain T_EX is the extent to which the value of \parindent
is involved in the definition of so many other features; features
which themselves seem to have little to do with paragraph indentation.

Equally, having seen the definition, it becomes obvious why it
has the side effects noted above, and also to infer that we could
keep nesting \narrower sufficiently that the line length for a
paragraph could become zero or less.

⇒*Exercise 12.5:*   Since \narrower has some distressing side effects,
devise a command pair, \beginnarrow, \endnarrow, which would be a
little more 'user friendly'.   ⇐

Item by item

There is another feature in T_EX which uses indentation. Often
when lists are prepared, it is useful to have them itemized. T_EX
provides a \item command which allows the 'key' to the item
to be printed and then all the information which goes with it
to form an indented paragraph. The itemized information is in
the form of an *indented paragraph*, and the whole paragraph has
an indentation equivalent to that of \parindent. If you have set
\parindent=0pt then \item will give unsatisfactory results. The
use of \item is perhaps easier to demonstrate than to explain.
Several of the itemized lists used so far have used \item. The
following example gives some flesh to the basic ideas:
```
\item{1}What can go wrong will go wrong.
\item{2}What has gone wrong will get worse.
\item{3}For every complex problem there is a simple,
easy to understand solution which does not work.
```

This yields:

1 What can go wrong will go wrong.

2 What has gone wrong will get worse.

3 For every complex problem there is a simple, easy to understand solution which does not work.

Note that the continuation of the paragraph is indented, as would have been anticipated from a glance at the definition of \item, which is considered in a moment. When a new paragraph begins after the last item, it will be indented. This can often appear a little confusing, since the item and the paragraph share the same amount of indentation. This is the main reason for the usual recommendation that some extra vertical space is added, like a \smallskip or \medskip. One conclusion is that a list is not considered by TeX to be part of a paragraph, but constitutes a paragraph in its own right.

Additionally, there is an \itemitem feature which allows sub-lists, or just twice as much indentation. For example

```
\item{$\bullet$}Publishing
\itemitem{$\triangleright$}publishers and
   the \TeX-using author
\itemitem{$\triangleright$}the production cycle
\item{$\bullet$}Document preparation
\itemitem{$\triangleright$}document structure
\itemitem{$\triangleright$}portability and
   interchange
```

In this particular example, rather than use a numbered list, symbols have been used. The 'best' symbols are those available from mathematics, which makes their use rather longwinded. This is a case where it might be more appropriate, and easier, to define

```
\def\bitem{\item{$\bullet$}} %bulleted item
\def\subitem{\itemitem{$\triangleright$}}
                    %sub-item, different symbol
```

and use these instead as \bitem and \subitem:

```
\bitem    Publishing
\subitem publishers and the \TeX-using author
\subitem the production cycle
\bitem    Document preparation
\subitem document structure
\subitem portability and interchange
```

Individual \items do not require to have blank lines or \par between them, since their definition starts with \par. Accepting plain TeX's defaults gives the same separation between items as between paragraphs. It is quite reasonable to expect these to be different values. In order to do so it would be necessary to group so that the value of `\parskip` was local to the itemized list.

Since `plain` TₑX only supports `\item` and `\itemitem`, what happens when we have a third level of itemization? Here we would have to invent our own. To do this, first examine how `\item` works.

```
\def\item{\par\hang\textindent}
\def\textindent#1{\indent\llap{#1\enspace}%
                         \ignorespaces}
```

This is quite interesting, since although `\item` itself does not have a parameter as part of its definition, it nevertheless does take an argument. An exactly equivalent definition could have been:

```
\def\item#1{\par\hang\indent\llap{#1\enspace}%
                         \ignorespaces}
```

but, as we will see next, `\textindent` is used elsewhere, and there is some value in defining it separately, rather than echoing the same set of commands.

Each `\item` starts a new hanging paragraph. Why is the `\indent` included? The first line of hanging paragraph will be indented by the same amount as the rest. Why do we need to specify it explicitly? And why is it not therefore indented even more? In fact, the `\indent` is here because of the nature of `\llap`. This command 'hides' an `\hbox`. Without the `\indent`, or to make it more obvious, a `\leavevmode`, we could get the sort of weird behaviour that follows from starting a paragraph with an `\hbox`, and which was discussed in Chapter 9. So all the `\indent` is doing is ensuring that we are in horizontal mode. An `\llap` is a way of 'back spacing'. The contents of the argument are placed to the left of the start of the paragraph. An `\enspace` is also included, so that there is a bit of white space between the argument and the beginning of the paragraph. This obviously carries the implication that if we wrote

```
\item{Antidisestablishmentarianism:} a long word.
```

it could project well beyond the left page limit. TₑX will not warn us of such a situation. And naturally, had we specified `\parindent` to be a small value (or even zero points), `\item` would not work very well at all. This is perhaps another case for distinguishing between the `\parindent` and the amount by which an itemized list should be indented.

The second-level item, `\itemitem`, is an elaboration:

```
\def\itemitem{\par\indent \hangindent2\parindent
                              \textindent}
```

In order to understand what is going on here, it is useful to realize that the definition of \hang is:

\def\hang{\hangindent\parindent}

so that when we used \hang in the definition of \item, we were setting up a hanging indent of a given amount, \parindent. At the second level, we double that value.

⇒*Exercise 12.6:*   The \item structure in plain TEX always seems a bit limited to me. It should be possible to define a \beginitem \enditem structure which allows you to have 'nested' items. While you are at it you may as well let it number the items consecutively at each level.   ⇐

⇒*Exercise 12.7:*   Since it can be rather tedious to number lists, and since TEX is well able to add, and to keep track of counters, it is also possible to create \nitem which automatically numbers the items. The TEX command \romannumeral will convert a number into its Roman form – for example, \romannumeral10 or \romannumeral\num where \num was a \count register. It would therefore also be possible to make \nitemitem increment as Roman numerals. There is one remaining problem. There has to be some way of turning the list on and off, otherwise every time \nitem is used the number will increment. Suggestions?   ⇐

One of the drawbacks of \item is that it is really only suited to 'short' items, which do not run over more than one paragraph. As soon as a second or subsequent paragraph begins, the 'hanging' nature of the item is lost. Perhaps this is suggesting that items should not be long, but it is possible to find counter-examples where it would be useful to have such features.

⇒*Exercise 12.8:*   Despite the implied prohibition to \items which contain more than one paragraph, devise a scheme where this would be possible.   ⇐

Floating

Many technical books require a mechanism where material can be placed at some 'convenient' point: for example, a diagram may be placed at the top of a page, or between paragraphs. Obviously, a diagram (or perhaps a table) does not obey the normal rules of text. We cannot simply break it into two at the page boundary and put part at the bottom of one page and the remainder at the top of the next. Some way must be found to accommodate these blocks of 'rigid' material, without distorting the text too much. One way would be to leave white space to fill up the page, and then start the diagram on the next page. This is rather ugly, and when a large amount of white space is encountered towards the bottom of page, it usually signals the end of that chapter.

TEX supports three mechanisms where arbitrary material may

be 'floated' to some convenient place. These are \pageinsert, \topinsert, and \midinsert. These are quite similar, in that they provide floating insertions. As you will guess, a page insert is where a whole page is given over to an insert. It will be the next one after the \pageinsert command is encountered. A top insert is inserted at the top of the page where the \topinsert is encountered (or at the top of the next one if that is not possible), and a \midinsert is placed immediately where it is encountered, or at the top of the next available page. They are unlikely to be inserted *exactly* where the command occurs, although this might happen from time to time. I have found these constructs to be of great use either in including tables at a convenient point within the text, or for leaving room for diagrams. Their use is slightly different from anything we have yet seen:

```
\topinsert
    lots of text,
    or a table,
    or even something like \vskip250pt
\endinsert
```

⇒*Exercise 12.9:*   The \endinsert is very important. Can you see why? What happens if it is omitted?   ⇐

Having raised the question of including material like tables and diagrams in some sort of 'floating' way, it is also worth considering whether TeX can also handle such material through the use of hanging indentation. If, for example, we had a small diagram (or perhaps a photograph), which was 144 pt square, could we take a corner out of the paragraph by

```
\hangafter-13\hangindent-150pt
```

and manipulate the photograph into the correct position? Yes, this is possible, but it could be tricky if that page was to be broken in the middle of the paragraph. The hanging would be there, but spread over two pages. Basically this is a rather difficult problem to solve with TeX. It is difficult (I hesitate to say impossible, since someone, somewhere, will find a way) to have TeX divulge how many lines of a paragraph it has processed before it breaks the page. TeX simply does not work that way. It is possible to find out how many lines there are in a paragraph through a built-in counter \prevgraf, but that does not help if the paragraph is broken over a page.

The paragraph building and the page building are handled somewhat separately: not entirely separately, since there are controls available to prevent 'widow', and 'orphan' or 'club' lines. An orphan or club line is one which appears on its own at the foot of a page: a widow line is a single line appearing at the top of page. TEX seeks to control these undesirable elements by associating penalties with them. We shall examine the penalty structure later. At the moment it is sufficient to know that they exist and that TEX has some way of dealing with them. Similarly, it is usually considered undesirable to break a page on a hyphen: TEX can also associate penalties with such eventualities. In fact, when a hyphen occurs on a left hand page, it is usually tolerated. It is only when it ends a right hand page, where the page has to be turned before the full word is revealed, that there is a real problem. TEX has no convenient way to distinguish these two cases.

But to return to the page and paragraph building: TEX simply does not have a mechanism to report back that when the page break was chosen, the paragraph that was spread over the pages had so many lines on one page, and so many on the next. This is rather unfortunate, and does effectively inhibit some uses of TEX. But do note that extremely sophisticated users of TEX can find ways round this problem. These are elaborate, involved, and by no means `plain`.

There is no 'bottom insert': perhaps part of the reason for this omission lies in the presence of the next structure:

`\footnote{*}{A simple footnote}`

creates a footnote containing the text 'A simple footnote', and using the asterisk as the marker. TEX is actually very good at footnotes, and can keep track of many, placing them correctly, and breaking pages sensibly to include them. This book use footnotes only to illustrate the ease and facility with which footnotes may be used.* Note how the footnote is handled by default. There are many variations which might be preferred. The line might be longer, or even absent. The line associated with the footnote is defined as

```
\def\footnoterule{\kern-3pt\hrule width 2truein
                                    \kern2.6pt}
```

(This is a nice example of the use of the `\kern` in vertical mode.) The default thickness of an `\hrule` is 0.4 pt, which helps account for the difference in the negative and positive `\kern` amounts. So, if we wanted no rule, we simply write

---

* Except for a few gratuitous ones: I find footnotes self-indulgent and believe that they destroy the flow of text; but apparently they are essential to some disciplines.

```
\def\footnoterule{}
```
The footnote itself uses whatever font is current. This means that
if a footnote occurs within a block of italicized text, then the
footnote itself will also be italicized. It might therefore be wise to
begin each footnote with `\rm`, or whatever font was to be used:
```
footnotes may be used.\footnote*{\rm Except for...
```
If we decide to have each footnote in a smaller font, then we must
take account of a great many other factors (if we wish it to have
general application). For example, simply using
```
footnotes may be used.\footnote*{\eightrm Except for...
```
where `\eightrm` has been set up to reference 8 point Computer
Modern Roman, will not take account of the smaller `\baseli-`
`neskip` that should occur between lines, nor will it help if the
footnote itself contains a font change. An apparently simple change
like this starts to take on the appearance of major surgery. One of
the simpler ways to tackle it is to define a new command `\foot`
which uses `\footnote`. Let us assume that there is already a
command `\eightpoint`, which will handle the changes in fonts,
baseline skip, and paragraph skip (if needed). Then
```
\long\def\foot#1#2{{\eightpoint\footnote{#1}{#2}}}
```
will provide a solution. Once we have described what it is we
really want, an answer becomes more apparent.

　　If a footnote is long, and contains several paragraphs, the paragraphing is maintained. An 'intuitive' style of footnotes might be
to have the footnote symbol project to the left of the footnote text
(like `\item`), with the first paragraph having no indentation, but
any other paragraphs in the same footnote taking some suitable
indentation amount. The simple solutions of
```
\long\def\foot#1#2{\hang\footnote{#1}{\eightpoint#2}}
```
or
```
\long\def\foot#1#2{\footnote{#1}{\eightpoint\hang#2}}
```
just do not work.

⇒*Exercise 12.10:*　　Try these last two definitions to ascertain what it
is they do, assuming you did not work it out from first principles, or
intuitively.　　　　　　　　　　　　　　　　　　　　　　　　　⇐

　　A glance at the `\footnote` command in the *The* TEX*book* is
unlikely to throw much light on the problem, but a clue is presented by something which almost works:
```
\long\def\foot#1#2{\everypar{\hang}\footnote{#1}%
                        {\eightpoint#2}}
```
The second and later paragraphs are not indented, just as we
might have expected from the action we associate with `\hang`. A

fairly simple, though rather inelegant solution is:

```
\long\def\foot#1#2{{\everypar{\hang}\def\par
                {\hfil\break\indent}%   see page 212
                \footnote{#1}{\eightpoint#2}}}
```

An even more inelegant solution would be to begin each of the paragraphs in the footnote with appropriate indentation.

⇒*Exercise 12.11:* Try out these alternative footnote styles, and confirm the way in which the hanging indentation does work. A more elegant scheme would be welcome too.   ⇐

In the examples above, the font change was moved to affect only the second parameter, the text of the footnote. This does not mean that the symbol used to mark the footnote would be in the 'prevailing' font. Although it is not immediately apparent, the first parameter is reused, and any font changes affecting the second parameter will also affect the first when it is used in the footnote as a marker.

In general there are two sorts of marker used in footnotes – symbols and numbers. The asterisk is commonly used, and even the double asterisk. TEX does have a set of useful symbols which may be used and include † and ‡. Numbers are also often used, either incrementing throughout the chapter, or being reset to zero with each page. This latter case is very difficult for TEX to handle, although Mike Spivak implemented it with L$A_{M}S$-TEX. Again we return to the fact that TEX does not really provide the information on where exactly it breaks a page, and consequently the point at which any footnote counter should be modified.

⇒*Exercise 12.12:* Write a version of \footnote which automatically increments a counter and which uses that, rather than a symbol, at each footnote. The footnote will only require text, since TEX will be keeping track of the details.   ⇐

Footnotes normally do not contain footnotes (although for a counter-example, see Pratchett, 1989), which is just as well for TEX. However, tables sometimes do, and here TEX has a little difficulty. The difficulty is even more general. Any material which appears in an insert (or in a box) may not contain the \footnote command. If we simply use the normal \footnote approach, the marker symbol appears, but the footnote itself disappears. There is a rather inelegant way out of this, with the \vfootnote command. Essentially this breaks the footnote down into two components. The first component is the marker, which appears in the text, and which may be written like the first argument – for example, an example^2 – while the second component looks just like a conventional footnote, but must appear outside the insert or boxed material – in other words, among the text. This means we may have to guess that the insert and the footnote will appear on the same page. This is taking optimism a long way. We shall encounter a fairly practical example of this situation later when we examine tables.

Fine tuning the layout

By default TᴇX prints a page number at the bottom of each page, centred within the 'footer' line. The number will be an ordinary Arabic number, starting at 1. To switch off this facility, say
`\nopagenumbers`
before the start of your text. If you do not want page numbering to start at 1, you can change the page number by saying
`\pageno=3`
or some other suitable value. This is the starting value. Therefore, by default, TᴇX has a starting page number of 1. Sometimes you will need to use Roman numerals for page numbering – usually for the 'front matter' of a book or thesis. Specifying
`\pageno=-1`
will produce a series of page numbers which are in lower-case Roman numerals. Don't worry, they won't be negative numbers. It is rather unusual to see negative page numbers, on any document. It is even possible to obtain upper-case Roman numerals, but that's a bit more tricky. A daunting incantation is squirreled away in one of the appendices of the *The* TᴇX*book*. For example,
`\uppercase\expandafter{\romannumeral\year}`
could give us MCMXCII. This introduces two commands which will be tackled a little later, and is merely included here for completeness.

It is useful to know just a little about TᴇX's page-building technique here. TᴇX is organized on an individual paragraph basis (not the basis of a 'galley' or continuous steam of paragraphs). Until a paragraph has been completed, TᴇX does not consider page breaking. This means that you can break TᴇX fairly easily by writing a 'stream of consciousness' novel with only one paragraph in it. In general though, TᴇX will have gathered together more than a pagefull of paragraphs when it comes to create the page. It is uncommon to break pages at the end of paragraphs, especially if the pages are each supposed to be the same length. Therefore it is common for TᴇX to be part way through the next page when it starts to look for a 'good' break point. Just as in building a paragraph TEX 'optimizes' the line breaks to ensure that the inter-word spacing is even, and within some specified tolerance, when building a page TEX seeks to optimize, ensuring that there are no club lines or widow lines. And, of course, the paragraph spread around two pages is being optimized too. Once TEX has decided where to break the page it 'ejects' the first page and starts work on the next. The page numbers, header, and footer lines are added as each page is being ejected, using a special set of commands collectively known as 'output routines'. Output routines are the subject of a TUG 2 or 3 day course (for people who know their way round TEX). The output routine in `plain` is quite powerful, and sufficient for our immediate purposes.

The footer line – material printed at the bottom of *every* page – is specified in a `\footline`. Where is it actually placed? It is placed *outside* the body of the text, outside the zone delimited by the `\vsize`. There is a similar `\headline` command to permit material to be placed at the top of the page (also beyond the vertical text boundary). By changing the default definitions of `\headline` and `\footline` we can alter the characteristics of the material printed out with each page.

The definition for `\footline` in `plain` is
`\footline={\hss\tenrm\folio\hss}`
where `\folio` is itself a command which prints `\pageno` in either Arabic or Roman numerals, depending on how you have set things up (if `\pageno` is negative, we get Roman numerals, else Arabic). We have already met `\hss`. Here it ensures that the page number is centred. The `\tenrm` simply ensures that the page number is printed in 10 point CM Roman.

The footer line I usually use is set up by redefining `\footline` as
`\footline={\sl\today\hss\folio}`
We met the `\today` command earlier. Placing the `\hss` between the elements has the effect of placing them as far apart as the `\hsize` will allow.

The `\headline` and `\footline` are token strings. This is one of the few examples in `plain` of the use of token strings. Recall that to use the contents of a token string it is necessary to place the command `\the` before it:
`\the\headline`   *or*   `\the\footline`
A little thought will reveal that these two token strings must be part of a horizontal box which is set to the width of the page. As they stand, they are of indeterminate width. Somewhere that width must be specified.

A further consideration comes from the rather simplistic way I have specified the font. Consider the following situation: assume that we have a block of text in a different point size – a quotation, or perhaps an example or an exercise. The size change could be achieved by a command like `\eightpoint`, which would ensure that `\rm` is (say) an 8 point roman, `\it` is an 8 point italic, `\sl` is an 8 point slanted font, and so on (note that this command is hypothetical; it does not exist in `plain`, although a strategy is introduced in Chapter 18). If it happens that the page-building commands are invoked while TEX thinks that `\sl` means 8 point slanted, then the slanted text in the footline will also be 8 point. It is at this point that we have to know that what we really wanted was `\tensl`. The `plain` commands set up the default commands `\rm`, `\it`, `\bf`, `\sl`, and `\tt` indirectly by, for example, first nominating

`\font\tenrm cmr10`

and subsequently defining `\rm` to be `\tenrm`. When `\rm` is used, it really does mean 'roman' and not necessarily '10 point roman'.

Often it is desirable to have different headlines or footlines on even and odd pages. Books in European languages tend to have the odd-numbered page on the right and the even-numbered on the left. The page number itself tends to be on the outer edge of the page, away from the bound edge. Remember conditionals? They can be used here to good effect:

```
\footline={\tensl\ifodd\pageno
            \hss\folio
        \else\folio\hss
        \fi}
```

would assist here. The `\ifodd` command, followed by a number, or a counter, determines whether the value is odd or even. If the condition is true, the first path is chosen, else the second one. Note that there is no `\ifeven` command. Note too that we test `\pageno`, but centre `\folio`. Testing `\folio` would avail us little, since it is not a counter. The nub of the `\folio` command is

`\number\pageno`

There is a little more to it, since if the page number is negative, it should appear as a Roman numeral.

⇒*Exercise 12.13:*   Can you construct a footline which would allow for positive page numbers appearing as Arabic numbers, and negative as Roman?   ⇐

The `plain` output routine allows about 1 inch of white space around each printed page. Some of this space is used for printing

`\dag`	†	dagger mark
`\ddag`	‡	double dagger mark
`\S`	§	section mark
`\P`	¶	paragraph mark *or* pilcrow
`\#`	#	hash – known as *pounds* sign in the USA
`\$`	$	dollar symbol
`{\it\$}`	£	sterling symbol (pounds sign)
`\&`	&	ampersand
`\%`	%	per cent symbol

Figure 12.1
More symbols

the `\headline` or `\footline` (and sometimes for marginal notes). It is a simple matter to reposition the whole of your output, including headers and footers with respect to these page edges. The overall page layout (and dimensions like `\hsize` and `\vsize`) will not be affected. It is the position of the whole printed page which is moved. Use `\hoffset` to adjust pages horizontally, and `\voffset` to move them vertically. The commands
`\hoffset=1.5cm \voffset=-0.5in`
would cause each page of output to be shifted 1.5 centimetres to the right and 0.5 inches up in relation to the paper edges.

Use `true` dimensions if you are using `\magnification` but do not want these offsets to be magnified.

Naturally this prompts a question 'Where is the page origin by default?' The origin is defined to be 1 inch in and 1 inch down from the top left-hand corner of the page. Imperial measures die hard. It is not immediately clear whether this position refers to the baseline or not, but these details are considered in Chapter 20. Anyone who changes from one output device to another will know that this definition is not always honoured. Many printer drivers allow you to change the position of the text on the page, without having to alter the TEX input.

Some strange characters

There are a few characters which you may need to use in everyday typing (especially if you use footnotes). Figure 12.1 gives the ones that might be most useful.

The odd way the sterling symbol is handled raises a few practical points. In some ways, we should be grateful to have the #, $, and £ together, but the question does arise, what happens if the 'body' text is in the typewriter font, or in slant. Will the `\$` sequence give a dollar or a sterling symbol? The short answer, as you may guess, is that the dollar triumphs.

There is one further relevant issue reintroduced by the commands \& and \%. Recall that a command in TEX may be made up *either* entirely of one or more alphabetic characters, *or* a single non-alphabetic character. Thus \1, or \; are legitimate, and potentially meaningful commands, just like \hsize, \1, or \nopagenumbers. A command made up of alphabetic characters may be conveniently terminated in a number of ways, including by a space. This space will disappear on output. The other class of commands need not be terminated by a space. If it is formed of non-alphabetic characters, the command may contain only one such character. Therefore any space which follows will be treated as a 'real' space, and will appear on output. If we wished to typeset the sentence 'Processor speed has been increased by 140%.', we type

`Processor speed has been increased by 140\%.`

Had we terminated the sentence by \%␣., there would be a space between the '%' and the '.': 'Processor speed has been increased by 140% .'

There is of course at least one exception. If the command in question is a diacritical, the spaces just get swallowed up. TEX knows that an accent has an accompanying letter, and goes and finds it. Therefore \'␣␣elan still produces élan. But this is because \' is defined as a command with a single parameter. This is not necessarily obvious to the uninitiated.

Let's be punctual out there

There are one or two niceties of text control which can be added here. Firstly, revision: the so-called 'italic correction' accounts for the fact that italic and slanted fonts slope to the right. This means that a word in an italic or slanted font, followed by one in an upright font such as roman or bold, may look rather squashed together – for example, *small* letters: to avoid this Knuth suggests the use of a correction – \/. The amount of the correction is different for different letters in different fonts. This is all a bit messy, since there turn out to be extra rules which are rather context sensitive. In general we adopt the correction before switching back to an upright font, *except* where the next character is either a comma or a full stop. Although this is described as an *italic* correction, setting '{\bf half}' will look clumsy unless you say '{\bf half\/}'! To try to see what this means, work out whether '**half**' or '**half**' has the italic correction. Rather than trying to remember these special cases, look at your output and see if it looks right, and then incorporate corrections if you think you need them. This is again an anathema to the idea of declarative markup. But then, the notion of allowing the author to select a bold font is already chipping away at any such pretensions. The author ought merely to be saying 'this type of emphasis' (in some more 'meaningful' way).

One other aspect of the italic and slanted fonts is that a block of text set in such a style may appear to be moved slightly to the right when compared with text set in an 'upright' font. If this worries you, there is no very easy solution, but it would be possible to use \leftskip and \rightskip to move that block of text slightly rightwards. Remember though that these commands affect the whole paragraph, so that performing this sort of action on part of a paragraph will be much more difficult.

You may notice that some books use the em-dash where this book uses a 'spaced' en-dash. If the em-dash is used, no white space is left at the ends. There is an aspect of using the em-dash in this way which must be addressed. If you use the em-dash in this conventional way, for example do---they, and TEX breaks this sequence at a line end, it will be broken between do and --- they, never between do--- and they. In order to signal this latter case as a possible breakpoint, you must write something like
do---\allowbreak they
The easiest way to do this is with a global edit after the manuscript is complete. Similarly, TEX feels that phrases like 'right/left' and 'input/output' are all one word. We can use a similar strategy to place potential breakpoints:
right/\allowbreak left
input/\allowbreak output
You could always define commands \rl and \io if you were using these frequently.
\def\rl{right/\allowbreak left}
\def\io{input/\allowbreak output}
You would find a global change of / to /\allowbreak rather dangerous. There is a special control sequence \slash which provides the oblique symbol, but also allows a breakpoint. The 'best' way to express these compound 'words' would therefore be
right\slash left
input\slash output

... period

T_EX treats the period in a special way. It permits the glue after a period to stretch at a faster rate than that after a word, provided of course the period is followed by a space. The same applies to the exclamation mark. Space after commas also stretches slightly faster too, but not as much. The implication of all this is that periods in the middle of sentences, which signify abbreviations rather than sentence ends, have too much glue associated with them. *Unless* they are preceded by capital letters, T_EX assumes that these are initials. Thus Prof. R. A. Bailey would have 'normal' glue after her initials, but extra glue after her title. How do we regularize this? One way is to use a control space – \␣ after `Prof.`. But in this case, a further subtlety intrudes. We would prefer that the name was not broken at the end of lines: that is, there should be no line end break in the midst of Prof. R. A. Bailey, and as we have written it, there could be. T_EX supports a tie character, which prevents separation, but provides white space. The tie character is ~. Thus what we probably wanted was

`Prof.~R.~A.~Bailey`

This is a bit long and difficult to hyphenate, so it could lead to overfull box problems. Be warned.

⇒*Exercise 12.14:*   There are several other ways to solve this last problem. How else can you ensure that the name is not broken, and that the full stops are treated as abbreviation symbols rather than full stops? ⇐

Ties are also useful in situations like 'Fig. 6', where we would not like the two parts 'Fig.' and '6' to appear on different lines. Some manuals of style claim that abbreviations like e.g. or cf. should be followed by a comma (how absurd), so the problem does not arise if you wish to be bound by antique prescriptions.

⇒*Exercise 12.15:*   Does the sentence termination space stretching apply to the question mark?   ⇐

If this seems all a bit overwhelming, help is at hand. For once, the French have provided us with something useful! (European joke, not to be taken chauvinistically.) If you use \frenchspacing, you get something which is not at all daring, but sensible. All spaces have the same stretch, whatever the punctuation. This primer uses \frenchspacing, as a gesture to European unity. There is a matching \nonfrenchspacing which turns it back on again. Do note that negating \frenchspacing uses `non` rather than `no`. In passing, if you are wondering what Knuth has to say about interword glue, it is that 'the details are slightly tricky, but not incomprehensible'. No comment.

One more feature of periods: three dots in a row are termed ellipsis. If you simply type three dots, they appear on output to be too close together. In order to get ... rather than ... , TEX uses \dots. Why was it not called \ellipsis I wonder?

```
He went on, and on, and on\dots\ about ellipsis.
```

Now I don't have to say anything more about ellipsis. Hmmm...

⇒*Exercise 12.16:*　　Unfortunately that is not true. Use \dots to create ellipsis when you change font or change the font size. Compare the dots you obtain with the dots normally created in that font and size. Comments?　　　　　　　　　　　　　　　　　　⇐

Lines

There are often situations where you may wish to control the structure of your document, down at the line level. If you are setting verse or poems, you would be rather unhappy to have TEX use its usual paragraphing – although this might just do for some blank verse, or prosy passages. We need some way of forcing each line to be treated by TEX as a separate entity. We already have a suitable mechanism. If each line was a paragraph in its own right, we could emulate the desired effect:

```
As easily I should miss the spring,\par
certain, no need to mark or pace.\par
```

This has certain consequences: since each line is a paragraph, the values of \parskip and \parindent are brought into play, and should any line exceed the \hsize, it will be broken as normal and the residue will start at the left margin. In general poems right justify continuation lines. TEX has a special control sequence \obeylines which saves having to put the \par at the end of each line. The existing 'carriage return' is made to substitute for the explicit command (you could of course leave a blank line between each line instead of writing \par). Thus

```
{\obeylines
what's fixed, is, though the world turns
and turning, returns
where you and I are, no matter
the angles, orbits set.
}
```

This is exactly equivalent to the earlier solution, illustrating both the effect and the limitations of the command. This is a useful example of one of the drawbacks of plain TEX. Often the paragraph is exploited for other purposes, purposes for which it may not be truly appropriate. \obeylines implicitly accepts the current paragraph settings of skip and indent. It might be more appropriate in many situations to redefine these. The \parskip might be better as the same value as \baselineskip, and the indentation might be some entirely different value:

```
{\obeylines\parskip=\baselineskip\parindent=0pt
We merely wheel in this our own
made heaven, nor can we quit it,
}
```

Since this is grouped, the values of \parskip and \parindent are local, and are in effect only for that group. You will have to group \obeylines anyway, or every time you type a carriage return TₑX will start a new paragraph.

There is an alternative strategy: we could \break every line:

```
(nor would I, should or could)\break
still it goes, though never still\break
```

but by itself, \break is insufficient. Applying it in the way shown above would give:

poise   gained   from   movement
constant   encircling,   an   escapement,

which is really not very attractive. What we wanted was to \hfil it before breaking:

```
but no escape save seconds.\hfil\break
I'll await the spring.\hfil\break
```

which would give:

but no escape save seconds.
I'll await the spring.

If we were doing something like this at all seriously, we would probably redefine \hfil\break to \\, or something similar.

⇒*Exercise 12.17:*   Rather than redefine \hfil\break in the way suggested above, dabble in active characters again. Select some underused character and turn it into a suitable command.   ⇐

Give me a break

Time for an aside: you rarely need to \break a line in this way, far less break a page and start a new one. But for some reason, people expect to have an explicit mechanism for breaking a line or a page. This is largely a hangover from the days of the typewriter. Besides anything else, it suggests a lack of faith in TₑX. Apart from the explicit use of \break above, there is no use of such \break commands in this entire book. There are, however, a few page breaks: after all, you do need some means of terminating Chapters or Appendices. How do we obtain them? The command \eject forces a page break (ejects a page), just as \end or \bye forces the end of processing. Again, \eject by itself is probably insufficient, just as \break by itself is inadequate. We need to fill the page with white space:

\vfill\eject

is a suitable strategy. If we omit the \vfill any glue between paragraphs will come into operation. Similarly, any glue associated with the \baselineskip may allow lines to be further apart than they really ought to be. Outside of this very deliberate chapter or appendix end (or perhaps some other sectioning requirement), \eject is rarely required. Many books require that a new chapter starts on a right-hand (or odd) page. Thus if every chapter starts with

\ifodd\pageno\else\null\eject\fi

we can ensure that TEX takes care of this detail. Of course, no-one would really write that. They would have written a command which includes those instructions, together with instructions on how the chapter title was to be handled, and if there were any special instructions for the headline and footline on a title page.

In relatively informal documents, like for example memos or reports, it sometimes seems desirable to encourage page breaking at the end of paragraphs. This seems especially true if the paragraphs tend to be short. TEX has a trio of commands, \smallbreak, \medbreak, and \bigbreak, which provide a little extra flexibility in building a page, but they also add a skip (small, med, or big) if the page is not broken there. More drastic is the \goodbreak which is even more encouragement to break. There is one more variation, which most closely approaches the problem introduced at the end of this paragraph. The command \filbreak is particularly interesting: if a paragraph terminates with \filbreak, the *next* block of material which is itself terminated with a \filbreak will either be placed on the same page, if there is enough room, or start a new page.

⇒*Exercise 12.18:* Really these commands only start to make sense when you come to use them in a variety of situations. If you can also arrange to have a deadline loom over you, you will soon find the trying cases when they don't quite do what you expect, and where practice and experience would have been a great boon. ⇐

command	amount	defined by
\␣	normal space	\fontdimen
~	normal space	\fontdimen
\enskip	$0.5\,\text{em} \pm 0\,\text{em}$	\hskip
\enspace	$0.5\,\text{em}$	\kern
\quad	$1\,\text{em}$	\hskip
\qquad	$2\,\text{em}$	\hskip
\thinspace	$0.1667\,\text{em}$	\kern

Figure 12.2
Spaces

Spaces

In text we may have to control the spacing between words or characters. There are a number of ways of doing this (Figure 12.2). Most have been introduced in a slightly different context already. Not one is an absolute measure, but is related in some way to the current font. In Computer Modern Roman at 10 pt, the normal space is 3.33333 pt plus 1.66666 pt minus 1.11111 pt, and an em is 10 pt. These values are to be found in the \fontdimen parameters associated with every font (Chapter 18). For example, those first three values, associated with the way a normal space is handled, are stored in \fondimen2, 3, and 4. The value of 1 em (a quad width) is stored in \fontdimen6. Although we may not normally wish to change these, they can be manipulated. In general, the \fontdimens themselves are not manipulated directly, but, for example, \spaceskip may be reset to change the interword spacing:

\spaceskip 4pt plus1pt minus1pt

and the 'extra' space, associated with sentence endings, can be reset through \xspaceskip. You would have to have a really good excuse to want to change things like this.

⇒*Exercise 12.19:*   What differences are observed between starting a paragraph with \enskip and \enspace?   ⇐

Tables by tabs

One reason for tackling matrices before tables was to demonstrate how straightforward it is to obtain aligned entries. There is very little difference between a matrix and a table – at least, not from the way it is laid out. From a mathematical point of view they may have rather different properties, if they do indeed contain numerical information. Of course, many tables will contain no numerical information at all. Two elements will be preserved in any discussion of TeX's tabular facilities, the & and the \cr.

Before looking at TeX's handling of tabular material, consider this quotation from Richard Beach (1986):

> Designing table typography is a hard problem. There are many formatting details to get right and there is only a small amount of space with which to work. The two-dimensional nature of tables requires alignment of information in both directions at the same time. It is very important to maintain control over placement because the organization of information in tables is part of the message. Juxtaposition and other spatial relationships within tables have an important impact on the way in which tables convey information.

At least one of the things this suggests is that you should have some idea of what you are trying to achieve when you commit yourself to using a table. A small amount of forethought may cut through many layers of layout, and you could end up with something which is easier to understand. This should be a thread which runs throughout this primer. There is no point having the world's most sophisticated text layout software at your fingertips, if the message you are conveying is woolly, garbled, or unclear. TeX will allow the clearest message to shine through unfettered: it will not burnish a pig's ear. Software is no substitute for brainware.

As usual we will start with some of the simpler cases. TeX has a very simple and crude method of aligning text through the command \settabs

```
\settabs 3\columns
\+ column one & column 2 & column 3 \cr
\+ next one   & and the next & and more \cr
```

Interpretation is not too difficult, since we already know what & and \cr do. In this very special instance, they have non-deleterious effects on ordinary text. The new expression is \+ which starts every line in the alignment. The command \settabs itself needs some extra information – the number of columns that the aligned text occupies, followed by the command \columns. The sequence above would give us

column one   column 2   column 3
next one   and the next   and more

The line is merely divided into three *equal* parts. Notice that each of the columns is 'left justified'. Do not be misled by the name \settabs to assume that this command works in exactly the same way as typewriter 'tabs'. In particular, we should be careful that the content of any column does not overwrite that of another column. Selecting the next tab on a typewriter just jumps to the next available, relative to the current position – \settabs goes to the next, even if that means backtracking. Equally, note that the command does not 'wrap' a longer entry into several shorter 'lines', in the way that TeX normally handles paragraphs. For example, some of the line

```
\+ an extremely long entry which is really not
   a good idea&short&also short\cr
```

will probably end up being printed in the same space as the second and third columns. 'Probably' because this will depend on the current \hsize.

⇒*Exercise 13.1:*   Set up a simple \settabs and by changing the \hsize show how wider entries can lead to overwriting.   ⇐

⇒*Exercise 13.2:*   There is a way to make the entries behave as 'normal' paragraphs by boxing them. See if you can make it work.   ⇐

An interesting feature of \settabs is that it remains in operation until a new \settabs is set up. The \settabs could be set up at the beginning of the file, to be utilized whenever needed:

```
\+ yet another & penultimate & the end \cr
```

simply produces

yet another   penultimate   the end

You might also cheat a little and park something in a mythical fourth (or even fifth, sixth. . .) column. What happens then?

```
\+ Stop! & Don't do it!! & I warned you & Aargh!\cr
```

See for yourself.

Stop!   Don't do it!!   I warned you   Aargh!
A block of tabbed alignments will split over a page boundary. They are not seen as an integral unit, but of course, if the whole block is \vboxed, the \settabs may be local to that box, and they cannot be split over pages. But note that it is also possible to write

```
\settabs3\columns
\vbox{
\+ column one & column two & column three \cr
\+ next one & and the next & and more \cr
}
```

The feature of equal width columns may be unsatisfactory. You can get round it by nominating a sort of 'template' line – a line which exhibits the 'worst' (longest) features of the individual entries, or adopts some other appropriate set of guidelines. To illustrate this, the example of a table of contents will be used:

```
\settabs\+LXXXVIII\quad&The Pequod Meets the Samuel
                        Enderby\quad&999\cr
\+ I      & Loomings        & 1     \cr
\+ II     & The Carpet Bag  & 9     \cr
\+ III    & The Spouter Inn & 16    \cr
\+ .      & .               & .     \cr
\+ CXXXV & The Chase -- Third Day & 806 \cr
\+       & Epilogue         & 825   \cr
```

The line

```
\settabs\+LXXXVIII\quad&The Pequod Meets the Samuel
                        Enderby\quad&999\cr
```

will never appear anywhere. In fact, there will be no page 999. The entries simply represent the maximum size to be allotted to their columns. TEX's digits have the quality that they are all of the same width (half a quad, or an \enspace). This produces

I	Loomings	1
II	The Carpet Bag	9
III	The Spouter Inn	16
.	.	.
CXXXV	The Chase – Third Day	806
	Epilogue	825

How might we have placed the entries in another font, for example italics? It is worth remembering that simply saying \it Loomings does not then bring \it into play for the whole of the rest of the alignment, either horizontally or vertically. Each of the individual entries between \+, &, and \cr is grouped. In passing, this implies that an arrangement like

```
\+{\it...&...}&...\cr
```
is doomed to failure. To make all the entries italic, you could do something like:
```
{\it
\+......\cr
\+.......\cr
\+.......\cr
}
```
or even
```
\+......\cr
{\it\+.......\cr}
\+.......\cr
```
to turn a single line into italics. If the \settabs occurs *within* the braces, it will be local. The \global command has no effect on \settabs, although it does not generate an error message.

What happens to spaces within the aligned material? 'Ordinary' spaces which occur between words are handled in the normal TₑX way – as space. The leading or trailing spaces are simply ignored. It does not matter whether you write
```
\+I& Loomings&1\cr
```
or
```
\+ I      & Loomings          & 1  \cr
```
The fact that \+I and \+ I work in exactly the same way may seem a little anomalous. After all, \+ is a command made up of \ and a single non-alphabetic character, where one might expect the space to be therefore significant. Not so. If, though, space occurs in a template, leading spaces are ignored, but trailing spaces count as 'space'. That is, the lines
```
\settabs\+LXXXVIII &The Pequod Meets the Samuel
                              Enderby &999 \cr
```
and
```
\settabs\+LXXXVIII&The Pequod Meets the Samuel
                              Enderby&999\cr
```
result in slightly different spacing of the following alignments.

In order to do something a little more useful, let's take a real example, published in Lesk (1979). This table is too large to present in detail, especially since once a couple of lines have been done, the remainder fall out naturally. The first few lines are given in Figure 13.1.

This actually starts to look like a table (at last). How do we do it? Looking first at the body of the table, it is obvious that taking three equal width columns:

New Jersey Representatives
(Democrats)

Name	Office Address	Phone
James J. Florio	23 S. White Horse Pike, Somerdale 08083	609-627-8222
William J. Hughes	2920 Atlantic Ave., Atlantic City 08401	609-345-4844
Edward J. Patten	Natl. Bank Bldg., Perth Amboy 08861	201-826-4610
Frank Thompson Jr.	10 Rutgers Pl., Trenton 08618	609-599-1619
Peter W. Rodino, Jr.	Suite 1435A, 970 Broad St., Newark 07102	201-645-6363

Figure 13.1
Table begin-
ning

```
\settabs3\columns
```
is rather absurd. What is needed here are different length alignment entities:
```
\settabs\+Frank Thompson Jr.\enspace&
Suite 1435A, 970 Broad St., Newark 07102\enspace&
-999-9999&\cr
```
This will set up the template that is to be repeated. We are choos-
ing the widest entries which occur in column one, column two, and
column three. Column three is the easiest to deal with, since all
digits are known to have a constant width. Otherwise we have to
scan down the entries and make an educated guess. This may not
be easy for real-life data. After all, the actual width of an entry
depends on the typeface and font being used. The original is set in
a sort of Times typeface, but there is no guarantee that Computer
Modern will have the same width characteristics. If the original
had been typed, or had been handwritten, it would have been
even more problematic to estimate the significant entry. Note the
inclusion of an \enspace in the first two entries, to ensure that
there is some space between the columns.

A rather odd feature is the 'extra' & which immediately precedes the \cr. What is going on here? In broad terms, the way
that \settabs works is to create a number of \hboxes, which each
contain the argument (the material in the alignment), left justified by an \hss. The command \hss is an interesting one, since
it is the mechanism which allows material to spill over the fixed
width of the \hbox. There is one exception to this pattern. The
last \hbox in the alignment contains no glue at all. It is simply
an \hbox to its natural width. Thus in order to be able to modify
the entry to do anything other than left justify it, the only real

option is to add an extra alignment which becomes the one with the \hbox to its natural width. This 'extra' column has to be added to any line where the rightmost 'real' entry is to be centred or right justified – a rather ugly way to handle the problem. For the bulk of the table, these strategems are irrelevant, since the entries are intended to be left justified. However, the line

       Name   Office Address   Phone

has entries which are centred over their columns. Since the \set-tabs uses an \hss command, it can most easily be overridden by \hfil or \hfill. If centering is required, it is sufficient to write

\+\hfil Name &\hfil Office Address &\hfil Phone&\cr

since this will counterbalance the \hss. Obviously, although sufficient, this does not appear intuitive when we come across it in a chunk of text. It would be far clearer to write

\+\hfil Name\hfil&\hfil Office Address\hfil
   &\hfil Phone\hfil&\cr

where the centering is made explicit. If we wished to right justify within an entry, the command to use is \hfill. A pair of balancing \hfills could also have been used to centre.

   This accounts for the bulk of the table, but not for the first two heading lines. It turns out that these cannot easily be handled as part of the \settabs already set up. The problems are similar to those encountered with the other centred material. One way to tackle these is

\settabs\+Frank Thompson Jr.\enspace
    Suite 1435A, 970 Broad St., Newark 07102\enspace
    999-999-9999&\cr
\+\hfill New Jersey Representatives\hfill &\cr
\+\hfill\it(Democrats)\hfill&\cr

There are tidier ways to do this, since we know that an \enspace is half a \quad. On the other hand, by far the easiest way is to take the template for the \settabs already discussed, and just edit it, by dropping out the &s between the entries, remembering that the template line should end with a &\cr. If we happened to have some idea of the width of the table that was to follow, we could of course just write

\settabs\+\hskip334pt&\cr

To me this illustrates one of the weaknesses of \settabs, since it emphasizes how important it is to know the characteristics of the material to be formatted. This is not "declarative markup' if we have to take into account the current \hsize or individual entries. We can plead for clemency on the grounds of the particular

```
\settabs\+Frank Thompson Jr.\enspace
  Suite 1435A, 970 Broad St., Newark 07102\enspace
  999-999-9999&\cr
\+\hfil New Jersey Representatives\hfil &\cr
\+\hfil\it(Democrats)\hfil&\cr
\smallskip
\settabs\+Frank Thompson Jr.\enspace&
Suite 1435A, 970 Broad St., Newark 07102\enspace&
-999-9999&\cr
\+\hfil Name\hfil & \hfil Office Address\hfil & \hfil
Phone\hfil&\cr
\+ James J. Florio & 23 S. White Horse Pike, Somerdale
 & 609-627-8222\cr
\+ William J. Hughes & 2920 Atlantic Ave., Atlantic
    City 08401 & 609-345-4844\cr
\+ Edward J. Patten & Natl.\ Bank Bldg., Perth Amboy
    08861 & 201-826-4610\cr
\+Frank Thompson Jr.\enspace&10 Rutgers Pl., Trenton
    08618 & 609-599-1619\cr
\+Peter W. Rodino, Jr.&Suite 1435A, 970 Broad St.,
    Newark 07102\enspace&201-645-6363\cr
```

Figure 13.2
A portion of
the input of
Lesk's table

nature of tabular material, but it does raise some uncomfortable questions.

What does this give us? Figure 13.2 provides a summary of all the components which have been introduced. It accounts for the headings and the first few entries. The results of this have already been given. There are a couple of small items to be accounted for: a \smallskip appears in the table, just to spread out some of the headings. Perhaps of more interest are the ways that periods are handled. Recall that under TEX's default settings additional space is added after a period. Periods are used in (at least) two different senses, as the terminator to a sentence and as an indication that abbreviation has taken place – for example, after an initial in a name, or in common abbreviations like 'etc.' TEX attempts to handle these differently. If a period follows a capital letter, a space that follows is a 'normal' interword space. If it follows a lower-case letter, it is assumed to be a sentence terminator, and some extra space is added. This accounts for the different handling of periods in the table. Whenever a period is used as in an abbreviation, but follows a lower-case letter, a 'control space' can be entered: for example, Natl.\␣. In the case of the abbreviation Bldg., the period is followed by a comma rather than a space, and no special action has to be taken.

Indirectly this raises a couple of other points. If a sentence ends with a capital letter the following period will be followed by a normal interword space, rather than an intersentence space. The actual amounts of space are not large. In the standard `cmr10` an interword space is 3.33 pt, while 4.44 pt is placed after a full stop which ends a sentence. These quantities are skips, and therefore have associated glue too. Many acronyms are presented in upper-case letters: names like CAD-CAM, CGM, TEX, and so on spring readily to mind. If we really care about this finesse, what should we do? One way to handle the problem is to insert a null group, `{}`, between the last upper-case letter and the period, so that we 'normally' write `CAD-CAM{}`, or `\TeX{}`. Again, this looks ugly, but it does 'solve' the potential problem. The solution adopted in this primer is to adopt `\frenchspacing` throughout. This makes spaces after a period (or any other punctuation) be treated as normal interword spaces. To return to the default TEX spacing, issue the command `\nonfrenchspacing`. Opinion appears to be divided about the appropriate gap to be left at a period which indicates a sentence end. Alison Black (1990) notes 'In typeset documents, all punctuation should be followed by a single space', while all typists appear to have been taught to leave two spaces (and therefore most word processors do this by default).

⇒*Exercise 13.3:*   In the original of the 'New Jersey Representatives' table, the first column, 'Name', was set in a bold typeface. Modify the table template(s) and entries to do this.   ⇐

⇒*Exercise 13.4:*   Returning to the earlier example (the table of contents), the first column, the chapter numbers, would be better set right justified: similarly, the page numbers would be much better right justified. Modify the components of this table of contents to take these details into account.   ⇐

More control

Very often we wish to centre the displayed material across the page. There is a simple way to do this. At first it seems a little perverse and perhaps a little contradictory, but it merely exploits some aspects of TₑX's nature:

I	Loomings	1
II	The Carpet Bag	9
III	The Spouter Inn	16
.	.	.
CXXXV	The Chase – Third Day	806
	Epilogue	825

may be set through

```
$$\vbox{\settabs\+LXXXVIII \quad&The Pequod Meets the
                         Samuel Enderby \quad&999\cr
\+ I     & Loomings            & 1\cr
\+ II    & The Carpet Bag      & 9\cr
\+ III   & The Spouter Inn     & 1\cr
\+ .     & .                   & .\cr
\+ CXXXV & The Chase -- Third Day & 806\cr
\+       & Epilogue            & 825\cr
}$$
```

Essentially all the maths mode contributes is the centering. But since we have textual material it has to be \vboxed to be handled properly. The use of maths mode also inserts extra skip above and below the table. TₑX uses its normal mechanism for vertical space between text and displayed maths, as discussed earlier.

There are some further implications. Since the material is boxed, it will not be split over pages: it will be treated as a single integral block. Thus its applicability to a table of contents of indeterminate length is suspect. In this example the \settabs is inside the \vbox and would be local (the inclusion within the $$ signs also makes a local group). The \settabs could have preceded the $$\vbox if desired.

⇒*Exercise 13.5:*   Take this last example, and compare what you would have obtained by removing the maths setting, and then the \vbox. Also place the \settabs outside the $$\vbox.   ⇐

Would this strategy also work with the use of \settabs when it is used with a fixed number of \columns? Recall that the final aligned entry is an \hbox to its natural width. Thus a line is not really to the full \hsize, but can be a bit shorter. The 'shortness' will depend on the particular number of columns and the entries. But if an extra & has been added to allow the final column to be centred or right justified, then no apparent centering will take place. A way to handle this would be to nominate an extra column: that is to say,

```
\settabs4\columns
```
when only three were going to be used.

Although placing material in maths mode will, by default, centre it across the width, so too does `\centerline`. This also gives us rather better control over vertical spacing. Why not simply place the tabular material into `\centerline`? This raises some interesting points.

Taking the straightforward approach of experimentation,
```
\centerline{\settabs3\columns
\vbox{
\+ column one & column two & column three \cr
\+ next one & and the next & and more \cr
}}
```
we find the rather forbidding error message
```
Runaway argument?
{\vbox {\settabs 3\columns
! Forbidden control sequence found while scanning
          use of \centerline.
```
Asking for more information through typing `help` at the ? prompt yields little to help us:
```
I suspect you have forgotten a '}', causing me
to read past where you wanted me to stop.
I'll try to recover; but if the error is serious,
you'd better type 'E' or 'X' now and fix your file.
```
In fact this is misleading. The problem lies with the `\+` command, since it turns out that this is defined with the aid of `\outer`. It cannot therefore appear as an argument in a command. There are two ways out of this dilemma. The command `\centerline` takes one argument, but the command `\line` takes none. How can this be? Looking at the two commands in detail:
```
\def\centerline#1{\line{\hss#1\hss}}
\def\line{\hbox to \hsize}
```
the definition of `\line` is quite elegant. It could have been written as
```
\def\line#1{\hbox to\hsize{#1}}
```
but why bother, when the material to be used by `\line` ought to be grouped anyway? In other words, when
```
\line{Some text}
```
is used, it expands to
```
\hbox to \hsize{Some text}
```
a simple substitution macro. If therefore we write

```
\line{\hfill\vbox{\settabs3\columns
\+ column one & column two & column three \cr
\+ next one & and the next & and more \cr
}\hfill}
```
which 'feels' like \centerline, the desired effect will result.

The other approach is to use a version of \+ which is not \outer. Knuth provides another command, \tabalign, which may be used in these circumstances:
```
\centerline{\settabs3\columns
\vbox{
\tabalign column one & column two & column three \cr
\tabalign next one & and the next & and more \cr
}}
```
⇒*Exercise 13.6:* Centre either the table of contents or New Jersey Representatives table. ⇐

A specialized extension

There is one more feature to be taken into account before leaving the commands in the \settabs suite. Perversely, it does not involve the direct use of \settabs at all, since it is possible to use \+ without first referencing \settabs. This feature is really most appropriate for the formatting of computer programs, or some similar sort of exercise where the alignment positions change from line to line. The following example from Stig Hanson (1990) may help to give some flavour of this:

column=**Id**
table =**Transpose** ∘
      (**all** i: **Insert**[place=first
                element=word(**Arabic**(i))]) ∘
      (**all** i: **Layout**[dimension=horizontal...]) ∘
      Layout[dimension=vertical...]

may be obtained from
```
\+column&=\bf Id\cr
\+table &=&\bf Transpose $\circ$\cr
\+      & &(\bf all $i$: Insert{\rm []}&place=first\cr
\+      & &                    &element=word(%
    {\bf Arabic}($i$))]) $\circ$\cr
\+      & &(\bf all $i$:
    Layout{\rm[dimension=horizontal\dots])}
                                    $\circ$\cr
\+      & &\bf Layout{\rm[dimension=vertical\dots]}\cr
```

There is quite a lot of work here, but it is possible to see that more &s are added as the 'program' is developed. Since it is often inconvenient to be stuck with the alignment markers which are selected for a couple of lines, a command \cleartabs allows resetting of the alignments. From the same source,

bottom-num$[i, r]=$**Singleton** ∘
     Insert[place=last
         element=word(**Arabic**(i))] ∘
     Layout[orientation=vertical
         alignment=r **with** r
         glue: between=*foot-sep-glue*
         reference: ref=ref(first)]

is given from the following commands:

```
\cleartabs
\+bottom-num[$i,r$]=&\bf Singleton $\circ$\cr
\+    &\bf Insert\rm[&place=last\cr
\+    &                &element=word({\bf Arabic}($i$))]
                                             $\circ$\cr
\+    &\bf Layout[\cleartabs&orientation=vertical\cr
\+    &                &alignment=$r$ {\bf with}
                                             $r$\cr
\+    &                &glue: between=%
                          {\sl foot-sep-glue}&\cr
\+    &                &reference: ref=ref(first)
                                             &]\cr
```

The \cleartabs command is used here only in order to remove the alignments. Without this command, the previously set up alignment would have been used.

⇒*Exercise 13.7:* The last examples might have been better handled if the entries which included mathematical symbols like = and ∘ were handled completely in maths mode in order to ensure that the spacing was 'correct'. Rework them in order to accommodate this refinement. ⇐

Tables again 14

There is quite another way entirely to tackle tables. TEX has two commands, \halign and \valign, which provide an enormously flexible way of handling tabular material. With the exception of the two 'programming' examples from the last chapter, all the tabular material presented so far would (in my opinion) be more easily handled through this alternative technique. I confess that I very rarely use \settabs. The \halign command in particular seems to lend itself to a variety of problems. To begin with, its use gives the illusion of awkwardness. This is more a function of unfamiliarity, rather than intrinsic difficulty.

A very simple template for a numeric table is

```
\halign{#&#&#\cr
1 & 270 & 9 \cr
2 & 39 & 16 \cr
3 & 4 & 126 \cr
}
```

This is rather rudimentary, but it serves to illustrate the notions. The command \halign merely means a horizontal alignment is being set up. The next set of commands are an alignment 'preamble' or 'template' which serve to describe the form the table will have. Essentially all it is saying is 'three entries per row', and making no pronouncement about placement within a column. This table comes out as:

```
1 270 9
2 39  16
3 4   126
```

It would have been rather nicer either to centre or right justify the entries. If we change the preamble to

```
\halign{\hfil#&\hfil#&\hfil#\cr
```

the individual entries would have been right justified:

```
1 270   9
2  39  16
3   4 126
```

The \hfil is propagated down the column, but it does not filter 'sideways' through to the other columns. This feature is very powerful. Positioning, font changing, boxing, and many other sorts of commands may be incorporated into an alignment preamble.

There are some other interesting features associated with the \halign command. The occurrence of an \halign within text will begin a new line, not a new paragraph. But when the alignment is finished, any following text continues as if a new paragraph had been begun. The # indicates the replacement text. Any blank spaces after the & in the preamble (or the individual entries) are ignored, but any spaces after the # are regarded as the inclusion of 'space'. In the example, the spaces between the columns are generated by virtue of the spaces which follow the numbers (not those preceding them). That is, taking ␣ to mean 'significant space' in this context, what TEX sees is

```
\halign{#&#&#\cr
1␣& 270␣& 9␣\cr
2␣& 39␣& 16␣\cr
3␣& 4␣& 126␣\cr
```

The space between the columns was generated by the table entries, but space may also be inserted into the preamble. The preambles

\halign{#&#&#\cr and \halign{ #& #& #\cr

are equivalent, but

\halign{# &# &# \cr

is different, since in this case an extra space will be added after the replacement text.

If other material occurs in the preamble, it is not necessary to include separators between any commands and the #, nor is it necessary to shield the replacement text in braces. Thus when

```
\halign{\hfil#&\hfil#&\hfil#\cr
one&two&three\cr}
```

is typeset, although it might appear that one is merely inserted immediately after the \hfil to give \hfilone, TEX is friendlier and recognizes that the \hfil is a command separate from whatever follows. But equally, it would have done no harm to express the preamble as

\halign{\hfil #&\hfil #&\hfil #\cr

since the space after the \hfil disappears, in common with any other TEX command.

Should we decide to group some of the replacement text, it does become possible to insert extra space in entries. As you might expect { one} manages to insert a little extra space too, since it is contained in the group.

There is some conflict going on here. On the one hand, it seems a good idea to lay out tabular material clearly, mimicking the eventual layout. In this way it is far easier to keep track of what goes where. On the other hand, if the contents of the table are presented in a way which eliminates the leading and trailing space, then the table may become less readable and more prone to error. There are straightforward strategies which can help. In a trivial example,

```
    one&    two&    three\cr
   four&   five&      six\cr
  seven&  eight&     nine\cr
    ten&eleven&    twelve\cr
```

ensures that no inadvertent spaces are introduced. In general, any such space would hardly matter if the entries were to end up left justified: if the preamble was

```
\halign{\hfil#&\hfil#&\hfil#\cr
```

then an extra space between the replacement text and an & could lead to a small amount of extra space being introduced, and as a result, the entries not being spaced as expected. For example, with this 'right-justified' preamble the entries

```
one  &two    &three \cr
four &five   &six   \cr
seven&eight  &nine  \cr
ten  &eleven&twelve\cr
```

could give a rather irregular spacing between the columns.

⇒*Exercise 14.1:*   Experiment with the preambles in the examples already given in this chapter. Modify them to centre entries in a column. Show the effect of omitting all spaces in the entries and the preamble. ⇐

To illustrate the font-changing capability, we could have the first column in italics, the second bold, and the last in the default font through the alignment

```
\halign{\it#&\bf#&#\cr
```

This is much more flexible than anything \settabs has to offer.

⇒*Exercise 14.2:*   Take the 'table of contents' from the previous chapter and create a suitable preamble.   ⇐

Headings

But we surely expect much more out of a table than just a simple set of entries. If the entries were numerical, we could as easily

have obtained that from one of the \matrix forms – we could
have written

```
$$\matrix{1& 27&  93\cr
          2& 39& 106\cr
          3& 47& 126\cr}$$
```

As with some \settabs examples, we require headings. Approaching the problem simply,

```
\halign{\hfil#&\hfil#&\hfil#\cr
order& height& length\cr
1& 27&  93\cr
2& 39& 106\cr
3& 47& 126\cr
```

gives some headings, but they will each be right justified in the
column:

orderheightlength

1	27	93
2	39	106
3	47	126

It might be better to centre those individual entries, and they
certainly need spacing out more. Tackling the centering first, we
can do this by giving each individual alignment in the preamble
its own \hfil:

```
\halign{\hfil#&\hfil#&\hfil#\cr
order\hfil&height\hfil&length\hfil\cr
1& 27&  93\cr
2& 39& 106\cr
3& 47& 126\cr
}
```

There are several ways to tackle the introduction of space between
the columns. It is worth emphasizing the need for consistency yet
again. Had we written

```
order &height &length \cr
1& 27&  93\cr
```

the headings would have had a bit of space associated with them,
and they would not have (right) aligned with the numbers which
followed. But provided we treat the heading row in the same
way' as each of the following rows, by consistently introducing
space or not, the table should contain no unexpected anomalies.

One of the easiest ways to include space is to introduce a \quad
or an \enspace in the template. Gradually, we are building up to
something useful:

order	height	length
1	27	93
2	39	106
3	47	126

Since the alignment preamble is a sort of template, we could use it to convey other information, which would be repeated in each entry. For example, if we wished the first column to be in a different typeface, we could

```
\halign{\it\hfil#\quad&\hfil#\quad&\hfil#\cr
order & height & length \cr
1& 27&   93\cr
2& 39& 106\cr
3& 47& 126\cr
}
```

This chapter began by saying that there was a similar path, through the use of \valign. In truth, this is rarely used. Knuth notes that 'people usually work with TEX at least one year before they find their first application for \valign'. This may even be a conservative estimate. The only examples I have ever seen were rather forced (and could probably have been done another way).

Approaching the problem

The easiest way to approach tables is by gradually building up the elements until we achieve all the bits and pieces we want. In doing so we will encounter many other features which are of a more generally applicable nature. It seems almost impossible to teach (or learn) TEX in a 'linear' fashion. There always seem to be little diversions and loops which, in the end (if it is ever reached), make the path look like macramé or lace.

There are many ways to illustrate the creation of tables. The approach that will be adopted from now on is to tackle some 'real' tables, and later to examine some more specific problems. One of the alternatives, creating only a very few, fairly complex tables, as exemplified by Knuth, will not be adopted. The first few tables will be drawn from Lesk's paper on tbl (which is also where Knuth borrowed the AT&T example in *The TEXbook*, and from which the \settabs example in the previous chapter is derived). There is a slight drawback in this approach. While the tables are reasonably comprehensive, the originals were 'solved' with tbl, and it is by no means clear whether they were chosen to clarify the power of tbl, or even whether other, more tricky tables were omitted as being outside its power. We don't really have any idea what compromises were made. Therefore one or two extra examples are included, which illustrate some particular point.

No rules

Firstly, a table without any rules at all (Figure 14.1). It is a fairly simple two-column table with a left-justified textual column followed by a right-justified numeric column – almost. There are subdivisions which are offset to the left by about a quad (the amount hardly matters); and there are some numbers which are handled in a rather different manner.

In constructing the table, note that the alignment character is a category 4 character. That is to say, somewhere there exists in `plain` the statement
```
\catcode`\&=4
```
This may be useful to us later. The `\cr` is a primitive command. As Knuth notes 'it may be dangerous to redefine (it)'.

The nub of most tables is a specification line like:
```
\halign{#&#\cr
```
Looking first at the information and ignoring headings and subdivisions, we can tackle the table as:
```
\halign{#&#\cr
Tube & 244 \cr
Sub-surface & 66 \cr
Surface & 156 \cr
}
```
What this chiefly omits is the information describing the position of the elements with cells. The way that tables 'work' is to process all the entries in all the rows, calculating the very widest cell in all rows: This information is then used in the spacing. This indicates one feature of tables: they can lead to TₑX running out of memory. All the information is effectively held in memory. Large tables can indeed be a problem. There are ways of circumventing this, but they really do start to make TₑX complicated. In the case of this table, the left column is left justified, and the right is right justified:
```
\halign{#\hfil&\hfil#\cr
Tube        & 244\cr
Sub-surface & 66\cr
Surface     & 156\cr
}
```

Some London Transport Statistics
(Year 1964)

Railway route miles	
Tube	244
Sub-surface	66
Surface	156
Passenger Traffic – railway	
Journeys	674 million
Average length	4.55 miles
Passenger miles	3,066 million
Passenger Traffic – road	
Journeys	2,252 million
Average length	2.26 miles
Passenger miles	5,094 million
Vehicles	12,521
Railway motor cars	2,905
Railway trailer cars	1,269
Total railway	4,174
Omnibuses	8,347
Staff	73,739
Administrative, etc.	5,582
Civil engineering	5,134
Electrical eng.	1,714
Mech. eng. – railway	4,310
Mech. eng. – road	9,152
Railway operations	8,930
Road operations	35,946
Other	2,971

Figure 14.1
A simple table without rules (from Lesk, 1979)

By now this is pretty close to what we want. But this says nothing about the spacing between the columns. On the face of it, it is conceivable that a row could consist of two columns which abut straight into one another (if we had the worst case event of both widest cells occurring on the one row). In fact, TeX puts 'tabskip glue' between columns. By default the tabskip glue is zero. Unfortunately, merely stating `\tabskip=1em` does not automatically separate the columns by extra white space. But the 'simplest' way to achieve this is

```
\halign{#\hfil&\quad\hfil#\cr
Tube          & 244\cr
Sub-surface & 66\cr
Surface       & 156\cr
}
```

In other words, manually insert the space.

What width is the table? The table will be its 'natural' width, just in the same way that a box takes its natural width (and depth and height). Where will it be on the page? It is just a box, and will be placed wherever it is you leave it. But even if it is a paragraph in its own right, it will not be indented by the current \parindent value.

Time to see what it looks like so far:

Tube   244
Sub-surface 66
Surface   156

Now we can start to solve some of the problems associated with this table: in particular, the cases which do not quite match the template. The numeric values which have an associated dimension 'hang' out into the right margin. There are a great number of ways that this can be handled. To some extent the one selected depends on just how you perceive the relationship between the ways these cells and the others are handled. Is the longest example cell centred with respect to the longest of the other cells in the column? Do the dimensions merely project 'beyond' the present right limit? Or put another way, is the way we have handled this column actually in error, and these 'long' entries are right justified, but the others, though right justified, are followed by a quad of space? This latter suggestion seems the simplest. How does it affect the template?

`\halign{#\hfil&\quad\hfil#\quad\cr`

Provided we can find some way of overriding the template for these particular cells, this may be a solution. Of course, there is a way of overriding: \omit. This command (which must be the first to appear in the contents of a cell entry) says 'omit the template information in this cell of the alignment'. You cannot easily be selective here. You omit it all, or obey it all. Having once omitted the information on how to treat the cell, you must provide cell-specific information for that particular entry.

```
\halign{#\hfil&\quad\hfil#\quad\cr
Journeys          &\omit\hfil 674 million\cr
Average length  &\omit\hfil 4.55 miles\cr
Passenger miles &\omit\hfil 3,066 million\cr
```

Since we are repeating the `\omit\hfil` it could be made into a
simple substitution command:

`\def\rt{\omit\hfil}`

Before we put this together, there is the matter of the subdivisions. Again, there are several ways these can be handled.
If we treat them as 'genuine' row entries we could again redefine
the template:

`\halign{\quad#\hfil&\quad\hfil#\quad\cr`

and this time `\omit` before these headings:

`\halign{\quad#\hfil&\quad\hfil#\quad\cr`
`\omit Railway route miles \hfil&\cr`

An alternative to the `\omit` approach is to use `\noalign`. After
a `\cr`, that is once a row is terminated, non-aligned material may
be included. This is particularly useful for adding white space,
and one solution here could have been

`\halign{\quad#\hfil&\quad\hfil#\quad\cr`
`\noalign{\smallskip}`
`\noalign{Railway route miles}`

Again, the solution chosen depends on how you perceive the relationship between the elements. In the example, there seem to be
three main groups (Railway route miles; Passenger Traffic; Vehi-
cles and Staff), with one group, Passenger Traffic, divided into
two subgroups – railway and road. Putting all these bits together,
we obtain:

```
\def\rt{\omit\hfil}
\halign{#\hfil&\quad\hfil#\quad\cr
\noalign{\smallskip}
\noalign{Railway route miles}
Tube        & 244\cr
Sub-surface & 66\cr
Surface     & 156\cr
\noalign{\smallskip}
\noalign{Passenger Traffic -- railway}
Journeys         &\rt 674 million\cr
Average length   &\rt 4.55 miles\cr
Passenger miles &\rt 3,066 million\cr
}
```

Lastly, the overall title to the table may be specified as a row or
rows, or may just be external to the alignment. My own preference
is often to include the title as a part of the table: this allows the
introduction of another variation. The title spans two columns.
In order to do this we may `\multispan`. This command takes a

numeric argument which says just how many columns to span. In fact, `\multispan1` and `\omit` are functionally equivalent. A `\multispan` is an `\omit\span`. At any point, `\span` may be used in place of an `&`, and the two adjacent cells will be merged, obeying whatever template rules happen to be in force. (But in the template or preamble, `\span` means something slightly different: it means 'expand' the next token.)

```
\halign{#\hfil&\quad\hfil#\quad\cr
\multispan2\hfil Some London Transport Statistics
                                       \hfil\cr
\multispan2\hfil \it (Year 1964) \hfil\cr
```

Note again that the `\it` operates only within its group, where the group is defined in a table as being bounded by `&` and/or `\cr`.

So there we have it.

⇒*Exercise 14.3:*   Put all these pieces together to create the table. ⇐
⇒*Exercise 14.4:*   Tackle this table through `\settabs`.   ⇐

The basic template for this table,

```
\halign{\quad#\hfil&\quad\hfil#\quad\cr
```

is rather inflexible. We have automatically fixed the width of the rows. Recall the `\tabskip` glue which may be placed between the columns. Actually it is also placed before the first column and after the last one. Since it is usually zero, it won't be noticed. When a positive value of `\tabskip` is present, *and* when the `\halign` is adjusted in some way, so that the row widths are made greater than their 'natural' widths, then we can adjust the distance between columns in a more dynamic way.

```
\tabskip 0.5em plus 0.25em minus 0.25em
\halign to \hsize{\quad#\hfil&\quad\hfil#\quad\cr
```

The rows will now be made longer by inserting the specified glue before and after each row, and also between each cell. If the 'new' size fails to reach the `\hsize`, underfull boxes will be generated, while if it exceeds the `\hsize` we get overfull boxes; but you won't get an overfull rule message in the log file and a blob in the margin. Perhaps a nicer solution would be something like

```
\halign to 0.9\hsize{%
           \tabskip 0.5em plus 0.25em minus 0.25em
#\hfil&\quad\hfil#\quad\cr
```

which could then be centred easily, or

```
\tabskip 0.5em plus 0.25em minus 0.25em
\halign spread 1em{\quad#\hfil&\quad\hfil#\quad\cr
```

which is 'spread' 1 em more than its 'natural width'. The glue is flexible enough to do this here.

The tabskip glue can be changed between entries in the template. The tabskip glue which is in force when the { after the \halign is encountered is used before the first cell; then the tabskip glue which is in force before the next & is used to separate the columns, and so on, until the \cr is reached.

```
\tabskip 0em % default
\halign spread1em{\tabskip1em plus 0.25em minus 0.25em
\quad #\hfil&\tabskip0em\quad\hfil#\quad\cr
```

This has the effect of placing the tabskip glue between the two columns, but making the glue zero at the beginning and end of each row.

⇒*Exercise 14.5:*   Change your table to use tabskip glue. And centre it horizontally on the page.   ⇐

We should be watching the use of space carefully. Provided the entries in the table are handled consistently, few problems arise. Recall that

```
Tube & 244 \cr  and  Tube&244\cr
```

yield rather different results. The spaces preceding the entry are ignored, but any after are indeed treated as 'space'. Therefore the width of the 244 as passed into the table is different (by the width of a space in that font). Similarly the width of Tube is different in this example. My own preference is to include spaces in order to line up the cells making them easier to read on input, but more important, to try to be consistent. But the space is also taken into consideration when the width of the fields is calculated. This may lead to ill-balanced output, or it may be unnoticeable to all but the most fanatic. One possible, though rather dangerous, alternative is to redefine the space for the duration of the table:

```
\catcode'\ =9
```

This redefines the space character to category code 9: in other words, the particular character is ignored.

⇒*Exercise 14.6:*   Why is this dangerous?   ⇐

There is a side issue of where to place the table. Recall that TeX supports two main insertion mechanisms, \topinsert and \midinsert. These are invoked by

```
\topinsert
 lots of stuff
\endinsert
```

and they will try to place the material at the top of the page on which the insert 'occurs' (or a following page if there is no room). The \midinsert works in a similar way, but places material somewhere on its 'reference' page, between paragraphs. One of the features of these inserts is that any definitions (or modifications to tabskip glue) will be local to the insert. There is no bottom insert.

⇒*Exercise 14.7:*   Why is there no apparent bottom insert?   ⇐

Maths

Since TEX is well known for its mathematical abilities, we should demonstrate fairly quickly that we can easily incorporate mathematics into a table (Figure 14.2).

There is not a great deal new here, except to note that the notion of the template is extended slightly. The preamble runs

`\halign{#\hfil&$\displaystyle{#}$\hfil\cr`

so that the equations are all set in maths mode display style. It is therefore unnecessary to repeat these instructions in each entry. This can often simplify matters, but the column title 'Definition' should not be set in maths display style. An `\omit` will solve that problem. There is one other thing to consider. The spacing between rows is too small by default. TEX puts the normal interline glue between the entries. There are a number of ways to increase the space between rows. We have already seen the use of `\noalign`. This is perhaps the easiest way. To remove the need to put

`\noalign{\smallskip}`

between each line, it is easier to do something like

`\def\crex{\cr\noalign{\smallskip}}`

and to terminate each row with this control sequence instead of `\cr`. There is a better solution in this circumstance, though, through the use of `\everycr`:

`\everycr{\noalign{\smallskip}}`

Whenever `\cr` is used, the token string `\noalign{\smallskip}` will be appended. This is probably the most elegant solution here.

⇒*Exercise 14.8:*   Despite the suggestion of using `\everycr`, another alternative is to use `\openup`. Implement this. You will have to 'guess' a suitable value. Recall that you do not have to use `\jot`.   ⇐

The original of this table was enclosed in a ruled box. It would not have been difficult to introduce horizontal and vertical rules at this point. Rules are the subject of the next chapter. There is an easier way to put things in a ruled box. Knuth gives a little command, `\boxit`, to do just this (note that we have already defined a command very similar to this, with a similar name):

`\def\boxit#1{\vbox{\hrule\hbox{\vrule\kern3pt`
`  \vbox{\kern3pt#1\kern3pt}\kern3pt\vrule}\hrule}}`

In fact, the original was enclosed in two ruled boxes, so we may just

Name	Definition
Gamma	$\Gamma(z) = \int_0^\infty i^{z-1} e^{-i}\, dt$
Sine	$\sin(x) = \dfrac{1}{2i}(e^{ix} - e^{-ix})$
Error	$\mathrm{erf}(z) = \dfrac{2}{\sqrt{\pi}} \int_0^z e^{-i^2}\, dt$
Bessel	$J_0(z) = \dfrac{1}{\pi} \int_0^\pi \cos(z \sin \theta)\, d\theta$
Zeta	$\zeta(s) = \sum_{k=1}^{\infty} k^{-\zeta} \quad (\mathrm{Re}\ s > 1)$

Figure 14.2
Mathematics
displayed in
tables (from
Lesk, 1979)

```
\boxit{\boxit{%
\halign{rest of table}
}}
```

⇒*Exercise 14.9:* Centre and box this last example. ⇐

Diagrammatically

Although we shall consider diagrams later, it is worth pointing out that `\halign` may provide the possibility of creating some sorts of diagrammatic layouts. The structure of Figure 14.3 is quite straightforward, although the manipulation of the arrows and text is not immediately obvious. The left-hand entry, WEAVE↙, was

`\llap{$\vcenter{\hbox{\tt WEAVE}}$}$\swarrow$`

demonstrating, among other things, the first serious use of `\vcenter`. The `\llap` ensures that the text is considered to have no width, so that when it comes to placing that entry, it is only the width of the arrow which is taken into account. In this way the entries balance.

WEB document
WEAVE↙   ↘TANGLE
Pascal source   TₑX document

Figure 14.3
Tables or
diagrams?

⇒*Exercise 14.10:* Recreate this diagram. ⇐

Rules 15

But there is something fairly important missing. What about the rules? We normally expect tables to be boxed in. This we can do, but the alignments tend to get even more hidden in the welter of extra detail.

The use of the horizontal rule to divide some rows is still quite common, but vertical rules are now infrequently found. A curious inversion of reality has occurred. The latest edition of the *Chicago Manual of Style* says

> One style that has changed since the last edition of this manual was published is the use of vertical rules in tabular matter. In line with a nearly universal trend among scholarly and commercial publishers, the University of Chicago Press has given up vertical rules as a standard feature of tables in the books and journals that it publishes. The handwork necessitated by including vertical rules is costly no matter what mode of composition is used, and in the Press's view the expense of it can no longer be justified by the additional refinement it brings.

From this quotation it is clear that the loss of the vertical rule is on economic rather than aesthetic grounds. But TeX allows us vertical rules at no great additional cost. Now we will start to include them.

As usual, there are many ways to tackle a problem like this. Choosing the optimum really depends on many factors. Although we present tables here as 'one-off' operations, in many cases they are really repetitive, so that the templates or preambles developed are used in a number of situations, where the headings and various other 'stubs' remain fairly constant (or consistent), and only the cell entries change from table to table, report to report, year to year. In such cases, the effort put into developing the preamble starts to show dividends. There can be no doubt that getting everything right is not trivial, and very few manage to get everything approximately right first time.

A simple ruled example

One of the first differences to be noted in the input for this first ruled table (Figure 15.1) is that the vertical rules are treated as if they belonged to their own cells – a cell which contains *only* a vertical rule. Perhaps the other point to be made is that we build the vertical rules one row at a time. A single vertical rule may be made up of many row-high components. It is indeed possible to put the rules in as single longer lines, but it then becomes necessary to know exactly where to put them, and if there is glue in the table, it all starts to get very difficult. So we'll tackle things an 'easier' way. An advantage of treating the vertical rules on a row by row basis is that it becomes possible to include or omit them as required. In general, the horizontal rules span the whole table, separating some rows. They are usually handled as single horizontal rules.

To begin with, the tabskip glue will be omitted from the preamble, since it initially obscures the simplicity of the design:

```
\halign to\hsize{%
\strut\vrule#&#\hfil&
\vrule#&\hfil#&
\vrule#&\hfil#&
\vrule#&\hfil$#$&
\vrule#\cr
```

It is perhaps worth noting why the preamble is laid out the way it is. Firstly, the % at the end of the \halign line is placed there to ensure that no extra space is absorbed. The 'phrase' ␣\strut\vrule is one space wider than the phrase \strut\vrule. In very general terms it is worth terminating every line in a preamble with a %. Often they are not necessary, but few things are more frustrating than to have extra space in the middle of a table. Eliminating it afterwards can take a great deal of time and effort. Taking prophylactic action as you go along ('safe TEX') can avoid tears. On the other hand, the & characters are like commands, which tend to gobble up space after themselves, and we do not actually need to put a % at the end of their lines. Equally, there is nothing to stop you doing so; it won't hurt. The only real danger of littering your preambles (and commands) with % symbols are editors which wrap automatically. From time to time a little editing leads them to rewrap your preamble text, with the result that the %-ending lines are combined into the rest of the text, with rather frustrating results.

1970 Federal Budget Transfers (in billions of dollars)			
State	Taxes collected	Money spent	Net
New York	22.91	21.35	−1.56
New Jersey	8.33	6.96	−1.37
Connecticut	4.12	3.10	−1.02
Maine	0.74	0.67	−0.07
California	22.29	22.42	+0.13
New Mexico	0.70	1.49	+0.79
Georgia	3.30	4.28	+0.98
Mississippi	1.15	2.32	+1.17
Texas	9.33	11.13	+1.80

Figure 15.1
A ruled table
(from Lesk,
1979)

What does this preamble mean? For example, what is the
\strut? A \strut is defined as a type of vertical rule. In plain
TEX the definition is a little sly, but what it boils down to is
\vrule height8.5pt depth3.5pt width0pt
In other words, an invisible vertical line 12 points in length. What
use can that be? Before the preamble started the interline skip
was switched off with the command
\offinterlineskip
As it suggests, this turns off the normal interline skip. This is
done to ensure that the distance between each line in the table
is constant – or to be more precise, is zero; the glue is still there,
it is just zero. It is worth pointing out that to switch the normal
interline skip back on, the command is
\normalbaselines
There is a further way of switching off the line skip – the command
\nointerlineskip
This is really intended as a one-off command to suppress the
normal interline glue between two boxes in vertical mode.

This still does not quite explain all the fuss. We have to go back
to TEX's model of box building. Recall that the vertical extent of
a box is made up of a height and a depth. The depth effectively
takes into account the descenders. A box made up of words with
no descenders may have no depth. Similarly, the 'height' of a box
is affected by the ascenders. The boxes surrounding sea, seal, and
squeal are each of different vertical extent. In a table, with the
interline skip switched off, we merely butt the boxes immediately
against one another, so that the boxes containing sea and swan

will appear much closer together than `squall` and `squeal`. The ascenders and descenders in the last two have the effect of keeping the 'words' further apart, although in reality the boxes are just the same distance apart. Therefore we insert an artificial 'strut' or divider to ensure that the baselines are actually kept the same distance apart. This is where it becomes important to bear in mind the definition of `\strut`. If you change font (or typeface), it may be best to alter the definition of `\strut`, or to introduce another sort of strut with different characteristics. If it helps, you will find that the ((the parenthesis symbol) in Computer Modern Roman just happens to have a height of 8.5 pt and a depth of 3.5 pt. This was a deliberate artefact by Knuth. It is consistent for all other CM fonts. It means that if you change to `cmr7` you can reconstruct an appropriate strut by boxing the (and finding its height and depth. This relationship is not guaranteed for non-CM typefaces.

The strut is therefore only there to ensure even spacing. If we ignore it in the template for the meantime, the design looks even simpler:

```
\halign to\hsize{%
\vrule#&#\hfil&
\vrule#&\hfil#&
\vrule#&\hfil#&
\vrule#&\hfil$#$&
\vrule#\cr
```

If the first 'real' column had been right justified too, it would have looked even more repetitive. One of the columns which holds numbers has been given a maths mode template, just to ensure that the minus signs come out looking good. Two of the lines in the template are identical. Is there no shorthand way of saying 'two identical blocks of template', or better still, 'n identical blocks'? Yes there is, but it does not help us here, since the shorthand is rather more restrictive. If an extra `&` is inserted before any template, that block of template between the following `&` and the `\cr` will be repeated indefinitely until the actual information in the table is exhausted. If therefore we truly do have a repeated segment, it becomes easy to simplify the template. However, in this case we do not wish the template to be repeated indefinitely. There are some repeated elements, but they are followed by some slightly different material. With some manipulation, we could use repetition:

```
\halign to\hsize{%
\vrule#&#\hfil&
\vrule#&\hfil#&
\vrule#&\hfil#&
\vrule#&\hfil$#$&
\vrule#\cr
\cr
```
could easily be reorganized to
```
\halign to\hsize{\vrule#%
&#\hfil&\vrule#%
&\hfil#&\vrule#%
&\hfil#&\vrule#%
&\hfil$#$&\vrule#%
\cr
```
which could be expressed
```
\halign to\hsize{\vrule#%
&#\hfil&\vrule#%
&&\hfil$#$&\vrule#%
\cr
```
After all, it does not matter whether the two other numeric columns are handled in maths mode or not. In this case we can indeed exploit the repeated structure. Often, though, the last column is treated in a different way, and this technique is inadequate. To begin with it is often easier and clearer to specify each element of the template explicitly.

Once we have accepted that the vertical rules can exist in their own columns, and we also accept that the interline skip is switched off, relying on the \strut to separate lines, the rest of the table starts to fall out.

The body of the table will be of the form:
```
&New York&&22.91&&21.35&&-1.56&\cr
&New Jersey&&8.33&&6.96&&-1.37&\cr
&Connecticut&&4.12&&3.10&&-1.02&\cr
```
Although the separators && look rather untidy, a way of simplifying this and making it look 'nicer' will be introduced later. This merely leaves a couple of items to be considered. Firstly, the \multispans, which we have met already anyway. This time we have to recall that we are spanning extra columns (the ones with the vertical bars in too). People often make mistakes in just adding up the number of columns. If you span too few you will usually still get a table, which looks oddly incomplete, but if you span too many, the error message looks like:

```
! Extra alignment tab has been changed to \cr.
```
and often you can just continue and something will appear. Of
course, if you have used the **&&** feature in the template, it is difficult to span too many, since TEX dutifully provides them. But
sometimes the error just compounds and you have to exit and
edit the table. Since tables can be a little tricky until you master
them, it is often worth while tackling them individually and using
the **\input** command to include them in your text later. Tables
are often rather slow in execution, since TEX has to do quite a lot
of work. There is therefore some point in isolating tables and text
and only combining them when you are reasonably confident that
you are close to a final draft.

Headings

The second point, which now constitutes 'new' information, is the
way some of the headings are handled. The width of the individual
numeric columns should really be determined by the information
in the columns, and not by the headings to the columns. We need
some way of telling TEX to ignore the width of those particular
pieces of information. This can be done with **\hidewidth**. This
command has some peculiarities. As Knuth notes, it is equivalent
to
```
\hskip-1000pt plus 1fill
```
If you precede an entry by **\hidewidth**, the entry will be left justified within its box, and if you follow an entry with **\hidewidth**
it will be right justified. In ordinary text **\hidewidth** gives rather
odd, but perhaps not unexpected, results. Putting **\hidewidth**
both before and after has the effect of making TEX ignore the
width of that entry in calculating the column width. (To be a little more accurate, the entry has a very negative width, and thus
never enters into the calculation). The expression used here for
the two lines involved was
```
&\omit\hfil State\hfil&
&\omit\hidewidth Taxes\hidewidth&
&\omit\hidewidth Money\hidewidth&
&\omit\hidewidth Net\hidewidth&\cr
&&&\omit\hidewidth collected\hidewidth&
&\omit\hidewidth spent\hidewidth&
&&\cr
```
The alert will perhaps notice a potential problem. What hap-
pens if the width of the numeric fields is less than that of these

particular stubs? The answer should be intuitive. Murphy's Law continues to hold.

It might also be worth while defining a command \hide
\def\hide#1{\hidewidth#1\hidewidth}
which would make this last extract look a little tidier and perhaps easier to understand.

Between the columns

This starts to approach the last major element of this table, the \tabskip. Although we have tackled \tabskip already, when we start to use it with vertical rules and with \hidewidth it requires a more precise understanding. The relevant pages in *The TEXbook* are 243 and 245. The key is the way in which the tabskip is distributed.

It may be simpler to take this in two parts: the tabskip is a skip quantity, comprising a 'fixed' amount and the glue which is permitted. Provided the alignment is allowed to be set at its 'natural' width, it will be the fixed amount which is used. Only when we align to a particular amount, or spread by an extra amount, is the glue called into play. This provides us with two slightly different problems.

Tackling the easier one first, where the alignment is set to its natural width, it is fairly obvious to see that
\tabskip 1em plus 2em
at least ensures a minimum of 1 em between entries, while
\tabskip 0em plus 3em
will not separate the columns at all. So it seems obvious always to use a tabskip amount which was positive, ensuring column separation. Unfortunately, that is not quite the case. There is a little bit more to tabskip: it needs to be switched off and on. Remember the rule: the tabskip in effect when the { after the \halign is read is placed *before* the first column; the tabskip glue in effect when the & after the first template is read is used *between* the columns; and the tabskip glue in effect when the \cr is read is used *after* the last column: and, equally important, although the individual alignments act as groups, tabskips are exempt from this rule – there is no tabskip glue grouping *within* template elements. The main point is that some glue goes before, some goes between, and some goes after, depending on where we are. We end up having to switch it on and off. In a practical example this translates to something like

```
\tabskip0em    \halign{%
\strut\vrule#\tabskip1em \relax&#\hfil&\vrule
#&\hfil#&\vrule
#&\hfil#&\vrule
#&\hfil$#$&\vrule
#\tabskip0em\cr
```

The initial `\tabskip0em` is redundant, since it is the default, but
it is here for clarity. After the first entry is dealt with, the one
which creates the leftmost vertical rule, the tabskip is set to the
value of 1 em, and retains that value until the last entry is read,
where it is reset to 0 em; then the alignment is ended. In this way,
no skip precedes the first rule, nor follows the last one, although
skips are placed between the remaining entries. If there were no
vertical rules the problem would not be so glaringly apparent.
This also helps to demonstrate why it is often difficult to use the
template repetition feature effectively, when the final entry in the
template has to be treated differently.

So far this seems straightforward, but a complication can arise
when we have a situation where there are spanned columns, and
the width of those spanned columns may exceed the 'natural'
width of the other rows. In this case the tabskip glue may be
accumulated in the last entry of those spanned, leading to a rather
uneven separation between columns, although we appear to have
taken great pains to ensure that there will be adequate separation – instead of being distributed evenly between all spanned
columns, the excess may be placed in the last of those columns. In
the example that is currently being used, turning the first heading
into '1970 Federal Budget Transfers (in billions of dollars)' would
make this entry considerably in excess of the width of the bulk of
the table, and could lead to this:

1970 Federal Budget Transfers (in billions of dollars)			
State	Taxes collected	Money spent	Net
New York	22.91	21.35	−1.56

The critical line in this is

```
&\multispan7\hfil 1970 Federal Budget Transfers
 (in billions of dollars)\hfil&\cr
```

The long entry is spanned over seven columns. When T*E*X cal-
culates the width of the eighth column (that is, the last of the
spanned columns), what it does first is to take the width of the
spanned entry, together with the skip which precedes and follows

that entry – 1 em either side in this case; then each of the other six columns are set to their own width, with their appropriate skips; the difference between these two values is the width of the remaining column in this part of the table – if the width calculated here would be less than the width obtained by the entry and its skips, this would have been used. It seems a little convoluted, but basically all that is happening is that, given the constraints that have been placed implicitly, TEX has to put the space somewhere, and the somewhere is the last available place. Perhaps the intuitive response is to expect that the glue portions would be employed, but unfortunately this is not the case.

The 'easy' way out of this is to hide the width of the spanning entries, but this may lead to the spanning entries being larger than the rest of the table. An alternative is to ensure that the tabskip is big enough. Both of these solutions demand that you have a very clear notion of what is going on in the particular table.

The alignment preamble actually used was

```
\tabskip 0in\hsize0.75\hsize
\offinterlineskip  \halign to\hsize{%
\strut\vrule#\tabskip1in plus1in minus1in&#\hfil&\vrule
#&\hfil#&\vrule
#&\hfil#&\vrule
#&\hfil$#$&\vrule
#\tabskip0in\cr
```

The initial `\tabskip 0in` is not strictly required, since it is a default, but it makes things a little clearer here. Before the first column, and after the last one, the tabskip glue is zero. For the remainder of the table it is set to have some flexibility (probably a little too much). This also helps to illustrate why I did not want to use the `&&` repetition form. It would have prevented me from resetting the tabskip glue after the last column. Why am I so bothered about this? Let's use just one value for the glue throughout the table – the flexible one – and see what happens:

```
\tabskip1in plus1in minus1in\hsize0.75\hsize
\offinterlineskip   \halign to\hsize{%
\strut\vrule#&#\hfil&\vrule
#&\hfil#&\vrule
#&\hfil#&\vrule
#&\hfil$#$&\vrule
#\cr
```

This would have given us the table in Figure 15.2. The problem revolves around the way in which the horizontal rule is specified.

It is given as a

```
\noalign{\hrule}
```

which has the effect of placing the rule across the entire `\hsize`
permitted. This width includes the tabskip glue placed before and
after the first and last entries. At some point we will have to look
at ways of spanning only some of the horizontal cells.

There is one other thing we should have done. In the original,
the stubs containing 'State' and 'Net' are in fact centred vertically. Tackling this turns out to be sufficiently clumsy as to be
worth treating later too.

⇒*Exercise 15.1:*   Quite a lot has been covered here. Show your understanding of what you have learned by creating a version of this table. If
you are satisfied with your attempt, modify the way that you handle the
`\tabskip` glue, and create a table which is spread by an extra 50 pt. ⇐

Sometimes it seems far easier to work without tabskip glue,
and to specify each element more or less exactly. Let us see how
that might be done with the last example. Again, the nub is the
preamble, which can be expressed as

```
\halign{\vrule\strut\quad#\quad\hfil\vrule&&
\quad\hfil$#$\quad\vrule\cr
```

This time it is straightforward to reap the benefit of the repetition.

It is worth asking what the relative advantages and disadvan-
tages of these two approaches are – with and without tabskip
glue. It has always seemed to me that the tabskip glue is rather
fiddly and gets stuck to the most unlikely objects. But the second
approach is very rigid. If we do have the situation where tables
should be a particular width, then setting up an

```
\halign to0.9\hsize
```

really does demand that some flexibility is built into the table to
satisfy this demand. Of course, eliminating the tabskip glue does
make the template so much easier.

One way of tackling the `&&`s in this table and making them
look a little less awkward is to arrange for TeX to use a different
character which is then expanded to the pair of alignment tabs.
A rather obvious candidate is the vertical bar. If this is made an
active character (just like the ~), it can then be defined as the
double alignment tab:

```
\catcode'\|=13
\def|{&&}
```

and then the table can be constructed with vertical bars in place
of the `&&` characters.

⇒*Exercise 15.2:*   In true pedagogic style, adding all the extra items

1970 Federal Budget Transfers (in billions of dollars)			
State	Taxes collected	Money spent	Net
New York	22.91	21.35	−1.56
New Jersey	8.33	6.96	−1.37
Connecticut	4.12	3.10	−1.02
Maine	0.74	0.67	−0.07
California	22.29	22.42	+0.13
New Mexico	0.70	1.49	+0.79
Georgia	3.30	4.28	+0.98
Mississippi	1.15	2.32	+1.17
Texas	9.33	11.13	+1.80

Figure 15.2
Not what was
wanted

which turn the last preamble into a 'real' example is left as an exercise.
If this sounds too trivial, change the 'table' part of the input so that it
could accept either tabs or vertical bars as the column dividers.   ⇐

Vertical spans: Composition of Foods

We have already fudged the major issue of this table by ignoring
it in a previous table – namely material which spans several rows
vertically. Often we can 'get away' with ignoring the problem, but
clearly that is unethical. In Figure 15.3 the interest lies in the
stubs rather than the body of the table. How do we make Food,
Protein, and Fat straddle several rows vertically? This is only one
solution, and its lack of generality makes me hesitate to show it.
Still, it demonstrates lots of other things too. The preamble is still
unspectacular
```
\halign{\vrule\strut\quad#\hfil\quad\vrule
&&\quad\hfil#\quad\vrule\cr
```
The table is to be handled 'as normal'. The 'tricky bits' look like:
```
\omit\vrule\hfil\vspan3{Food}\hfil\vrule&
    \multispan3\hfil Percent by Weight\hfil\vrule\cr
\omit\vrule\hfil\vrule&\multispan3\hrulefill\cr
&\omit\hfil\vspan2{Protein}\hfil\vrule&
    \omit\hfil\vspan2{Fat}\hfil\vrule&
        \omit\hfil Carbo-\hfil\vrule\cr
&&&\omit\hfil hydrate\hfil\vrule\cr
```
The new features are the \vspan commands. These are somewhat
analogous to the \multispans. Now these are not plain commands, but have been defined for this example. The idea here is

that the contents of the vertical span are spread over n rows. The way it was chosen to do this was as follows:
```
\def\vspan#1#2{\parindent0pt\setbox0
\vbox to#1\normalbaselineskip
    {\null\vfill#2\vfill\null}%
    \ht0\ht\strutbox
    \dp0\dp\strutbox
    \setbox1\hbox{#2}\wd0\wd1\box0}
```
There is quite a bit of footwork going on in here, so let's take it fairly slowly. The principal feature is that the material to do the vertical spanning is placed in a box at the beginning of the command; its dimensions are manipulated; and then it is output. What could be simpler? The vertical box in which the text occurs spans n rows: this is specified through the `#1\normalbase-lineskip`. The material is 'floated' to the middle of that box by the `\vfill` commands. However, if we left things as they are, the box would have very unfriendly dimensions. Its width would be the width of `\hsize`, for example. In order to find its 'real' width, the text is `\hbox`ed, and the width of the enclosing `\hbox` is assigned to the width of the vertical box. TₑX doesn't mind us cheating shamelessly like this. If we left the vertical box with the vertical extent based on the `to#1\normalbaselineskip`, when it came to be placed in a cell in the table it would really be that height and depth. So we have to reset its height and depth to something a little more reasonable. The values chosen here are the height and depth of `\strutbox`. Where did `\strutbox` come from? Recall the `\strut`; part of its definition involves a `\strut-box`, which is created as a vertical rule with a height of 8.5 pt and a depth of 3.5 pt. Why don't we just use those values? Well, that loses a bit of generality. So far, the command has no specific 'hard-wired' dimensions. Should we want to change the typefaces in the table (say, replace the `cmr10` with `cmr12`) then we should really have to change any hard-wired values. If we do the type size change properly, it should involve resetting the baselines and the `\strutbox`, among other things. We would be insulated from such changes. Another example of 'safe TₑX'.

The use of `\hrulefill` to obtain a partial horizontal line is examined more fully in the next chapter.

$\Rightarrow$*Exercise 15.3:*   The rest of the table is dull. Put the pieces together and reproduce the table. Then return to Figure 15.1 and make the stubs for 'State' and 'Net' be centred vertically as they ought to have been. $\Leftarrow$

Composition of Foods			
	Percent by Weight		
Food	Protein	Fat	Carbo-hydrate
Apples	.4	.5	13.0
Halibut	18.4	5.2	...
Lima beans	7.5	.8	22.0
Milk	3.3	4.0	5.0
Mushrooms	3.5	.4	6.0
Rye bread	9.0	.6	52.7

Figure 15.3
Vertical spans
(from Lesk,
1979)

Thick rules

The last example given here (Figure 15.4) uses \vrule in a new way. Whenever a \vrule appears in a preamble, it can be used to modify the thickness of the vertical line. Just as
\noalign{\hrule height0.5pt depth0.5pt}
would give us a thicker horizontal line than the default, the contents of the cell passed through to the preamble can also contain width information. Consider the following preamble:
\halign{\vrule#\vrule\cr
When the information passed through is
width 1pt
we would obtain a vertical rule of that width for the left-hand rule. The right-hand rule would be unmodified. This starts to illustrate just why the \vrules are often assigned their own columns. It becomes much easier to control them. This example merely mentions the possibility of widening the rules. We could also change their height and/or depth. There is no \strut in the previous alignment preamble. The \vrule therefore 'stretches' to the height and depth of any other information present. We can influence that by providing height and depth information:
height 10pt depth 5pt
will ensure that we have a vertical rule of those dimensions.

One of the commonest uses of this strategy is where there are horizontal rules which vary in thickness across the table. The first line which spans the entire table was created by
\multispan2\hfil\vrule&
    \multispan6\thickrulefill&
        \omit\vrulethick\cr
The vertical rules all have their own cells in the preamble. The \thickrulefill is simply an \hrulefill (stolen from Chap-

Figure 15.4
Enthalpy of
evaporation for
chlorine (from
Angus *et al.*,
1985)

	Estreicher and Schnerr	Giauque and Powell	Equation of State
$\Delta H/\mathrm{Jmol}^{-1}$	18292	20406 ± 17	20427
T/K	237.3	239.10 ± 0.05	239.166

ter 16) made thicker by increasing its height:
```
\def\thickrulefill{%
    \leaders\hrule height0.8ptdepth0.0pt\relax\hfill}
```
The `\relax` is there just in case by accident the next word happens to be 'width'. TeX would then get rather confused and expect a number followed by a dimension.

The preamble needs to be considered before these details make much sense. The degree of apparent repetition is high. It can be exploited quite neatly if we repeat two elements:
```
\halign{&\vrule#&\bigstrut\ctr{#}\cr
```
The reason the rule is not included is mainly because we want to exploit the ability to vary the thickness of the rule by passing through an argument like `width0.8pt` when it is required.

Some effort was expended in this example to ensure that the thicker elements 'bounded' the table. This helps to explain the way the second line is expressed:
```
\multispan2\hfil\vrule&& Estreicher&& Giauque and&&
                    Equation of&width0.8pt\cr
```
and although that first rule appears thick, it actually makes up two adjacent default vertical rules: one is explicit, the other is obtained from the alignment preamble. Since the thickness of the thick rules is 0.8 pt, two default rules of 0.4 pt gives the same thickness.

The horizontal line is by far the most complex of all, since it varies in thickness:
```
\multispan2\thickrulefill
    &\multispan2\vrule\hrulefill
        &\multispan2\vrule\hrulefill
            &\multispan2\vrule\hrulefill
                &width0.8pt\cr
```
The 'extra' `\vrules` are there because of the thick horizontal rule. If we omit them, little notches appear again.

$\Rightarrow$*Exercise 15.4:*   Create this table and omit the 'extra' `\vrules`. Can you discern the notches? $\Leftarrow$

$\Rightarrow$*Exercise 15.5:*   There are probably too many horizontal and vertical lines in the body of the table. While retaining the thick surrounding lines, and the thinner ones separating the 'stubs', try to eliminate those in the body of the table.   ⇐

⇒*Exercise 15.6:*   A slightly more logical way to portray this table may be to have the names of the sources (Estreicher etc.) down the left-hand side, while the quantities are across the top. In this way, the values could be aligned around their decimal points, or the rightmost significant digit. Make this modification.   ⇐

Further rules 16

Partial horizontal rules

The next example (Figure 16.1) is deceptively simple. What it introduces are two quite important topics. The 'lesser' is that it is relatively straightforward to align on a decimal point, simply by treating the integer part as one column and the fractional part (including the decimal) as another column. There are possible refinements on this so that the decimal point itself is always included, but this is inappropriate in this example.

	Stack
1	46
2	23
3	15
4	6.5
5	2.1

Figure 16.1
Partial
horizontal rules

The major feature this example introduces is how to manipulate horizontal rules so that they span only part of the table. The preamble is unspectacular

```
\halign{\small#\quad&\vrule\strut\enspace\hfil#&
                    #\hfil\enspace\vrule\cr
```

There are three elements to a row, to account for the \small number on the left and the two parts of the decimal number. The two columns containing the decimal number are 'surrounded' by vertical rules. If we were to use the 'old' technique of placing an \hrule between the rows, the rule would extend under the first column too. Perhaps the 'obvious' solution is to place an \hrule in a row:

```
&\hrule&\hrule\cr
```

Curiously, although this is not going to work, it can help to point out what will. The error message which is generated is

```
! You can't use '\hrule' here except with leaders.
```

and if that does not make sense, and you wish to pursue it, the extra information which TₑX will provide is

```
To put a horizontal rule in an hbox or an alignment,
you should use \leaders or \hrulefill
(see The TeXbook).
```

This is arguably the most accurate and helpful message which TₑX manages to provide.

Since the pattern is a repeated one in this example, it is possible to take a shortcut by defining

```
\def\partline{\omit&\multispan2\hrulefill\cr}
```

The important part is the `\hrulefill` which merely extends a horizontal rule over the required horizontal 'gap'. Just in case the definition of `\hrulefill` is not at your fingertips, it is worth having a brief look at leaders and fill.

There are a couple of 'fills' already available in plain TₑX. They are `\hrulefill` and `\dotfill`. Of these, the `\hrulefill` is the most interesting here:

```
\def\hrulefill{\leaders\hrule\hfill}
```

When used in a box (such as within a cell in a table), it works in the same way as an `\hfill`, except that the box is 'filled' with an `\hrule`, rather than blank space. Recall too that all the rules have default 'characteristics'. The default for an `\hrule` is a height of 0.4 pt and a depth of zero: its width is context sensitive. The `\vrule` has a width of 0.4 pt: both its height and depth are context sensitive. So far we have always accepted the default dimensions for rules.

⇒*Exercise 16.1:*   Solve the last example yourself, but with the additional finesse of making the lines 'within' the table thinner than those which surround the 'Stack' values.   ⇐

Ruling and filling

Horizontal and vertical rules which extend over an arbitrary, or implicitly specified, interval have been treated in a rather cursory manner. They have mostly been presented in circumstances where a simple `\hrule` or `\vrule` works without difficulty. The one major circumstance where this is not sufficient, in the last example, was rather sidestepped by reference to the help facility which TₑX has, and its suggestion of `\leaders`. It is time to look at this aspect in more detail.

The manipulation of rules is usually straightforward: to specify a horizontal or vertical rule completely, the height, width, and depth can be given. It will have been apparent that it is seldom necessary to specify the full form of a \vrule or \hrule. For example, in vertical mode, an \hrule would extend across the full page width (that is, the current \hsize). How is the width and depth determined? By default, the height will be 0.4 pt and the depth will be 0 pt. Similarly a \vrule, like the one used in producing the rules ·in an alignment, will also be 0.4 pt wide. Its height and depth are derived from the context. In creating ruled tables, the \vrule normally extends through the vertical extent of the row (especially if you have remembered to set \struts in the alignment preamble). The default of 0.4 pt is not accessible. If you want to change it, it must be done manually at the time.

In a general context, it may seem that the following ways of creating a rule 20 pt long (or wide) are equivalent:

```
\hbox to 20pt{\hrule}
\hrule width 20pt
```

but they are not. The first does not work at all. In order to place a rule in an explicit box, we have to use \hrulefill, not \hrule. In a sense, we are trying to put a form of glue in the box, one which expands to fill the space available. This is not glue, but 'leaders'. The definition of \hrulefill exploits the command \leaders:

```
\def\hrulefill{\leaders\hrule\hfill}
```

At the very least this gives us the opportunity to develop other definitions where the thickness of the embedded \hrule can be changed. For example,

```
\def\thickrulefill{\leaders\hrule height1pt
                               depth0.5pt\hfill}
```

In broader terms, leaders can be used in other ways. There are already a few commands in **plain** which do this. For example, \dotfill, which creates 'fill' of dots; and a few used in maths, \rightarrowfill, \leftarrowfill, which create right and left arrows in a similar way to an \hrulefill, and \upbracefill and \downbracefill, which form ⌣ and ⌢. There is a special restriction with these last two: they must be used either in vertical mode in an \hbox by themselves, or in an alignment.

Of these, the \dotfill requires some further comment. Its full definition is

```
\def\dotfill{\cleaders
 \hbox{$\m@th\mkern1.5mu.\mkern1.5mu$}\hfill}
```

This illustrates a new form of a leader, \cleaders, and a limitation. There are three different sorts of leader: \leaders, \cleaders, and \xleaders. The \cleaders is a 'centred' leader, the

\xleaders are 'expanded', and the \leaders are aligned. A relatively easy way to grasp the differences between these different leaders is to use them in three versions of \dotfill, but substituting the different forms of \leaders:

$$\left.\begin{array}{l} \text{Leading}\ldots\ldots\ldots\text{Lights} \\ \text{Before}\ldots\ldots\text{Your Eyes} \end{array}\right\} \texttt{\textbackslash cleaders}$$

$$\left.\begin{array}{l} \text{Leading}\ldots\ldots\ldots\text{Lights} \\ \text{Before}\ldots\ldots\text{Your Eyes} \end{array}\right\} \texttt{\textbackslash leaders}$$

$$\left.\begin{array}{l} \text{Leading}\ldots\ldots\ldots\text{Lights} \\ \text{Before}\ldots\ldots\text{Your Eyes} \end{array}\right\} \texttt{\textbackslash xleaders}$$

Perhaps the key feature to note is that the \leaders version aligns the dots between lines. In general, this is the form we require if we want to produce a table of contents. The basic notion is that each dot (in this case) is contained in a box, and the boxes placed, or packed, in line. The space that the boxes will occupy will seldom coincide exactly with some multiple of the box width. In other words, there is likely to be 'some' extra space. How that extra space is distributed is then determined by the choice of \xleaders or \cleaders. With \xleaders any extra space is distributed between the boxes; with \cleaders the extra space is distributed before the first and after the last. Thus \cleaders are the same distance apart, while \xleaders are unlikely to be. How then does \leaders distribute the 'extra' space? Unevenly. With \leaders, we see only a 'window'. The boxes are distributed across the 'whole' box, but only those which appear in the window between its left and right extent appear. In this way, the boxes (or their contents) line up.

⇒*Exercise 16.2:*   In Chapter 13, one of the examples used was the creation of a table of contents (based on *Moby Dick*). How would you create a line of dots between the individual chapter titles and their starting page numbers?   ⇐

Most of the applications of leaders are likely to be enclosed in other commands (like \hrulefill and \dotfill), and most times it will be a rule or dots which are used to spread across the space.

It was suggested that the standard definition of \dotfill contains an inherent limitation. What limitation? The dots of \dotfill are those found in the cmsy font. If we were preparing a table of contents in which the chapter or section titles were in (say) the bold font, we might reasonably argue that the dots ought also

New York Area Rocks		
Era	Formation	Age (years)
Precambrian	Reading Prong	> 1 billion
Paleozoic	Manhattan Prong	million
Mesozoic	Newark Basin, incl. Stockton, Lockatong, and Brunswick formations: also Watchungs and Palisades.	million
Cenozoic	Coastal Plain	On Long Island 30,000 years: Cretaceous sediments redeposited by Recent glaciation.

Figure 16.2
Included
paragraphs
(from Lesk,
1979)

to be in this font. What can we do to make the definition font
sensitive? A first estimate might be

```
\def\dotfill{\cleaders
  \hbox{\kern.833333pt.\kern.833333pt}\hfill}
```

but while this is more font sensitive, it is not completely so. The
figure for the \kern value is derived by knowing that 18 mu are
10 pt. Equally of course, 10 pt is 1 em, in the standard 10 pt text
font. The most general definition would be

```
\def\dotfill{\cleaders
  \hbox{\kern.0833333em.\kern.0833333em}\hfill}
```

⇒*Exercise 16.3:*   Create a \dotfill command which responds to
maths mode and the current font.   ⇐

Paragraphs: New York Area Rocks

One frequent requirement of tables is to incorporate some text,
but to permit that text to obey the 'normal' paragraphing rules
(Figure 16.2). The naive approach is to divide each line by hand,
but obviously this is not very attractive, since it depends on having
some feeling for where the lines should break. And after all, TEX
has a nice sophisticated line-breaking algorithm. Why not use it?

The only really new element in this example is the introduction of the \vtops. The \vtop is just a vertical box which will
(in loose terms) be aligned at its top, rather than its bottom.

The introduction of the \normalbaselines into the paragraphed material is obvious once seen (it is salutary to omit it sometimes). This gives us an alignment preamble of the form

```
\halign{\strut\vrule\enspace
  \vtop{\hsize0.75in#}%
  \enspace\vrule
&\enspace
  \vtop{\normalbaselines\hsize1.25in#\strut}%
  \enspace\vrule
&\enspace
  \vtop{\normalbaselines\hsize1.25in#\strut}%
  \enspace\vrule\cr
```

The use of tabskip glue has been avoided since it is necessary to specify a width for the boxes anyway – through the \hsize command. The \normalbaselines command has been included since in the full example the interline skip has already been switched off. If we were to proceed with creating a paragraph with the line skip switched off, we could end up with some odd spacing. Similarly, the inclusion of the \strut at the end of the 'argument' – the paragraph – is there just in case the last line has no characters with descenders. It might be wise to have one at the beginning as well, but since each entry has either a number or a capital letter, it probably is not strictly needed here. The truly cautious will probably want to insert one, though. There really is not a great deal more to say, except to note that the paragraphs are squeezed into a rather narrow measure. In these cases it is wise to help TₑX a little by the application of \tolerance. You might also be prepared to permit some raggedness.

⇒*Exercise 16.4:*   There are at least two things which bear further investigation here. The first is the importance of restoring the normal baselines, and the other is the inclusion of the struts. Demonstrate what happens when they are omitted.   ⇐

Some syntheses: Major New York Bridges

The following example, 'Major New York Bridges' (Figure 16.3), merely builds on things we already have uncovered. There is, though, one very minor catch, which can be troublesome if we are not careful. The separation of the 'title' from the rest of the table with what looks like a double line is a fairly common feature in tables created with tbl. It is not clear to me whether this reflects a US usage in table construction, or whether the target output

Major New York Bridges		
Bridge	Designer	Length
Brooklyn	J. A. Roeblineg	1595
Manhattan	G. Lindenthal	1470
Williamsburg	L. L. Buck	1600
Queensborough	Palmer & Hornbostel	1182
Triborough	O. H. Ammann	1380
		383
Bronx Whitestone	O. H. Ammann	2300
Throgs Neck	O. H. Ammann	1800
George Washington	O. H. Ammann	3500

Figure 16.3
Major New
York Bridges,
(from Lesk,
1979)

device had problems in creating a thicker line, and that this 'feature' became ossified when the development of the underlying troff software was frozen at Ossana's death. The double lines are also a common feature in LATEX tables.

The naive preamble could be

```
\halign{\vrule\enspace#\hfil\enspace
    &\vrule\enspace#\hfil\enspace
        &\strut\vrule\enspace\hfil#\enspace\vrule\cr
```

which allows a fairly straightforward table construction of

```
        Williamsburg&           L. L. Buck&1600\cr
\noalign{\hrule}
        Queensborough&             Palmer \&&1182\cr
                & \enspace Hornbostel&      \cr
\noalign{\hrule}
\vspan2{Triborough}&\vspan2{O. H. Ammann}&1380\cr
                &               &\omit\hrulefill\cr
                &               & 383\cr
\noalign{\hrule}
    Bronx Whitestone&           O. H. Ammann&2300\cr
```

(just showing the most 'complex' part). The \vspan crops up again, but there is also the use of \hrulefill. Note that it is preceded by an \omit. If this were not present the current alignment entry would be used, with rather disastrous results. Because there are no \tabskips in operation, the \hrulefill works quite nicely. Of course, having omitted the alignment, we also omit the \vrules which fitted at either side of the last entry. If we did not reinsert them, we might see a rather tiny notch in the table where they ought to be. Given that the vertical rule will only be 0.4 pt in height, it might be practically invisible – it corresponds to less than two dots on a 300 dpi laser printer, and on a preview screen it is probably below the resolution of a 'readable' size. But it *is* there, or rather, it should be there, especially if we plan to output on a higher-resolution device.

Since the preamble given looks temptingly repetitious, we could replace it with something similar, but more compact:

`\halign{\vrule\strut#&&\enspace#\hfil\enspace\vrule\cr`

If we do this, we again have to add an extra & at the beginning of each row of entries. We also have a problem with the rightmost column, since it is right-justified, while the preamble left justifies it. The direct way out of this is to precede each of the numeric entries with an `\hfill`. The following specimen lines show this at work:

```
&\vspan2{Triborough}&\vspan2{O. H. Ammann}&\hfill
                                             1380\cr
\omit\vrule&         &                &\omit
                                       \hrulefill\cr
&                    &                &\hfill
                                       383\cr
```

Again note that where a cell is omitted, the `\vrule` has been carefully reinserted. If we do not omit the entry in the second of those lines, the `\strut` will remain in operation, and give rather unsatisfactory vertical spacing.

⇒*Exercise 16.5:*   A great deal has been made of the need to reinsert the `\vrule`s if they have been `\omit`ted. Create one of these tables without the inclusion of these particular rules. Can you see the difference in preview or in whatever final output form you have available. If you can't see it, is it important? One way to highlight the problem is to change the definition of `\hrulefill` so that it is much thicker than the default. For example:

```
\def\hrulefill{%
        \leaders\hrule height1pt depth1pt\hfill}
```

quickly reveals those frustrating gaps.   ⇐

AT&T at last!

One of the classic tables which appeared first in Lesk (1979), and which was then adopted by Knuth as the means of explaining the mysteries of `\halign` and `\tabskip` in *The* T_EX*book*, is the AT&T Common Stock table (Figure 16.4). Clearly Knuth provides a T_EX solution for this, but it will also be looked at here, with the intention of illustrating some points which have been omitted so far.

AT&T Common Stock		
Year	Price	Dividend
1971	41–54	$2.60
2	41–54	2.70
3	46–55	2.87
4	40–53	2.24
5	45–52	3.40
6	51–59	.95*
7	101–102	10.00

*(first quarter only)

Figure 16.4
A classic table

Sometimes we wish the columns of a table to have a fixed width. Normally, we allow TEX to work out the widths, find the maximum, and then create the table based on that width. This is not always what we need. When the same 'shape' of table occurs frequently, it may be necessary to fix the widths. One fairly obvious example might be where a table spans more than one page. Normally, TEX is not amenable to this situation. Although an \halign is not set as a single block, and will break at page breaks, it is usually placed within a \vbox where there is no way to insert page breaks part way through. On the other hand, if we derive the tabular data from a database, or from some other 'automatic' source, it is not difficult to have the report generator generate the TEX commands for alignment, and to keep track of the number of lines processed so that when it is clear that the page will have been filled, that table is terminated, a page eject is generated, and the continuation of the table on the next page is begun. The 'flaw' is that the information about 'widest entry' is calculated anew on each page. It is possible to develop some complex scheme where the widest entry is calculated and stored, with the entries being processed a second time to be typeset in the table. Such multi-pass systems are feasible, if a little awkward. A simpler approach is to fix the widths of the columns in advance: this is likely to work best in a situation where we have some idea of the likely range of entries in the table. This is not so unlikely.

In the context of this table, it is not necessary to worry about the appearance of continuation pages, but it is possible to indicate how the problem can be tackled. The simplest way is to put each column in an \hbox of some predetermined width. How to determine the width though? Provided we have some notion of the likely maximum number of numerals, we can estimate the maximum width. At least, we can for Computer Modern fonts, since the numerals are half a quad wide (that is, an enspace). It is not uncommon for numerals to have a fixed width, but this is by no means a rule in different typefaces. But even in the worst case, it should be possible to determine what width the widest numeral is (through some box work and \showbox) and use that information. No-one ever said that tables were going to be easy. Each alignment in the preamble could therefore be something like

`\hbox to50pt{\hfil#\hfil}`

In this case each column will be 50 pt wide, and be centred. That is not completely satisfactory here – certainly not for the first column or the third column. It could do for the middle one, though. The first and third columns need to be right-justified, but they do need some space to their left and right. If we assume that the columns are first placed in right-justified \hboxes, and that those boxes are then centred, we could end up with something suitable. That is,

`\hbox to 50pt{\hfil\hbox to 20pt{\hss#}\hfil}`

Again the columns are 50 pt wide, but the numerals are placed in a box which is up to 20 pt wide. This ensures 15 pt of space on either side. Obviously another strategy is to place \hskips on either side of the inner box:

`\hskip15pt\hbox to 20pt{\hss#}\hskip15pt`

Note the use of \hss rather than \hfil. The reason for this choice was to insure against an odd large entry (or my failing to guess the maximum width correctly). An \hfil could lead to an overfull box, while the \hss will remain commendably silent and invisible.

The only other remark to make is about the asterisk on the very last entry. This appears to be a footnote, but of course footnotes do not work in boxed alignments (or inserts). The \vfootnote would place the 'footnote' at the bottom of the page, not the bottom of the table. The way to handle this is the hard way, by inserting the relevant information physically in the table. There is more than one way of handling this. Obviously \noalign is one way, since it is material outside the alignment rules; perhaps slightly less obvious, the material could be handled as a \multispan. Equally, since it ocurrs right at the end of the table it could be placed after it entirely. The three alternatives may look identical when typeset, but there are some implications lurking around: with a \noalign, the material is set as a paragraph, with any paragraph indentation. Since it is set without regard to the alignment, it takes the \hsize which is current, and may bear no relation to the table width. Note there is a real difference here between the way a \noalign{\hrule} works and a \noalign with text or other material in it. The \hrule merely expands to the table width. Since the textual material is set with the current \hsize, centering a table with a \noalign which contains text and not an \hrule may be tricky. If the \offinterlineskip has been used, it will apply to the \noalign too. In some circumstances it will be advisable to insert a \normalbaselines. If the \multispan strategy is used, a long entry may widen the table inadvertently. If the material is placed at the end, after the table has been completed, it could, under some circumstances, be separated across a page boundary (this is not a serious problem, since there are several ways to inhibit the breaking). Again, if the table is to be centred the textual material may pose a problem, since it uses the current \hsize, bearing no relation to the table width.

We could therefore expect to see
```
\noalign{\smallskip
   \noindent{$^\ast$}(first quarter only)}
```
or
```
\multispan3{$^\ast$}(first quarter only)\cr
```
or even
```
\smallskip\noindent{$^\ast$}(first quarter only)
```
This avoids the problem of how to make the asterisk have no influence on the right justification of that last column. One alternative, but crude, technique could be to introduce a further column just for such markers, but a simpler alternative is to give the asterisk no width at all. Before we go assigning it to boxes of zero width, recall that \rlap and \llap were designed for such situations. A simple
```
\rlap{$^\ast$}
```
is all that is needed.

We now have most of the elements. The preamble may be:
```
\halign{\strut\vrule
  \hbox to 50pt{%
      \hfil\hbox to 20pt{\hss#}\hfil}\vrule
&\hbox to 50pt{%
      \hfil#\hfil}\vrule
&\hbox to 50pt{%
      \hfil\hbox to 20pt{\hss#}\hfil}\vrule\cr
```

and the headings:
```
\noalign{\hrule}
\multispan3
  \strut\vrule\hfil AT\&T Common Stock\hfil\vrule\cr
\noalign{\hrule}
\hidewidth Year \hidewidth
&\omit\hidewidth Price\hidewidth\vrule
&\omit\hidewidth Dividend\hidewidth\vrule\cr
\noalign{\hrule}
```
and the 'variable' matter which is the key material (together with the 'footnote') is:
```
&41--54&\llap{\$}2.60\cr
   2&41--54&2.70\cr
   3&46--55&2.87\cr
   4&40--53&2.24\cr
   5&45--52&3.40\cr
   6&51--59& .95\rlap{$^\ast$}\cr
\noalign{\hrule}
\noalign{\smallskip\noindent
               {$^\ast$}(first quarter only)}}
```
The only point not really covered earlier was the `\llap` for the dollar sign. Had each element in the third column been preceded by a dollar sign, I would have been inclined to include it as part of the number to be centred.

⇒*Exercise 16.6:*　Try out the various forms of the table 'footnote'. Some neat work with a box could allow the `\hsize` to be set for a note which follows a table. Do this. Any suggestions on how a suitable `\hsize` might be selected for similar `\noalign`ed material?　　　　⇐

⇒*Exercise 16.7:*　Some effort was expended to ensure that, when the price of the stock rose above 99, and that if the dividend rose, the table would still look sensible. Can you discern what these things were? Is it worth taking such precautions?　　　　⇐

End table

Why then do tables look difficult? Often the basic problem is difficult, and difficult things are seldom easy. The major problem stems from the two-dimensional layout of tables. This poses certain intrinsic constraints. Once we start wanting to have horizontal and vertical rules which join nicely, the problems are compounded. Nevertheless, the problems are certainly not insurmountable, and really occur mainly with the headings. The body of the table (the part which holds the useful information) is usually very straightforward. In a great many cases, the headings remain constant, but the contents change. Once having mastered the headings, the contents are easily generated or provided with the minimum of effort. Ideally, they are the parts which are generated by a database or some other program.

Creating tables in TEX requires some attention to detail, and does tend to focus on the very small details: it is far removed from the notion of declarative markup. There are many macro packages available which help simplify the input of tables. In the end they have to be agreed to have a little less generality. In this instance, it is not easy to generalize into agreed templates. There seems to be too much going on, and each pattern of table is sufficiently distinct as to seem to want individual treatment.

⇒*Exercise 16.8:* By now you have probably qualified as a TEX Master – 'i.e. a person who can create complicated tables' (*The TEXbook*, page 253). Congratulations. As a 'passing out' test, reproduce these. You don't have to put them side by side.

January	February	March
April	May	
June	July	Month
August	September	
October	November	December

	%BP		
λ_{ij}	L_{R-I}	DAR	L_{R-P}
70	4.60	6.80	5.10
80	10.70	12.10	11.20

⇐

Conclusion

Tables constructed in TEX have quite erroneously gained the reputation of obscurity and perversity. The 'problems' of tables stem from a number of roots. The first is their intrinsic difficulty. Creating tables is, put simply, not straightforward. While Knuth was able to create a reasonably straightforward linear language for mathematics, no-one, so far, has been able to do anything similar with tables. Tables are usually two-dimensional structures, and in some cases may take on the appearance of another half dimension or so. Part of our problem stems from trying simultaneously to align horizontal and vertical elements, where each element may have a different 'structure'. There may be some relationship between all elements in one column (let's say 'all mathematical expressions') and those in another (right-justified text), but looked at in the sense of the rows, the relationship is not structural, but perhaps functional. Merging these disparate elements is usually non-trivial. But a table consists of more than just elements on some sort of grid. There are often components which should 'span' several columns, or several rows (usually titling information). Another problem is that we often include 'positioning' information in order to emphasize some of the relationships between elements (usually) in columns. This sort of 'typographic' or 'procedural' markup is rather against the more general notions of declarative markup. One further complication is the role of horizontal and vertical rules within the table.

Graphics 17

To a very large extent, TEX was designed for the placement of characters on a page. It was implicitly assumed that the characters were probably alphabetic or mathematical. Nevertheless, Knuth notes

> If you enjoy fooling around making pictures, instead of type-setting ordinary text, TEX will be a source of endless frustration/amusement for you, because almost anything is possible...

While it is well able to draw horizontal and vertical lines, or even to plot dots more or less at random (see, for example, Knuth, 1986, p.389, and Figure 17.1), most people expect a little more from their graphics. There is also an architectural limitation: although TEX could easily simulate an arbitrary continuous curve by placing a very large number of small dots (or rules) on the page (or screen), TEX was only granted a finite memory. You quickly run out of memory. This is all the more distressing since there now exist versions of TEX with small and large amounts of memory (basically related to the addressing ability: 64-bit TEX on a Cray has potentially much more memory than 16-bit TEX on a pc: TEX-in-UNIX is generally somewhere in between). Sadly, this has had the effect of making TEX documents *less* portable, and seriously undermines TEX's claim to universality. TEX is universal, but the documents may be restricted to certain versions – and you won't necessarily know until you try to process them (and run out of memory, or not).

All sorts of diagrams have been created using TEX. References to some of these are given in the bibliography.

There are three major ways in which graphics may be made part of TEX documents. For simplicity and brevity, 'graphics' is restricted principally to line graphics, but most of what is covered can be generalized. As with most things, the more limited the capabilities, the closer they may be to universality. High degrees

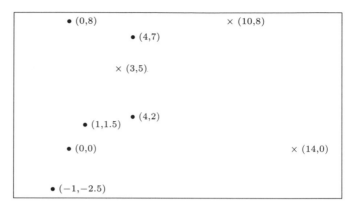

Figure 17.1
Simple graphics
within TEX

of sophistication usually mean greater restrictions are present. Attention is directed here to techniques which have some claim to generality: the 'running on my Sun workstation using propri- etary software' solution is ignored as far as possible. The vain hope is that someone working on their Macintosh will be able to exchange TEX documents with someone working on an IBM pc, an Amiga, an Atari, a NeXT, a Vax under VMS, and so on up the scale until we reach the supercomputer league. We do not wish to present solutions which only work on specific boxes. UNIX may be the *de facto* operating system, just as POSTSCRIPT is the *de facto* page description language. But there are more non-UNIX boxes out in the world than there are UNIX boxes. Similarly, there are more non-POSTSCRIPT output devices than there are POSTSCRIPT out- puts. If everybody were to standardize on the same computing box many problems of interchange would go away, but this is unlikely to happen.

Special fonts

This first approach is limited, but very general – it will work with TEX and any of its drivers. It is possible to use special fonts to build pictures. Again there are three main ways to do this: the first is through simple font elements (that is, straight line segments, or curves) which can be assembled to give (fairly simple) pictures. The second is through METAFONT. Here, we use METAFONT to create a single character which is our graph (or whatever). This seems intimidating, but need not be. And lastly, we can create special fonts without METAFONT.

Simple font elements

So, start with the simple font elements. Knuth gives an example in *The TEXbook*, pages 389–391, but the font he uses is not generally available. Alternatively, LaTeX already does this, in its `picture` environment (cf. Lamport, 1986, pp.101–111). Unfortunately Lamport did not develop this to the same extent as the rest of LaTeX, and it has a distinctly 'squared graph paper' feel. But it is certainly possible to create quite attractive graphs. Any vertical and horizontal elements are just standard TEX rules, while rounded corners and circles can be made from the LaTeX circle fonts $-\,\diagdown\diagdown\diagup\diagup$ (Figure 17.2). A small range of diagonals is possible through other special line fonts $-\diagup\diagup\diagup\diagup$.

The LaTeX `picture` environment is amazingly modular. In other words you can rip it out of LaTeX and run it in `plain` TEX, using the same basic commands which are documented in the LaTeX book. Although creating pictures this way is time consuming, it can give quite pleasing quality (at least on the laser printer). Quite acceptable bar charts may be created, as Nagy (1989) shows (Figure 17.3). It is possible to tackle chemistry through the use of these fonts, as Figure 17.4 demonstrates. In this case some of the tedium is removed by creating the ring structure only once, storing it in a box, and then copying that box when it is needed. Besides making the procedure less long winded, it cuts down on the effort needed by TEX itself, since copying a box requires no new manipulations.

The creation of diagrams like this can be amazingly tedious, but the approach still achieves a generality and portability which cannot be ignored. Because of this generality, there are some preprocessor programs which will allow you to create something interactively which is then transformed into LaTeX commands. If you have access to a UNIX system, `gnutex` can assist. On an MS-DOS system, part of the emTEX package does just this (although it adds a few extra features of its own). The key drawbacks of the LaTeX special font approach are centred around the limited fonts which are available, both in the slope of lines and their thicknesses, and the limited range of curves. These very limited resources can be encouraged to generate quite an amazing range of possibilities. But an enormous amount of time and effort is also required. Having said this, traditionally a tremendous amount of effort had to be expended to create diagrams like these anyway. In this way we have a single document, and the opportunity to revise.

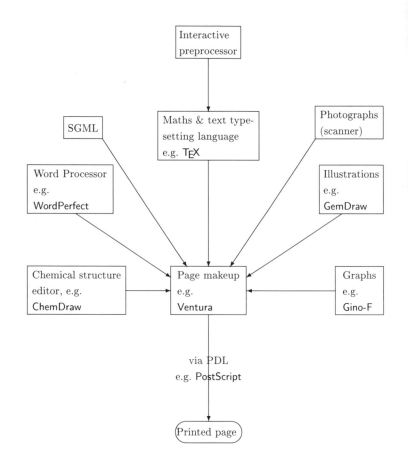

Figure 17.2
Using the
L^AT_EX fonts,
from Norris and
Oakley (1990)

An advantage of course is that everything is in (L^A)T_EX, so that we can ensure that the relative weights of lines, the font sizes, the symbols, blend in well with the rest of the document. This is a feature which we should not ignore.

A further advantage is the ability to preview the diagram on the screen. Since the METAFONT descriptions of the fonts are available, the screen fonts may also be generated.

The use of the rules might indicate that you could build the most complex curves out of small rectangular boxes: make them small enough and it will not be possible to see the join. In fact, an extension to L^AT_EX picture environment is the bezier style,

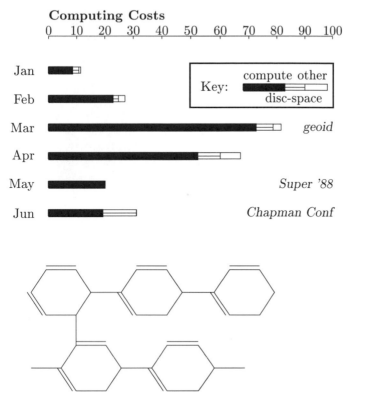

Computing Costs

Figure 17.3
Bar chart, from
Nagy (1989)

Figure 17.4
Simple
chemistry with
LATEX fonts,
from de Bruin
et al. (1988)

which allows a bézier curve to be plotted (see Figure 17.5). Make too many of them and TEX runs out of memory.

Resolution becomes an issue if we try to create continuous curves from small elements. If TEX memory fills up quickly at 300 dpi, it will fill up even more quickly at 1270 dpi. It is difficult to claim device independence when we must take resolution into account. We can of course ignore the resolution problem, but on those times when we want to produce high-quality graphs, we may be disappointed by the faithful rendition of those 300 dpi blobs, and the angular 'staircasing' which is all too obvious at the higher resolution.

The creation of bézier curves is a remarkable achievement, given TEX's limited arithmetic capability. Adding two numbers together is awkward enough, and when we realize that TEX will only use

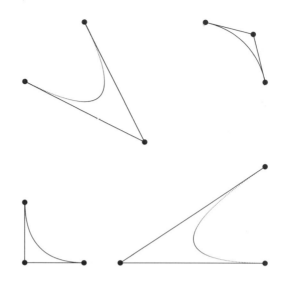

Figure 17.5
Bézier curves
and control
points, from
Beebe (1989)

integers in a rather limited range, the results are all the more surprising.

Since the `picture` environment is rather crude, one or two people have put higher-level commands around them. The two best known are PiCTeX and `epic`. PiCTeX (Wichura, 1987) can be run with both TeX and LaTeX (Figure 17.6).

The commands for PiCTeX are distributed freely, but the 85 page manual is essential in order to use it sensibly. This chapter has already loaded quite a few picture-drawing commands and many of the allocation registers are becoming filled up. While it is no real problem to stick to (say) the `picture` environment, once we start mixing in extra commands the limitation to 256 counters, boxes, dimensions, and token strings starts to hurt.

The syntax of the commands required by PiCTeX seems quite reasonable, if quirky at times. It is no worse than many commercial plotting packages like SAS or SPSS. But even if we have enough room for allocation of the registers, running with PiCTeX and LaTeX, on a 32-bit TeX, it is still possible (but not easy) to exhaust the available memory. And given the amount of arithmetic going on in the background, these diagrams tend to be slow.

Olivier (1989) describes an amalgam between S, the UNIX statistical package, and PiCTeX. Clearly this is restricted to UNIX in the first instance, although the PiCTeX would be portable.

Although `epic` (Podar, 1986) was targeted for LaTeX it can also be used in TeX. It lacks the generality of PiCTeX, but is

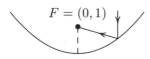

The parabola $y = x^2/4$
before rotation

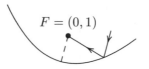

After rotation about the
focus F by 15°

Figure 17.6
P$_I$CT$_E$X
graphics, from
Wichura (1987)

a useful extension. Podar added some higher-level commands in order to provide a 'friendlier and more powerful users interface'. In particular he managed to reduce the amount of manual calculation required. For example, he introduced a `\drawline` command which allows specified points to be connected. In order to avoid the problem of slope segments outside LaTeX's ability, he uses the closest slope available. This can lead to rather jagged lines. If the lines are dashed, this problem appears less acute.

There are several collections of commands which draw all sorts of rather nice graphs. My favourites are those of Michael Ramek (Ramek, 1990). Figure 17.7 is taken from his paper and helps illustrate the scope that is possible. Besides the 'normal' graph requirements, he provided some other commands to draw chemical structures as shown in Figure 17.8.

Other fonts

So far we have been discussing the use of special fonts. Of course, we can also generate our own. There are two different directions here. On the one hand we can use some suite of other fonts; on the other we could generate METAFONT descriptions somehow and use those descriptions. In both cases there is appreciable generality. In the final analysis, METAFONT is as portable as TeX, and once the descriptions are made available we are as free to use those as we would be to use (LA)TeX commands.

Knuth (1987) introduced some halftone fonts which allow grey-scale 'pictures' to be typeset in a completely device independent way. Adrian Clark (1987) also made some contribution to this, and Hoenig (1989) shows some interesting examples. Since the descriptions are available, anyone may 'borrow' them quite easily. Adrian used a FORTRAN program as a pre-processor. This is fair, since for all sorts of reasons we would normally expect the data to be provided in a digital form from some other source. There are problems of TeX memory here again. Even with a 'big' version,

A plain TₑX primer

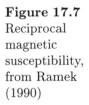

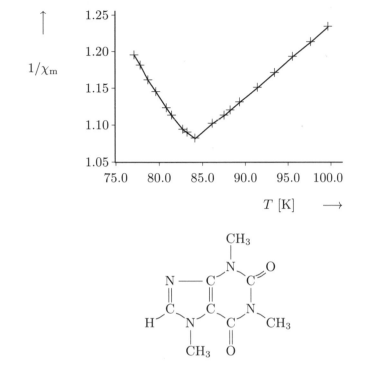

$1/\chi_{\mathrm{m}}$

T [K] $\longrightarrow$

Figure 17.7
Reciprocal
magnetic
susceptibility,
from Ramek
(1990)

Figure 17.8
Caffeine

TₑX may only handle one 512×512 picture (or four 256×256 pictures). Knuth's paper discusses some manipulation techniques which would allow greater clarity from lower-resolution pictures. This is a fairly general and well-understood aspect of image processing which need not concern us here. The point is that it is quite possible and represents no new addition of hardware or software.

An alternative use of METAFONT is to view it as a means of describing an arbitrary picture, not a typeface. All the tools are there to do it, and in fact it is really a lot simpler than creating fonts. Of course, you do not really do it in METAFONT; you do it in something else, which is then translated to METAFONT. The something else at the moment is one of several programs by Rick Simpson (Simpson, 1990), which works on the IBM RT (running AIX, a UNIX lookalike), or Metaplot (Pat Wilcox, 1989). This latter was written in C, and is available in a number of forms. There is at least a pc version, an Amiga version, and lots of UNIX versions.

In both cases, what comes out at the far end is a single (very large) character (or even a set of characters which are 'tiled' together), which you plot wherever you want. The disadvantage is that scaling the picture is tedious (just like scaling a 'normal' character), and editing it requires a re-run of METAFONT. But it is device independent. The only proviso is that the device driver be able to handle these very large characters. This is not a trivial expectation, since many drivers were written expecting that they would be dealing with letters, and that there was some reasonable maximum size to a letter.

Wilcox did not really expect the user to write in her 'Metaplot'. The notion was that a variety of other, arbitrary, plotting languages could be mapped onto the Metaplot commands, which were then shipped to METAFONT.

CGM, or Computer Graphics Metafile, is worth considering too. It has a couple of features which we ought to bear in mind. It is an international standard. Nominally, every graphics package ought to have the facility to generate CGM, and also to read it in. The metafile should also be able to be transmitted over electronic networks with the minimum of fuss. The other feature is that CALS (Computer-aided Acquisition and Logistics System) has adopted CGM as one of its components: while we may worry about the militaristic background of CALS, it has done much to revitalize and make acceptable SGML, and we can expect it to help in the adoption of CGM. One other component of CALS is that it has adopted another 'graphics' standard, IGES. IGES is usually described as a *de facto* standard; it was developed principally for use with CAD-CAM software. Nevertheless, it does offer another routeway. In essence there is no real reason why Metaplot could not read an IGES file and transform it to METAFONT form. Since we are in the real world of 'standards', Heinz (1990) notes that GKS (Graphics Kernel Standard) may also be transformed into TeX.

Another route to create a character

If we look a little more closely at what a driver actually requires to set a character, we note that there are two items: the pixel file, and the TeX font metric file. Conventionally, the route to produce these is METAFONT, but there is no particular reason why we should have to adopt this route. Provided the `tfm` and `pk` contain appropriate information, the driver should be able to typeset. The underlying idea here is that we can have another program take (say) a grey-scale picture and process it to produce both the required files. The `tfm` file should be simple enough to produce, even by hand, since we might make this 'font' have only one character at a time. The property list would be fairly simple. A traditional pixel (or `pxl`) file only contains binary information, so we are back in the realms of image processing or half toning if we wish to do something rather fancy. Most drivers now accept 'packed pixel' rather than 'pixel' information. This is simply a far more compact form of the same information.

Simpson (1990) also describes an application of this approach. The example he chooses takes a raster image and turns it into a font. The program `imtopk` converts an IMPART image processing file into a `pk/tfm` pair. `impart` handles the image scaling, allowing for device pixel density, does any filtering necessary, and converts an n-level grey scale to two levels. TeX positions the image on the page, typesets any annotation, and handles any other typesetting. At Texas A&M University, a similar approach is used where output from a number of graphics programs, but especially the graphics software package 'Disspla', is processed to produce the `pk/tfm` pair. This has some appeal since Disspla runs on a very wide variety of machines, and may even be called from programming languages. A drawback of this approach is that it is difficult to annotate the diagrams with fonts similar to the ones used in the TeX document.

Special

Now to the less general: any sort of material may be incorporated in a `\special`. Whatever appears there is passed directly to the `dvi` file, where it will be handled by the `dvi` driver. For example, we could have POSTSCRIPT commands in there (or even a reference to a file containing a POSTSCRIPT-created graphic). The problem is that you also need a driver which knows what to do with the information, and a device (printer/screen) which can display the information. While POSTSCRIPT is described as a *de facto* standard, not everyone has access to a POSTSCRIPT device, and in fact more Hewlett Packard (and compatible) machines are out there in the real world than anything else.

This actually opens up another route. While we could easily include a complete graphic produced by another approach (one of the vast array of graphics packages which will produce POSTSCRIPT), and probably scale or otherwise modify it, we can also pass simpler information to the `dvi` file for processing by the driver. Maus and Baker (1986) extended the LaTeX `picture` environment by adding a whole host of commands, which, when examined closely, are little 'specials' which do things like draw a line of arbitrary slope through POSTSCRIPT commands. Now TEX does not process anything; therefore TEX's memory does not fill up. When printed (on a POSTSCRIPT device), the line is there. Unfortunately, only a few screens are POSTSCRIPT devices, and so we don't usually expect to see these elements previewed.

One other disadvantage of using specials is that the form of specials is by no means standardized. Although there is a working party (TUG, 1992) attempting to standardize and issue recommendations, they are facing the usual problems of standardization committees. One of the recommendations is that a level 0 driver should be able to place at least 1000 rules and 20,000 characters on a single page, unless the output device is constrained in some way. On-board device memory may be limited and limit these ideal minima.

Recall that well over half of the drivers written for use with TEX reside in the public domain. No commercial forces come into play with them, nor can the TEX Users Group impose rules (it is there to serve its members, not police them: in general this sort of anarchy works, since there is enough goodwill around). What we are coming to is the fact that specials have to be written with a specific driver in mind. To give an example: imagine we want to ship out a couple of POSTSCRIPT commands, represented by <command>. Using *Textures* on the Macintosh, which has its own built-in driver, you could say
\special{postscript <command>}
Using ArborText's (1987) POSTSCRIPT driver, DVILASER/PS, the command is
\special{ps:: <command>}
Using the public domain DVI2PS, the structure is
\special{pstext=<command>}
or using another public domain driver DVIPS (Tom Rokicki), the equivalent is
\special{ps: <command>} *or* \special{ps:: <command>}
while Nelson Beebe's driver (Beebe, 1987) appears to have no way of including a single command (you could obviously use the facility to read in a file, which itself contained only one command); similarly, Personal TEX's POSTSCRIPT driver (Personal TEX, 1987) appears to lack the 'in-line command' feature.

Trevor Darrell (1987) wrote a useful set of commands, **psfig**, which greatly ease the problems of incorporating POSTSCRIPT into a document. The POSTSCRIPT is really 'encapsulated', since the 'bounding box' information is required. 'Encapsulated' also implies that the POSTSCRIPT should not change the state of commands – in other words, that any changes should be local (in TEX terminology). The portion of `psfig` which deals with the `\specials` is well separated, and it is possible to modify that part of the command suite for particular drivers.

You could reasonably ask why we do not include CGM files in `\specials`. In fact, this has been done (Andrews, 1989). Provided the driver can handle the commands and change them into the correct form for the output device, any sort of file can be processed. As noted earlier, the `dvi` is itself a sort of metafile. Andrews' extensions work for UNIX and VMS environments.

POSTSCRIPT is not yet ubiquitous. Fortunately, there is also an approach which allows us to use a Hewlett Packard LaserJet – CAPTURE (Pickrell, 1990). Any program which produces output for a LaserJet can have that output processed with CAPTURE to produce a file which may be input to TEX, through some suitable commands (which will, somewhere, employ `\specials`). Again, this sounds longwinded, but there are a great many programs which will do this. Even more remarkable, there are programs which can take POSTSCRIPT and turn it into LaserJet form (Freedom of the Press, GoScript, Ghostscript, etc.). This means that we are now relatively independent of POSTSCRIPT.

In betweens

A few years ago the notion of 'little languages' became current. This is a scheme which is found most generally in UNIX. Instead of adding features to troff, 'little languages' were created: preprocessors which massaged some reasonable form of input into troff. These include chem (for chemistry), tbl (for tables), eqn (for equations), grap (for general graphs), and pic (for pictures). The one we are interested in is pic and perhaps grap: pic has a language which allows creation of line diagrams with embedded text. Sounds simple. Of course, with the way that UNIX works, it is 'easy' to write a command line which hides all the 'little language' bits and pieces from the end user.

How is this relevant? Recall that TEX passes `\special` information straight to the `dvi` file. That information could easily be special commands which the driver could interpret. If we pass POSTSCRIPT commands, then the driver can handle POSTSCRIPT (maybe). What if we pass higher-level commands which the driver then processes to produce a new `dvi` file? In other words, a `dvi` to `dvi` processor. The new `dvi` file would, among other things, be able to be previewed, or be sent to any suitable printer (provided you had the correct `dvi`-to-printer driver). So what we end up with is a *device independent* method.

There are a couple of attempts to do this. There is a program around called `dvidvi` (Rokicki, 1989) which processes a `dvi` file, but only so that you can rearrange the pages – say to shrink them to thumbnails and arrange them all on a single sheet (actually very useful for book make-up). Mike Spivak (1989) has provided `dvipaste` which allows you to 'paste' a `dvi` file into another `dvi` file, so that you can put a table (which gobbles up space in TeX) where you want (equally it could paste in a large picture – and that is why it has been mentioned here). And lastly, the one that really does pictures, Rolf Olejniczak's `texpic` (1989). This is a TeX implementation of pic which does all the things that pic does and more, and works in just the way outlined.

What is the snag? The driver has to be implemented on all sorts of different machines. We are gnawing away at the portability. Including POSTSCRIPT or Hewlett Packard's laser printer language seems also eminently non-portable. At least this localizes the problem and in the longer term gives a far more general solution. Olejniczak's program is available only for MS-DOS, and is currently proprietary, although it is not especially expensive. It is the restricted platform which is the real problem.

Closing comments

Beebe (1989), Rahtz (1989), and Heinz (1990) have all contributed to the discussion of incorporating graphics into TeX documents. The adoption of the METAFONT and `pk/tfm` solution goes some way to ensuring the transportability of documents. None of the other approaches yet comes close enough to being capable of being transmitted over fairly arbitrary networks. Another advantage of this approach should be the capability of viewing the diagrams on the screen, as well as on paper. The tools which enable these transformations ought to be part of the standard TeX distributions. Within a closed environment, any solution which works is to be applauded. But one of the major features of TeX is its 'open'-ness, and the portability of documents created with TeX.

It will have become apparent that we are always in the hands of the drivers available. This is perhaps the weakest link in the whole chain. Whether you regard the drivers as part of TEX or not depends on your viewpoint.

It is perhaps wise to remind ourselves that even in the days of Johann Gensfleisch zum Gutenberg the integration of text and illustration (through woodblocks) took some time, and could only be achieved after agreement with the professional woodblock cutters.

Fonts 18

In this chapter we will look at some of the aspects of dealing with fonts. To some extent the basics have already been covered. As already related, a simple

`\font\tenss=cmss10`

loads the Computer Modern Sans Serif font at 10 pt. There are potential problems since `plain` is only guaranteed to set up the basic 16 fonts. These are the eight Computer Modern fonts in Figure 18.1. All are at 10 pt, but four of them are also loaded at some other sizes:

Font	Sizes (pt)
Roman	5, 7, 10
Bold Extended	5, 7, 10
Slanted Roman	10
Text Italic	10
Typewriter Type	10
Math Italic	5, 7, 10
Math Symbols	5, 7, 10
Math Extension	10

Figure 18.1
The default fonts in `plain` TEX

A number of others are `\preloaded` in `plain`. All that `\preloaded` means is that the font information is read in so that should we need those fonts sometime there is no overhead. But why? What is the problem? Knuth says:

> it is desirable to keep the total number of fonts in plain TEX relatively small, because plain TEX is a sort of standard format; it shouldn't cost much for someone to acquire all the fonts of plain TEX in addition to those he really wants. Second, it is desirable on many computer systems to preload the information for most of the fonts that people will actually be using, since this saves a lot of machine time.

Neither of these reasons seems current. Practically every distributed version of TEX comes with all of the fonts in the Computer

Typeface	Sizes (pt)
Bold Extended	9, 8, 6
Maths Italic	9, 8, 6
Math Symbols	9, 8, 6
Roman	9, 8, 6, (scaled $\approx$ 14.5)
Sans Serif	10
Sans Serif Bold Extended	(scaled = 14.4)
Sans Serif Italic	10
Sans Serif Quotation	8
Sans Serif Quotation Italic	8
Slanted Roman	9, 8
Text Italic	9, 8
Typewriter Text	9, 8, (scaled = 14.4)

Figure 18.2
The default
'preloaded'
fonts in `plain`
TₑX

Modern family, and processors are quite fast enough that we are unlikely to notice a few nanoseconds here or there as the font information is read in.

The \preloaded fonts are listed in Figure 18.2. They fall into two main categories: extra sizes of loaded fonts – filling in the other sizes to give 1 point increments between 5 pt and 10 pt; and other 'useful' fonts. An exception to this are the three fonts loaded at particular \magsteps. These are used by Knuth for some titles. It is odd to see them here. Do note though that he says:

> different machines can be expected to differ widely with respect to preloaded fonts, since the choice of how many fonts to preload and the selection of the most important fonts depend on local conditions.

It is only in this area of preloaded fonts where Knuth permits changes to be made to `plain` without his authorization.

The Computer Modern family of typefaces is quite large. In fact, it must be one of the most comprehensive range of practical, working fonts. There are very few typeface families which have serif and sans serif faces, varieties of bold, italic, 'typewriter', slanted, as well as the oddities like Fibonacci, Dunhill, and Funny. It is far more common to have to use a serif typeface with some suitable sans serif typeface, and perhaps a monospaced 'typewriter' typeface. It should not be assumed that any arbitrary *mélange* will be satisfactory. Fortunately, the Computer Modern family fits together, by and large.

Each distribution of TₑX should have the fonts in Figure 18.3. The prefix to which the 'suffix' is prepended is 'cm'. The name will

Computer Modern name	Point sizes available	Suffix
Bold	10	b
Bold Symbol	10	bsy
Bold Extended	5, 6, 7, 8, 9, 10, 12	bx
Bold Extended Text Italic	10	bxti
Bold Extended Slanted	10	bxsl
Caps and Small Caps	10	csc
Dunhill	10	dunh
Extension	10	ex
Funny Font	10	ff
Funny Italic	10	fi
Fibonacci	8	fib
Italic Typewriter Text	10	itt
Inch	72.27	inch
Math Extension	10	ex
Math Italic	5, 6, 7, 8, 9, 10, 12	mi
Math Italic Bold	10	mib
Math Symbols	5, 6, 7, 8, 9, 10	sy
Roman	5, 6, 7, 8, 9, 10, 12, 17	r
Slanted	8, 9 10, 12	sl
Slanted Typewriter Text	10	sltt
Sans Serif	8, 9, 10, 12, 17	ss
Sans Serif Italic	8, 9, 10, 12, 17	ssi
Sans Serif Bold Extended	10	ssbx
Sans Serif DemiBold Condensed	10	ssdc
Sans Serif Quotation	8	ssq
Sans Serif Quotation Italic	8	ssqi
Symbol	5, 6, 7, 8, 9, 10	sy
Text Italic	7, 8, 9, 10, 12	ti
Typewriter Caps and Small Caps	10	tcsc
TEX Extended	8, 9, 10	tex
Typewriter Text	8, 9, 10, 12	tt
Unslanted	10	u
Variable width Typewriter Text	10	vtt

Figure 18.3 The full range of the Computer Modern family

be followed by a point size in the range shown, for example `cmr10` or `cmss17`. The one exception to this, `cminch`, may not be found in all distributions. It is a rather large font, and takes up lots of disk space. Since its use is rather specialized, it can probably be omitted with relative immunity. There is no guarantee that each font will be available at all `\magstep`s. Your user manual or local details should be able to fill in this essential information.

Recall that TEX is only interested in picking up the basic `tfm` information. It does not care whether the fonts are scaled or not. Only the output driver cares about that and usually only when it tries to use them.

⇒*Exercise 18.1:*   It may be noticeable that the longest font name will be eight characters long. Which fonts are these? Why should this characteristic be present?   ⇐

⇒*Exercise 18.2:*   Using the information in Figure 18.3, generate some samples for all the Computer Modern fonts available to you.   ⇐

It is also possible that other Computer Modern sizes will be available. It is quite possible to 'interpolate' extra sizes from the METAFONT descriptions and use these to generate both the `tfm` and `pk` (or `gf`) files needed. The `pk` file is a 'packed pixel' file which contains the font itself: it is used by the output driver. In fact, METAFONT will have generated a 'generic font' file (the `gf`), but this is usually transformed into the more compact `pk` file. There is no fundamental reason why a `cmr13` could not be generated, if required. Interpolating between two existing sizes is relatively straightforward, but extrapolating to a larger (or smaller) size may be a problem. It may turn out that `cmr25` or `cmssq10` is not at all satisfactory, unless you truly understand what you are doing. But this is well outside the scope of this primer.

Inspection of the table of the standard (or canonical) fonts shows that 10 point is well supported, and, really, all else revolves around this size. But we do not have to be tied too closely to this fact. It is not difficult to arrange that TEX becomes a little more flexible, and provide some commands which allow easy changes in the base size.

When `plain` sets up fonts, it does not use names like `\rm`, `\it`, and all the others with which we are familiar. Instead, they are set up in a much more specific way. For example,

`\font\tenrm=cmr10 \font\sevenrm=cmr7\font\fiverm=cmr5`
`\font\teni =cmmi10\font\seveni=cmmi7\font\fivei=cmmi5`
`\font\tenbf=cmbx10\font\sevenbf=cmbx7`

                                    `\font\fivebf=cmbx5`

and at some later point a definition associates the command `\rm` with `\tenrm` (and similarly for the other fonts). These assignments are examined more closely later in this chapter.

A careful scrutiny of *The* TEX*book* will reveal some rather interesting font manipulation commands, notably `\tenpoint` and `\ninepoint`. These are not part of `plain`, but are part of example formats discussed in Appendix E of *The* TEX*book*. From them we will be able to generalize to other convenient base sizes. The

notion is, for example, that we should be able to say `\ninepoint`
and from then on our text would be in a 9 point size, with suitable adjustment of the symbol fonts for maths, and of all the
other fonts, like slanted, italic, and so on. This would then make
it simple to switch back into `\tenpoint` (or some other size), in a
more or less arbitrary way. In order to understand what is going
on, it is useful first to go back into `plain`. There are a set of
commands in `plain` which set up many details concerning fonts.
The fundamentals are:

```
\textfont0=\tenrm \scriptfont0=\sevenrm
                  \scriptscriptfont0=\fiverm
  \def\rm{\fam0\tenrm}
\textfont1=\teni  \scriptfont1=\seveni
                  \scriptscriptfont1=\fivei
  \def\mit{\fam1}
  \def\oldstyle{\fam1\teni}
\textfont2=\tensy \scriptfont2=\sevensy
                  \scriptscriptfont2=\fivesy
  \def\cal{\fam2}
\textfont3=\tenex \scriptfont3=\tenex
                  \scriptscriptfont3=\tenex
```

We see some things which look vaguely familiar, although not
totally so. The `\textfont0` has a familiar ring, and clearly ties
into `\textstyle` in maths mode. The new concept is that of family, abbreviated by TEX to `\fam`. This has nothing to do with the
conventional typographic notion of 'family', but is a term introduced by Knuth to account for a particular usage of TEX within
maths. It has no specific meaning outside maths.

There may be up to 16 families of fonts, numbered from 0 to
15. Each family has three fonts, the `\textfont`, the `\scriptfont`,
and the `\scriptscriptfont`. As the extract above hints, family
1 is maths italic letters, family 2 is ordinary maths symbols, and
family 3 is for large symbols (the extension font). Maths fonts
usually have a little more information in them than normal text
fonts. This is one reason why it is difficult to make fonts other
than Computer Modern work properly in maths: the other reason
is the paucity of symbols in most other typefaces. Note, however,
that Knuth recently used the Concrete typeface, together with
Euler for maths, and that Lucida may also be available. Lucida
has a range of maths symbols equivalent to that of Computer
Modern. Spivak has also created a set of symbol and extension
fonts (MathTime) suitable for use with the Times typeface.

Although that goes some way to accounting for the commands, it does not quite describe the definitions of \rm, \mit, \oldstyle, and \cal. It does, however, highlight plain's preoccupation with mathematics, since none of this would be really necessary outside maths. Only \rm is met outside mathematics. Associating \rm with \tenrm, the 10 point Computer Modern Roman, is to be expected, but why the \fam0? When TEX enters maths mode, \fam is set to -1. In other words, each beginning \$ or \$\$ has an implied \fam-1. Font changes are controlled through the \fam value in maths mode. In order to obtain cmr style letters it is necessary to set \fam to zero – which is what \rm is doing. In horizontal mode, \fam0 has no effect, and the 'current font' (whatever is currently being used outside maths) has no meaning within maths, except in a couple of fairly obvious cases: material in an \hbox will refer back to the current font, and so too would a direct reference to a dimension through ex or em.

If the value of \fam is -1 when maths is entered, how does TEX know to pick up the appropriate style? Each mathematical character has an 'associated' code which, among other things, contains information on the family which is to be used. There is an implicit font which can (usually) be overwritten by the \fam value.

This begins to provide an explanation for the definition of the \mit and \cal commands too, although the \oldstyle requires a little more discussion. This command refers only to the numerals: in a sense it is similar to some of the commands like \cal and \bf in maths. It is fairly restricted in its range of operation. It applies only to the 10 numerals. It does, however, work inside and outside maths – the \teni sees to operation in normal text. So-called \oldstyle numerals look like this: 0123456789.

⇒*Exercise 18.3:* Given the information presented above, in what way will \$\oldstyle A9\$ differ from \$\oldstyle\cal A9\$? ⇐

⇒*Exercise 18.4:* How would you obtain calligraphic characters in ordinary text without explicitly going into maths? ⇐

There are some additional commands. Recall that \bf works in maths too. From our description above, it is obvious that \bf has to have some similarity with the way in which \rm is set up:

\newfam\bffam \def\bf{\fam\bffam\tenbf}
\textfont\bffam=\tenbf \scriptfont\bffam-\sevenbf
\scriptscriptfont\bffam=\fivebf

The only new command here is \newfam. Instead of deliberately choosing a family number for bold, TEX has the ability to choose the first available one, rather in the same manner as \newbox,

\newtoks, and the rest, allowing for the fact that \newfam is restricted to the range 0–15. The remaining fonts in general use by plain are set up with reference to \newfam too:

```
\newfam\itfam \def\it{\fam\itfam\tenit}
\textfont\itfam=\tenit
\newfam\slfam \def\sl{\fam\slfam\tensl}
\textfont\slfam=\tensl
\newfam\ttfam \def\tt{\fam\ttfam\tentt}
\textfont\ttfam=\tentt
```

⇒*Exercise 18.5:*   We now have the capability of changing the way in which TEX handles sub- and superscripts. Assume that we wish the progression to be 10 pt for the equivalent of text style, 8 pt for script style, and 6 pt for script script style. Alternatively, let there be only one level of script styles, at say 7 pt. Is there any way to extend the progression of sub- and superscripts to three or more levels?   ⇐

We now have the sort of information which makes the \tenpoint and \ninepoint commands easier to understand. The \tenpoint is slightly easier to recognize since it refers to the 10 point fonts with which we are more familiar:

```
\def\tenpoint{\def\rm{\fam0\tenrm}%
  \textfont0=\tenrm \scriptfont0=\sevenrm
                    \scriptscriptfont0=\fiverm
  \textfont1=\teni  \scriptfont1=\seveni
                    \scriptscriptfont1=\fivei
  \textfont2=\tensy \scriptfont2=\sevensy
                    \scriptscriptfont2=\fivesy
  \textfont3=\tenex \scriptfont3=\tenex
                    \scriptscriptfont3=\tenex
  \def\it{\fam\itfam\tenit}%
    \textfont\itfam=\tenit
  \def\sl{\fam\slfam\tensl}%
    \textfont\slfam=\tensl
  \def\bf{\fam\bffam\tenbf}%
    \textfont\bffam=\tenbf \scriptfont\bffam=\sevenbf
    \scriptscriptfont\bffam=\fivebf
  \def\tt{\fam\ttfam\tentt}%
    \textfont\ttfam=\tentt
  \normalbaselineskip=12pt
  \let\big=\tenbig
  \setbox\strutbox=\hbox{%
    \vrule height8.5pt depth3.5pt width0pt}%
  \normalbaselines\rm}
```

Only the last few lines introduce anything noteworthy. (In passing, this \tenpoint command is almost identical to the commands which Knuth developed for Appendix E of *The TEXbook*.) The \normalbaselines is there to ensure that should we be changing from another size, the baselines will be appropriate for 10 point sizes. In executing the command \normalbaselines, \baselineskip is reset to \normalbaselineskip. The command \tenbig is derived from plain's \big and deserves a little extra explanation: looking back into plain, we will see that \big is defined as:

```
\def\big#1{{\hbox{%
   $\left#1\vbox to 8.5pt{}\right.\n@space$}}}
```

Most of this seems quite sensible, and makes the use of \big in maths quite logical. It is interesting that the apparent dichotomy between the use of the delimiters generated by \left and \right and those which use \big (and its variants) is more apparent than real. In the same set of commands that Knuth includes \tenpoint he defines \tenbig exactly as the \big above. The \n@space requires a little further explanation:

```
\def\n@space{\nulldelimiterspace=0pt \m@th}
```

Obviously it is a 'guarded' command which is not to be used by the normal user without some effort. The width of a null delimiter (a \right. or \left.) is 'normally' 1.2 pt. This particular null delimiter is zero. The other command here, \m@th, is shorthand for \mathsurround=0pt. Again we are ensuring that no space is inserted in this context. If we were really obsessive, we might wish to ensure that \Big, \bigg, and \Bigg are also reset here. The \strutbox is just the standard one used for setting up \strut. If we look through plain, we will find a definition of the versatile \strut:

```
\def\strut{\relax
   \ifmmode\copy\strutbox\else\unhcopy\strutbox\fi}
```

This is remarkably robust, and demonstrates a use for \unhcopy. It also demonstrates that if we change the definition of \strutbox, the size of \strut will change quite conveniently.

⇒*Exercise 18.6:*   Be obsessive and add \Big and the other 'large' delimiters.   ⇐

⇒*Exercise 18.7:*   Add the CM Caps and Small Caps font to this \tenpoint command, and enable it to be used in maths.   ⇐

⇒*Exercise 18.8:*   Now that the structure of the delimiters given by \big through to \Bigg has been revealed, it is possible to add more, for example, \BIG and \BIGG. Do so.   ⇐

From eight fifty

A very similar \ninepoint command can be defined as:

```
\def\ninepoint{\def\rm{\fam0\ninerm}%
  \textfont0=\ninerm \scriptfont0=\sixrm
              \scriptscriptfont0=\fiverm
  \textfont1=\ninei  \scriptfont1=\sixi
              \scriptscriptfont1=\fivei
  \textfont2=\ninesy \scriptfont2=\sixsy
              \scriptscriptfont2=\fivesy
  \textfont3=\tenex  \scriptfont3=\tenex
              \scriptscriptfont3=\tenex
  \def\it{\fam\itfam\nineit}%
    \textfont\itfam=\nineit
  \def\sl{\fam\slfam\ninesl}%
    \textfont\slfam=\ninesl
  \def\bf{\fam\bffam\ninebf}%
    \textfont\bffam=\ninebf \scriptfont\bffam=\sixbf
    \scriptscriptfont\bffam=\fivebf
  \def\tt{\fam\ttfam\ninett}%
    \textfont\ttfam=\ninett
  \normalbaselineskip=11pt
  \setbox\strutbox=\hbox{%
    \vrule height8pt depth3pt width0pt}%
  \let\big\ninebig
  \normalbaselines\rm}
```

This is very similar to the definition of \tenpoint. Clearly there have to be substitutes for the 10 and 7 point fonts used in maths. Note the different values in \strutbox. Equally, \big has been set equivalent to \ninebig. The definition of \ninebig is:

```
\def\ninebig#1{{\hbox{%
    $\textfont0=\tenrm\textfont2=\tensy
    \left#1\vbox to7.25pt{}\right.\n@space$}}}
```

The maths italic font, \textfont1, is not mentioned, since it does not contain any parentheses.

Of course, all these references to \ninebf and so on imply the presence of commands like

```
\font\ninebf=cmbx9
```

There must be a reference where that particular font is set up. It may be necessary to manipulate the way the fonts are set up a little in order to get things to come out approximately right. Not every font is available at a variety of sizes. How do we try to solve that problem? There are ways. We might decide to load the fonts at different scale factors:

`\font\twelvesc=cmcsc10 scaled\magstep1`

but this runs into difficulties when we need smaller sizes, since few implementations will keep, for example, a `cmcsc10 at 9pt`. They might, but it is unlikely. T_EX will not complain, but the output (if you do get any) won't look too good. Is there a solution? META-FONT! There is no real reason why you should not generate your own fonts at the sizes you want. After all, the METAFONT descriptions are public. Of course, generating your own means that the portability of your document is compromised. Another possibility exists. In some cases, fonts may be scalable. This implies that if we ask for `cmcsc10 at 9pt`, the driver will create such a font for you. This does not have to involve METAFONT, if the fonts themselves are stored in an 'outline' form. The most common scheme which employs this form of encoding is POSTSCRIPT. POSTSCRIPT fonts are stored as outlines, not as raster images. Traditionally, Computer Modern was a raster image (or bit-map), but recently it has been rendered as an outline, in conventional POSTSCRIPT form. If you have a POSTSCRIPT output device, this gives great flexibility.

⇒*Exercise 18.9:*   You should have about enough information to generate a `\twelvepoint` or an `\eightpoint` equivalent.   ⇐

If we are going to use this sort of `\ninepoint` command, then we really ought to look at `\magnification`. T_EX comes with a command which sees to it that a basic document can be magnified by a series of factors. The defaults are all to the ratio of 1.2, in steps of half, one, two, three, four, and five. Thus simply saying

`\magnification\magstephalf`

right at the beginning of a document magnifies every dimension (including the fonts) by $1.2^{0.5}$ or $\sqrt{1.2}$ – approximately 1.1. This is what I almost always do, except I use `\magstep1`, giving me a basic 12 point look. I would really rather use `\twelvepoint`, but I would loose a few fonts and have to do a bit more work. When I am typesetting a book I usually use 10 point, but course notes and drafts are easier to read on standard paper sizes at about 12 point. As I get older I shall start to use `\magstep2`.

It is worth glancing at the command for `\magstep`. It runs

```
\def\magstep#1{\ifcase#1 1000\or
   1200\or 1440\or 1728\or 2074\or 2488\fi\relax}
```

and there is another 'special' one for `\magstephalf`:

```
\def\magstephalf{1095 }
```

Really then, \magsteps are only a convenient shorthand, and there is nothing (well, not much) to stop us saying \magnification500 or even \magnification1095.

⇒*Exercise 18.10:*   You might like to make \magstep a little more friendly: what happens if I inadvertently say \magstep7?   ⇐

Why go to all the trouble of using \twelvepoint and so on when we could just use \magnification? The main reason revolves around the concept of the design size. Going back to the tfm files, you may recall that a font has a 'design' size. This is the size at which it was meant to be read. In the old days, every letter in every size was 'different'. It was not just scaled up or down geometrically, but there were subtle non-linear changes as we went up the scale from a 6 pt to a 24 pt character. Photosetting rather killed this idea, since in photosetting there is often just one master shape, from which all sizes are generated optically. In some cases there may be three or four 'masters', each applicable to a particular range. The Adobe fonts are examples of scalable fonts. Their Times Roman was based on a 14 point master, which partly accounts for its ugliness at 10 pt. In their Type 1 fonts Adobe include 'hints' which alleviate some of the scaling problems, although they were mainly intended to tackle the problems of low resolution.

Recall that if I had put

\font\five=cmr5 at \magstep5

TEX would have taken the existing magnification and added it to any existing one, perhaps giving a magnification of 6. Many implementations have a \magstep6. Mine does not. This additivity illustrates a problem with magnification. If we used \magstephalf, combining it with something at another magnification would give us the rather odd magnification of 'something and a half'. Beware.

Another dimension

Every font has associated with it a number of \fontdimen parameters. We have touched briefly on these already. All fonts have at least a basic seven dimensions associated with them. The maths fonts have rather more: the extension fonts have at least 13, while the symbol fonts have at least 22. The details of these \fontdimens are not essential unless we want to do something rather sophisticated, but it is still worth providing some account of the seven dimensions associated with the fonts most likely to

\fontdimen	Description
1	slant factor; for positioning accents – relevant for slanted and italic typefaces. This is actually a slant per point figure, and is therefore unaffected by changes to the magnification, unlike the other \fontdimens.
2	normal interword space; this may be altered by reference to \spaceskip.
3	interword stretch; the interword space normally has a stretch and shrink component. Since \spaceskip is a true \skip quantity, it has a plus and minus part associated with it. This is the plus part.
4	interword shrink; this corresponds to the minus part of a \spaceskip.
5	the x-height; the height of lower-case characters without ascenders. Whenever you use a distance ex, this will be the value used – it is therefore font specific. Even between fonts of the same notional 'size' the x-height may vary. The most obvious example is between bold and normal weight characters. The bold characters tend to have a larger x-height.
6	quad width; this is the width given to a \quad; the em is also set through this dimension; they are therefore font specific.
7	extra space; this is the additional space which is added at the end of sentences. There are two ways to alter this value; indirectly through the use of \frenchspacing, and directly through \xspaceskip.

Figure 18.4
The first seven
font dimensions
and their
descriptions

occur in ordinary text. Since we will refer to these a few times, the descriptions of the 'essential' \fontdimens are given in Figure 18.4.

Any of the \fontdimen values may be changed: for example,
```
\fontdimen2\tenrm=3.5pt
\fontdimen3\tenrm=1.25pt
\fontdimen4\tenrm=1.15pt
```
have the effect of changing the interword spaces for 10 point Computer Modern Roman. An equivalent would be

	cmr10	cmti10	cmsl10	cmbx10	cmtt10	cmmi10
1	0.00	0.25	0.17	0.00	0.00	0.25
2	3.33	3.58	3.33	3.83	5.25	0.00
3	1.67	1.53	1.67	1.92	0.00	0.00
4	1.11	1.02	1.11	1.28	0.00	0.00
5	4.31	4.31	4.31	4.44	4.31	4.31
6	10.00	10.22	10.00	11.50	10.50	10.00
7	1.11	1.02	1.11	1.28	5.25	0.00

Figure 18.5
The font dimensions of the 'basic' fonts

`\spaceskip=3.5pt plus1.25pt minus1.15pt`
Of the two, changing the \fontdimens is global in its scope, while the \spaceskip refers only to the current font, is local, and can of course be grouped.

What does Figure 18.5, the table of font dimensions, tell us? Among other things, it highlights the fundamental differences embodied in both the Typewriter Text font (cmtt10) and the Math Italic font (cmmi10). Taking the Typewriter Text font first, the key value is the \quad width (\fontdimen6). The normal interword space (\fontdimen2) and 'extra space' are each half this value. The x-height is of little consequence. All the other dimensions are zero: the slant value, like that in all the other non-slanted fonts, is obviously zero, but there is no stretch and shrink associated with the interword skip. Since we generally wish the typewriter style to be a monospaced style, it is logical to restrict the spaces to units which correspond to the width of the characters in the font. Note though that if we were setting a whole paragraph of typewriter text, it would be surprising if the limited flexibility that we have permitted here was sufficient. It is probably appropriate to set typewriter (or any other monospaced) fonts with ragged-right. The default \raggedright is not entirely sympathetic, and **plain** provides \ttraggedright. This difference is not directly related to fonts, but still worth pursuing here. The ragged-right commands are
`\def\raggedright{\rightskip=0pt plus2em`
`    \spaceskip=0.3333em \xspaceskip=0.5em}`
`\def\ttraggedright{\tt\rightskip=0pt plus2em}`
The \spaceskip and \xspaceskip dimensions are quite clear, but the \rightskip requires more explanation. There are two commands, \rightskip and \leftskip, which we have met through \narrower. There, they were both \advanced by the extent of the \parindent. No glue was involved. In this context, these skips are all glue. In building lines, TeX normally places an amount of

glue equivalent to the \leftskip and \rightskip amounts on the left and right respectively. Permitting the \rightskip to be glue is a way of making the right margin ragged. In 'normal' text the raggedness should not be too great. Hyphenation is normally permitted. But in a monospaced font we might be inclined to allow much more flexibility at the margin, especially if we want to suppress hyphenation too. In the typewriter version it is not necessary to include the space skips, since they have already been given appropriate values in cmtt and have no glue associated with them.

An even more attractive proposition is to attempt to detect whether a typewriter font is in use, and set the \rightskip appropriately. How might this be done? The 'number' of the typewriter family is normally 7. There is no reason we should know this, and going back into the various font-related commands, we will recall a \ttfam. This is a more flexible approach. Provided that there is a \newfam\ttfam, and that the definition of \tt is something like
\def\tt{\fam\ttfam\tentt}
so that both a text and mathematical context have been set up, we can test the value of the family:
\ifnum\fam=\ttfam
Note that we are interested in the 'family', not the expression of the typewriter font. Employing this strategy can give far greater flexibility. It is possible to pick up the actual font through a command \fontname, but that would yield something like cmtt10, or cmtt9. We would therefore have to devise a test structure which looked at only the cmtt part, somehow ignoring the numeric value which might follow. Testing the \fam is far easier. This allows us to create a new \raggedright command:
\def\raggedright{\rightskip0pt plus2em
\ifnum\fam=\ttfam
\else\spaceskip0.3333em \xspaceskip0.5em\fi}
⇒*Exercise 18.11:*   There are a couple of refinements we might make to this new definition. It would be useful to be able to turn off the hyphenation in typewriter. Setting \hyphenchar\fontname-1 has this effect. Unfortunately, this requires that we insert \ninett, or \tentt, or whatever for \fontname. This seems to put us back a step in generality. Fortunately, \font gives the name of the current font, so that \hyphenchar\font-1 would be satisfactory. Another useful feature would be to give much more flexibility on the right margin, or to permit the interword space to have some flexibility in the glue: suitable values might be 0.5em plus.25em minus.15em. Incorporate some of these changes. ⇐
⇒*Exercise 18.12:*   The information you have about \rightskip and \leftskip may enable you to create an environment where text is 'cen-

\fontdimen	Description
13	vertical movement of superscripts in display style (relative to the horizontal maths axis).
14	vertical movement of superscripts in text style.
15	vertical movement of superscripts in display mode when in 'cramped style', for example below a root or a vinculum.
16	minimum distance between subscripts and the baseline when there is no superscript.
17	minimum distance between subscripts and the baseline when there is a superscript.

Figure 18.6
A few extra font dimensions and their descriptions

tred' in each line. The only real problem you may encounter is with the very last line in any paragraph. The last line is normally left justified. In order to accomplish this TEX has a command, \parfillskip, which is normally set to 0pt plus 1fil. That is to say, all glue. This glue ensures that the text on the last line is pushed to the left. In the case of centering text, this glue will have to balance exactly the glue of the \leftskip. ⇐

Let's return briefly to the \fontdimens, but only to a few which are especially relevant, and touch on a subject which was raised much earlier. In Chapter 4 we noted that the position of subscripts depended on whether superscripts were present or not. This positioning is also controlled through \fontdimen values. In this case, the two relevant values are 16 and 17 (see Figure 18.6).

In order to control these minimum distances, it should be sufficient to reset the values of \fontdimen. For example,
\fontdimen16\tensy=\fontdimen17\tensy
For this particular font, the value of \fontdimen17 is 2.47 pt.

⇒*Exercise 18.13:*   An alternative way of controlling the positioning of the subscripts could be to choose another value altogether, perhaps between the value of \fontdimen16 and \fontdimen17. It should be possible to devise a way of establishing this missing dimension. You may also alter the height of the superscripts.   ⇐

More detailed fonts

There is an area which we have hardly touched, that of the position of characters in a font. The characters in a font may be accessed in a number of ways. We are accustomed to the 'normal' way, by actually specifying the character – a, b, c, ... : similarly, some characters are accessed through commands – \ae, \o, \l, \clubsuit, ...

At the very simplest level, the command \char permits you to access any of the 256 characters in a font. For example, \char97 references character 97 in a font: this is 'a' in many fonts. Checking back into the font table, Figure 19.1, note that the numbering starts at 0.

	$'0$	$'1$	$'2$	$'3$	$'4$	$'5$	$'6$	$'7$
$'00x$	Γ	Δ	Θ	Λ	Ξ	Π	Σ	Υ
$'01x$	Φ	Ψ	Ω	ff	fi	fl	ffi	ffl
$'02x$	ı	ȷ	`	´	ˇ	˘	¯	˚
$'03x$	¸	ß	æ	œ	ø	Æ	Œ	Ø
$'04x$	´	!	"	#	$	%	&	'
$'05x$	(	)	*	+	,	-	.	/
$'06x$	0	1	2	3	4	5	6	7
$'07x$	8	9	:	;	¡	=	¿	?
$'10x$	@	A	B	C	D	E	F	G
$'11x$	H	I	J	K	L	M	N	O
$'12x$	P	Q	R	S	T	U	V	W
$'13x$	X	Y	Z	[	"	]	^	·
$'14x$	`	a	b	c	d	e	f	g
$'15x$	h	i	j	k	l	m	n	o
$'16x$	p	q	r	s	t	u	v	w
$'17x$	x	y	z	–	—	"	~	¨

Figure 19.1
Font table
for Computer
Modern Roman

Why are only 128 characters shown in Figure 19.1 when we can use 256 characters in a font? Although TEX3 allows us to input 256 characters from the keyboard, this is an 'input' character set, not an output one. The Computer Modern typeface has only 128 output characters. However, 256 character output fonts have been developed as extensions to Computer Modern.

Since there are 128 characters in Computer Modern, it is convenient to divide the table into groups of eight or 16. There is a convenient way to refer to octal (base 8) or hexadecimal (base 16) numbers, rather than decimal numbers. For example, the following are equivalent: \char'152 and \char"6A. An octal number is preceded by a ', while a hexadecimal number is preceded by a ". Note that the hexadecimal numbers use the upper-case alphabetic characters. Using lower-case will lead to trouble.

⇒*Exercise 19.1:*   The font table is indexed in octal. Try to create a similar table indexed in hexadecimal.   ⇐

If you were truly determined, you could write text by referring to the character positions in the fonts. In fact, as far as text is concerned, you need only have access to the individual characters \, c, h, a, r, and either 0–7 and ' or A–F, 0–9, and ". But it is not possible to use commands through this mechanism. Writing

\tt\char'134\char'101\char'101

yields \AA, rather than Å. Note that most fonts do not contain the backslash character. This is why we changed to \tt here, since it does contain this character. The standard text fonts have characters which are given in Figure 19.1. Naturally the maths symbol fonts and the extension fonts are very different. So too are the maths italic. The typewriter text font contains a number of variations too. The bulk is identical, but as noted earlier in Chapter 6, there are some key differences. These fonts are illustrated in Appendix A.

How then might we define \ae? The obvious way, based on the commands we have met so far, is:

\def\ae{\char'032}   *or*   \def\ae{\char"1A}

but in fact plain has a more terse way, through a command which simultaneously defines and references a character:

\chardef\ae='032   *or*   \chardef\ae="1A

This has the useful feature, from a command writer's point of view, that it uses slightly less of TeX's memory. How would you know that it used more or less memory? Tracing commands will report how much memory has been used.

⇒*Exercise 19.2:*   Find out how many words of memory you save by using \chardef rather than a 'conventional' \def.   ⇐

There is yet another way to define characters, although its use is restricted to individual characters or to commands whose 'name'

is a single character. For example, in order to define `\&` as a way
of accessing &, we may write

`\def\&{\char38}` *or* `\def\&{\char'46}` *or* `\chardef\&='&`

as already discussed. But in addition, both

`\def\&{\char'&}` *and* `\def\&{\char'\&}`

will do exactly the same job. The left quote character followed by
either a character or a command given by a single character is
understood by TEX to represent the internal code of that character. To some extent it is not necessary that you know the corre-
spondences given in the font table. When is the 'extra' \ needed,
and when may it be omitted? Its inclusion never does any harm,
but the rule is that it is mandatory when the category code is 0, 5,
9, 14, or 15 (see Figure 7.1). In short, that's the escape character,
the end of line character, an ignored character, the comment character, and an invalid character. These cases are intuitively obvious.

TEX font metrics

In order to discuss font metrics effectively, it is useful to introduce
another piece of TEXware, which you may or may not have available. It is not essential to have access to this, but some background
information is enlightening. Traditionally, there is a utility named
TFtoPL. With the introduction of 'virtual fonts', coincidental with
TEX3, though not directly related to it, a new utility, VFtoPL,
replaced it. For the purposes of this description, either of these
utilities is valid. Both convert TEX font metric (`tfm`) files into
equivalent property list (`pl`) files. The property list file output by
this utility has the advantage that it can be edited with a normal
text editor, and the result can be converted back to `tfm` format
by using the companion utilities PLtoTF or PLtoVF.

The idea behind `tfm` files is that TEX and the host computer
need a compact way to store the relevant information about fonts.
The `tfm` files are compact and most of the information they contain is highly relevant, so they provide a solution to the problem.
⇒*Exercise 19.3:* If you do have VFtoPL or TFtoPL available, generate
a property list for one of the `tfm` files.   ⇐

Rather than go through all the elements of a property list, only
the major parts will be covered here. Essentially they comprise a
header, with some general information (some of which TEX will
not actually use, but a device driver might), and various blocks
of information: one contains the font dimensions; another the
ligaturing information; another the character information which

includes details of the dimensions of individual characters; and lastly, a block which indicates how large 'extensible' characters are to be built.

Header

The property list begins with a block of header information. It includes

1 a check sum; the check sum is simply an identification number. Incompatible fonts almost always have distinct check sums. Some drivers will pick up check sum information and will report if it is untoward.

2 the design size of the font, in units of TEX points (72.27 points to the inch). This number is fairly arbitrary, but usually the design size is 10.0 for a '10 point' font, that is, a font that was designed to look 'best' at a 10 point size. It is the amount by which all quantities will be scaled if the font is not loaded with an 'at' specification. For example, `\font rm=cmr10` would lead to the design size being used, but if you use `\font rm=cmr10 at 15pt` the design size is ignored and replaced by 15 points. The quantity is always points.

3 the design units. Normally this would be 1: that is, how many units equal the design size (the eventual 'at' size if the font is being scaled).

4 identification of the character coding scheme; for example, are `ascii` for standard ASCII, `tex text` for fonts like `cmr` and `cmti`, `tex math extension` for `cmex`, `graphic` for special-purpose non-alphabetic fonts `unspecified` for the default case when there is no information? Actually TEX ignores this information; it is included in case other software might find it useful.

5 the name of the font family (for example, `cmr` or `concrete`). Again, TEX ignores this.

6 an identification of the font within its family (family is used here in the wider typographic sense). Ignored by TEX.

Font dimensions

The font dimensions which were explored earlier in this chapter are part of the `tfm` files. The first seven of the `FONTDIMEN` properties correspond exactly to the first seven `\fontdimens` which we have already met. There are up to 22 font dimensions, but those numbered from eight to 22 are not used in text. To reiterate, the first seven in the `tfm` nomenclature are:

SLANT: the amount of italic slant, which is also used to help position accents.

SPACE: the normal spacing between words in text.

STRETCH: the amount of glue stretching between words.

SHRINK: the amount of glue shrinking between words.

XHEIGHT: the x-height is the height of lower-case characters without descenders, or, put another way, the height of letters for which accents do not have to be raised or lowered.

QUAD: the size of one em in the font (or one quad).

EXTRASPACE: the amount added to SPACE after a full stop at the end of a sentence.

When the character coding scheme is `tex mathsy` the font has fifteen additional parameters. When the character coding scheme is `tex mathex` the font is supposed to have six additional parameters. Curiously, there is no reason why you should not store numerical information in these 'unused' locations and retrieve them for some very specialized application, (for example, see Hoenig, 1991).

Ligature information

The LIGTABLE contains instructions in a simple programming language which explains what to do for special letter pairs. The two key instructions are LIG and KRN. It should not be difficult to guess that LIG is a command to indicate how to ligature pairs of characters. For example, in many fonts, an 'f' followed by an 'f' would be replaced by 'ff'. If this new character was itself followed by an 'i' it could be replaced by 'ffi'. This is controlled through this part of the property list. The KRN allows us to kern pairs of characters. This implies that kerning in TEX will only ever be on the basis of pairs of characters. The LIGTABLE is terminated by a STOP statement.

Character

The value is an integer followed by a list of properties. The integer represents the number of a character present in the font. The elements of the property list may be:

CHARWD: the character's width in design-size units.

CHARHT: the character's height in design-size units.

VCHARDP: the character's depth in design-size units.

CHARIC: the character's italic correction in design-size units.

NEXTLARGER: specifies the character that follows the present one in a list of characters.

VARCHAR: specifies an extensible character: the elements of this property list are top, bot, mid, or rep, indicating whether the character code is used to make up the top, bottom, middle, or replicated piece of an extensible character.

Extension

Extensible characters are assembled through a recipe which uses the character codes of individual pieces to build up a large symbol.

Numbers

Values in a property list can be expressed in several ways:

R is used to express a real number;

D is used for a decimal integer;

O is an octal integer;

H is a hexadecimal integer;

C is used for an ASCII character, provided it is a standard 'visible' character, *except* a parenthesis.

There is another code, 'a Xerox face code', which probably has only historical interest.

As examples, a check sum might be expressed as an octal value:

(CHECKSUM O 11374260171)

while many other values might be real numbers:

(DESIGNSIZE R 10.0)

This last example could be expressed as D 10 or O 12 or even H A. The character notation is often used in the ligature tables. For example,

(LABEL C v)

(KRN C a R -0.055555)

specifies that firstly we are dealing with the character 'v', and that when this letter is followed by an 'a', it will be kerned by −0.55555 pt (the fundamental unit revealed above). When it is not possible to use C, it is possible to specify characters in one of the other ways. For example,

(LIG C i O 14)

indicates that when this character 'i' is ligatured with another (in this case, an 'f'), it is replaced by a new character with the octal value of 14. An inspection of the font table for Computer Modern shows that this is the 'fi' ligature (as you would expect).

Property list description of font metrics

A property list file is a list of entries of the form

(`propertyname value`)

where the 'property name' is one of a limited set of names, and
the value may itself be a property list. It is easier to look at an
example. Figure 19.2 contains a fragment of the property list from
Computer Modern Roman at 10 point. This example says that the
font whose metric information is being described belongs to the
CMR family; and `codingscheme` states that the characters appear
in the TEX TEXT code positions. The `designsize` is 10 points (the
R states that this is expressed as a real number); all other sizes in
this property list are given in units such that the units are multi-
ples of this design size. The font is not slanted (a slant would have
some effect on the position of accents). The normal space between
words is 3.33334 pt (in this case one-third of the 10 pt design size),
with glue that shrinks by one-third of this or stretches by one-
half. In other words, if we take the shrink (and extra space) as
2 units, all the other horizontal dimensions are integral values –
for example, the ratios of shrink:stretch:space:quad are 2:3:6:18.
This last value, 18, is a clue. The original Monotype system had
its fonts built on a 9 unit grid (and later, an 18 unit grid). The
letters for which accents do not need to be raised or lowered are
4.3 pt high, and one em is a fraction of a whisker over 10 pt.

The example ligature table specifies that the letter 'f' followed
by 'i' is changed to code octal 14, while 'f' followed by 'f' is changed
to octal 13, and so on. Further, when 'f' is followed by the code 41
(an exclamation mark), or 51 (a right parenthesis), an additional
0.77779 pt of space should be inserted after the 'f'. Note that this
is where the notion of an 18 unit matrix for Computer Modern falls
down, but kerning values are generally quite small, and a restriction to a minimum of one-eighteenth of 10 pt would be unrealistic.

Character 'f' itself is 3.05557 pt wide and 6.94445 pt tall. Its
italic correction is 0.77779 pt. Again, the widths are not constrained to match the traditional Monotype structure.

Beyond Computer Modern

It is not particularly difficult to use fonts other than Computer
Modern with TEX. As we have commented earlier, all that TEX
requires are the `tfm` files to be available. To illustrate this, let's
take the relatively easy case of 'ordinary' text fonts. Let us assume

that we have a font family 'Aldine'. How do we set it up for use
with T_EX?

```
\font\tenrm=Aldine   at 10pt %a 'roman'
\font\tenit=AldineI at 10pt %an 'italic'
\font\tenbf=AldineB at 10pt %a 'bold'
```

In fact we could simply ensure that this was read in before the text
was typeset (remembering to issue the command \rm, or T_EX will
start off in CM Roman). We would then have available the basic
\rm, \it, and \bf fonts. For most text that will probably be quite
satisfactory. If we wanted to become more sophisticated, we could
also substitute various other fonts for others of Computer Modern. It is unlikely that this Aldine will have a Sans Serif (the first
Sans Serifs appeared about 1816, while the Aldine might go back
to 1499). But essentially there is no real problem here. If we want
to try to incorporate mathematics, there are problems. Assuming
that all the characters are available, we also need to ensure that
all the \fontdimen values that we need are available. In maths we
need an extra 12 \fontdimen values. The \fontdimens needed
for text are not too difficult to determine, and will generally be
available in some form. Knowing what we do about property lists,
we can always create tfms by hand, if necessary. Finding, or even
estimating, the additional dimensions which are required in maths
is by no means straightforward. Often the information is proprietary, but over the last few years font suppliers have become rather
more relaxed in releasing the details.

Extending Computer Modern

There are already some extensions to Computer Modern with
which you may already be familiar. The L^AT_EX fonts have already
been introduced. In order to use them in plain, you have to load
them yourself. Their use is rather specialized, but for reference
sake, they are listed in Figure 19.3. Similarly, there are extra sym-
bols available for use with $\mathcal{A}_{\mathcal{M}}\mathcal{S}$-T_EX. These extra symbols seem
quite esoteric to me, but may be needed, and can also be used
within plain. Both these sets of fonts are designed to be used
alongside Computer Modern. There are two main categories of
AMS fonts: there are the 'normal' extra symbols in the msam and
msbm fonts, and the extra alphabets, which are termed the 'Euler'
fonts, and which include a Fraktur. Fraktur is a Gothic typeface,
similar in style to T_EX's $\Re$ and $\Im$. In addition the Euler family has
a script and a cursive font. They are all available in a bold and a

```
(FAMILY CMR)
(CODINGSCHEME TEX TEXT)
(DESIGNSIZE R 10.0)
(COMMENT DESIGNSIZE IS IN POINTS)
(COMMENT OTHER SIZES ARE MULTIPLES OF DESIGNSIZE)
(CHECKSUM O 11374260171)
(FONTDIMEN
   (SLANT R 0.0)
   (SPACE R 0.333334)
   (STRETCH R 0.166667)
   (SHRINK R 0.111112)
   (XHEIGHT R 0.430555)
   (QUAD R 1.000003)
   (EXTRASPACE R 0.111112)
   )
(LIGTABLE
   (LABEL C f)
   (LIG C i O 14)
   (LIG C f O 13)
   (KRN O 41 R 0.077779)
   (KRN O 51 R 0.077779)
   (STOP)
(CHARACTER C f
   (CHARWD R 0.305557)
   (CHARHT R 0.694445)
   (CHARIC R 0.077779)
   )
```

Figure 19.2
Fragments of
a specimen
property list

medium weight. There are also the 'blackboard bold' fonts in msbm. Blackboard bold has always seemed a strange font to me. Approximately, its history is this: in order to indicate a bold font when writing an expression on a blackboard, certain conventions arose, basically writing certain strokes as double strokes. This is only an expedient since a true bold font is difficult to write. In a printed formula, we would expect a true bold font to be used. But true to the unwritten code of mathematicians, there are never enough symbols available, and they began to demand a typographic version so that they can use both true bold and this other manifestation. The analogy in conventional typewriting is underlining, which is used to indicate stress, and usually translates into italics.

There are some pitfalls. The first pitfall may be in the names of the LATEX fonts. They ought all to begin with the letter 'l'.

Font name	Sizes available (points)
lasy	5, 6, 7, 8, 9, 10
lasyb	10
line	10
linew	10
lcircle	10
lcirclew	10

Figure 19.3
The LATEX
fonts

When they were first released, they were named more naturally. For example, lcircle10 was originally circle10. It is possible that these conventions are still adopted by the implementation you use. Should TEX come back to you with the message

! Font \rm=Aldine at 10.0pt not loadable:
                    Metric (TFM) file not found.

it will mean either that TEX is unable to locate the appropriate font, which may be because you mistyped the name of the font, or that it is one of those which has undergone this change in name. The addition of the 'l' threw up at least one rather distressing problem. The font circlew (wide circle) is available at 10 points, and the logical name is therefore lcirclew10. This leads to a name of nine characters. In order to reduce it back to the 'normal' maximum of eight characters the trailing zero may be dropped, giving lcirclew1, which is rather inconsistent with any other font name.

There may also be a pitfall with the names of the AMS fonts. There are essentially two versions of $\mathcal{AMS}$-TEX; the more recent version has had new fonts designed for it, with correspondingly different names. The old style names were msxm and msym to which the fonts sizes 5–10 were appended. Why the difference? The old fonts were designed with the previous version of METAFONT, and had been released for only a limited range of resolutions (and for a particular type of laser printer). The second round of fonts, designed with the current METAFONT, was released with its METAFONT description files, making it possible for anyone with access to METAFONT to generate their own fonts, suitable for whatever output devices they might have. This makes the new descriptions immeasurably more useful. But equally, your implementation may have the old versions. In general this will not worry you if you wish to use the symbols. If you have access to the fonts, you will have access to a file mssymb.tex (the 'old' $\mathcal{AMS}$-TEX), which references the fonts and sets up the names which will be used too.

The remaining pitfall is that you might just run out of font memory. TEX sets aside a certain amount of its memory for loading fonts. The \preloaded fonts take up some of this memory, and loading lots of others may mean that that area of memory is exhausted. What can we do then? Well, the problem is not quite as serious as it may at first sound. All that is required is to create a new format, or fmt file. First locate plain.tex and edit out the fonts which you think you are never likely to use. Many of the \preloaded fonts are likely to fall into this category. It is most unlikely that you will want all 75 fonts in a single document. Next you have to find a special version of TEX called INITEX. This is a version of TEX which has some interesting properties, the major one being its ability to create format files through the use of a new command, \dump. This particular command may only be used in INITEX. The edited version of plain ought to be renamed if you do more than merely eliminate preloaded fonts. Knuth says 'files like plain.tex should not be changed in any way, except with respect to preloaded fonts, unless the changes are authorized by (their) author'. Run your new version of plain.tex through INITEX. It will respond with a few messages, and you may note that it also reads hyphen.tex, a file which contains information on hyphenation. Should you wish to create a version of TEX for use with another language, you could use a hyphenation file appropriate for that language, and create a corresponding format file. But whatever you do, remember to type \dump at the end of the file. INITEX will then create a file with the file name extension fmt.

The usual way to make TEX use this new format file (let's call it fancy.tex) is to write

```
tex &fancy
```

although most operating systems will have a way of creating a more elegant way of incorporating the alternate format file. Information on this should be available with your implementation.
⇒*Exercise 19.4:* It is straightforward to create new format files. Locate your plain.tex, eliminate the \preloaded fonts, and create a new format. Using \tracingstats=1, find out how much font memory is saved by this. ⇐

One last group of fonts is normally available, the logo fonts. These are the fonts which provide the characters necessary to write METAFONT. They are rather basic since they contain only seven characters. They are available in three basic styles – upright, slanted and bold, respectively logo, logosl, and logobf. All three

are available at 10 point, but only `logo` is available also at 8 and
9 point.

⇒*Exercise 19.5:*   How would you create a command for the META-
FONT logo?   ⇐

Making pages 20

Although we have looked at some aspects of building pages, we have not tackled this in a systematic way. In this chapter we will look at the default arrangements that TeX has for page building, and the ways this may be modified for more specialist requirements. In particular, we shall examine some of the techniques which may be employed in order to achieve double-column output. This seems a perennial problem, not least since the most common size of paper available, generally of the order of just over 8 inches, or about 750 points, requires some alternative to the default strategy when faced with 10 point fonts.

How does `plain` tackle output? In some ways, this is not the best place to start. As we have noted before, the `plain` commands represent a working model which includes many embellishments which take it beyond a pedagogic level. But in any case, output requires attention to sufficient details that a 'simple' version is illusory anyway – at least a simple version which does anything at all interesting. It is still worthwhile trying to build up to a version of the `plain` output routine, but some of its details will be deferred, omitted, or simplified.

There is an underlying conceptual consideration. How do you use the output routine? The answer is that *you* do not. Although there is a command called \output, you will never invoke it in any of the commands you write, nor will you wish to include that command in any of your own. If you do not get to use it, how does it get used? As TeX processes your text and handles paragraphs it is contributing to a structure known as the 'main vertical list'. At some point TeX will hand over that list to the output routine and let it arrange the output. Arranging the output can mean things like adding headlines and footlines, including the footnotes, and perhaps adding any 'inserts' (like \topinsert and \midinsert, Chapter 12); what it almost certainly means is having TeX write out (or *ship out*) the page to the `dvi` file. This simply re-emphasizes the fact that TeX does not process the text (in the sense of sending it out to 'output') paragraph by paragraph, or line by line, or even character by character, but page by page. Given our short descriptions of how paragraphs are handled, it should also be obvious that the page boundary is influenced by the paragraph handling. Until the structure of the paragraph is 'decided', the structure of the page cannot be determined fully. There is therefore some interaction between the two processes. We may therefore be well into the succeeding page when the \output routine is exercised. This feature is sometimes referred to as 'asynchronous' output.

The very simplest possible output routine is

`\output={}`

which appears to do very little, and is actually equivalent to

`\output={\shipout\box255}`

This should illustrate a number of points. Firstly, the \output routine is actually a token list, that \shipout may be inferred to be the 'active' component, the command which actually ensures that the page is sent off to the dvi file, and that \box255 is where the page of text resides. Since the page is stored in a box, we can treat it just like any other box (it is a vertical box, as you will probably have realized). If we wish to add extra things, like headlines and footlines, or footnotes, keep incrementing the page number, and so on, we have to add these features to the \output routine.

A page is just a box

If the 'page' is held in a box, it can be manipulated just like any other box. For example, it is fairly straightforward to employ the 'boxing' command which we have already introduced (see page 156):

`\output={\shipout\Boxit{\hsize}{\box255}}`

and each page will be surrounded by rules.

⇒*Exercise 20.1:* Create an output routine which places the text within a pair of boxes. This is just a simple extension, but begins to build up some confidence in the ease with which output can be handled. In attempting these exercises, it is quite useful to decrease the \hsize and \vsize to something manageable, especially so that we ensure that we create a few pages. ⇐

In passing, note that I tend to call it an output 'routine', rather than an output command. This is, I suspect, partly out of respect for the complexity that output routines appear to contain. And also perhaps the fact that they are not used as most other commands in TEX. Nevertheless, there are other complex commands which could be constructed which also might qualify for a term like 'routine' rather than command. But the nomenclature is largely irrelevant. The structure and components of \output differ in no essential ways from any other TEX command.

Breaking boxes

If it is straightforward to take the box and add something to it, is it also possible to take the box apart? We already have a command \unvbox, which will allow us to take a box apart. There is another command which can be useful in this context: \vsplit. This is actually a sort of boxing command. It allows us to 'split' a box into two elements. It provides a strategy for building double-column pages. We could take \box255, split it into two \vboxes, and then place the reassembled \vboxes side by side. To split we have to say something like

\setbox254\vsplit255 to 0.5\vsize

The \box254 would now contain the 'top' 0.5\vsize of \box255. The splitting must be a whole number of lines: \box254 may therefore not contain quite half of \box255. We now have two vertical boxes whose height is equivalent to half the original \vsize (or, in the case of \box254, perhaps slightly less). The total vertical extent might be a bit different, when we consider the depth as well.

⇒*Exercise 20.2:* Using the \showthe mechanism, check the vertical extent of \box255 before and after it has been \vsplit into \box254. ⇐

We may have to ensure that half the \vsize is a sensible value: as noted above, TEX has to split on a whole number of lines. Ideally we want each box to contain the same number of lines, and even more ideally, we wish that the lines in the left-hand box line up with those in the right-hand box. I remain unconvinced that this last requirement is fully valid: we normally have a tiny amount of glue between paragraphs, and as a result it is quite feasible that the horizontal alignment will not be perfect. In order to ensure that the alignments are 'correct' we really ought to ensure that the \parskip is zero and has no glue.

The more acute problem is that the split may lead to a different number of lines in each column. This is a necessary consequence of trying to do something unreasonable. Given that we are trying to decant a fixed number of lines – determined by the \vsize

– which may be an odd number, into two boxes, it should come
as no surprise that naive use of \vsplit will not always work
as anticipated. We can take precautions by choosing a value of
\vsize which is likely to encourage an even number of lines. In
other words, a value like \baselineskip$\times 2n$, when we expect to
end up with n lines in each column. Of course, even this precaution
will not ensure success. If we have display maths, there are likely
to be 'blocks' which are essentially indivisible; if we have removed
the flexibility of the \parskip, there may still be problems; and if
there are section headings or subsections, which do not adhere to
the same sort of dimensions as \baselineskip, it may be awkward
to balance columns properly.

⇒*Exercise 20.3:*   Try to do something with \box255 so that you split
it into two and present a double-columned page. In order to do this, you
need to place the boxes side by side: for example,

```
\output={\setbox254\vsplit255 to0.5\vsize
    \shipout\hbox{\box254\box255}}
```

is a rudimentary though rather crude attempt. The \shipout ships out a
box. We therefore have to ensure that the two boxes are placed in a box.
Why an \hbox?   ⇐

Since the \box255 (and here, \box254) are \vboxes, it is the
baselines of the bottom line which are used as the reference point.
That may very well mean that the top lines do not align. This
tends to be far more noticeable than any other mis-alignment. If
we were to unbox these vertical boxes and then reassemble them
into \vtops, we could guarantee that the top baselines were where
we want them:

```
\output={\setbox254\vsplit255 to0.5\vsize
\shipout\hbox{\vtop{\unvbox254}\quad
              \vtop{\unvbox255}}}
```

This looks rather cumbersome, but it is a fairly straightforward
extension. And after all, it will be hidden away in the output
routine. You will probably be the only person to be embarrassed
by it. Note the addition of a \quad to separate the two boxes –
this 'gutter' ought to have its own value.

⇒*Exercise 20.4:*   It is useful to separate columns by a vertical rule
rather than an 'empty' gutter. How would this be done?   ⇐

⇒*Exercise 20.5:*   If we were doing this seriously, we would want to
specify the eventual horizontal and vertical extent of the text, rather
than making the \vsize twice the value we really want. Similarly, we
would wish to specify the gutter. Write the commands you would need in
order to make the specification more intuitive to someone else.   ⇐

Extras

So far, we have ignored the extras – the page 'furniture' that we normally expect to see. We need headlines and footlines: at the very least we expect to see page numbers. You may have noted when TEX was grinding away with these last few \output routines that the page number reported by TEX remained at 1 (or [1]). What TEX is reporting is the value of \pageno, and therefore \count0. Unless we increase this value, it will remain 1.

In order to add the information, we do not have to take \box255 apart. The extra items need not be added to \box255 itself. Just as easily (*more* easily) we could simply \shipout the page 'furniture' and the \box255: very roughly

\shipout{*headline*\box255 *footline*}

gives the sort of structure that can be adopted. In **plain**, the main structure is fundamentally

\shipout{\vbox{%
    \makeheadline\box255\makefootline}\advancepageno}

where \makeheadline and \makefootline are further commands which create vertical boxes which contain (among other things), the \headline and \footline token strings which were briefly discussed on page 205. The command \advancepageno increments the page number. Although

\advance\pageno by 1

is a suitable ploy, \advancepageno is more convenient, since it can account for the case for both Arabic and Roman page numbers (see page 204). There is another flaw with the simple \advance shown here. It is not immediately apparent, but \output inserts an extra pair of braces around the token string. Thus 'really' it is closer to

\output={{\box255}}

There are quite sound reasons for this localization, since it helps to ensure that any purely local changes in the manipulation of the output remain so, and are not propagated into the text. Imagine that there was a font change in the footline. We would not wish it to affect the main bulk of the text. The \output routine is invoked at some point in the 'next' page: if the \headline and \footline commands are not localised, any font or other changes could easily end up influencing the 'next' page. It is also important to realize that local changes within that 'next' page can influence the \output routine. Imagine that the \footline reads

\footline{\hss\sl\folio\hss}

In the event that we had a command which altered the meaning

of \sl (for example, \let\sl\sevenit, where \sevenit has been
defined to be a 7 point italic font), the footline could end up with
a 7 point italic page number instead of the 10 point slanted we
think we asked for. If you want 10 point slanted (as the next chapter will show, the appropriate command is \tensl, not \sl), ask
for it. Whatever else you do, ensure that you select a font for the
headline or footline. Assuming that \rm is current at \shipout is
asking for trouble. A consequence of the grouping, or localization,
is that simple advancing of the page number will also be local. We
should therefore be wary of any manipulations within the \output
routine which are intended to be global. They must be preceded
by the command \global:

\global\advance\pageno by 1

Again the default \advancepageno has taken care of this.

Note that this is described as the fundamental structure: in truth
there are some other commands in the \output routine as well,
but largely these are commands which are relevant only when we
have insertions (like \footnote, \topinsert, and \midinsert).
These will be tackled later in this chapter.

For the moment, let us construct our own headline and footline:
for example,

\output={\shipout\vbox{%
  \rightline{Making pages}\medskip
  \box255\medskip
  \centerline{\folio}}\advancepageno}

Although this is not the way that plain handles the headline and
footline, it is a possible strategy.

⇒*Exercise 20.6:*   Modify this last output routine so that it employs
the normal \headline and \footline token strings. Make sure you select
an appropriate font.   ⇐

The way that plain handles the footline is not completely intuitive, but some of the elements are rather inevitable:

\def\makefootline{%
      \baselineskip24pt\line{\the\footline}}

The \baselineskip may be unexpected, but it merely ensures
that the baseline of the footline is suitably distanced from the
'bottom' of the text on the page. It also reinforces the need to
have the implicit braces around the output routine, else that new
\baselineskip figure would be used in the text. Naturally, it
would have been possible also to use \vskip (or a \kern) to
position the footline. The headline is more involved:

```
\def\makeheadline{\vbox to 0pt
    {\vskip -22.5pt\line{\vbox to 8.5pt{}\the\headline}
        \vss}\nointerlineskip}
```

Once seen, it does make sense. The \vbox to 0pt makes the headline a box of no depth. It therefore does not affect the position of the bulk of the text on the page. The footline did not have quite the same problem. Where do these values of $-22.5\,\text{pt}$ and 8.5 pt come from? Like the \baselineskip of 24 pt, they are related to the default font size of 10 pt. In general terms, the sizes of text fonts we normally use imply that these values are reasonably acceptable over the expected range. Recall first that the height and depth of a strut are 8.5 pt and 3.5 pt. If we subtract 8.5 pt from 22.5 pt, we find a value of 14 pt. A distance we have not introduced is the \topskip. This is the distance between the top of the text area and the baseline of the first line. By default, \topskip is 10 pt. Adding the \topskip value to 14 pt gives us the same value as that used in the \baselineskip of the \footline. So at last we begin to see a symmetry between the foot- and headlines. The distance between the baseline of the headline and the first line of text is the same as the \baselineskip set for the footline. Lastly, the \vbox to 8.5pt{} ensures that even if the \headline is null, the positioning is maintained consistently. The inclusion of the \nointerlineskip ensures that no extra space is inserted between the headline and the text area.

⇒*Exercise 20.7:*   With this knowledge it should be possible to construct appropriate \makeheadline and \makefootline commands for pages which are set in 5 pt fonts on 6 pt baselines. Alternatively, a large-print book, for those with poor vision, might have 14 pt fonts on 16.5 or 17 pt baselines. How would the commands change, while maintaining the same sorts of proportions as the default styles?   ⇐

⇒*Exercise 20.8:*   Sometimes the headline or footline is made more complex by including two lines of information. The most common example of this is when the furniture is separated from the body of the text by a line, or the whole information may be placed in rules: for example

Making Pages	*319*

or

Making Pages   *319*

Emulate these two alternatives, and modify them to allow for larger (and probably bolder) fonts in this information.   ⇐

Many boxes

This introduction of the furniture and some more details of the
way in which \shipout works lays the groundwork to extending
the techniques by which we can handle multiple columns. There
is no real problem in placing 'virtual' pages (as understood by
\box255) side by side on the same physical page. For example,
each odd-numbered page could be decanted into another box but
not physically output, and then when the even-numbered page
came to be created, both boxes could be output. In this case,
something like

```
\count1=1
\output{\ifodd\count1\global\setbox254\box255
   \else\shipout\hbox{\box254\quad\box255}
   \advancepageno\fi
\global\advance\count1 by 1}
```

could be employed. Taking this apart, rather than employ the page
counter as a way of determining whether we are on the even or
odd 'page', a column counter has been used instead. This makes
discussion a little more straightforward. Using \count1 has an
interesting side effect, as you will find when you come to try this
out. TEX will report not only the value of the page number (stored
in \count0), but also the value of \count1. This therefore provides
a handy confirmation that things are going as planned, since the
reported values of \count1 should all be even. The log file should
be reporting a sequence like

```
[1.2] [2.4] [3.6]
```

The first digit of each pair is \count0. The second is \count1. If
any other of the counters up to \count10 are being used, they will
also be reported in this way.

The essence is the

```
\global\setbox254\box255
```

which stores the odd columns in another box. The \ifodd structure restricts the \shipout to occur when we have the even
columns. Note that the page number advance is included in the
same group as the \shipout, but that the column counter is incremented with each invocation of the \output routine. It should be
apparent that this is necessary. Lastly, the use of \global is a necessary consequence of the implicit grouping of an output routine.

⇒*Exercise 20.9:*   Take either of the two approaches to double-columning
and add the page furniture. This will likely require some rewriting of the
way the headlines and footlines are controlled.   ⇐

Both of these approaches may be generalized to multiple columns, where multiple implies a value greater than or equal to two. In the \vsplit case, the total \box255 would be split $n-1$ times to form \vboxes, each of height \vsize/n, and then manipulated. In the second approach, the virtual pages are simply stored until required. For example, for three columns

```
\count1=1
\output{\ifcase\count1
   \or\global\setbox253\box255
   \or\global\setbox254\box255
   \or\shipout\hbox{\box253\quad\box254\quad\box255}
   \global\count1=0 \advancepageno\fi
\global\advance\count1 by 1 }
```

Modifying that to four or more columns is trivial.

These are not general solutions, in the sense that they are not easily modified to a situation where it would be possible to issue a command like \setcolumns=5 and the column structure would change. That is outside the scope of a primer, although there are sufficient clues around that you might be able to do it. But it seems more of an intellectual exercise than something with practical value. A report or book set in multiple columns rarely needs to change that structure. If it does, it is often sufficient to provide a subsequent \output routine which replaces the 'normal' one. Undoubtedly there are legitimate examples which can be put forward – the one which springs to mind is an index, where the space saving and ease of use of double or triple-columning can be very significant. Normally an index appears at the end of the text, where introducing a new \output routine would have no knock-on effects.

Since \topskip has been introduced, its relationship to \vsplit should be discussed. A variant of \topskip is \splittopskip. Just as \topskip standardizes the position of the baseline of the first line of text on a page, \splittopskip performs the same task for the box left when some material has been \vsplit from it. By default, both of these skips have the same value, 10 pt.

Balance

One of the things which has been deliberately omitted in this discussion of multiple columning is balancing the columns. Should the last page have its columns balanced so that they are all the same length? If the 'virtual' page approach is used, this is probably

impossible (or, at least, very difficult), but if the \vsplit approach
is used it can be done fairly readily. Instead of splitting to some
proportion of the \vsize, it is possible to split to a proportion
of the total accumulated height of the box which goes to making
up the page, recalling that any page can be treated as a box, and
therefore its dimensions may be determined. Personally I do not
share the desire to balance columns like this. However, it does
open the way to finish off one section of multiple columning and
start another one or to mix single and double-columning.

⇒*Exercise 20.10:*   Manipulate the 'last' page to make the columns
balance. If there are unequal numbers of lines, the right-hand column is
normally the shorter.   ⇐

   If we return to the plain output routine, we will note that it
contains several levels: it is rather like a Russian doll. A simplified
version is:

```
\output={\plainoutput}
\def\plainoutput{\shipout\vbox{%
  \makeheadline\pagebody\makefootline}
  \advancepageno}
\def\pagebody{\vbox to \vsize{\boxmaxdepth=\maxdepth
  \pagecontents}}
\def\pagecontents{\unvbox255}
```

Most of this seems reasonable, although the depth of the 'hiding'
may be surprising. Part of the reason lies in the material which
has been omitted. The setting of \boxmaxdepth to \maxdepth is to
ensure that the \vbox in \pagebody is constructed under the same
conditions as the \box255 which we are just about to \unvbox. If
this seems rather arbitrary, it is because we have not tackled the
building of \box255 in all the detail that we might have. The last
element here, \pagecontents, is amplified by taking into consideration the inserts which may have been accumulated.

   TEX wraps up so many of the parts of the output routine in
definitions to make it easier to change component parts, without
having to tackle the whole output routine at once. This modulari-
zation is quite useful in the case of involved commands. As we
have seen, it is not necessary to understand fully the routine in
order to change well-defined components.

Inserting more extras

It is appropriate to tackle inserts. By default, plain recognizes
four categories of inserts, the \topinsert, \midinsert, \page-

`insert`, and `\footnote`. These have to be accounted for in any well-tempered output routine.

The top insert material is stored in a vertical box named `\topins`. To include the `\topinsert`s, the structure of `\pagecontents` has to include something like

`\unvbox\topins\unvbox255`

While TEX is processing the text, it is dealing with a quantity known as `\pagegoal`. This is the desired height of the page. It normally starts out as equal to `\vsize`. An insert will reduce the `\pagegoal` by its own vertical extent. Therefore the body of the text will not take up the full page height. While `\pagegoal` is modified by inserts, `\pagetotal` is the vertical height of the 'main vertical list', where TEX is storing the lines of text. It is increased every time a box or some glue is appended to the main vertical list. Once `\pagetotal` exceeds `\pagegoal`, TEX will know that output is imminent. Output will not be invoked, however, until the end of a paragraph is encountered (and one or two other cases, like encountering an `\halign` or at the end of a display equation). In the default output routine, the situation is a little more involved:

`\ifvoid\topins\else\unvbox\topins\fi`

We have not previously introduced `\ifvoid`, but in this context it is easy to see that it is a way of testing to see whether a box contains anything or not. It will come as no surprise that the footnote insertion, held in a box `\footins`, is also tested to see if it is void:

```
\ifvoid\footins\else
    \vskip\skip\footins
    \footnoterule
    \unvbox\footins\fi
```

but this time some extra work is also done. The footnote rule is added, after skipping down the page by `\footins`. Although not explicitly expressed, in creating an insert (which is a box), a skip, a counter, and a dimension are also created, all with the same name. To use these implicit quantities, precede them with `\skip`, `\count`, or `\dimen`. For example, in this context, the `\skip\footins` is a skip quantity. By default it is a `\bigskipamount` or 12 pt. The TEX output routine inserts this skip in any page which has at least one insert of this class, as shown above. A word of warning about these quantities: they must be handled carefully. The dimension is the maximum amount of either footnotes or other insertions on a page: it turns out that TEX treats `\topinsert`, `\midinsert`, and `\pageinsert` as if they were all varieties of `\topinsert`. By default, `plain` allows the `\topinsert` to take up any amount of the page, while the footnotes may only take up to 8 inches: when you change `\vsize`, you really ought to change `\dimen\footins` to be some other value. Recall that, by default, `\vsize` is set to be 8.9 inches.

⇒*Exercise 20.11:*   A more flexible way to determine `\dimen\footins` would be to make it some function of the vertical extent of the page. Attempt to do so.   ⇐

Similarly, the `\count` quantity has a very special meaning. It is described as a 'magnification' factor. That should be distinguished from `\magnification`, since what this magnification is doing is indicating the contribution the vertical extent of the insert makes to the overall page. In essence this is a way of letting (say) a footnote be handled in two or three (or even more) columns. If the `\footnote` command is altered to permit double-columning, the appropriate value of `\count\footins` is 500. By default the value of both `\count\footins` and `\count\topinsert` is 1000.

Since the default output uses `\unvbox` to decant the contents of the various boxes, any glue which is 'contained' can be used in rebuilding this page as a complete unit. We are not constrained by the various elements. Clearly this has some advantage. But if it was not your wish, you should be able to see how to control it more precisely.

There is one more thing added to the page. This accounts for the situation where `\raggedbottom` has been set. In other words, where we do not insist that the bottom lines of each page occur at the same position (this is one way to avoid the message about underfull `\vbox`). In some ways this is about the most complex part of this section:

`\ifr@ggedbottom \kern-\dimen0 \vfil \fi`

The `\dimen0` has not been introduced before. Immediately before unboxing `\box255`, T_EX records the depth of the box (probably a rather small value). All `plain` is really doing then is 'removing' this depth and filling up the bottom of the page with glue, eliminating any glue associated with `\topskip`. The `\topskip` is the glue inserted to keep the tops of pages even. The `\ifr@aggedbottom` should not be intimidating. It is possible to create your own `\if` commands in T_EX, a topic which will be examined later. The `@` merely reveals that this is one of the commands defined in `plain` for 'private' use.

You may be wondering where the `\midinsert` belongs in all of this. In fact, the inserts, with the exception of the footline, share a very similar structure. The key manipulations are in the way that the top and mid inserts handle the \pagegoal and the \pagetotal. If the \midinsert cannot be included on the page, it becomes a \topinsert on the following one – or rather, joins any other top inserts. The question of inserts is perhaps one of TeX's weakest areas. It can be frustratingly difficult to anticipate just where an insertion will be located. If there are a few insertions, well dispersed through the text, then there are generally few problems. Naturally when you need three or four in a short space, it is difficult for any automated system to come up with an aesthetic solution – especially when the aesthetics are poorly understood. We can all recognize when things are in the wrong place; working out the rules which ensure that they may be well placed is considerably more difficult. LaTeX recognizes the inadequacy of the default plain insertions and replaces them entirely to provide its own; but even then, it can provide layout which is just as quirky and unstable. There are many apocryphal tales of satisfactory page layout which suddenly goes awry when a typographic error is corrected: the tiny change in line breaking may modify the page breaking, which in turn affects the location of the inserts. But it must be stressed that the commands controlling the inserts are part of plain. There is nothing to stop you from writing your own commands (except skill). Good luck.

It is possible that the last inserts are not flushed out properly if you end the text with a simple \end or \vfill\end. Since it is more 'normal' to terminate with \bye, this is probably not a frequently observed problem. Perhaps more acutely, it would be possible, if a chapter ended with a \vfill\eject, that inserts which have not yet been used may end up at the beginning of the next chapter. The key to the problem is to see how \bye manages successfully. The definition of \bye is

\outer\def\bye{\par\vfill\supereject\bye}

The new command here is \supereject. This is a command which rather cleverly sets up a penalty value which is then tested in plain's own \output routine and goes on to determine whether any insertions are being retained. It has the advantage of flushing out all of TeX's classes of inserts – \topinsert, \midinsert, and \footline. Penalties will be considered in some more detail in the next chapter.

Insert it yourself

T_EX allows you to create new classes of inserts through the
\newinsert command. A class of insert which is often used is
one which collects indexed entries and writes them out in the
margin during the draft stages of a manuscript, switching then off
for the final version. A rudimentary version of such an insertion
could be

```
\newinsert\margins
\dimen\margins=\maxdimen
\count\margins0
\skip\margins0pt
\def\margin#1{\insert\margins{%
                \vbox{\margindetail\strut#1\strut}}}
```

Note that we have to take account of the \dimen, \count, and
\skip quantities associated with \margins. The effect here is to
place no limits on the number or extent of marginal notes, and
adding no \skip when this insertion is placed on the page. The
\margindetail is a command which sets up a few of the other
details necessary to typeset the marginal insertions. For example:

```
\def\margindetail{\raggedright\emergencystretch5pt
              \tolerance1000\hsize0.2\hsize\noindent}
```

The \output routine will have to be enlarged in order to take care
of this new insertion. This time we will take the default plain
definition and modify it. First we can reveal what plain's \page-
contents really looks like:

```
\def\pagecontents{\ifvoid\topins\else\unvbox\topins\fi
\dimen0=\dp255
\unvbox255
  \ifvoid\footins\else
    \vskip\skip\footins\footnoterule\unvbox\footins\fi
\ifr@ggedbottom\kern-\dimen0\vfill\fi}
```

One possible strategy for the location of the marginal insertion is
to place

```
\rlap{\kern1.05\hsize\vbox to0pt{\box\margins \vss}}
```

before the \unvbox255. This will position the insertion at the
top right of the page. Alternatively, some vertical space could
be included before the \box\margins. A \kern could be appropriate here. Note that \ifvoid is used to check whether there
really are any insertions. The insertions are placed in a box which
has no height. If we do not do this the placement will be very
unsatisfactory.

⇒*Exercise 20.12:* Since placement appears rather tricky it is perhaps worth while to make some simple changes by setting the marginal inserts (a) in a slightly different style, and (b) in a completely different position. Placing the insertion in a 'balanced' position with respect to the body of the text provides an attractive alternative. How may these two alternatives be implemented? ⇐

⇒*Exercise 20.13:* The whole insertion strategy is more complicated when we try to provide insertions with multiple column output. Do not solve the problem, but see how the insertions work with the two types of double-column output which we have already tried. ⇐

Adjustment

One of the possible weaknesses of the marginal insertion shown here is that the insertions are swept up into a single block which will appear at a specific place on the page. Should we wish to guarantee that the marginal note occurs close to the position in the text where the note was placed, a different strategy has to be employed. TEX supports a command, \vadjust, which goes some way to meeting this need. The material in a \vadjust is placed in the internal vertical list. It is passed to the vertical list enclosing the paragraph in which it occurs, so that it occurs immediately after the line containing the position of the \vadjust. This can mean that ensuring that the marginal material aligns precisely with the baseline requires some further adjustment. A failing of this sort of marginal note is that it is feasible to have several which overlap. As usual, the underlying notion seems to be that you use no feature to excess.

The use of \vadjust to append marginal notes is fraught with problems: the following solution owes much to an example provided by Knuth:

```
\def\strutdepth{\dp\strutbox}
\def\marginalnote#1{\strut\vadjust{\kern-\strutdepth
   \vtop to\strutdepth{\baselineskip\strutdepth \vss
   \hskip1.02\hsize{#1 }\null}}}
```

The major point of this is the very careful attention paid to the depth of the box so that the nothing is added to the height of the paragraph. The manipulation is very canny, and any slight deviation can lead to disaster.

⇒*Exercise 20.14:* This command \marginalnote puts a note in the right margin. Can you suggest how to put one in the left margin? ⇐

The \vadjust has some other uses. To guarantee that a page break will occur at a given point you may \vadjust{\eject}.

The page break will follow the line on which this command occurs (even if it is in an absurd position).

⇒*Exercise 20.15:*   Can you mix marginal insertions created with insertions with those created with \vadjust?   ⇐

Breaking up 21

Some topics, although essential, have been treated in a rather diffuse manner. In particular the problem of line, paragraph, and page breaking requires closer examination. It reveals some fascinating aspects of TeX.

In order to be able to tackle this, we need to have some knowledge about three kinds of costs associated with this activity. In a nutshell, TeX seeks to minimize some function of the costs incurred in dividing a paragraph into lines. The three costs are termed badness, penalties, and merits (or demerits). Penalties have at least been introduced in a rather loose and informal way. The function of a penalty is to modify TeX's 'normal' or default behaviour. All of these behaviour characteristics can be modified either globally or locally by either modifying global penalty values, or by locally introducing specific penalties. Only penalties may be specified or altered. The other costs are determined by TeX itself. 'Badness' is associated with individual lines (or potential lines) within a paragraph, while 'merit' is calculated over the whole paragraph. TeX can report their values, but you have no mechanism for altering them directly. The merit figure may be altered indirectly through manipulation of \penalty.

Where exactly may TeX break lines? In normal test, there are four places where TeX will break:

1 at the left edge of glue; in many cases this means after a word or punctuation which is itself followed by a space (there are two exceptions which need not concern us here);
2 at a kern followed by glue, but not simply after a kern, since a kern is unbreakable;
3 at a penalty (penalties are examined in more detail later); commands like \allowbreak are actually a way of inserting a penalty;
4 at a discretionary break; in the majority of cases this means at a discretionary hyphen, at a \- or a hyphenation point which TeX determines.

In very general terms these boil down to 'between words and after hyphens'.

The break has a penalty associated with it. In the first three cases, between words, the penalty is zero. In the fourth case, at a hyphen, there is a penalty invoked. If T_EX inserts a hyphen itself, the value of `\hyphenpenalty` is inserted; by default this is 50. If the word is broken at an existing hyphen, `\exhyphenpenalty` is invoked ('explicit' or 'existing' `\hyphenpenalty`). Again this has a default value of 50. There could be a case made for altering these values: for example, it can be distracting or ambiguous to allow a line break at an explicit hyphen since there is no typographic distinction between the expression of an explicit hyphen and one inserted by T_EX.

Hyphenation of words is fairly well understood at an intuitive level, but maths may appear within a paragraph, as text maths. And it may be necessary to break an expression. There are two relevant penalties and a command which may be useful. In general, T_EX prefers not to break up text maths. This is quite sensible, since breaking maths at the right place is likely to be prone to error. By default, breaking after a relation has a penalty value of 500; it is controlled by `\relpenalty`: breaking after a binary operator carries a slightly higher penalty of 700. It is influenced by `\binoppenalty`. The command which may be used is analogous to `\-`, the discretionary hyphenation command. The command `\*` is a discretionary multiplication symbol. It is therefore the binary operator $\times$. If this is included in a text maths expression, the $\times$ will only appear if the expression is broken. The symbol appears at the end of the line. Curiously, `\*` may be used in text without complaint. In display maths it has no meaning, since there is no line breaking in display maths.

Although the last paragraph starts with the implication that hyphenation may be 'fairly well understood', there is an important peculiarity which very occasionally presents a problem: hyphenation of a word only takes place if the word is preceded by glue. Why is there this restriction? Normally, such a word is the first on a line: the probability of having to hyphenate the first word on a line is usually very low. This is not infallible. Narrow columns in technical texts may lead to a problem in this area. The command to insert marginal notes in the previous chapter may also exhibit this sort of problem, since very narrow 'columns' are being set. Tables including paragraphs of information may also suffer. Solving the 'problem' is not very elegant; all that is really practical is to insert some glue, for example \hskip0pt. But since it is likely that the problem is bound up in a command, these unpleasant facts can usually be well hidden from the user of the command. Equally, a word immediately followed by a rule will not be hyphenated. Again, the solution is to insert glue after the word.

⇒*Exercise 21.1:* Return to the marginal insertion command in the previous chapter and modify it to allow for hyphenation of the first and last words of the material to be inserted. Any command which includes a \strut should be modified to take this feature into account. ⇐

Should you ever have a need to switch off hyphenation, this can be achieved, as shown in Chapter 17, by \hyphenchar. This has to be specified for each font. On the other hand, suppressing hyphenation on words beginning with an upper-case letter is not font related: it is accomplished by \uchyph-1. By default this has a positive value, and all words are hyphenated.

You may easily adjust the values of penalties, or even introduce some new penalties of your own. If, in the text, you include \penalty50 you are charging a penalty of 50 'demerits' to break here; similarly \penalty-50 encourages TEX to break, since this cost will be deducted from the overall figure (making it more attractive).

This diversion into hyphens is slightly distracting: in establishing the line breaking, TEX performs a number of passes; on the first pass, no attempt is made to hyphenate. Knuth reports that in the vast majority of paragraphs hyphenation is not required; in this case, TEX does not proceed to the second pass, where hyphenation would be considered. This removes the need to identify the hyphenation points, and helps reduce the overall time taken to process the document. This is partly a function of line measure. If the lines were narrow, it is almost certain that hyphenation would be required, and it would be better, from the point of view of the overall processing time, to omit this pass. This is possible.

Let us recap the calculation of badness introduced in Chapter 3. There is glue between word boxes. The line has a fixed length – it is a sort of 'line box'. The words have fixed lengths; the lines have fixed lengths; the only thing that can change is the space between words. This is where the glue comes in. As Knuth points out, a better metaphor would be a spring, but the notion of glue seems to have stuck. The available stretch or shrink will depend on the number of words in the line (which is why \tolerance should be related to the measure). TEX will not allow the gaps between words to be shrunk below the minimum value.

If there are n words on a line, the badness value will depend on whether TeX has to stretch or shrink the interword gaps. Firstly, assume that TeX has to shrink, using some proportion of the glue determined by `\fontdimen4` or `\spaceskip`. Using the notation x^- to indicate the total amount of shrink on the line, and f_4 as the shrink component of the interword gap, the badness, b, is calculated as:

$$b = 100 \left(\frac{x^-}{(n-1)f_4} \right)^3$$

On the other hand, when the glue on a line is to be stretched by a total of x^+, and the stretch component of the interword gap is f_5, then

$$b = 100 \left(\frac{x^+}{(n-1)f_5} \right)^3$$

If the badness is 12 or less, then the line is described as 'decent'. If it is greater than 12, then it is loose or tight, depending on whether it has been stretched or shrunk. If it has been very stretched, where the badness is over 100, it is described as very loose. There are therefore four categories: tight, decent, loose, and very loose.

The `\tolerance` figure is a badness. If, for example, `\tolerance` is 1000, then lines may have a badness up to this figure, but if this is not possible, an overfull box will be set. On the first pass, TeX will assess not the `\tolerance` figure, but a `\pretolerance`. The default value of `\pretolerance` is 100. TeX therefore accepts a paragraph if none of the lines have a badness up to this figure. On the second pass, the `\tolerance` is used. This has a default value of 200. In order to omit the first pass, set `\pretolerance` to a negative value.

⇒*Exercise 21.2:*   Take a paragraph and change the defaults so that hyphenation is inhibited. Make the measure narrow and reintroduce hyphens. Try to eliminate overfull boxes.   ⇐

⇒*Exercise 21.3:*   If there was no penalty at all for hyphenation, just how many would TeX tend to introduce?   ⇐

These individual line badnesses are an intermediary step in deciding which potential paragraph to accept. An acceptable paragraph combines the individual line badnesses together with any appropriate penalties into an overall demerit figure. In broad terms, the demerit is the sum of the badness squared and the penalties squared. There will be a minimum demerit through the `\linepenalty`, which has a default value of 10. In a sense this penalty has the effect of making TeX work harder to achieve the desired results. There is also a precondition: if the penalty associated with a breakpoint at the end of a line exceeds 10,000, or if the badness is greater than the current \tolerance (or \pretolerance), TEX would not have considered the line in the first place. The formula that TEX uses in calculating the (de)merit is almost

$$demerit = (linepenalty + line\ badness)^2 + penalty^2 \times \mathrm{sgn}(penalty)$$

where $\mathrm{sgn}(x)$ is the 'signum' function, -1 when x is negative and $+1$ when it is positive (just a ruse to make the equation a little more straightforward – it allows negative and positive penalties to be distinguished after being squared). The 'real' formula is very slightly different, but this form does not obscure the essential nature.

The nature of adjacent lines can influence the total demerit at this point. TEX attempts to ensure that any two adjacent lines are of adjacent classes. For example, successive tight and decent lines are acceptable, but if a tight line is next to a loose or very loose line (or a decent line next to a very loose one), then TEX brings in an extra demerit, \adjdemerits. TEX is attempting to make lines look visually similar by means of this parameter. A loose line next to a tight line is really noticeable.

One unfortunate consequence of TEX's line-breaking algorithm was that it can concentrate all the badness on one single line. In other words, rather than have several lines with (say) very loose lines, it may have one with truly awful looseness. This defect has been taken care of with TEX3, by using a new command termed \emergencystretch. This is used on a third pass through the paragraph. The \emergencystretch is invoked 'pretending' that extra stretch equal to \emergencystretch is present on each line. This scales down some of the badnesses and allows TEX to find an 'optimum' solution. This extra stretching is not actually there at all. In essence it allows the badness to be distributed over more lines, and makes it less noticeable. But always remember that TEX's notion of badness is a numeric one: in general it will provide a reasonably aesthetic solution. It is extremely doubtful that the correlation between TEX's badness and aesthetic quality is exact. The default plain has no value set to \emergencystretch. A likely value seems to be about 5 pt.

As noted earlier, TEX accumulates demerits for hyphens: since two (or more) consecutive hyphenated lines are thought to look rather ugly, more demerits for adjacent hyphens are accumulated through \doublehyphendemerits, normally set to 10,000. Nevertheless, with narrow measure you may still see two or more hyphens together at the end of lines. Similarly, ending the second last line with a hyphen does not look pretty, and would attract a default penalty of 5000 through \finalhyphendemerits.

There is yet another command which interacts with all of these. Although TEX seeks to minimize the number of lines in a paragraph, it is sometimes necessary to interfere and tighten or loosen paragraphs just a little. The command is \looseness. This command instructs TEX to try to make a paragraph longer, when it is followed by a positive number, or shorter, if it is followed by a negative one. Therefore \looseness-1 instructs TEX to attempt to shorten by one line. Whether or not TEX will succeed depends on the structure of the paragraph – in particular, its length. The longer a paragraph, the more scope there is to lengthen or shorten without the interword spacing beginning to become noticeably different. It is often tempting to use \looseness-1 as part of the token string of an \everypar in order to shorten a document.

From time to time it is necessary to try to lengthen or shorten a paragraph. Perhaps a paragraph has been rewritten but it is essential that succeeding pages retain the same page breaks. There are inelegant ways of doing this with forced page breaks (discussed later), but the alternative is to use \looseness. Alternatively, changing the \linepenalty from its default of 10 will instruct TEX to try harder to create a paragraph with the minimum number of lines. It is more difficult to gauge the effect of \linepenalty.

⇒*Exercise 21.4:*   Try comparing the effect of these two techniques for shortening paragraphs. As suggested, a long (or a thin) paragraph will tend to respond more obviously.   ⇐

⇒*Exercise 21.5:*   Examine the effect of altering the value of \looseness on a paragraph of moderate length. Can you determine a difference in the interword gap?   ⇐

If this all seems very involved, in truth it is all rather transparent. You need never know what is going on in the background. On the other hand, it can occasionally be useful to have some inklings of what is going on, especially when you have to deal with an apparently aberrant situation. Perhaps the more important features are that there are a number of hard-wired values, ones that you cannot modify: the cubic power in the evaluation of badness; the badness breakpoints at 12 and 100; the power of 2 in the evaluation of demerits. This at least indicates that any additional demerit values will generally have large values if they are to have an effect, while penalties may generally be of a lower magnitude, since they are likely to be squared when they are used in the value of the demerit.

The interaction between all these demerits, penalties, and tolerances is not easy to fathom. We seem to be operating in a multidimensional (hyper-)space, where the axes are anything but orthogonal. If you really want to know the gory details, use `\tracingparagraphs=1`. But be prepared for an awful lot of output, and a fair amount of thinking. It is possible to follow TEX's logic in line breaking through the output from this tracing command. Examples may be found in Knuth and Plass (1981) and Brüggeman-Klein (1989).

⇒*Exercise 21.6:*   It is worth while running a paragraph or two through with alterations made to the default tolerance, penalty, and demerit values. If you make the measure tolerably narrow things do start to happen. Very wide page sizes tend to show very little, since a great deal of flexibility is available for TEX to perform its paragraphing miracles. You will probably find lots of overfull `\hbox`es. If they upset you, this is a good time to revise ways of eliminating them.   ⇐

Breaking pages

Breaking paragraphs between pages follows a very similar strategy to breaking lines. There is one very significant difference. While TEX looks at all feasible breakpoints in determining the paragraph, it does not look at page breaks in the same detail. Pages are created one at a time and there is no attempt to see how the next page break will influence the current one. Knuth notes that there is insufficient high-speed memory capacity to handle several pages. This is probably no longer a completely valid consideration. If TEX were to be recreated today, it is likely that some attention would have been given to optimizing page breaks in a more global way. Asher (1990) describes a system based on TEX which does this.

Firstly, where may page breaks occur? The rules applicable to line breaking are echoed here, in a muted form. Within a vertical list, breakpoints may occur:

1 at glue preceded by a box, a mark, or an insertion; since there is normally glue between the boxes of a vertical box, a paragraph can be broken between the lines;

2 at a kern followed by glue;

3 at a penalty.

Although page breaking has been introduced in terms of finding a suitable place within a paragraph to divide between pages, one very suitable place will also be between paragraphs.

Instead of manipulating the space between words, TₑX will attempt to manipulate the vertical space between boxes. If there are vertical skips between paragraphs, with associated glue, this can give the scope for satisfactory page breaking. The `\parskip` by default is zero, but it has a positive glue amount of 1 pt. Normally there is no glue associated with `\baselineskip`.

Page breaks have some similar penalties. When the first line of a paragraph becomes adrift and is left at the end of a page, it is termed an orphan, or in TₑX terminology, a club line. The `\clubpenalty`, with a default value of 150, tends to dissuade this from happening. Similarly, the last line of a paragraph held over to the beginning of a new page is termed a widow, and is controlled by `\widowpenalty`, with the same default value. The astute will appreciate that if we demand that TₑX creates pages of fixed length, but equally insists that there shall be no club or widow lines, we have the beginnings of a potential conflict. There is sometimes the suspicion that TₑX's paragraphing algorithm is a physical expression of Knuth's writing style – a tendency to 'medium' length paragraphs. If you insist on writing short paragraphs you may not be giving TₑX sufficient flexibility.

⇒*Exercise 21.7:*   It is said that by removing a word in a paragraph, it is possible to increase the overall length of the text. Suggest how this apparent paradox may be resolved.   ⇐

Breaking a page at a hyphen is also regarded as unsatisfactory. To influence this, TₑX employs `\brokenpenalty`, which is set by default to 100. TₑX also has some controls over the relationship between display maths and page breaking. Assuming we have such a display, breaking a page after the display is influenced by `\post-displaypenalty` with a default value of zero; on the other hand, breaking the page immediately before a display is influenced by `\predisplaypenalty`, with a default value of 10,000. One last penalty comes into this class: `\displaywidowpenalty`. This is a special case of a widow line. A display may occur within a paragraph: if breaking leads to a single line being placed on the next page, followed by a display, this looks rather like a conventional 'widow' line. The default value is 150. Quite logically, there is no corresponding 'club' version.

⇒*Exercise 21.8:*   Some grasp of the page breaking may be gained by creating a sequence of small pages. This will also allow you to experiment with the various penalties which influence page breaking.   ⇐

A page break can be forced explicitly by \eject. This command is a penalty of −10,000, or, more accurately, contains a penalty of this value. Similarly, the \break command which is sometimes used to force a line break is a shorthand for \penalty-10000. There is in fact an interesting exploitation of TEX's modes here. Typing \break (or \penalty-10000) while in horizontal mode (for example, while building a paragraph) forces a line break, while typing the same command in vertical mode (for example, after a \par or a blank line) forces a page break.

⇒*Exercise 21.9:*   What does \vadjust{\break} do?   ⇐

As you will anticipate, \eject works by first forcing the change into vertical mode by issuing a \par, and then specifying the penalty.

The values of 10,000 may require some explanation. In many TEX contexts, 10,000 is broadly equivalent to infinity. A value of over 10,000 is often replaced by 10,000 in calculations. A penalty of 10,000 inhibits breaking, while a penalty of −10,000 forces it. Using numerical values greater than these do not make the behaviour 'more certain', although smaller values might have some perceptible effect. If a box is overfull, it has a real penalty of infinity associated with it.

The default commands which come with **plain** also have a few other ways of influencing page breaks. The command \goodbreak is a shorthand for \par\penalty-500, that is, a 'good' place to break a page: of course, this is a place between paragraphs. More subtle is \filbreak. This command is equivalent to writing \vfil\penalty-200\vfilneg. The penalty is nothing new, nor is the \vfil. The \vfilneg was introduced briefly in Chapter 9; in a sense it is equivalent but opposite to \vfil. If the page break occurs at the \filbreak, the \vfilneg is carried over to the top of the next page, where it disappears. Glue at the top of a page (with the sole exception of \topglue) disappears. If there is no page break the \vfil and \vfilneg cancel one another out. So what is the overall effect? Essentially, if we terminate each paragraph with a \filbreak, all pages will tend to be broken between paragraphs.

⇒*Exercise 21.10:*   Why is this 'tend to' and not a guaranteed way of ensuring that paragraphs are not broken across pages?   ⇐

⇒*Exercise 21.11:*   Beckett's 'Molloy' starts with a single paragraph of about 90 pages. If TₑX breaks paragraphs, and has a finite memory, how would we go about setting it?   ⇐

Since \break encourages breaking, it will seem logical that \nobreak inhibits it. This command is a shorthand way of writing \penalty10000. If the break occurs at that point, a massive penalty would be incurred. Again the mode is relevant. Within this spectrum, a variety of penalty values may be set, in order to favour or discourage breaking of lines or pages. The trio of \smallbreak, \medbreak, and \bigbreak contain penalties of -50, -100 and -200 respectively. They are vertical mode commands (deliberately, they also contain a \par), and do some neat footwork to remove the last skip which TₑX performed (provided it is bigger than a \small, \med, or \big skip), insert the penalty, and then reinsert a \smallskip, \medskip, or \bigskip.

⇒*Exercise 21.12:*   When starting a new section or subsection, it is appropriate to manipulate any command you introduce so that the vertical space immediately preceding the (sub-)section title is 'breakable'. And equally that the vertical space after is not breakable. Otherwise the title may come adrift and be left at the bottom of a page. Create such a command.   ⇐

A bigger penalty

In looking at output routines, \supereject was introduced, but not explained. This command is especially interesting since it indicates a use for very high penalties, as a way of passing information to an output routine. An \eject is defined as

\def\eject{\par\penalty-10000 }

but the \supereject uses a higher penalty:

\def\supereject{\par\penalty-20000 }

As soon as TₑX finds a penalty of −10,000 or higher, it will invoke the output routine. The higher value explicitly included in the \supereject has precisely the same effect, but now the value is retained (although in any calculations it would be treated as being −10,000). In the \output routine the value of \outputpenalty, which is the value of the penalty at the current breakpoint, is tested. If it is less than −20,000 (that is, if \supereject has been used), then the default TₑX output routine will invoke a further command \dosupereject. This is the nub: this is what really does the work. TₑX now checks to see whether there are any inserts left over: or rather it checks both for whole and part inserts which may be left over. A footnote might easily be split.

If you design your own output routine, and use inserts, you will have to include some scheme like this so that any 'dangling' inserts are flushed out. If no special measures are taken, it is quite possible that some inserts appear to be forgotten.

There are two ways to finish off TEX, to tell it to terminate. TEX itself will suggest that \end can be typed (if you have not already included a termination in the file). This is rather brutal. A better technique is to use \bye. The full form of this command is revealed through

\outer\def\bye{\par\vfill\supereject\end}

Since \bye is \outer it cannot be incorporated within other commands you might like to create. But the main point of this is that it contains a \supereject before the \end. Clearly this ensures that insertions are cleared up.

In a similar way, if you are writing a book and dividing it into chapters, it would be very wise to ensure that a \supereject terminates every chapter. Thus no insertions will be held over to interfere with the beginning of the next chapter.

Delays and deferments 22

The action of page creation has some interesting consequences. There are certain matters which TEX deliberately delays until a page has been created. Clearly, the \output routine makes explicit certain actions, but there are a few implicit actions too. To be specific, the \mark command has several compatriots, namely the triad \topmark, \firstmark, and \botmark whose meaning is determined through page breaking. The contents of these three will change automatically, without any 'human' (or even explicit command) intervention. The basic strategy is this: somewhere in the text, there will be some \marked text. The first time that \mark is used, all of the \mark triad take the same value. Taking an example,

\item{\mark{aardvark}Aardvark}: has the first word

Should we refer to \topmark or \firstmark or \botmark, the text which will be inserted will be 'aardvark'. When there is a second reference to \mark, the triad will change. Quite how the triad changes depends on where the page boundaries fall. These 'definitions' are in force as the current page is boxed. That is, in essence, when the \output routine is invoked:

\topmark contains the text of the last \mark *before* the current page was boxed;

\firstmark contains the text of the first \mark encountered on the current page;

\botmark will contain the text of the very last \mark on the page; it is the \topmark of the next page.

This may all seem a little esoteric, although the example above may give a clue to a potential use. The most 'obvious' use of these marks is in a headline or footline. Dictionaries often bracket the range of words which are included on each page. These 'guide' words are intended to make the dictionary easier to use. Similarly it is common to see the section (or chapter) title in the headline. The use of \mark is not necessarily the sole way to solve this last problem. There are subtleties involved in this use of the \mark

Page	\topmark	\firstmark	\botmark
1	*empty*	*empty*	*empty*
2	*empty*	*i*	*i*
3	*i*	*ii*	*ii*
4	*ii*	*iii*	*v*
5	*v*	*v*	*v*
6	*v*	*vi*	*vi*

Figure 22.1
Marks: see
the text for an
explanation

and the triad. Should `\topmark` or `\firstmark` go into the headline? Or to be even more complex, should left- and right-facing pages have different structures? Examples do help a little. Note that using the triad of marks before `\mark` has actually been used does not generate an error: TEX will simply insert nothing.

Looking at a theoretical instance, imagine the following arrangement, where the text contains six instances of `\mark`, where `\mark{`*i*`}` occurs on page 2, `\mark{`*ii*`}` on page 3, `\mark{`*iii*`}`, `\mark{`*iv*`}`, and `\mark{`*v*`}` on page 4, and `\mark{`*vi*`}` on page 6. Note that this deliberately avoids placing a `\mark` on the first and fifth page, and has three on page 4. What will the values of the triad or marks be? Figure 22.1 attempts to summarize the position.

⇒*Exercise 22.1:* Attempt to confirm the arrangement which is summarised in Figure 22.1. ⇐

If `\mark` is used within a box, it may be difficult to retrieve. Knuth notes that 'a mark that is locked too deeply inside a box will not migrate', and that a mark in internal vertical mode will not be accessible. But how deep is too deep? A `\mark` within an `\halign` will be heeded, but not if that is itself embedded within a `\vbox`. As you would expect, a `\mark` within an insert (remember that includes footnotes) will be ignored too. For the purposes of creating section headings which are echoed in a `\mark` which will be used in a `\headline`, it is convenient that embedded in a simple `\leftline` or `\centerline`, the `\mark` is heeded. But if there had been any deeper boxing, it would not work. In general terms, though, it would be as convenient to write a rudimentary command like:

`\def\section#1{\leftline{\bf #1}\mark{#1}}`

where no boxing of the mark takes place. A problem may arise with more complex commands that the marked text *might* become separated from the text it is supposed to represent, if a page break intervenes.

Reading and writing

The other major area where page building has a major effect is when we attempt to write to a file. Besides being able to read the current text file, and input other files through \input, or write to the log and dvi files, TEX can read and write to other files. This can be useful when we wish to create a table of contents, or an index, among many possibilities. Before indicating the interaction with pages, we can look at the commands available for this sort of file manipulation. Reading in from a file can be accomplished by \read. The command must be followed by a number indicating the input file (or stream) number. This number is normally between 0 and 15. If it lies outside this range, TEX will assume you wish to input from the keyboard. But first you should 'open' the file with the \openin command. This has the structure

\openin1=extra

where some file extra (or extra.tex if a file extra does not exist: it is difficult to guarantee the way different implementations, or different operating systems, will accommodate this) is linked to the stream number 1. It may not be a surprise that there is a \newread command which allows TEX to choose the input stream number. What happens if the chosen file does not exist? You may by now be aware of what happens when you try to \input a file which is not available. But this is different: TEX just assumes that the input stream is not open. A wise decision could be to test to see if the end of the file had been encountered. TEX supplies an \ifeof for this purpose.

If you start to think about this seriously, you will realize that the behaviour of \read has to differ in substance from \input. What a \read enables us to do is to define a command with the contents of a line from the nominated input file: in other words

\newread\aux

\openin\aux=stream

\read\aux to\information

The new command \information has no parameters (and no definition). Although this has been stated as if a single line is read in, if there are enclosing braces, TEX keeps reading successive lines until it balances the braces. Perhaps the most obvious use of this sort of reading is to request input from the keyboard. This gives a pleasing illusion of interactivity. For example,

```
\def\draft{draft }
\read-1 to\version
\ifx\version\draft
\input draftmac.tex \else \input finalmac.tex \fi
```
would allow selection of the appropriate set of commands (already stored in an appropriately named file) depending on whether we were preparing a draft or final version of some text. The `\read-1` is to read in from the keyboard. In fact, this is rather imperfect, since there is no indication in the log file that TEX is waiting patiently for 'draft' or something else to be typed in. A 'better' idea is to issue a prompt:
```
\message{draft or final version? }
\read-1 to\version
```
The command `\message` writes out text immediately to the screen. In the example here, the extra space after the ? is quite deliberate. It too will appear at the screen.

⇒*Exercise 22.2:*   Examine what will happen if `\read16` is used in place of `\read-1`.   ⇐

A further command, `\closein`, when given the appropriate file number (or 'name'), closes down the file or stream. In general terms, when TEX encounters a `\bye` or `\end` it will close down any files which have been opened, but it is always more satisfying to do this yourself. Apart from anything else, there is bound to be some aberrant operating system somewhere which does not do this sort of automatic housekeeping. It would be distressing to find TEX producing different behaviour simply because you were not tidy.

Writing out information is a far more common requirement than trying to use `\read`. The examples already noted are a table of contents and an index. The strategy is very similar, though: we have `\newwrite`, `\openout`, `\closeout`, and `\write`. Let's look at a real example where we try to create a table of contents:
```
\newwrite\toc
\openout\toc=\jobname.toc
\def\section#1{\leftline{\bf#1}%
        \write\toc{#1:\the\pageno}}
```
This introduces the command `\jobname`. It expands to the same name that TEX is currently using for the `dvi` and `log` files. This is not necessarily the same name as the currently `\input` file. It does mean that later we can use
```
\input \jobname.toc
```
to read in the contents of this automatically created file, without having to nominate a name within the commands.

But there is a flaw: the three commands \openout, \closeout, and \write are deferred until the page is built. After all, until TEX decides the page break the appropriate page number will not be determined. However, this will work:

\newwrite\toc
\immediate\openout\toc=\jobname.toc
\def\section#1{\leftline{\bf#1}%
        \write\toc\expandafter{#1:\folio}}

The \expandafter, which is discussed briefly in Chapter 23, is needed to change the expansion order so that the correct page number is inserted. The use of \immediate forces the \openout to take place before the page building – in fact, to take place immediately. But note that if there is an \immediate before the \closeout the file may be closed before some last remaining \writes have taken place. It is usually sufficient to put the \closeout after an \eject, so that page construction has taken place before the file is closed.

⇒*Exercise 22.3:* Confirm the need for \expandafter in the definition of \section. Check what happens if you use \immediate\closeout. ⇐

⇒*Exercise 22.4:* A similar arrangement can be made for the production of a simple index. Do so. ⇐

If an index is created, it will be necessary to sort the entries. This is not a task to which TEX is well suited. In general terms, the strategy is to employ a sorting program, and then typeset the index later. Since an index is generally the very last thing which is done in the production of a book, this should be no real hardship. Some features of using \write pose problems for both an index and (sometimes) for tables of contents. TEX will expand any commands as it writes out text. This can lead to some quite intriguing results, especially when there are font changes. Expanding font changes locks them into the precise expression of the current font. For example, \bf will probably become \tenbf and there will be a reference to the \fam (an attribute explained Chapter 18); for example,

\fam \bffam \tenbf

would appear in the file which is written out. If you do want to use the information again (which is usually why you bother writing it out), it can be quite distressing to find these commands.

⇒*Exercise 22.5:* Experiment with the use of \write when there are commands written to file. ⇐

Since the file is usually being read in again, perhaps through an \input of the entire file, it can be useful to include commands in what is written. But we do not wish the commands to be expanded at this point. How can we delay them? TEX supports a command \string which will write out the next token into the file. Recall that a token is (among other things) a command, or a character. In other words if we

\write0{\string\bf\space Janis Joplin}

the \string\bf will write out \bf into the file. The \space is needed, since the space after \string\space is needed to delimit the \bf. If \space is omitted, what will be written into the file is \bfJanis, and of course, when we come to use it, an error will appear. This \string mechanism is also useful for including braces.

Since commands embedded in a \write are deferred until the page is constructed, any redefinition of a command may result in something different being written into a file. Be warned.

More messages

This chapter has been aimed principally at writing out information to files which may be read in subsequently, but has already addressed a way of obtaining a message on the screen, through \message, which is almost the same as \immediate\write16. Both will display some text at the screen. There is a slight difference, in that 'messages' are not printed out on separate lines. Each \write will be on a separate line. In both cases, the text is displayed on the screen and written into the log file. If you do not wish the text to be written on the screen, but just to appear in the log file, you must use an \immediate\write, with a file number which is negative. There is no way to suppress the text of a \message in the log file. TEX has a default command, \wlog, which writes to the log file, should you want to use it.

To provide a concrete example, the following was written in order to ensure that any use of a command \title might be used only once:

```
\newif\iftitle      \titlefalse
\def\title#1{\iftitle
   \message{incorrect, title may only be used once}
            \else
   \goodbreak\centerline{\bf#1}\global\titletrue
            \fi}
```

Besides this and the use suggested earlier, as a prompt, it can be very helpful to use \write and \message to inform you of what is going on. Sometimes a particularly recalcitrant command can be examined more closely through the use of \message. If you read in files containing lots of commands it is often very useful to include a \message. Although the name of any \input file will be recorded in the log file, a more meaningful explanation will always be appreciated – especially when something goes wrong!

Errors

There is another class of messages which can be used when errors occur. The \errmessage is similar to \message, but when it is encountered, it stops TEX and invokes the standard error processing machinery. If you should ask for help in response to TEX's offer, you will be entertained by

```
This error message was generated by an \errmessage
command, so I can't give any explicit help.
Pretend that you're Hercule Poirot: Examine all clues,
and deduce the truth by order and method.
```

But you can add your own help too. When \errmessage is used, any text stored in \errhelp can be used to provide the help message obtained by typing help at the ? prompt. Such features tend to find most use when more complex commands are created.

Collections   **23**

The purpose of this chapter is to draw together some of the commands which have been uncovered in the evolution of the primer. From time to time it has been necessary to introduce members of various classes of commands in a somewhat unstructured way. They were needed to solve particular problems, but elaborating upon them and introducing similar commands would confuse the flow of the text.

Conditionals

The account of TeX's primitive conditionals has been rather scattered throughout the preceding chapters. It is useful to draw all the variations into a more ordered exposition, augmenting them with examples where appropriate. Some of the conditionals are used infrequently, although it may be comforting to know that they are available. Naturally these tests would not occur in 'normal' text: they would be located within more elaborate commands.

Comparing numeric values

`\ifnum`⟨number₁⟩⟨relation⟩⟨number₂⟩ compares two numeric values (including integers and counters). The ⟨relation⟩ may only be `<`, `>`, or `=`. An example was used in the calculation of the time of day in Chapter 7. For example,

`\ifnum\time<720 before noon\else after noon\fi`

Recall that it is wise to leave a blank after the numeric value. Otherwise TeX has to go on reading to make sure that whatever follows is not a command which might expand to a numeric value which is really part of the number.

    `\ifdim`⟨dimen₁⟩⟨relation⟩⟨dimen₂⟩ compares two dimensions. Again the ⟨relation⟩ may only be `<`, `>`, or `=`. A practical application of this might be

```
\def\caption#1{\smallskip\setbox0\hbox{\bf#1}%
 \ifdim\wd0<0.9\hsize
 \line{\hfil\box0\hfil}\else
 \line{\hfil\vbox{\hsize0.9\hsize\noindent#1}\hfil}\fi
\bigskip}
```

where a caption is written out as a single centred line when it is 'short enough', but set as a centred paragraph if it is wider than some particular proportion of the horizontal width.

\ifodd⟨number⟩ tests for an odd integer. The condition is true when the integer is odd, false when even. Note there is no \ifeven command. This command is most often used in creating left and right headlines and footlines. Normally we expect the left-hand page (*verso*) to be even numbered and the right-hand page (*recto*) to have different characteristics. For example, part of the \output routine might contain

```
\ifodd\pageno
        \footline{\rectofoot}\headline{\rectohead}\else
        \footline{\versohead}\headline{\versohead}\fi
```

where \rectofoot, \rectohead, \versofoot, and \versohead are previously set up token strings appropriate for the headlines and footlines of the right and left pages.

\ifcase⟨number⟩ is TEX's implementation of the 'case' statement often found in programming languages. It will be found with \or, and perhaps with \else. It allows a many-way branching by testing the value of ⟨number⟩, and then takes the action corresponding to the ⟨number⟩. The values of the number must be non-negative, but the first branch corresponds to zero. A practical example already encountered is \today:

```
 \def\today{\ifcase\month\or
    January\or   February\or    March\or    April\or
    May\or           June\or     July\or   August\or
    September\or  October\or November\or December\fi
\space\number\day, \number\year}
```

The value of \month must lie between 1 and 12. Therefore the first branch, corresponding to zero, is 'ignored' by having no text appropriate to it. The truly cautious might have followed December by an \else and an error message. In this context this caution is perhaps excessive, but the plain command \magnification would be much more robust with such a trap. Exercises 6.12 and 17.10 examined this in more detail.

Testing modes

`\ifvmode` tests for vertical mode. If TEX is in vertical or internal vertical mode, the condition is true. Since a command which starts with an `\hbox` may be interpreted anomalously when it is the first token in a paragraph, it may seem appropriate to begin with a test for mode. For example, a reasonable definition of ␣ (for space) might be

`\def\]{\hbox{\tt\char`\ }}`

Should a paragraph begin with `\]`, TEX would be in vertical mode, and would continue to be so until the text token occurred. This would make `\]` a paragraph in its own right. It might seem that some `\ifvmode` structure was needed to force TEX into horizontal mode. A far simpler solution is

`\def\]{\leavevmode\hbox{\tt\char`\ }}`

The `\leavevmode` is legitimate in both horizontal and vertical mode.

A slightly more plausible example might be connected with the use of `\centerline`. If you use this command within a paragraph, the contents will not be set on a separate line and centred, but will be incorporated into the text, with rather unfortunate consequences. A possible alteration of the command to make it robust under these circumstances could be:

`\def\centerline#1{\ifvmode\par\fi\line{\hss#1\hss}}`

`\ifhmode` tests for horizontal mode. If TEX is in horizontal or restricted horizontal mode the condition is true. Obviously the `\centerline` example could have been rewritten as

```
\def\centerline#1{\ifhmode\par\line{\hss#1\hss}%
                  \else\line{\hss#1\hss}\fi}
```

It looks more clumsy. It also takes up more space within TEX's memory.

`\ifmmode` tests for text maths or display maths mode. This has been used in several examples which help to extend the ease of use of TEX. For example,

```
\def\,{\ifmmode\mskip\thinmuskip\else\thinspace\fi}
\def\dots{\relax
        \ifmmode\ldots
        \else.\thinspace.\thinspace.\thinspace\fi}
```

give us two useful definitions which work well in both maths and ordinary text.

⇒*Exercise 23.1:* The underscore character is not usually available, since it has already been taken by the maths 'subscript' character. Knowing that a substitute for _ is `\sb`, and that a _ may be obtained from

`\tt\char'137`, create a way of making _ provide an underscore character, yet still work in maths.   ⇐

`\ifinner` tests for internal or restricted mode. If TEX is in internal vertical, restricted horizontal, or text maths mode, the condition is true. Since `\marks` are sensitive to 'inner' conditions, it
could be wise to include such a test, if only to warn the unwary
that the mark may not appear. It will certainly not appear if used
in internal vertical mode, but *may* appear if used in restricted
horizontal mode.

Comparing tokens

`\if`⟨token₁⟩⟨token₂⟩ tests if two character codes agree. In order
to do so, TEX will expand any commands following the `\if` until
two unexpandable tokens are found. The use of `\if` has already
occurred in the answer to Exercise 7.5. For example, take this
abbreviated version:
`\def\pion#1{$\if#1+\pi^+\else\pi^-\fi$}`
The key feature of `\if` is that it expands the tokens: therefore
`\let\a+`   *or* `\def\a{+}`
`\pion\a`
would give the same result as `\pion+`.

`\ifx`⟨token₁⟩⟨token₂⟩ tests if two tokens agree, but does not
expand commands. The condition is true if the two tokens are
not commands and they represent the same character code and
category code pair, *or* the same TEX primitive, *or* the same `\font`
or `\chardef` or `\countdef`, etc.; *or* the two tokens are commands
and have the same status with respect to `\long` and `\outer`, both
have the same parameters, and the same top-level expansion. A
practical example of the use of `\ifx` is to test whether a set of
commands in a file has already been read in:
`\ifx\commandsfile\undefined\else\endinput\fi`
`\let\commandsfile\null`
If these two statements are at the beginning of a file of commands
(a macro file), or indeed, any other file, whenever it is read for
the first time, `\commandsfile` will be a token which agrees with
`\undefined` – in other words, two tokens which have not yet been
defined. The command `\undefined` must not have been defined
for this to work. Next, `\commandsfile` is assigned some contents:
it hardly matters what, but `\null` is a good compact value.

Should this sequence be re-read, `\commandsfile` will have been
made equivalent to `\null`, and will no longer be `\undefined`.

Therefore the \else condition will be obeyed. Once \endinput is encountered, the file is left and TeX returns to reading from the file in which the \input statement occurred.

Note that expansion of the tokens does not take place, unlike \if. If \pion had been defined as

\def\pion#1{$\ifx#1+\pi^+\else\pi^-\fi$}

then

\def\a{+}

\pion\a

would give π^-. Using \if rather than \ifx in the definition would have given π^+.

\ifcat⟨token₁⟩⟨token₂⟩ tests if the category codes agree. This works in a similar way to \if.

Testing boxes

\ifvoid⟨number⟩ tests whether the box with that number is void. In this context ⟨number⟩ includes the name of a box, as well as its number. It is possible to collect material in a box by \unvboxing it and then adding new material at the end: the first time round, there is nothing in the box – it is void – and therefore no unboxing is required:

\newbox\collect

\def\beginnote{\setbox\collect\vbox\bgroup

        \ifvoid\collect\else\unvbox\collect\fi

        \strut}

\def\endnote{\strut\egroup}

This simple structure needs more attention to make it really useful, but still illustrates the basic point, and the use of \ifvoid. At some point the material will have to be written out. The simplest way is to \unvbox\collect.

\ifhbox⟨number⟩ tests whether the box with that number is an \hbox.

\ifvbox⟨number⟩ tests whether the box with that number is a \vbox or \vtop.

These last two seem rather esoteric. After all, under what circumstances is it at all likely that you do not know whether a box is horizontal or vertical? TeX has a command \lastbox which, as its name suggests, will contain the contents of the last box. More precisely, if the last item on the last horizontal or vertical list is a box, it is removed and becomes \lastbox. Under these circumstances, we might not know in advance whether the box was a \vbox or an \hbox, and the test could be quite meaningful. Note that there is no way to distinguish between a \vbox and a \vtop (the astute will appreciate that there are indirect ways to infer whether the vertical box is likely to be a \vbox, with lots of height, or a \vtop, with lots of depth).

File test

\ifeof⟨number⟩ tests for end of file. The number must be between 0 and 15. The condition is false when the input stream is open and not fully read. Again, ⟨number⟩ could also be the name of the file. Reading and writing to files is addressed later in this chapter.

Fixed tests

\iftrue and \iffalse are always true or false. The self-defined conditions covered next account for these apparently superfluous features.

Self-defined conditionals

The condition that has been omitted is the condition you may create for yourself. Setting up
\newif\ifprev
first defines a conditional \ifprev, which is set to have the value \iffalse, but also creates two related commands, \prevtrue and \prevfalse. This is the 'real' explanation for the presence of \iftrue and \iffalse. They are necessary for the construction of this more flexible command. As an example, consider the following situation. The beginning of a section or subsection is a good place to break a page. T_EX has a command \goodbreak which will encourage a page break, and another one, \nobreak, which tends to inhibit page breaking. These are essentially ways of inserting particular \penalty values. A section or subsection would then normally be bracketed by a \goodbreak and a \nobreak, since we do not wish the title of the (sub-)section to be separated from the text which follows. But if a section title is immediately followed by a subsection, we would not wish the \goodbreak to be operative. How might we achieve this? A sketchy outline of a possible solution is:

```
\newif\ifprev
\def\section{\goodbreak
  \leftline{\sl Section}%
  \prevfalse\nobreak\smallskip\nobreak
  \everypar{\prevtrue}}
%
\def\subsection{\ifprev\smallskip\goodbreak\fi
  \leftline{\sl Sub-section}%
  \nobreak}
```

The notion is that immediately after a \section, \ifprev is set to false; if the subsection command is found before a paragraph, then \ifprev will still be false. If a paragraph had been encountered before \subsection is used, the \goodbreak will be used.

Besides creating your own conditions, it is possible to associate your own help text which can be used when an error occurs. This starts to be of major advantage when you attempt to exploit the structure of the document. For example, in general terms, a book will generally have only one bibliography. Should we try to include a second bibliography, there is likely to be an error.

Looping

It is possible to create a looping structure based on conditionals. The syntax looks something like
```
\loop text (optional)
  \if some condition, text and commands\repeat
```
Clearly there has to be some way to get out of the loop, otherwise it will just cycle round for ever. But there is no \fi command here. The \repeat is constructed of a number of commands, including a \fi. A minor problem of this construction is that in passing it defines \body. Should you define a command \body, looping will not work properly. It is inexplicable why \body was not written \b@dy by Knuth, in order to make it a private command, inaccessible to the rest of the world.

The looping mechanism is used by \multispan. Recall from Chapter 14 that \multispan takes a numeric argument and is said to be equivalent to repeating \omit\span. Effectively, plain uses \loop to repeat the two commands. It therefore looks similar to:
```
\def\multispan#1{\omit\mscount=#1 \loop\ifnum\mscount>1
    \span\omit \advance\mscount by-1 \repeat}
```
Note that this means that a \multispan 'really' expands to \omit\span\omit\span\omit...

since the actual entry in the table has to begin with an \omit, and the 'spare' one at the end does no harm. Of course, \mscount has been defined somewhere to be a counter.

⇒*Exercise 23.2:*   Once every schoolchild could rattle off her or his multiplication tables by rote. Since this is now regarded as a misuse of the educational process, these tables come to have a certain period charm. It is not difficult to have T_EX perform the mechanical functions necessary for the creation of multiplication tables. Do so.   ⇐

A mathematical condition

In maths, there is a command which has some similarity to the \ifcase. There are four possible states in maths: text, display, script, and scriptscript. While it is not possible to identify which of these states T_EX is in at any particular time, T_EX is obviously aware of this. Much earlier, we noted that plain, using the Computer Modern fonts, has no convenient way of creating a 'triple dot' mathematical accent. Using \dot and \ddot is straightforward, but there is no \dddot. While $\mathcal{AMS}$-T_EX does have such an accent, and obviously METAFONT could be used to create one, an alternative is to take three dots and place them physically above the character involved. To do this satisfactorily, we must have a version of \dddot which works for superscripts and super-superscripts (in other words, in script and scriptscript as well as text and display). In order to do this, we have to identify how the dots should be placed in all possible states. The command \mathchoice contains four different paths; these cover the four possible states. The command looks like

\mathchoice{*display*}{*text*}{*script*}{*scriptscript*}

There are four arguments, one for each state, in the order given here. This is a very expensive procedure, since T_EX generates every single one. At the very least it will take about four times as long as evaluating one branch, and of course, it will also take about four times as much space. One of the features of accents in maths is that any superscripts are relative to the symbol, not to the position of the accent. If we place some dots over a symbol, we must ensure that it does not add to the apparent height. A simple approach is to \halign three suitable dots over a symbol (supplied as an argument to the command). Done simply, any subsequent superscript would be placed relative to the accent. One way to handle this is to pretend that the accent has no vertical extent (unlike a \vphantom which has height and depth, but no physical expression, we want the physical expression but no height and depth). First define the three dots:

```
\def\ddd{.\mkern-1.8mu.\mkern1.8mu.}
```

An advantage of using `mu` is that it alters according to the mathematical state, saving us the trouble of having to do it. The actual values used here were found by trial and error. A way to 'crush' the vertical extent is

```
\setbox0\hbox{\ddd}\dp0=0pt ht0=0pt \box0
```

The box is there, but has had its vertical extent modified. This is just standard box manipulation.

We now have most of the information that we need. A suitable command may be written as:

```
\def\dddot#1{{%
\def\ddd{.\mkern-1.8mu.\mkern-1.8mu.}%
\def\crush##1{\setbox0\hbox{##1}%
               \ht0=0pt \dp0=0pt \box0 }%
\offinterlineskip\mathchoice
%
{\vbox{\halign{\hfil##\hfil\cr
\crush{$\displaystyle\ddd$}\cr
\noalign{\vskip0.4ex}%
$\displaystyle{#1}$\cr}}}
%
{\vbox{\halign{\hfil##\hfil\cr
\crush{$\textstyle\ddd$}\cr
\noalign{\vskip0.4ex}%
$\textstyle{#1}$\cr}}}
%
{\vbox{\halign{\hfil##\hfil\cr
\crush{$\scriptstyle\ddd$}\cr
\noalign{\vskip0.28ex}%
$\scriptstyle{#1}$\cr}}}
%
{\vbox{\halign{\hfil##\hfil\cr
\crush{$\scriptscriptstyle\ddd$}\cr
\noalign{\vskip0.2ex}%
$\scriptscriptstyle{#1}$\cr}}}}
}
```

Most of this should be fairly apparent. The doubling of the `#` in the definition of `\crush` and the expression of the template for the `\halign` is needed so that when the 'outer' command is expanded these are treated properly. If the argument is to be used, it will have the form `#1`: in order to distinguish the uses of `#`, the stratagem is to double the symbol. Should we get into a situation where a command was defined within a command which was itself quoted, its arguments would have to be expressed in the form `####1`, and so on, deeper and deeper. At each level, a pair of these symbols is interpreted as a single symbol.

The `\noalign` values were obtained by trial and error. They are in proportion with one another, assuming that the relation for 10, 7, and 5 point fonts are proportional. To some extent this can be verified by comparing the result with the behaviour of `\dot` and `\ddot`.

⇒*Exercise 23.3:*   Sometimes a vector is indicated by placing a tilde under a symbol. Can you create such an 'under-tilde' which will work appropriately with super- and subscripts?   ⇐

Looking into the future

There are a group of T_EX commands which have some rather interesting properties, and which can allow you to tie yourself up in the most awkward knots. One of these is `\futurelet`. As its name suggests, it has something to do with `\let`. It allows you to inspect commands in input to see what future input to expect. The syntax looks like

`\futurelet\next\test\future`

where `\next` is just a convenience command which will receive the value of `\future` by the equivalent of `\let\next=\future`; but `\future` still remains in the input stream (we have our cake and have it eaten!). Then `\test` can check the contents of `\next`.

Consider the following piece of code, where the notion is that when `\testing` is followed by the letter 'T' it will turn what comes next into **bold**, but anything else will result in `\sl` being selected.

```
\def\testing{\futurelet\next\fred}
\def\fred{\ifx\next T
   \bf
 \else  \sl
   \fi}
```

Note that the `\testing` command only defines *part* of the syntax we expect. The third element is the one which we will test, and is therefore the part which varies. When the argument supplied is examined by `\ifx` it is either equal to 'T', when the test selects `\bf`, or it is not, when it will select `\sl`:

```
\testing T Eiffel Tower?
\testing Q Tower of Pisa!
```

Now this is a painfully trivial example, since it removes all but the most essential parts. It also has the distressing feature of echoing the first character it finds. Most working examples of \futurelet are involved. Let's try to make it just a bit more realistic. A more common sort of construction is:

```
\def\change{\futurelet\next\switch}
\def\switch{\if\next *
   \def\action##1{\bf}
          \else
   \def\action{\sl}
          \fi
\action}
```

Now we are starting to get closer to something which might be useful. The command \action takes one argument if \change is followed by *, but no argument if it is not.

⇒*Exercise 23.4:*   Modify the \testing command to eliminate the echo of the first character it finds.   ⇐

This time, just elaborating on the existing structure, we peek ahead to see if what follows is a [. If it is, we assume that it must be an optional argument, and therefore \macopt must be used. Otherwise it is ordinary, and \macone is used:

```
\def\macopt[#1]#2{#1; #2}
\def\macone#1{#1}
\def\change{\futurelet\next\switch}
\def\switch{\if\next[
                \let\action=\macopt
            \else
                \let\action=\macone
            \fi
\action}
```

This is the basis by which LATEX does lots of its work with optional parameters. And partly why it is such a brain-damaging experience to meddle with LATEX style files.

⇒*Exercise 23.5:*   Awkward or not, let us borrow another idea from LATEX. There are a number of commands which have a *-form. There must be at least two ways you could make \fred and \fred* work differently. Implement and compare them.   ⇐

Besides reordering the arguments, we can reorder the expansion of the commands. If we say

```
\def\nextbf#1{{\bf #1}}
\def\text{Some arbitrary text}
```

then
```
\expandafter\nextbf\text
```
will give 'Some arbitrary text', while
```
\nextbf\text
```
gives '**Some arbitrary text**'. What has happened? The command \text has been expanded first: thus its braces are removed. The \nextbf command then takes the first token of the string, the 'S', and uses that as its argument. Note that the ordering of the tokens is not changed. Really all we have done here is to expand \text by one level of expansion, before expanding \nextbf at all.

Let's look at another example:
```
\def\two{{Alpha}{Omega}}
\def\choose#1#2{#1}
```
As it stands, saying \choose\two and hoping to obtain the first of the two arguments of \two is doomed to failure. The command is unable to find a second argument. It has to be expanded first, to become {Alpha} and {Omega}. To do that, we could say
```
\expandafter\choose\two
```
where \two would be expanded first, revealing two nicely packaged arguments which \choose will then process.

A further example of \expandafter, which has already been introduced, is to modify the effect of \romannumeral so that it expands a number to be upper-case characters, not the default lower case. In other words, the normal action of
```
\romannumeral\year
```
is mcmxcii. The command \uppercase will turn its argument into upper case, and its companion \lowercase will turn an argument into lower case. These apply only to alphabetic characters: anything else is ignored. If we wanted MCMXCII we would have to ensure that the expansion was modified. A simple
```
\uppercase\romannumeral\year
```
will not do, but
```
\uppercase\expandafter{\romannumeral\year}
```
should do nicely, since it ensures that the \year has been turned into Roman numerals before we apply the command \uppercase.

Last words   24

What will the future of TeX be? Will there be a TeX4 to follow
the TeX3 of 1989? It is clear from the statements made by Knuth
that he is unwilling to consider this possibility. It may not be
impossible, since the change to TeX3 seemed impossible immediately before the Stanford conference at which Knuth announced
his intention to make one last major change (the ability for TeX
to handle 8-bit characters rather than 7-bit), and a number of less
significant (though sometimes extremely useful) changes. Nevertheless, Knuth has said that TeX3 is 'frozen', or at least, the only
changes which will be made are corrections to the code. A quirky
side effect has been that the version numbers of the TeX 'corrections' will be 3, 3.1, 3.14, 3.141, ..., and that when Knuth dies, no
further changes will be made and TeX, bugs and all, will become
TeX π. In a similar way, METAFONT, currently version 2.71...
will become METAFONT e. (Both π and e are irrational numbers,
which gives one insight into the fate of TeX and METAFONT!)

If there is to be no development of TeX, does this mean that
TeX is doomed? On the contrary, the stability of TeX is one of its
strongest and most attractive features. TeX is complete. No new
features are about to be added. Everything which is there, works.
It is almost bug free. It is remarkably well tested: it has been
exposed to the TeX-hacker (hacker is not a perjorative term in the
TeX world) as well as the TeX user. It emerges unscathed from
their ravages. It is solid. A quotation from Knuth is appropriate:

> I wanted to design something so that, if book specifications
> are saved now, our descendants should be able to produce
> an equivalent book in the year 2086 ... I designed TeX and
> METAFONT themselves so that they will not have to change
> at all: They should be able to serve as useful *fixed points* in
> the middle, solid enough to build on and to rely on.

It is therefore clear that it was not Knuth's intention that TeX
(or METAFONT) would gradually evolve, slowly acquiring new

features (Knuth terms this 'creeping featurism'). This is in stark contrast with 'commercial' documentation systems, who must keep producing 'new' versions, simply in order to keep themselves in the public eye.

But Knuth does not dismiss the possibility that TEX may form the basis of some new piece of software: there may indeed be an evolved TEX (see, for example, Mittelbach, Poppelier, Spivak, and Vulis, among others), but it will not be called TEX. The code is available and anyone may tinker with it: what is clear is that the name of this hybrid may not be TEX. It remains to be seen whether this injunction can be enforced, but the high regard in which Knuth is held, plus the assignment of the term 'TEX' to the American Mathematical Society (and 'METAFONT' to Addison Wesley) will likely ensure that these wishes are observed.

One other 'attribute' contributes to the stability of TEX. An implementation may only call itself 'TEX' once it passes the `trip` test. This has a rather interesting history. A complex set of TEX input was developed to guarantee that every part of the TEX program was exercised, that every single line of code was used at least once. The ability to do this at an early stage in the TEX project was dependent on some particular software available on the TOPS system on which TEX was originally developed. As features have been added to or corrected in TEX, the `trip` suite has been augmented. Unfortunately, the `trip` test requires a special version of TEX, with some extra features switched on when the program is compiled. It is not possible for the ordinary TEX user to *validate* the program they have. It is slightly ironic that after passing `trip`, the implementation must then be recompiled, perhaps with the reintroduction of some non-conforming effects or features. META-FONT has a similar philosophy, with a `trap` test. The output from both `trip` and `trap` – in particular, that contained in the `log` file – are to be compared with Knuth's standard.

This reference to an acknowledged standard provides one useful base level: once you have learned TEX, you will never have to relearn it. From my own point of view I have to confess I am still learning TEX, but I have only been using it since 1984. Your investment is unlikely to be devalued.

Various components of TEX have been adopted by other docu mentation systems: in general, it is often rather difficult to identify the systems which have 'borrowed' TEX: they seldom note this fact in their advertising or technical material. But sometimes it is possible to identify the presence of TEX by the excellence of the typesetting (especially of mathematics). Since the internal TEX algorithms are published, and are generally available, it is understandable and appropriate that they should be used in other applications. This simply reflects their excellence and in a way helps to ensure a future for TEX.

There are two notable extensions to TEX which use the core. Knuth and MacKay produced an extension which could handle texts which are read both right-to-left (for example, Arabic, Hebrew, and also da Vinci's mirror writing) as well as the 'normal' for 'western' languages, left-to-right. The other major TEX extension is the one used in Japan, where it was necessary to implement a way of handling a character set of 6877 characters, and where text is read top-to-bottom. These two are clearly related to TEX.

TEX plus

There are developments based on TEX which remain TEX: the general increased availability of raw computing power, together with good-quality bit-mapped screens and a windowing environment, has tended to make highly integrated TEX 'environments' more available: in other words, the more traditional division into TEX, TEX screen drivers, TEX hard copy drivers, editors, and so on is becoming blurred. In some implementations it is possible to accomplish all TEX functions from within one application. As TEX is run, a 'typeset' page may appear in a window of its own as soon as it is available. The user can be viewing the screen version of the typeset text as TEX is working away completing the remainder of the text file. This is not an interactive TEX, in the sense that many 'desktop publishing' programs appear interactive. It will still not be possible to 'edit' the typeset version and have those changes reflected back into the original text file.

It is often the experience of those using TEX that the beginning of a document is typeset many more times than the end, as 'errors' (in a very broad sense) are slowly flushed from the document. If the first few pages do not change, why keep typesetting it? Could TEX not jump in at the 'corrected' position and continue from there? Clearly the paragraph and page make-up preclude a strict interpretation of this model, but a 'visually oriented TEX' (Chen *et al.*, 1986) has been developed which tries to do just this. This is not a commercial implementation, but it indicates what might be done as increasing computing power and disk space becomes available.

It is also reasonable to expect to see developments in the tools which are available with TEX. Already there are TEX-sensitive spelling checkers, editors, word counters, and so on. In general, these have tended to be system specific. One of the major strengths of TEX, its availability in a high-level generalized programming language which can be translated into machine-specific dialects, is seldom reflected in these tools. As a result, it is often difficult to translate the tools to other platforms. Therefore, although the core TEX remains constant, the surrounding components may be quite different. Nevertheless, it has been the experience of many TEX teachers that there is a great degree of commonality between different systems, and that transferring from one to another is not too difficult, even when faced with a class of TEX (and computer) novices. If we must point to an area of great concern, it is in the multiplicity of drivers: while I can guess that, to run TEX, I will likely type `tex` at the system prompt (assuming there *is* a system prompt!), working out how to obtain a hard copy is usually considerably more difficult. Added to this, the different drivers for different devices may provide a huge range of options – some more flexible than others. There appears to be limited success in 'standardizing' the range of options.

In the area of editors, it may be worth noting two examples which can provide models: the first of these is based on `emacs`. This particular editor has been around for many years, and can be obtained on (at least) UNIX and DOS versions. This is a very powerful editor, and it can be programmed (cf. van Bechtolsheim, 1988) so that it will, for example, insist that braces are balanced – apparently a very trivial need, and yet many TEX errors will be traced to this simple omission. It is straightforward to see other 'balancing' extensions, like `$` or `$$` for mathematics. Since some key combinations can be made to generate particular commands, it may also be possible to insist that, for example, typing the combination `<esc>` a generates `\alpha` in the text. A similar approach has been adopted with the VAX editor LSEDIT, although the best-known example of this (McPherson, 1985) supports LATEX rather than TEX. Nevertheless, the principles remain the same.

If we assume that mathematics is inherently difficult to input, we may wish support from editors which allow the typist (mathematician or not) the opportunity to place the symbols on the screen, and then have some transformation take place which turns this into 'raw' TEX. There are a number of such pre-processors: in 1989, Siebenmann noted more than 12, which he divided into 'text-oriented preprocessors' and 'equation editors'. In general these are targeted for the pc or Macintosh. I remain unconvinced by them. I still find it easier to write the TEX (but I have been writing the TEX for a long time and may be biased).

Approaching the problem from a slightly different direction, some other applications may generate TEX: the most obvious example of this is Wolfram Research's 'Mathematica', a widely available system which handles both symbolic and 'numeric' mathematics. Equations output from Mathematica may be turned into TEX form: similarly, two other major algebraic systems, Maple and Macsyma, can produce LATEX (Lavaud, 1991, and Chancelier and Sulem, 1989). Note that we should not expect machine-generated TEX (or LATEX) to be as concise, elegant, and understandable as a human-generated TEX (or LATEX) can sometimes be.

Extending the language

There are ways to 'extend' TEX without modifying the program. To some extent we have already been doing this. At its very rawest level, TEX is hardly usable: what we have been using is `plain`: that is, TEX with a fair number of commands (or macros) already loaded. While `plain` is just about house-trained, TEX without its `plain` commands (VIRTEX, or 'virgin' TEX) needs a great deal of careful attention. The point here is that `plain` is only one possible manifestation of TEX. It would not be very difficult to load quite different commands from those provided in `plain.tex`, but this does not seem to be a route chosen by many. Even the LATEX extension to TEX is currently built on top of `plain` (this is not quite true: LATEX is built on top of `lplain`, which is a slightly reduced version of `plain` omitting some commands or features which overlap some LATEX features or extensions). Most of the `plain` commands are still available. Similarly, $\mathcal{AMS}$-TEX 'sits on top of' `plain`. These two are extensive and comprehensive 'macro packages' which are quite widely available. There are literally hundreds of small add-ons to `plain`: extensions to meet particular requirements. These may vary from simple definitions similar to those in this primer, through to more developed and consistent additions, like Ray Cowan's `tables.tex` (which offers a straightforward interface for table creation), PICTEX (Michael Wichura's commands for the creation of pictures), `edmac` (John Lavagnino and Dominik Wujastyk's additions for 'critical editions), or `texinfo`, developed for use with the Free Software

Foundation's documentation (which, among other things, defines
the 'escape character' to be @ instead of \, and bears a passing
similarity to *Scribe*).

How can you hope to find out about these facilities? Most of the
packages were written at particular institutions, and only slowly
percolate to the outside world. It is only through the good nature
and cooperation of their originators that they escape at all. Practically all of these packages are available for free. This has two
very important consequences: information will tend to pass by
word of mouth – there will certainly be no organized advertising
to try to contact a potential audience. The documentation may
also be rather sparse, and corrections intermittent, although there
are notable exceptions to this rule. One way around the problem has been to allow the packages to be available freely, but to
market the documentation: for example, Knuth's *The* T_EX*book*,
Lamport's L^AT_EX manual, Spivak's $\mathcal{A}\mathcal{M}\mathcal{S}$-T_EX and L_A$\mathcal{M}\mathcal{S}$-T_EX
books, Wichura's P_ICT_EX documentation, and so on. This has
the additional advantage that copyright of documentation is well
understood, and usually observed, while copyright of the commands themselves (like most other computer software) tends to
be treated with much less respect.

But there are ways to find out what is available: in broad terms
there are likely to be four major sources: through publications,
through user groups, electronically, and on disk. The publications
of the T_EX Users Group (TUG), which includes the quarterly
magazine TUGBOAT, the Resource Directory, the T_EXniques
series (approximately monographs), and the recent TTN (T_EX
and TUG News), are the most widely available, and provide an
invaluable set of resources for the dissemination of information of
all matters T_EXnical, including the availability of macro packages.
In addition, the publications of the various national and language
groups provide similar services.

The various user groups (listed in Appendix C) generally provide some sorts of information flow, perhaps directly by telephone,
but also by having meetings where there is the opportunity to find
out what others know (or know about), and at which information
may be disseminated about the availability of T_EX facilities.

But even when a listing of the commands and their definitions
are included in TUGBOAT, no-one wishes to type them in again,
with the attendant problems of mis-types. The increasing tendency has been to circulate the information, or the commands
themselves, across electronic networks. This is further elaborated

in Appendix C. The evolving nature of electronic communication tends to make anything printed rather out of date. But it is probably true to say that anyone in North America or Europe probably has the capability of connecting with an electronic network, either directly through a connection to an academic host computer linked to a network, or through a modem to a commercial system like CIX, BIX, or CompuServe. This can permit downloading of much TEX-related material. The various 'conferences', 'bulletin boards', and electronic digests help keep people informed. Fortunately, TUG and the other user groups also tend to supply synopses of this information.

The last category, through the distribution of floppy disks, is generally organized through the various user groups, although some vendors will also help here. Information on this medium will be found through the previous three routes.

Keeping up to date with corrections to software is a problem, but again the electronic networks and the user groups do assist here. Version control of many of the packages is not exemplary. For example, version 2.09 of LATEX includes many corrections: the version number has remained constant, but the cognoscenti know that they should also look for the date (not earlier than `<7 Dec 1989>`).

Acquiring skills

As you use TEX, you will discover that there are things you wish to do which exceed your knowledge. If suitable commands, or similar commands, exist and are accessible to you, then you may be able to use or modify them to your requirements. Using TEX is one well-trodden path by which more TEX skills may be accumulated. Equally, there are courses which can often help. TUG runs courses at various levels, from introductory through to the truly arcane and obscure. Most of these include some amount of 'hands on' practice, although the more advanced courses tend to have a lower component of machine-oriented practice. TUG's courses tend to be the most structured and are run most regularly, but all the other user groups have some sort of educational programme, sometimes in the form of workshops, and sometimes as more formal courses.

There are other skills to acquire. Most computer users seem to be lamentably naive when it comes to typography. Those with a background in typewriting are often heavily influenced by the constraints and expectations of the typewriter, failing to appreciate that this is a very different medium, while the computer science end of the spectrum seems to have little aesthetic appreciation (there are notable exceptions). The typographic skills needed to create masterpieces are beyond the average author, and the availability of suitable tools does not guarantee their successful and aesthetic use. The development of a critical eye comes only slowly when it is untutored. There are some ways of short-circuiting this: there is a large literature in typography – some is directed towards type design, rather than the problems of legibility, but a reasonable literature exists, and it is well worth examining. A rather selective list is given in Appendix B. Courses are few and far between, and (anathema to the average TEX user) tend to be rather expensive.

In order to approach Knuth's exhortation, to 'create masterpieces of the publishing art', you need to know more than just TEX. There appears to be no substitute for practice, practice, a critical eye, and some sympathy for the end product. But these skills contain the seed of a problem. Many books become unreadable; their typographic infelicities obscure and conceal the content. Even the hyphenation becomes an issue. Form and content become so intimately intertwined that the reader becomes distracted. Be warned!

Although the desire to create masterpieces underpins Knuth's underlying objective in the creation of TEX, we must not lose sight of the fact that it has proved to be an effective workhorse for a wide variety of functions, many of which have little to do with traditional publishing. TEX is not just for books and journals, although many such have been produced with its aid. One of them might even be a masterpiece.

Appendix

A

Font tables

The Computer Modern typeface has over 70 individual fonts. As discussed earlier, in Chapter 18, some of these fonts are different design sizes of the same fundamental font. For example, Computer Modern Roman comes in design sizes of 5, 6, 7, 8, 9, 10, 12, and 17 points. There are really only about 31 basic designs. There are two main issues to be addressed in providing examples of the fonts. The first is 'what characters are available in each font?' The second is the 'shape': for example, what does Computer Modern Sans Serif look like? The first question is fairly straightforward to answer: the majority of the fonts have the same set of characters (with perhaps one variation). The font table for Computer Modern Fibonacci, given here, contains the same basic characters, in the same locations, that are used for the majority of the family. The Computer Modern fonts with the prefixes cmr, cmsl, cmvtt, cmbx, cmss, cmssi, cmssdc, cmssbx, cmssq, cmssqi, cmdunh, cmbxsl, cmb, cmff, and cmfib all share the same font table, shown in Figure A1.

There are two slight variations: firstly, the fonts with prefixes cmti, cmbxti, cmitt, cmu, and cmfi share this same table (Figure A1) except that they replace $ (dollar sign) with £ (the pounds sterling sign). Secondly, a very slight modification occurs with the 'Capital and Small Capital' fonts, cmcsc and cmtcsc, which do not have the usual lower-case characters, but, instead, smaller versions of the full-sized capitals. These 'smaller' characters are not merely reduced in a geometric progression: the weights of the strokes correspond appropriately to the upper-case characters. But the basic character positions remain the same.

There are other fonts with rather radical departures from the 'standard' pattern. The 'inch-high' font, cminch, has a denuded set of characters – only the capitals and the numerals, but these are found in the same positions as the previous fonts. In a similar way,

	'0	'1	'2	'3	'4	'5	'6	'7
'00x	Γ	Δ	Θ	Λ	Ξ	Π	Σ	Υ
'01x	Φ	Ψ	Ω	ﬀ	ﬁ	ﬂ	ﬃ	ﬄ
'02x	ı	ȷ	`	´	ˇ	˘	¯	˚
'03x	¸	ß	æ	œ	ø	Æ	Œ	Ø
'04x	˝	!	”	#	$	%	&	’
'05x	(	)	*	+	,	-	.	/
'06x	0	1	2	3	4	5	6	7
'07x	8	9	:	;	¡	=	¿	?
'10x	@	A	B	C	D	E	F	G
'11x	H	I	J	K	L	M	N	O
'12x	P	Q	R	S	T	U	V	W
'13x	X	Y	Z	[	“	]	^	˙
'14x	‘	a	b	c	d	e	f	g
'15x	h	i	j	k	l	m	n	o
'16x	p	q	r	s	t	u	v	w
'17x	x	y	z	–	—	˝	˜	¨

Figure A1
Character positions of the 'standard' CM fonts

	'0	'1	'2	'3	'4	'5	'6	'7
'00x	Γ	Δ	Θ	Λ	Ξ	Π	Σ	Υ
'01x	Φ	Ψ	Ω	↑	↓	'	¡	¿
'02x	ı	ȷ	`	´	ˇ	˘	¯	˚
'03x	¸	ß	æ	œ	ø	Æ	Œ	Ø
'04x	␣	!	"	#	$	%	&	’
'05x	(	)	*	+	,	-	.	/
'06x	0	1	2	3	4	5	6	7
'07x	8	9	:	;	<	=	>	?
'10x	@	A	B	C	D	E	F	G
'11x	H	I	J	K	L	M	N	O
'12x	P	Q	R	S	T	U	V	W
'13x	X	Y	Z	[	\	]	^	_
'14x	‘	a	b	c	d	e	f	g
'15x	h	i	j	k	l	m	n	o
'16x	p	q	r	s	t	u	v	w
'17x	x	y	z	{	|	}	˜	¨

Figure A2
Character positions of the 'typewriter' CM fonts

the logo fonts have only a few characters; these are not included here since they are not 'Computer Modern' fonts.

The bulk of the tables are the same for the 'typewriter' fonts, cmtt, cmtti, and cmsltt, but there are sufficient differences to require the generation of Figure A2. Conveniently, cmtti has a £ in place of the $. The major differences are the absence of the ligatures, and the substitution of certain other characters in their place. Note, however, that cmvtt is a typewriter type with ligatures and has its characters in the positions shown in Figure A1.

The maths italic fonts, cmmi and cmmib, have a recognizably similar layout but with notable changes, as shown in Figure A3. The maths symbol fonts, cmsy and cmbsy, have less similarity to what has gone before, and the only major correspondence is in the position of certain upper-case characters – see Figure A4. As would be anticipated, the maths extension font, cmex, has no characters which correspond to any of the other fonts. It is shown in Figure A5.

There is only one other font to consider, cmtex, the 'TEX extended' font. This is an expression of an extended ASCII code used at some US universities, including Stanford. It is shown in Figure A6.

Text type specimens

The majority of the Computer Modern family is not intended for text: it is intended for special uses, like headings, or perhaps for emphasis. For example, the bold fonts are unlikely ever to be used for setting blocks of text: they will prove far too difficult to read. The typewriter text fonts are also specialist fonts, with rather limited uses. The following specimens are therefore intended to provide some clues of what typographers and designers term the texture, colour, brilliance, and legibility of the 'reading' fonts. But it is important to realize that other factors will be significant, like the leading (or, in TEX terminology, the `\baselineskip`), the texture of the paper, and even the process to be used in the final printing – all of which helps to explain why professional advice can make the difference between excellence and mere competence. Most of the fonts are given in the 10 point design size, on 12 point baselines. Since the two 'Quotation' fonts have an 8 point design size, they have been set on 10 point baselines.

	'0	'1	'2	'3	'4	'5	'6	'7
'00x	Γ	Δ	Θ	Λ	Ξ	Π	Σ	Υ
'01x	Φ	Ψ	Ω	α	β	γ	δ	ε
'02x	ζ	η	θ	ι	κ	λ	μ	ν
'03x	ξ	π	ρ	σ	τ	υ	φ	χ
'04x	ψ	ω	ε	ϑ	ϖ	ϱ	ς	φ
'05x	↼	↽	⇀	⇁	`	'	▷	◁
'06x	0	1	2	3	4	5	6	7
'07x	8	9	.	,	<	/	>	⋆
'10x	∂	A	B	C	D	E	F	G
'11x	H	I	J	K	L	M	N	O
'12x	P	Q	R	S	T	U	V	W
'13x	X	Y	Z	♭	♮	♯	⌣	⌢
'14x	ℓ	a	b	c	d	e	f	g
'15x	h	i	j	k	l	m	n	o
'16x	p	q	r	s	t	u	v	w
'17x	x	y	z	ı	ȷ	℘	→	⌢

Figure A3
Character positions of the CM Math Italic fonts

	'0	'1	'2	'3	'4	'5	'6	'7
'00x	−	·	×	∗	÷	⋄	±	∓
'01x	⊕	⊖	⊗	⊘	⊙	◯	∘	•
'02x	≍	≡	⊆	⊇	≤	≥	⪯	⪰
'03x	∼	≈	⊂	⊃	≪	≫	≺	≻
'04x	←	→	↑	↓	↔	↗	↘	≃
'05x	⇐	⇒	⇑	⇓	⇔	↖	↙	∝
'06x	′	∞	∈	∋	△	▽	/	∣
'07x	∀	∃	¬	∅	ℜ	ℑ	⊤	⊥
'10x	ℵ	𝒜	ℬ	𝒞	𝒟	ℰ	ℱ	𝒢
'11x	ℋ	ℐ	𝒥	𝒦	ℒ	ℳ	𝒩	𝒪
'12x	𝒫	𝒬	ℛ	𝒮	𝒯	𝒰	𝒱	𝒲
'13x	𝒳	𝒴	𝒵	∪	∩	⊎	∧	∨
'14x	⊢	⊣	⌊	⌋	⌈	⌉	{	}
'15x	⟨	⟩	∣	∥	↕	⇕	\	≀
'16x	√	∐	∇	∫	⊔	⊓	⊑	⊒
'17x	§	†	‡	¶	♣	◇	♡	♠

Figure A4
Character positions of the CM Math Symbol fonts

CM Roman 10 pt on 12 pt

'In the leafy shade she lay all huddled and forlorn, the red-gold hair, the ivory of her in the cool and leafy shade by the river, her garments all disordered offering to the eye her shapeliness, her long and rounded limbs; splendid and sculptural she was, like a broken winged victory. The honeyed air droned and sang; the ivory of her, the pathetic and savage splendour of her beauty sang in my eyes as I knelt beside her. Gone she was and lost to me for ever, Eurydice! Eurydice!'

CM Text Italic 10 pt on 12 pt

'Yes. Weeping, weeping in the golden afternoon her voice came to me in the mottled sunlight by the river and I went to where she lay all huddled and forlorn, the red-gold hair, the ivory of her in the cool and leafy shade by the river, her garments all disordered offering to the eye her shapeliness, her long and rounded limbs; splendid and sculptural she was, like a broken winged victory.

CM Slanted 10 pt on 12 pt

The honeyed air droned and sang, the ivory of her, the pathetic and savage splendour of her beauty sang in my eyes as I knelt beside her. She looked at me not as one looks at a stranger but as if she expected me to comfort her. Full of desire and uncertainty I took her in my arms. She smelled of honey, it was like a dream, there was no strangeness in it; there already seemed to be a long history between us.'

CM Sans Serif 10 pt on 12 pt

It is difficult to describe someone who is surrounded by a special nimbus, perceived at once. But as this girl had the same effect, in one way or another, on many others, I must try. She had soft yellow hair, greeny-blue eyes, lovely eyebrows below a broad, quiet forehead and the most perfect mouth I have ever seen; underneath her skin there were golden lights.

CM Sans Serif Italic 10 pt on 12 pt

I am not a good physiognomist, I find it distorts a face to see it in detail, and I imagine the peculiar, extraordinary charm of her face lay in its proportions and in its expression. When I first saw the friezes in

A plain TEX primer

	′0	′1	′2	′3	′4	′5	′6	′7
′00x	(	)	[	]	⌊	⌋	⌈	⌉
′01x	{	}	⟨	⟩	∣	∥	/	\
′02x	(	)	(	)	[	]	⌊	⌋
′03x	⌈	⌉	{	}	⟨	⟩	/	\
′04x	(	)	[	]	⌊	⌋	⌈	⌉
′05x	{	}	⟨	⟩	/	\	/	\
′06x	(	\	⌈	⌉	⌊	⌋	∣	∣
′07x	(	)	⌊	⌋	{	}	.	∣
′10x	\	/	∣	∣	⟨	⟩	⊔	⊔
′11x	∮	∮	⊙	⊙	⊕	⊕	⊗	⊗
′12x	Σ	Π	∫	∪	∩	⊎	∧	∨
′13x	Σ	Π	∫	∪	∩	⊎	∧	∨
′14x	⊔	⊔	⌢	⌢	⌢	∼	∼	∼
′15x	[	]	⌊	⌋	⌈	⌉	{	}
′16x	√	√	√	√	\	∣	⌈	∥
′17x	↑	↓	⌢	⌢	`	´	⇑	⇓

Figure A5
Character
positions of
the CM Math
Extension font

	'0	'1	'2	'3	'4	'5	'6	'7
'00x	·	↓	α	β	∧	¬	∈	π
'01x	λ	γ	δ	↑	±	⊕	∞	∂
'02x	⊂	⊃	∩	∪	∀	∃	⊗	↔
'03x	←	→	≠	◇	≤	≥	≡	∨
'04x		!	"	#	$	%	&	'
'05x	(	)	*	+	,	−	.	/
'06x	0	1	2	3	4	5	6	7
'07x	8	9	:	;	<	=	>	?
'10x	@	A	B	C	D	E	F	G
'11x	H	I	J	K	L	M	N	O
'12x	P	Q	R	S	T	U	V	W
'13x	X	Y	Z	[	\	]	^	_
'14x	'	a	b	c	d	e	f	g
'15x	h	i	j	k	l	m	n	o
'16x	p	q	r	s	t	u	v	w
'17x	x	y	z	{	|	}	~	∫

Figure A6
Character positions of the CM TEX Extended font

the museum on the Acropolis I couldn't believe it, most of the girls are portraits of her. Her face, and above all her expression, belonged to the same ideal, golden time.

CM Sans Serif Quotation 8 pt on 10 pt

But beautiful girls are, in a sense, two a penny. There was something even more arresting, something unique in her face. She had the simplicity of a young girl who found life good; but it was a simplicity that had somehow been earned, was, as it were, on the second time round. This second simplicity has the directness and potency of a natural force.

CM Sans Serif Quotation Italic 8 pt on 10 pt

She had the kind of beauty that can change but not diminish – it depended for so much of its power on the kind of person she was that it could only end when she did. One trembled for her (it was too good to survive) and was humbled at the same tlme, by a face that was more strongly alive than anyone else's which contained an indestructible, fearless happiness. She shone.

Appendix   B

Annotated bibliography and references

Rather than present a bibliography in a strict order, some logic
has been imposed by dividing it into four sections. Some additional annotation attempts to provide the reader with a weighting
which often indicates the value that the author feels they have.
Some references are there merely since they appear in the text.
Others have influenced the text directly, for better or for worse. It
is inevitable that some essential material has been inadvertently
omitted.

Knuth

Since Knuth holds the pivotal position in TEX, this first section is
his, and his alone.

Donald E. Knuth, 1968–, The Art of Computer Programming,
    Addison Wesley Publishing Company, Reading, M. Volume 1,
    Fundamental Algorithms (1st Edition, 1968), 2nd Edition, 1973,
    634 pp.: Volume 2, Sorting and Searching (1st Edition, 1969);
    2nd Edition, 1981, 688 pp.: Volume 3, Seminumerical Algo-
    rithms (1st Edition, 1973), 723 pp. (Neither as quirky or amus-
    ing as the TEX books. However, since Knuth wrote TEX and
    METAFONT in order to aid the production of these volumes,
    they can be illuminating on several different levels. One exam-
    ple in volume 3 is that of calculating the date of Easter.)

Donald E. Knuth, 1979, TEX and METAFONT, New Directions in
    Typesetting, American Mathematical Society and Digital Press.
    Part 1, Mathematical Typography, 45 pp.: Part 2, TEX, a system
    for technical text, 201 pp.: Part 3, METAFONT, 105 pp. (Part 1
    is the printed text of the Gibbs Memorial lecture. Even if TEX

and METAFONT had never been written, it would be an essay worth reading.)

Donald E. Knuth, 1979, Tau Epsilon Chi, a system for technical text, American Mathematical Society, Providence, RI, 200 pp. (A version of Part 2 of the above.)

Donald E. Knuth and Michael F. Plass, 1981, Paragraphs into lines, Software – Practice and Experience, 11(11), pp.1119–1184. (A detailed description of how TₑX breaks lines in the construction of paragraphs. Some of the terminology has changed very slightly.)

Donald E. Knuth, 1983, The TFtoPL Processor *and* The PLtoTF Processor, in TₑXware, Stanford University Computer Science Report. (A detailed account of the structure of TₑX font metric files.)

Donald E. Knuth, 1984, The TₑXbook, Addison Wesley Publishing Company, Reading, Mass., 483 pp. (The source reference for TₑX-as-we-know-him/her. It delights many, and frustrates others. Another class of reader is both delighted and frustrated. The earlier editions do not reflect the changes made at TₑX3; use any edition from the 17th printing in softback or from the 11th in hardback.)

Donald E. Knuth, 1984, The METAFONT Book, Addison Wesley Publishing Company, Reading, M, 500 pp. (Still the only widely available text on METAFONT.)

Donald E. Knuth, 1984, Computer Modern Typefaces, Addison Wesley Publishing Company, Reading, M, 500 pp. (The illustrations of the Computer Modern typeface are an unexpected delight.)

Donald E. Knuth, 1984, Literate Programming, The Computer Journal, 27(2). (Explains some of the philosophy underlying the WEB system of structured documentation. DₑK regards this as one of the major developments from the TₑX project.)

Donald E. Knuth, 1986, Computer Science Considerations, Byte, (2), pp.169–172. (Text of an interview with DₑK. Helps fill in some of the gaps in the development of the TₑX project, in an anecdotal fashion.)

Donald E. Knuth and Pierre MacKay, 1987, Mixing right-to-left texts with left-to-right texts, TUGBOAT, 8(1), pp.14–25.

(Describes an extension to TₑX which allows 'bi-directional' texts to be set.)

Donald E. Knuth, 1987, Fonts for digital halftones, TUGBOAT, 8(2), pp.135–160.

Donald E. Knuth, 1989, The errors of TₑX, Software Practice & Experience, 19, pp.607–785. (A complete account of the errors noted down by Knuth while developing and maintaining TₑX. An incredible inventory of bugs, enhancements, and errors; the detail is probably unparalleled in the history of software development.)

Donald E. Knuth, 1989, The new versions of TₑX and METAFONT, TUGBOAT, 10(3), pp.325–328. (In which Knuth introduces the changes introduced at version 3. These features should be incorporated in all current implementations of TₑX and METAFONT.)

Donald E. Knuth, 1990, Virtual fonts: more fun for Grand Wizards, TUGBOAT, 11(1), pp.13–23. (Information about virtual, or composite, fonts.)

Donald E. Knuth, 1990, The future of TₑX and METAFONT, TUGBOAT, 11(3), p.489. (The definitive statement: 'I will make no further changes except to correct extremely serious bugs.')

The others

This section includes other TₑX books, many of the references within the text, and some material which may be worth pursuing if more information is required on the technical aspects of various support software and macro packages.

Paul W. Abrahams, Karl Berry, and Kathryn A. Hargreaves, 1990, TₑX for the Impatient, Addison Wesley Publishing Company, 362 pp. (A good reference manual for those who already have a few inklings. Use the second or later edition.)

Phil Andrews, 1989, Integration of TₑX and graphics at the Pittsburgh Supercomputing Center, TUGBOAT, 10(2), pp.177–178.

ArborText, 1988, DVILASER/PS User Manual, 56 pp. (Provides some useful examples of the capabilities of this driver, as well as the details of how \specials are used.)

Graham Asher, 1990, Type & Set: TₑX as the engine of a friendly publishing system, in: TEX applications, uses, methods, Malcolm Clark (ed.), Ellis Horwood Publishers, Chichester, England, pp.91–100. (This includes a post-processor for dvi files which optimizes page breaks over an entire document, following a simplified TEX line-breaking model.)

Richard J. Beach, 1985, Setting Tables and Illustrations with Style, Xerox PARC Technical Report CSL-85-3. (A discussion of the problems of setting tables and inserted illustrations.)

Richard J. Beach, 1986, Tabular typography, in: Text Processing and Document Manipulation, J. C. can Vliet (ed.), pp.18–33. (A more readable, shorter, and convincing version of the above.)

Stephan van Bechtolsheim, 1988, Using the Emacs editor to safely edit TEX sources, TEXniques 7, pp.195–202.

Nelson Beebe, 1987, A TEX dvi driver family (electronic document), University of Utah, 94 pp. (This 'family' is written in 'portable' C and can provide a fairly standard interface to a wide variety of output devices.)

Nelson Beebe, 1989, TEX and graphics: the state of the problem, Cahiers GUTenberg, no.2, pp.13–53.

Karl Berry, 1990, Filenames for fonts, TUGBOAT 11(4), pp.517–520.

Rob de Bruin, Cornelis G. van der Laan, Jan R. Luyten, and Herman F. Vogt, 1988, Publiceren met LATEX, CWI Syllabus 19. (Contains good graphics examples – some of which appear in Chapter 17. In Dutch.)

J. Ph. Chancelier and A. Sulem, 1989, MACROTEX: Un générateur de code LATEX implémenté en MACSYMA, Cahiers GUTenberg, no.3, pp.32–39. (A link between the algebraic system MACSYMA and LATEX.)

Pehong Chen, J. Coker, and Michael A. Harrison, 1986, An improved user environment for TEX, in: TEX for Scientific Documentation, Jacques Desarménien (ed.), Springer Verlag Lecture Notes in Computer Science, No. 236, pp.32–44. (With the next reference, useful sources of information about the VORTEX project. VORTEX takes a TEX input file, but reformats incrementally, as changes are made.)

Pehong Chen, J. Coker and Michael A. Harrison, Jeffrey W. McCarrell, and Steven J. Procter, 1986, The VORTEX document preparation environment, in: TEX for Scientific Documentation, Jacques Desarménien (ed.), Springer Verlag Lecture Notes in Computer Science, No. 236, pp.35–54.

Pehong Chen and Michael A. Harrison, 1987, Multiple representation document development, IEEE Computer, 21(1), pp.15–21. (Stresses the advantage of multiple 'views' of the underlying document.)

Adrian Clark, 1987, Halftone output from TEX, TUGBOAT, 8(3), pp.270–274. (An example of the use of halftone fonts, as described in Knuth, 1987.)

Adrian Clark, 1991, Practical halftoning with TEX, TUGBOAT, 12(1) pp.157–165. (An overview, with an extension to colour.)

Ray Cowan, undated, `tables.tex` (electronic document). (Straightforward but powerful set of commands for table creation.)

Trevor Darrell, 1987, Incorporating POSTSCRIPT and Macintosh figures in TEX (electronic document available with `psfig` commands). (Useful set of commands to ease the incorporation of POSTSCRIPT material into TEX.)

Hans Ehrbar, 1986, Statistical graphics with TEX, TUGBOAT, 7(3), pp.171–175.

Michael Ferguson, 1990, Report on multilingual activities, TUGBOAT, 11(4), pp.514–516.

P. Ferris and Geeti Granger, 1985, Apollo, pp.16–21, in: J. J. H. Miller (ed.), PROTEXT II, Boole Press, Dublin.

Donnalyn Frey and Rick Adams, 1990, !%@:: A directory of electronic mail addressing and networks, O'Reilly & Associates, Sebastopol, 420 pp. (Useful for information on how to get through to various electronic networks.)

N. Gehani, 1986, Tutorial: Unix document formatting and typesetting, IEEE Software, September, pp.15–24. (Gives some overview of nroff, pic, grap, and the rest.)

H. Gruber, E. Krautz, H. P. Fritzer, K. Gatterer, G. Sperka, W. Sitte, and A. Popitsch, 1988, Electrical resistivity, magnetic susceptibility, and infrared spectra of superconducting $RBa_2Cu_3O_7$ with R = Y, Sc, Tm, Ho, Eu, Nd, Gd, pp.83–88, in: H. W. Weber (ed.), High-T_c Superconductors, Plenum Press, New York. ('Source' of Figure 17.7.)

Michael A Harrison, 1989, News from the V_ORTEX project, TUG-BOAT, 10(1), pp.11–14.

Alois Heinz, 1990, Including pictures in TEX, in: TEX applications, uses, methods, Malcolm Clark (ed.), Ellis Horwood Publishers, Chichester, England, pp.141–151.

Alan Hoenig, 1989, Fractal images with TEX, TUGBOAT, 10(4), pp.491–498.

Alan Hoenig, 1991, Labelling figures in TEX documents, TUG-BOAT, 12(1), pp.125–128. (A rather clever way of using the 'other' font dimensions to store and use extra information.)

Don Hosek, 1990, TEX output devices, TUGBOAT, 11(4), pp.545–569. (Underlines the utility of TUGBOAT in providing material which is nowhere else available.)

ISO, 1985, Information Processing – Text and office systems – Standard Generalized Markup Language (SGML), ISO/DIS 8879. (Another approach to systematic, programmable text markup, but not very exciting.)

Brian W. Kernighan and Lorinda L. Cherry, 1975, A system for Typesetting Mathematics, Communications of the ACM, 18(3), pp.151–157. (Parallels to, and differences from, TEX.)

Brian W. Kernighan, 1979, A TROFF Tutorial, in: UNIX Programmers Manual 7th edition, vol. 2a, pp.237–250, Bell Laboratories.

Brian W. Kernighan, 1982, PIC – A Language for Typesetting Graphics, Software – Practice and Experience, 12(1), pp. 1–21.

Brian W. Kernighan, 1984, The UNIX document preparation tools – A retrospective, pp.12–25, in: J. J. H. Miller (ed.), PROTEXT I, Boole Press, Dublin.

Leslie Lamport, 1985, The LATEX Document Preparation System, Addison Wesley Publishing, 175 pp. (For many years the source textbook for LATEX. Its relative brevity is a blessing, but equally it could be regarded as terse in many essential areas.)

Leslie Lamport, 1987, TEX output for the future, TUGBOAT, 8(1), p.12.

John Lavagnino and Dominik Wujastyk, 1990, An overview of edmac: a plain TEX format for critical editions. TUGBOAT, 11(4), pp.623–643.

Michel Lavaud, 1991, AsTeX: an integrated and customizable multiwindow environment for scientific research, Cahiers GUTenberg no.10–11, pp.93–116. (Includes transformation from the algebraic system Maple to TeX.)

M. E. Lesk, 1979, Tbl – A Program to Format Tables, in: UNIX Programmers Manual 7th edition, vol. 2a, pp.163–180, Bell Laboratories. (Many of the examples in Chapters 14–16 are drawn from this report.)

Kent McPherson, 1985, VAX Language-Sensitive Editor (LSEDIT) Quick reference guide for use with the LaTeX environment and LaTeX style templates, TeXniques 1. (Applicable to TeX too.)

Doug Maus and Bruce Baker, 1987, DVILASER/PS extensions to LaTeX, TUGBOAT, 7(1), pp.41–47. (These extensions to DVILASER/PS can be employed for use with almost any other POSTSCRIPT driver.)

Frank Mittelbach, 1990, E-TeX: Guidelines for future TeX, TUGBOAT, 11(3), pp.337–345.

Peter and Linda Murray, 1963, The Art of the Renaissance, Thames & Hudson, London, 286 pp. (A helpful note on the integration of text and graphics before computing.)

Olivier Nicole, 1989, Un pilote graphique entre le logiciel statistique S et PiCTeX, Cahiers GUTenberg, 3, pp.21–31.

Olivier Nicole, 1990, A graphic driver to interface statistical software S and PiCTeX, TUGBOAT, 12(1), pp.70–73.

A. C. Norris and A. L. Oakley, 1990, Electronic publishing and chemical text processing, in: TeX applications, uses, methods, Malcolm Clark (ed.), Ellis Horwood Publishers, Chichester, England, pp.207–225.

Rolf Olejniczak-Burkert, 1990, texpic User Manual 1.0, interplan TB Software GmbH. (A dvi-to-dvi processor.)

Rolf Olejniczak-Burkert, 1989a, texpic – design and implementation of a picture graphics in TeX á la pic, Cahiers GUTenberg, 3, pp.9–20.

Rolf Olejniczak-Burkert, 1989b, *texpic* – design and implementation of a picture graphics in TeX á la pic, TUGBOAT, 10(4), pp.627–637.

Personal TeX Inc., 1987, PTI Laser/PS Manual, 28 pp. (Manual written by Mike Spivak. Another PostScript driver.)

Lee S. Pickrell, 1990, Combining graphics with TEX on IBM pc-compatible systems and LaserJet printers, TUGBOAT, 11(1), pp.26–31.

Sunil Podar, 1986, Enhancements to the picture environment of LATEX, Technical Report 86-17, Department of Computer Science, SUNY, 22 pp.

Nico A. F. M. Poppelier, 1991, Two sides of the fence, TUGBOAT, 12(3), pp.353–358.

Sebastian Rahtz, 1989, A survey of TEX and graphics, CSTR 89-7, Department of Electronics & Computer Science, University of Southampton, 51 pp.

Michael Ramek, 1990, Chemical structure formulas and x/y diagrams with TEX, in: TEX applications, uses, methods, Malcolm Clark (ed.), Ellis Horwood Publishers, Chichester, England, pp.227–258. (An elegant set of commands for graphics *and* for chemical formulae.)

Brian Reid, 1980, Scribe: A Document Specification Language and its Compiler, CMU-CS-81-1000, Carnegie-Mellon University. (On which LATEX was based.)

Tom Rokicki, 1989, `dvidvi`: read.me (electronic documentation), Radical Eye Software. (A dvi-to-dvi processor: its allows the rearrangement of pages, enabling 'signature' printing, for example, for booklets.)

Tom Rokicki, undated, DVIPS: a TEX driver, 41 pp. (A highly-rated PostScript driver, electronic documentation, `dvips.tex`, is available in the Aston TEX Archive, among others.)

Yasuki Saito, 1987, Report on JTEX: a Japanese TEX, TUGBOAT, 8(2), pp.103–116. (Another TEX extension. It will handle Japanese characters – katakana, hiranga, and kanji – and the 'traditional' western alphabets.)

David Salomon, 1989, DDA methods in TEX, TUGBOAT, 10(2), pp.207–216. (Implementation of Jack Bressenham's digital line drawing algorithms in TEX.)

David Salomon, 1990, Output routines: Examples and Techniques. Part I: Introduction and examples, TUGBOAT, 11(1), pp.69–86. (This and the next two articles provide the most extensive discussion on output routines currently available:)

David Salomon, 1990, Output routines: Examples and Techniques. Part II: OTR techniques, TUGBOAT, 11(2), pp.212–236.

David Salomon, 1990, Output routines: Examples and Techniques. Part III: Insertions, TUGBOAT, 11(4), pp.588–605.

Rainer Schöpf, 1989, Drawing histogram bars inside the LATEX picture-environment, TUGBOAT, 10(1), pp.105–107. (Transportable to TEX.)

Norbert Schwarz, 1988, Einführung in TEX, Addison-Wesley Verlag (Deutschland) GmbH, 272 pp. (A good, concise introduction. In German.)

Norbert Schwarz, 1989, Introduction to TEX, Addison-Wesley Europe, 278 pp. (Translation of the above.)

Raymond Seroul, 1989, Le petit Livre de TEX, InterEditions, 317 pp. (Excellent introduction to TEX. In French.)

Raymond Seroul and Silvio Levy, 1991, A Beginner's Book of TEX, Springer Verlag, 283 pp. (Translation of the above.)

Laurent Siebenmann, 1989, The evolution of the TEX user interface, TEXline 8, pp.11–13. (Describes a number of pre-processors which transform mathematics into TEX form.)

Richard Simpson, 1990, Nontraditional uses of METAFONT, in: TEX applications, uses, methods, Malcolm Clark (ed.), Ellis Horwood Publishers, Chichester, England, pp.259–271. (Makes use of METAFONT to create new characters – graphs, parts of graphs, special symbols. Also creates `pk`/`tfm` pairs.)

Michael D. Spivak, Michael Ballantyne, and Yoke Lee, 1989, HI-TEX cutting and pasting, TUGBOAT, 10(2), pp.164–165. (Another dvi-to-dvi processor: intended to allow TEX to handle large or complex tables, but it could equally be used to allow diagrams to be merged.)

Michael D. Spivak, 1990, The joy of TEX, 2nd edition, American Mathematical Society, 309 pp. (The source manual for the $\mathcal{AMS}$-TEX macro package, an extension to `plain` for hardened mathematicians.)

Michael D. Spivak, 1989, $\text{L}\mathcal{AMS}$-TEX the synthesis, The TEXplorators Corporation, Houston, 289 pp. (A specialized macro package merging of the functionality of both $\mathcal{AMS}$-TEX and LATEX, and with some extras.)

Michael D. Spivak, 1991, A contrarian view on TeX extensions, *TeXline* 13, pp.1–3. (A suggestion that many of the examples quoted of TeX's inadequacies are fallacious.)

TUG, 1991, Resource Directory, TeX Users Group, Providence, RI, 194pp. (Compilation of many of the resources available to the TeX user. One of the many benefits of TUG membership.)

TUG `dvi` Driver Standards Committee, 1992, The `dvi` driver standard, level 0, TUGBOAT, 13(1), pp.54–57.

A. J. Van Haagen, 1988, Box plots and scatter plots with TeX macros, TUGBOAT, 9(2), pp.189–192.

Michael Vulis, VTeX enhancements to the TeX language, 1990, TUGBOAT, 11(3), pp.429–434.

Michael Vulis, 1991, Should TeX be extended? 1991, TUGBOAT, 12(3), pp.442-447. (Provactively suggests that TeX could be 'a historical curiosity' by 1995.)

Michael Wichura, 1987, The PiCTeX manual, TeXniques 6, TeX Users Group, 83 pp. (The source manual: I find the syntax a bit quirky, but the commands certainly work well enough.)

Michael Wichura, 1988, PiCTeX: macros for drawing PiCtures, TUGBOAT, 9(2), pp.193–197.

Michael Wichura, undated, TABLE – The TABLE macro package, Personal TeX Inc. (A powerful alternative to building your own tables.)

Patricia Wilcox, 1989, Metaplot: machine-independent line graphics for TeX, TUGBOAT, 10(2), pp.179–187.

Dominik Wujastyk, 1987a, Chemical ring macros in LaTeX, *TeXline* 4, p.11.

Dominik Wujastyk, 1987b, Chemical symbols from LaTeX, *TeXline* 5, p.10.

Typography and style

This section is not TeX specific, but addresses some of the wider issues of typography. It is by no means comprehensive. Wider reading is essential if we are ever to be able to achieve success in Knuth's final exhortation in *The TeXbook*: GO FORTH now and create *masterpieces of the publishing art!*

Alison Black, 1990, Typefaces for desktop publishing, a user guide, Architecture Design and Technology Press, 106 pp. (Nicely designed and presented, this is nowhere as narrow as its title suggests. Substitute 'electronic' for 'desktop'.)

Horace Hart, 1986, Hart's rules for compositors and readers at the University Press Oxford, 39th edition, 182 pp. (First printed in 1893, this encompasses the house style still used at OUP. Still a mine of useful information, with lots of solutions to problems that the amateur does not know exist. Regarded as a standard by the English-speaking world.)

Linotype, 1988, The Pleasures of Design, Linotype Ltd, 33 pp. (A useful set of guidelines for layout and typography in general.)

Ruari McLean, 1980, The Thames and Hudson Manual of Typography, Thames and Hudson, 216 pp. (Explains some of the typographic detail that we ignore at our peril. Lots of good advice. Broadens your appreciation of type and typography enormously, and entertainingly.)

John Miles, 1987, Design for Desktop Publishing, Gordon Fraser, 103 pp. (TEX is hardly desktop publishing in the traditional sense, but there are many nuggets in here which will prevent you from making too many layout gaffes.)

Richard Rubinstein, 1988, Digital Typography, Addison Wesley Publishing Company, 340 pp. (Interesting, thought provoking, and by someone who knows something of TEX and METAFONT. Covers a wide field.)

Richard Southall, 1984, First principles of typographic design for document production, TUGBOAT, 5(2), pp.79–90. (Based on a course presented with Leslie Lamport. Richard occupies an important place in the TEX hagiocracy.)

University of Chicago Press, 1982, The Chicago Manual of Style, 13th edition, University of Chicago Press, 738 pp. (A comprehensive manual which describes the rules of style used by the Press. Not necessarily the rules used by other presses, but its all-encompassing nature does give it a claim to providing a relatively unambiguous standard.)

Sources for many equations and examples

Since real examples are more convincing and less tractable than invented ones, most of the equations in the text have been borrowed, stolen, or adapted from other published sources. In general these are from publishers other than Addison Wesley, since this introduces some variation in the way that the maths is handled. Simply reproducing an Addison-Wesley-style equation in TₑX is just too easy. One or two portions of text have also been borrowed, directly or indirectly. Some were referenced earlier. Naturally it is left as an exercise to the reader to locate the equations and examples in the sources.

S. Angus, B. Armstrong, and M. K. de Reuck, 1985, Chlorine: tentative tables, Pergamon Press, 162 pp.

Samuel Beckett, 1959, Molloy: Malone Dies: The Unnameable, Calder & Boyars, London.

William Blake, 1804, Milton, in: The Complete Poems, ed. Alicia Ostriker, 1977, Penguin Books.

Jorge Luis Borges, 1970, Labyrinths, Penguin Books, 287 pp.

Joe Bob Briggs, 1987, Joe Bob Briggs goes to the Drive-In, Penguin Books, 325 pp.

Lewis Carroll, 1965, The Annotated Alice (edited by Martin Gardner), Penguin Books, 352 pp.

Ruel V. Churchill, 1960, Complex variables and applications, McGraw-Hill Book Company, Inc., 297 pp.

W. E. H. Culling, 1989, The characterization of regular/irregular surfaces in the soil-covered landscape by Gaussian random fields, Computers & Geosciences, 15(2), pp.219–226.

R. W. Ditchburn, 1963, Light, Blackie and Son Ltd, 518 pp.

Rafael C. Gonzalez and Paul Wintz, 1977, Digital Image Processing, Addison Wesley Publishing Company, 450 pp.

Carol A. Gotway, 1991, Fitting semivariogram models by weighted least squares, Computers & Geosciences, 17(1), pp.171–172.

Bo Stig Hanson, 1990, A function-based formatting model, Electronic Publishing, 3(1), pp.3–28.

Yannis Haralambous, 1989, TₑX and latin alphabet languages, TUGBOAT, 10(3), pp.342–5.

Russell Hoban, 1987, The Medusa Frequency, Jonathon Cape, London, 143 pp.

Kiyoshi Horikawa, 1978, Coastal Engineering, University of Tokyo Press, 402 pp.

P. J. Kavanagh, 1966, The Perfect Stranger, Chatto & Windus, London, 182 pp.

Peter A. Lachenbruch, 1975, Discriminant Analysis, Hafner Press, 128 pp.

Gary Larson, 1984, The Far Side Gallery, Andrews and McMeel, unnumbered.

William S. Meisel, 1972, Computer-Oriented Approaches to Pattern Recognition, Academic Press, 250 pp.

Herman Melville, 1851, Moby Dick or the whale. (The examples in Chapter 3 are an amalgam of Chapter 2 'The Carpet Bag' from the 1982 Modern Library Edition and the 1967 Everyman's Library Edition. 'She was Rachel, weeping for her children, because they were not.')

Flann O'Brien, 1967, At Swim-Two-Birds, Penguin Books, 218 pp.

W. S. B. Paterson, 1969, The Physics of Glaciers, 1st edition, Pergamon Press, 250 pp.

Theo Pavlidis, 1982, Algorithms for graphics and image processing, Computer Science Press, 416 pp.

Terry Pratchett, 1989, Pyramids, Victor Gollancz Ltd, London, 272 pp. (But read 'The Colour of Magic' by the same author first.)

Henry Reed, 1946, Chard Whitlow, Jonathon Cape, London.

Azriel Rosenfeld and Avinash C. Kak, 1982, Digital Picture Processing, Volume 1, 2nd edition, Academic Press, 435 pp.

Azriel Rosenfeld and Avinash C. Kak, 1982, Digital Picture Processing, Volume 2, 2nd edition, Academic Press, 349 pp.

J. Serra, 1982, Image Analysis and Mathematical Morphology, Academic Press, 610 pp.

Appendix   C

Resources

TeX is widely available. There are versions of TeX which run
on practically any machine which is currently being produced.
Provided there is a Pascal or C compiler available, you could
probably compile your very own version from the sources which
are publicly available. In the mid-80s, this was indeed what you
were most likely to do. Fortunately it is now possible to find a
'plug'n'play' version of TeX for the majority of computing platforms. The popular platforms usually have both commercial and
public domain implementations available.

If there is a free (i.e. public domain, or better, publicly available) implementation, how do the commercial vendors survive?
And why? Purchasing a commercial version gives some assurance
that when something goes wrong, you have a friendly shoulder to
cry on (or a friendly telephone to cry over). Despite TeX's nature
as an unchanging *de facto* standard, there are upgrades from time
to time: the most notable of these was the significant change from
version 2.999... to version 3. The new features introduced circu-
lated fairly quickly through many parts of the TeX world, but in
the spirit of 'if it ain't broke, don't fix it', there are still bound to
be many 'old' versions around. But at least it was in the vendors'
interests to communicate with as many of their customers as they
could find, in the hope that they would want to upgrade. In the
public domain, the resources do not exist to do this sort of follow
up. But those who have good access to the TeX 'community' can
usually rely on their colleagues to find out what is going on. If you
are on your own, then this information nexus may not be present.

The vendors have other uses: larger companies may not be permitted to obtain software which is not 'supported' in some way. If
your business depends upon some software (to whatever degree),
the relatively small amount spent in purchase and support is an

insurance policy. There is, though, a minor problem lurking in the background. The 'versions' of TeX are not so very different – to be TeX the implementation must pass a fairly rigorous range of tests. The basic interface is fixed. What criteria are therefore used to choose between this range of very similar products? The vendors attempt to provide some added value – sometimes by hotline support (especially in the USA), sometimes by providing drivers for a wide range of output devices (although many purchasers mix and match their TeX implementations and drivers), sometimes by enhancing the TeX program by making it as fast as possible, or exploiting particular aspects of the platform's architecture, or by making the installation as easy as possible.

There can be no doubt that at one time the commercial implementations were likely to be better than the public domain ones (with perhaps the exception of the 'parent' installation on the TOPS-20 system at Stanford University). When the first commercial implementations on the IBM personal computer arrived, there were no public domain versions; the same was true of the Macintosh, and later the Atari and the Amiga. At a larger scale, the Sun workstation has had a fine commercial implementation since 1984 (it was this implementation by ArborText, together with its previewer, which convinced me of the utility of TeX). By and large, there are few commercial implementations for the very large mainframes. The market simply is not there to support a vendor. But once we migrate to Digital's VAX range, and then to UNIX workstations, and at last to the wide range of 'personal' machines, the vendors proliferate.

The following account of available versions of TeX is not comprehensive, nor does inclusion imply recommendation in any way. It just reflects an implementation that has been brought to my attention in some way. It concentrates on the 'popular' ranges of machines.

Personal machines

'Personal machines' tend to imply the IBM pc and its clones. This is shortsighted, since there are equally 'personal' machines around, like the Apple Macintosh, the Atari ST, and the Amiga (and some others too). All of these run TeX very well, and the superior graphics capability of these non-IBM machines does make them very attractive for preview.

The clones

There are more implementations on the 'clone' than any other platform. There are at least four commercial implementations, and probably an equal number of public domain versions. The commercial implementations pcTeX from Personal TeX Inc. and μTeX from ArborText (originally called microTeX and originally marketed by Addison Wesley) were the first practical implementations on 'small' machines. They have continued to develop. Since then, TurboTeX from Kinch Computer Company, Vector TeX from MicroPress Inc., CTeX from Micro Publishing Systems, and 'Complete System 1' from ScripTek have joined them. In the public domain field, the strongest versions seem to be Eberhard Mattes' emTeX and Wayne Sullivan's SBTeX. But there are others: Klaus Thull's PubliCTeX, Garry Biehl's DOSTeX, and Pat Monardo's Common-TeX. This last implementation was hand-translated into C, and forms the basis of some implementations on other platforms. All these are genuine full implementations of TeX, and all work in the 'normal' MS-DOS operating system with at most 640 Kbyte of memory (and a reasonable amount of hard disk). What else do you need? You need a screen previewer and other output drivers. In general these are extra items which have to be bought from the vendors, although the public domain versions do tend to include a good range of drivers. The multiplicity of alternative output devices in the pc world does make it difficult to be comprehensive, but almost all popular (and many rather unpopular) devices seem to be catered for.

Macintosh

Currently there are at least two public domain versions and one commercial. The most impressive of the public domain versions is Andrew Trevarrow's OzTeX. This begins to exploit the Macintosh interface and to provide a degree of integration. The Macintosh has the relative advantage of not having a wide variety of screens and output devices. This makes the implementor's job so much easier: he or she knows what devices to target. The commercial implementation, *Textures*, from Blue Sky Research, is even more highly integrated, and really feels like a Macintosh application.

Atari

The Atari has tended to be regarded as a games machine, but in some ways it provides an excellent engine for TₑX. There are commercial implementations from TₑXsys and from Tools, and public domain implementations from Christopher Strunk and from Stefan Lindner and Lutz Birkhahn. All these implementors are from Germany (a country which takes its Ataris very seriously).

Amiga

I only know of one commercial implementation for the Amiga, written by Tom Rokicki (otherwise known as Radical Eye Software, or $\sqrt{i}$). There is at least one public domain implementation. Like the Atari, this is an excellent platform for TₑX, and its support for true multi-tasking offers all sorts of really attractive possibilities.

Workstations

This almost always means UNIX. But even UNIX devotees will acknowledge that there is more than one UNIX. There is a 'vanilla' public domain UNIX distribution which comes through Pierre MacKay of the University of Washington. ArborText have a number of commercial implementations for various UNIX boxes. The NeXT machine comes complete with an implementation of TₑX by Tom Rokicki. Since workstations do not always mean UNIX, let us include Graham Toal's implementation on the Acorn Archimedes, and also Edgar Fuß' commercial implementation on the same machine.

VAX and bigger

For many years, David Kellerman of North Lake Software has provided both a commercial and a public domain implementation of TₑX for VAX/VMS systems. There are others around too, through Adrian Clark, Don Hosek, and others. There is an implementation on one of the DECUS distribution tapes. For many years Maria Code Data Processing Services have been stalwart providers of public domain TₑX. This includes a version for Vaxen.

   Beyond this point, all implementations appear to be in the public domain. This includes Prime, Data General, Cray, the various

IBM mainframe systems (VM/CMS, VMS, and even TSO), and the ageing DEC TOPS systems. Naturally there are some others out there. Provided you can find a Pascal or C compiler, the implementation is possible – not necessarily easy. Practically every one of the public domain implementations, and a few of the commercial ones, include the 'source' code. One interpretation of 'public domain' suggests that what it really means is 'publicly available' or 'freely available – but not necessarily free'.

TeX is not enough

Although various device drivers are almost inevitably included in most implementations, this is something which needs to be considered. There are some good commercial drivers, especially for the MS-DOS and UNIX implementations (and notably by ArborText for both and Personal TeX for MS-DOS). Outside this there are a few commercial drivers, but chiefly for very particular devices. The range of public domain alternatives is wide and bewildering. Nelson Beebe is responsible for a 'family' of drivers which have shown themselves to be modular and fairly readily enhanced to new devices which appear. Written in C they are often included in the various implementations.

From time to time tables of driver availability are published in TUGBOAT: see for example Hosek (1990). These tables cover both commercial and public domain drivers, but remain incomplete.

TeX and drivers are not enough

Even with a fully fledged TeX and a plethora of drivers, it is likely that you will need a few other things: these might include spelling checkers, although there are arguments against their use; syntax checkers – a way of balancing braces can often prevent much grief, and editors like EMACS (in the public domain and frequently found on UNIX machines) or the proprietary VAX LSEDIT can provide many useful features which make it much more difficult to make syntactic errors.

Information is also available: there are a number of ways of contacting other TeX users, either with problems of implementation, or with TeX problems. Of course, if you bought your implementation, you should reap the benefit of your investment and try out the vendor. Some are better than others, but if you don't ask, they won't provide. Unfortunately, there are two worlds: there are those with electronic access to the worlds, and those without. The widespread use of electronic mail is rather taken for granted in the academic and parts of the research world, but sadly is nowhere as widespread as those in electronically connected ivory towers believe. Marshal McLuhan's global village is still a fair way off. The expansion of TeX into the world of personal machines has taken it out of the hands of academics and placed it into the hands of the man on the Clapham omnibus, without his modem and portable telephone. But there are ways of accessing electronic mail services even if you are outside this academic world. Why would you want to? There are a number of distribution lists which accept TeX enquiries (in a very wide sense) and which are read by many other TeX users. In general, some response will be elicited (not always helpful, but you are dependent on the goodwill of interested volunteers who only benefit rather indirectly). A very generalized list, `texhax`, was started at Stanford University many years ago under the moderation of Malcolm Brown, was later under the auspices of Pierre MacKay at the University of Washington, and is now administered from Aston University. The electronic mail systems are extensive enough that many people throughout the world receive this digest, and it is common to see problems and solutions from all over the electronic world – Australia, New Zealand, Japan, Israel, Europe (now including Poland, Hungary, Czechoslovakia, and Russia), as well as the obvious Canada and USA. As yet, Africa, South America, Antarctica, India, and chunks of Asia do not appear to have reliable electronic links.

A rather similar system is run from the UK through a dedicated machine at Aston University – `uktex`. This has the remarkable feature that it is despatched with clockwork efficiency and timing every Friday evening. In Europe a number of language-specific lists exist.

UNIX users, with access to `uucp`, will also be familiar with this sort of world, and will also have access to the many 'lists', which include a number which have some relevance to TeX.

If you do not have immediate access to these sources, how can you use them? In general terms it is possible to access 'bulletin boards' or 'conferences' like BIX, CompuServe, and CIX (there must be more) through modems which provide the communication link between your desktop and the bulletin board. There should be a way of 'breaking out' of these to the wider email world. Since you have to pay for your use of space on these systems (as well as your connect time), there is an obvious overhead.

For a lower overhead, you could join a User Group. The largest and oldest User Group is the TEX Users Group. This started in 1980 as an implementors group, and now is an international group with over 4,000 members, many of whom would not know what a compiler is, let alone want to use one. They are indeed users. The group publishes TUGBOAT 'The Communications of the TEX Users Group', a journal of about 700–800 pages per year, containing articles on all sorts of levels on all sorts of TEX-related topics. It also contains advertisements from various vendors, and therefore provides a wide range of useful material. TUG organizes an annual conference (usually in North America), but it also provides other services to its membership. Its TEXniques series are monographs (usually) covering a wide range of TEX-specific topics; various other TEX-related publications are available to members; public domain TEX, notably for MS-DOS machines, and so on. It has also started to produce a Newletter, a more informal production than TUGBOAT.

This is not the only group.

German speaking

DANTE is the largest and fastest growing of the other TEX groups. Since they make the public domain versions of TEX for the pc available to group members, they have been able to ensure sustained growth, and recently have expanded their activities throughout 'greater' Germany.

Japanese

The next largest group is probably the Japanese group. The problems of the Japanese character set were addressed some years ago, and the Japanese progressed to a 2 byte input, adequately solving most of their character set problems. At least the twin features of diacriticals and hyphenation do not plague Japanese. Other interesting features of Japanese TEX and TUG life include *two* different implementations to handle Japanese – JTEX and pTEX – and a translation of *The TEXbook* into Japanese.

French speaking

GUTenberg, like DANTE, sees itself as a language group. Perhaps the most visible product of GUTenberg are the *Cahiers*. This journal has been produced for a number of years now, and continues a high standard of production and content. GUTenberg distributes disks for the pc.

Nordic

Now we come to the rather smaller groups. Firstly the Nordic group: a careful choice of title, since this now includes Finland, Sweden, Denmark, Norway, and Iceland. The observant will notice that this is neither a national nor a language group.

The TEX support provided by the group is decentralized to local systems groups at different sites. A central register is kept of TEX experts and contacts at different sites. Local courses, handouts, and instructions are offered by the various sites and made widely available. A mailing list has recently taken over the function of communicating news, problems, and questions from different sites. Since the majority of the group's members are in academic institutions, electronic mail is a good medium for communication.

Dutch speaking

The Dutch group, the NTG, is a 'Dutch-speaking group'. It produces a nice set of information – MAPs, or Minutes and APpendices – for its members, documenting the progress of various groups, reports from their own and other TEX meetings: a sort of annual, or semi-annual, report which provides a good record of what has been going on. Various bits crop up in other forms in other journals, but it serves well the function of keeping the membership informed and aware.

United Kingdom

This group has frequent and varied meetings, in a variety of locations. It also publishes 'Baskerville', the 'annals' of the group. Before reaching for your Sherlock Holmes and starting to worry about meetings next to the Grimpen Mire, note firstly that the book by Conan Doyle was 'The Hound of the Baskervilles', and secondly, that John Baskerville holds a position of great esteem among European type designers. His brief biography is interesting enough to be reiterated here: he was a japanner ('japan' is a sort of varnish), letter cutter, and writing master in Birmingham and went on to design a typeface which has been described as holding 'a central position in the transitional group of typefaces'. He also made innovations in printing inks, papermaking, and in printing itself. His book designs are also highly regarded. It is this remarkable conjunction of art and technology embodied in Baskerville which is echoed in Knuth's own achievements with TEX, and therefore makes the adoption of Baskerville's name so appropriate. The astute will also note that Birmingham is the home of Aston University, the site of the most comprehensive TEX electronic archive – further reinforcing this choice of name.

Czechoslovakia

Czechoslovakia must be counted as one of the notable successes of the newer groups. 'Československé sdružení uživatelů TEXu' was founded on May 9th, 1990. It grew out of two groups, one composed principally of mathematicians, and the other physicists. *CS* TUG is now able to provide its members with emTEX. It now produces a 'TEX Bulletin' for its membership.

Hungary

There are about six or so journals now produced in Hungary with the aid of TEX. This has helped to stimulate Hungarian TEX with typographically designed Hungarian letters and Hungarian hyphenation. At present the use of TEX is concentrated in academic institutions, perhaps much as one might expect.

Commonwealth of Independent States

A Russian-speaking TEX users group, probably to be called Cyr-TUG, now exists. TEX is in use by a number of publishers, although mainly in the production of texts in English. There are also groups in the Ukraine and probably elsewhere by now. Since Russia is big, there is also a Siberian group, a counterweight to those in the west of the country.

Ireland

Partly stimulated by the success of the 1990 TUG meeting in Cork, there are the stirrings of an Irish group, perhaps under the name of 'Italic'. Those with an eye for an acronym will manage to achieve 'Irish TEX And LATEX Interest Community'.

Others...

There are also stirrings in Turkey, Poland, Slovenia, Estonia, Mexico, Nigeria, and South Africa. There are probably others whose existence is as yet unknown. The point of this litany is that local groups do exist, and that they may be a useful source of information, provided there is one in your own area. The most likely source of information is the current edition of TUGBOAT, the TUG Resource Directory, or TUG itself.

Some user group addresses

International
TₑX Users Group
PO Box 9506
Providence
RI 02940
USA
tel: 401 751 7760
fax: 401 751 1071
email: `tug@math.ams.com`

French speaking
GUTenberg
BP 21
F78354 Jouy-en-Josas
France
email: `gut@irisa.fr`

Nordic
Nordic TUG
c/o Roswitha Graham
KTH
DAB
S100 44 Stockholm
Sweden
email: `roswitha@admin.kth.se`

German speaking
DANTE
Postfach 10 18 40
D6900 Heidelberg 1
Germany
fax: 06221 56 55 81
email: `dante@dhdurz1`

Dutch speaking
NTG
Postbus 394
1740 AJ Schagen
The Netherlands
email: `ntg@hearn`

Japan
Japanese TUG
Yoshio Ohno
Dept. Computer Science
Keio University
3-14-1 Hiyoshi
Kohoku-ku
Yokohama 223
Japan

United Kingdom
ukTEXug
c/o Information Systems
Aston University
Aston Triangle
Birmingham B4 7ET
UK
email: uktexug@tex.ac.uk

Ireland
Peter Flynn
Computer Bureau
University College of Cork
Cork
Ireland
email: cbts8001@iruccvax.ucc.ie

Czechoslovakia
𝒞𝒮 TUG
c/o MÚ UK
Sokolovská 83
CS186 00 Praha 8
Czechoslovakia

Appendix

D

Solutions to the exercises

3.1: Only 9. It's sad to begin on an ambiguity like this, but if it reinforces the notion that one way to find out is to experiment, perhaps not a complete disaster.

3.2: You can leave as many blank lines as you like. TEX only 'sees' the fact that you have left vertical 'space', and treats this 'space' as a paragraph separator. The same applies to multiple \par s. TEX actually looks for an end of line: somewhere TEX has made 'end of line' and \par equivalent. Extra blank lines or \par s do not give you extra vertical space, but if \parskip is zero, you would not expect extra space, would you?

3.3: The fact that TEX requires \end or \bye can alert you to the fact that you may not be tied to a single input file. If the 'end of file' marker indicated that TEX was to complete its typesetting, it could be more difficult to chain several files together. Since TEX will come up with a message like

`(Please type a command or say '\end')`

when it comes to the end of the input file, you could \input another one. Of course, the \input command can ocurr within a file, and you may assemble several files in a single job without having to type anything in.

3.4: Try some of the following:

`- - -      -{-}-       -{}-{}-     {-}-{-}`

Provided the - characters are 'separated', TEX will not jump in and impose its ligatures. Note that in the first, there will be some space between the hyphens. Thus the others more closely answer the question posed.

3.5: The easiest way is to use braces in order to disable the automatic ligatures:

```
dif{f}icult {f}lying
```
will do the trick. But the characters placed within the braces will not be kerned – the `tfm` files will not have kerning information for 'f' and 'i', since it will have expected to turn them into a ligature anyway. The question was biased towards the 'standard' Computer Modern Roman font: therefore the solution which suggests recreating the `tfm` files, where there was no ligaturing, is illegal (but it is possible: don't call it Computer Modern Roman).

3.6: This is apparently straightforward, but it is much more difficult to get the spacing right:
' ''Starboard'' ' and '' 'Starboard' ''
will result in ' "Starboard" ' and " 'Starboard' ", where at least there are single and double quotes which match. The space between the two sets of quotes is too large. The recommended amount of space is given by the command `\thinspace`. The 'correct' answer is therefore
''\thinspace'Starboard', he cried''
An advantage of this rather clumsy approach is that there will not be a line break between " and '.

3.7: To 'restore' justification once `\raggedright` has been invoked, ensure that the whole section of text to be set ragged right (unjustified/ranged left) is enclosed in braces:
```
{\raggedright.... . }
```
The braces can encompass whole paragraphs. Note that you will not be able to switch raggedright off and on within a paragraph (well, *you* can switch it off and on, but T_EX will only pay attention to whatever is 'active' at the end of the paragraph).

3.8: To obtain the backslash character, be intuitive: \\. Under some circumstances, `\backslash` will also work. The circumstance is maths, a condition you do not yet know how to invoke.

3.9: There is no convenient way to change these characteristics part way through a paragraph. T_EX sets a paragraph, and uses the relevant parameters which are still active at the end of the paragraph. Thus a paragraph starting with `\baselineskip10pt` and ending with `\baselineskip14pt` will be set with the last value – unless that last `\baselineskip` was enclosed in braces. This does not mean that baselines are a fixed distance apart: recall glue, `\lineskip` and some other parameters. But the paragraph is a fundamental unit. It is tricky to meddle with. On the other hand, there is a tendency to make some things paragraphs when they are not really. In a sense, a title or section heading can be treated as a special sort of paragraph. But is it really?

4.1: These examples may be typeset by typing:
```
Show that the volume $V$ is given by
$V=l(a-2b)(a+2b)$.\par
Common factors: $ab+ac=a(b+c)$.\par
$s=kP$, where $k$ is a constant.\par
If $y=kx$, and $y=15$ when $x=6$,
find the constant $k$.\par
```
Separate the lines either by blank lines, or by \par. This makes each 'line' a separate paragraph. Otherwise the sentences would run on into a single paragraph. Although the expressions within the \$ signs have no spaces within them, TEX would not have cared, since it decides on spacing within mathematical expressions.

4.2: The requires a simple edit of two of the examples in the previous exercise.
```
Show that the volume $V$ is given by
$$V=l(a-2b)(a+2b)$$\par
Common factors: $$ab+ac=a(b+c)$$
```
If a full stop follows the \$\$ at the end of the first line, TEX will place it at the beginning of the *next* typeset line. If you really want the period to be part of the mathematical expression, you will have to write something like
```
$$V=l(a-2b)(a+2b).$$
```
This is generally thought of as rather poor style. It is however a style used in many journals. Should you leave out the \par (or fail to leave a blank line) between the two sets of expressions, there will be a slight change in the formatting: it will all be a single paragraph. After the first display equation, the next section of text will start right at the beginning of the next line, with no indentation – that is, all part of the same paragraph.

4.3: The phrase \$\mit\sigma\$ gives σ: no change. Rather similarly, \$\rm\sigma\$ is no different to \$\sigma\$.

4.4: In traditional typesetting, with bits of metal type, the individual characters were kept in two cases. The 'lower' case contained the 'miniscules', or what we loosely call the small letters, while the 'upper' case held the majascules or capital letters. Quite why upper and lower case Greek do not seem to share the same slope is a subject lost in the mists of time. In *De Epidemia*, published in Venice in 1497 by Aldus Manutius' press, 'upright' roman text is mixed with 'slanted' greek text. Since the upper case greek letters are often identical to their roman 'equivalents', perhaps it did not seem worth cutting the extra characters, but acceptable to mix the two styles. Italic was a separate typeface, not merely some version of roman, and remained so for a couple of centuries. On the other hand, by 1501, Francesco Griffo had cut the Aldine italic, but the tradition, if it was, has continued. An apocryphal tale suggests that the custom arose in Oxford (inevitably) when a typesetter had lower case greek but no upper case greek characters. This sounds a bit implausible. Modern Greek has all sorts of typefaces and this custom is inappropriate.

4.5: If you tried this you will have obtained a comment from TEX that it inserted a missing $. It sensed that something was going on which had to do with maths, and therefore inserted the 'switch' immediately before the suspected maths expression. TEX had no way of knowing where the expression ended. Had you just allowed TEX to continue, everything up to the next $ (if there is one), will be turned into 'maths'. A way to tackle the problem is to delete the 'offending' tokens, and then insert what should have been there: for example

```
! Missing $ inserted.
<inserted text>
                $
<to be read again>
                \alpha
l.1 When \alpha
            =0, the dispersive stress is greatest.
? 4
l.1 When \alpha=0
              , the dispersive stress is greatest.
? i$\alpha=0$
```

Note that four tokens were deleted. The $ inserted by TEX had to be deleted too. The TEX command \alpha is considered a single token. After deleting the tokens, TEX allows you to do something else. The something else was to insert text.

In the other part of the question, because the text is acceptable outside maths, TEX does not consider there to be any obvious problem. But it does not look very good. It should have been:

```
In the case of $x+y-4x=0$, the longest arc is given by:
```

Remember the function, and the form generally falls out automatically. Form follows function.

4.6: The spacing does not look very good. Transliterated into the roman alphabet, it reads 'tekhne'. The tau-epsilon-chi should give things away. In general, a short greek tag in this alphabet is tolerable Why else why would Knuth have included ς, which is never (hardly ever) used in maths, but is needed when a sigma occurs at the end of a word?

4.7: We are comparing
> The surface is $y = h_s(x)$, the bed is $y = h_b(x)$; the slopes, if small, are $\alpha = -dh_s/dx$, $\beta = -dh_b/dx$. If α, β are small,

with
> The surface is $y = h_s(x)$, the bed is $y = h_b(x)$; the slopes, if small, are $\alpha = -dh_s/dx$, $\beta = -dh_b/dx$. If α, β are small,

As hinted earlier, it is considered bad practice to include the punctuation within the maths. In fact, since TEX considers the punctuation in maths to be a special category (math punctuation), it sets up different amounts of spacing than would be used for 'text punctuation'. By default, TEX will allow space after punctuation to stretch more than other space: a full stop 'within' maths will not be interpreted as a full stop. Thus the space here, `dx.$ If,` 'expands' as a normal interword space, while the space in `dx$.` `If` will be much stetchier (by default).

4.8: At first this seems a bit intimdating. When TEX encounters the blank line, it assumes that a paragraph is ending (it is equivalent to a `\par`). It is illegal to start a new paragraph within a text or display equation – in fact, the concept should be meaningless. Sensing that something is wrong, it inserts a `$`. Unfortunately, it only inserts one (it's not *that* smart). In order to recover, you can insert another `$` – in other words, type `i$` in response to the `?` prompt. But that may not help the next line. What we have done so far is to correctly terminate the first part. This leaves the second part dangling. Somehow we have to insert `$$`. We may anticipate and use `i$$`, but if the line starts with (say) a `\beta`, TEX, now in text mode, will insert a single `$` and come up with the `?` prompt. Now is your chance to insert another `$` and restore the balance. This should emphasise your desire not to leave blank lines in the middle of equations.

4.9: Braces: `{({({(a^4)}^3)}^2)}^1` gives $\left(\left(\left(a^4\right)^3\right)^2\right)^1$, and `({({({a^4})^3})^2})^1` yields $(((a^4)^3)^2)^1$.

4.10: A possible set of solutions are

```
$$h_0+\epsilon=h+p=h_0+h_1+p$$
$$(m+1)h_1/h_0+m\alpha_1/\alpha_0=0$$
$$h^{m+1}\alpha^m=h^{m+1}_0\alpha^m_0$$
$$\tau^2=\tau^2_{xy}+\tau^2_{zx}$$
$$\lambda=A\tau^{n-1}m=\rho $$
$$e M_\omega/PM_a=0.623\rho e/P$$
```
Of course there are many other solutions.

4.11: My solution was
```
The number of atoms of a radioactive element
at time $t$ years can be found from the original
number present at time zero by the relationship
$$P_t=P_0e^{-\lambda t}$$ where $P_t$ is the number
of atoms at time $t$,   $P_0$ is the original number
of atoms of the  parent nucleide, and $e$ is 2.7183.
```
Note that I used t rather than {\it t}. That was not just because it was quicker to type, since if we look very closely at t and t, we might detect some subtle differences.

4.12: The point here is that the \sqrt command merely takes the next 'token' or group. Therefore we obtain $\sqrt{4}ac$ and $\sqrt{16}c^4$. What we might have wanted is $\sqrt{4ac}$ and $\sqrt{16c^4}$. It's all in the braces (as usual).

4.13: The plain and obvious way is
```
$\overline{\sqrt{\underline{x}}}$
```
It is also the minimum way. Leaving out any of the pairs of braces leads to trouble. And sometimes interesting error messages.

4.14: An intelligible almost error message!
```
! Paragraph ended before \root was complete.
```
What it should have been was (probably) `$\root {n-1}\of {b^2}$`, unless you meant $\sqrt[n-1]{b^2}$. In this case, the n-1 need not be braced. The command is actually \root...\of... Anything which occurs between \root and \of will be the 'root'. The \of is not really a command at all. If you try to use it on its own it will not be recognised. What follows must be braced (unless it is a single token).

4.15: The following table shows the way in which these accents grow:

`\tilde x`	$\tilde{x}$	`\hat x`	$\hat{x}$
`\widetilde x`	$\widetilde{x}$	`\widehat x`	$\widehat{x}$
`\widetilde{xy}`	$\widetilde{xy}$	`\widehat{xy}`	$\widehat{xy}$
`\widetilde{xyz}`	$\widetilde{xyz}$	`\widehat{xyz}`	$\widehat{xyz}$
`\widetilde{wxyx}`	$\widetilde{wxyz}$	`\widehat{wxyz}`	$\widehat{wxyz}$

In general, the maximum size is suitable for three 'normal' symbols, but do note the difference between the **wide** form and the 'regular' form.

4.16: My solutions:
$$DT/Dt-k\partial^2T=H/\rho c$$
$$u=A'\tau_b^m$$
$$\vec{OA}'=k\vec{OA}'$$
$$\angle COQ=\theta$$
But look closely at the example which combines the `\vec` accent with a prime: the position of the prime will vary according to the combination of `\vec` and the braces, as the following example shows: `OA'`, `\vec{OA'}` and `\vec{OA}'` give OA', $\vec{OA}'$ and $\vec{OA}\,'$.

4.17: These are no more difficult, but sometimes it takes a while to master the vocabulary.
$${\partial\zeta\over\partial t}=$$
$$-{\partial M\over\partial x}-{\partial$$
$$N\over\partial y}$$
$$\psi_M={a\over r_1}e^{-i\kappa r_1}$$
$$\sqrt{\kappa\over2z_1}(x-x_0)=$$
$$\sqrt{\lambda\over2z_1}(x-x_0)$$
$${\partial\Im\over\partial s}=\pi s$$
$$C_d=a_1Re^{-1}+a_2Re^{-{1\over2}}+a_3$$
Probably the only 'catch' is to remember to brace the `\over` commands. Of course, this is an excellent opportunity to deliberately foul up the grouping, or omit it entirely (in the interests of practise).

5.1: For example, it may (or may not) be noticeable that in the case of text equations using large operators, TeX inserts a little extra space between lines, ensuring that there is no overlap.

5.2: After some experimentation, you should find that every one of the `\textstyle` large operators have their limits to the right. In the case of `\displaystyle` large operators, the limits are placed above and below, except for `\int` and `\oint`. To place the limits for `\int` and `\oint` above and below, you must use `\limits`, whether in text or display. All the others follow the same rule, 'extending' the vertical extent for display style.

5.3: This will do:
```
$$\overline{\eta^2}=
      {1\over2}\sum_{k=0}^\infty
                \sum_{\theta=0}^{2\pi}a_n^2$$
```
noting that `\bar{\eta^2}` is too short in this case.

5.4: The point of this exercise is the extra effort required to introduce negative thin space between the integrals and positive thin space between the *dy* and *ds*:
```
$$E_i(y')=
    \int\!\!\int A(s)e^{isy}\sigma(y-y')dy\,ds$$
```
Some would use more negative space.

5.5: For example
```
$$\overline{\nu^2}=
  \int\limits_0^\infty\int\limits_0^{2\pi}
    E(k,\theta)dk\,d\theta$$
$$\overline{\nu^2}=
  \int_0^\infty\!\!\int_0^{2\pi}
    E(k,\theta)dk\,d\theta$$
```
In the `\limits` example, introducing the negative thin space brings the limits on the integrals far too close together.

5.6: You should be able to observe that the spaces after the minus sight is smaller in the case of the monadic operator than the dyadic:

$$-4 - 2\pi i$$

Usually this is what we want.

5.7: A suitable rendering is
```
$$X\ominus\check B=X\cap X_{-h}$$
$$X\ominus B=\bigcup_i X_i\ominus B$$
$$\int_{-B/2}^{B/2}R''(y,y')\varphi''(y')dy'=
          \gamma''\varphi''(y)$$
$$\vec f^{(1)}=
    \vec f^{(0)}-{(\vec w_1\cdot\vec f^{(0)}
    -p_1)\over\vec w_1\cdot\vec w_1}\vec w_1$$
$$((A\lor \lnot B\lor C\lnot D)
        \land(\lnot E\lor\lnot F))$$
```
The degree sign may be obtained by `$^\circ$` and the 'times' operator as `$\times$`, hence: `$6^\circ$` Centigrade and `$9.46 \times 10^{12}$`.

5.8: Use \mid, since it is the operator:
$$\${1\over \pi}U(X)=\{1\over2\pi}$
$\int_0^{2\pi}L(X\mid\Delta_\alpha)\,d\alpha\$$
Had we used \vert, the spacing would have been different.

5.9: The recommended form is $\notin$, in the sense that Knuth bothered to create it rather than use $\not\in$. It is the second one.

5.10: There should be nothing particularly remarkable in this:
$$\tau_1/\tau_0\approx0.5p/h_0\$$
$$h/L\gg\partial h/\partial x\$$
$$\{\mit\Delta\over t}\ge\sqrt{2gh}\$$
$$\nabla^2f(i,j)\equiv$
$\delta_x{}^2f(i,j)+\delta_y{}^2f(i,j)\$$ %RK242
$$Q\in N(P)\iff P\in N(Q)\$$
It does take some skill to distinguish \iff and \Longleft-rightarrow, but again, provided you start with the meaning of the equation, the form usually follows. In this context, it is more tricky, when you may not know the meaning.

5.11: Again, there is nothing special, except perhaps an unfamiliar vocabulary:
$$(W\ominus \check B)\cap(W\ominus \check B)_{-h}\ne$
$\emptyset\Leftrightarrow B\cup B_h\subset W\$$
$$Y\subset X\Rightarrow\psi_\lambda(Y)$
$\subset\varphi_\lambda(X)\$$
$$X\rightarrow x_1\rightleftharpoons x_2\$$
$$2HCO_3{}^-\longrightarrow$
$\{H_2O+CO_2\uparrow}+CO_3{}^{2-}\$$
If you want to handle the chemistry in a better way, all you really have to do in this instance is ensure that the whole expression is preceded by \rm. Fortunately this does not influence the symbols:
$$\rm 2HCO_3{}^-\longrightarrow$
$\{H_2O+CO_2\uparrow}+CO_3{}^{2-}\$$

$$2\text{HCO}_3{}^- \longrightarrow \text{H}_2\text{O} + \text{CO}_2 \uparrow + \text{CO}_3{}^{2-}$$

If setting chemistry was a regular pursuit, you might be tempted to approach things in other ways, many of which may become possible in a few chapters.

5.12: Taking a manufactured example:
$$a\buildrel\rm def \over \not= b\$$

gives

$$a \mathrel{\overset{\rm def}{/=}} b$$

As might be anticipated, braces are the answer:
```
$$a\buildrel\rm def \over {\not=}b$$
```
to give

$$a \mathrel{\overset{\rm def}{\neq}} b$$

But in this case, \ne is an acceptable substitute for \not=:
```
\def\negrel{\rm def\over{\ne}}
$$a\negrel b$$
```
Once we discover how to create commands (in Chapter 7), it will be possible to abbreviate these lengthy descriptions.

5.13: Either of the following will give a reasonably satisfactory solution:
```
$${\textstyle A\over\textstyle B}          \over
{A-{\textstyle B\over\textstyle C}}$$
$${\displaystyle A\over\displaystyle B} \over
{A-{\displaystyle B\over\displaystyle C}}$$
```
Distinguishing between the two is possible, in theory.

5.14: For example:
```
The expected cost, $c(i|\vec z)$ is given by
$\sum_j p(j|\vec z)\lambda(i|j)$; if both
$\lambda(i|i)=0$ and the $\lambda(i|j)$'s are
equal when $j\ne i$, minimizing the expected cost is
equivalent to minimizing  $\sum_{j\ne i}p(j|\vec z)$.

The Laplacian $\partial^2f/\partial x^2 +
\partial^2f/\partial y^2$ is an orientation-invariant
derivative operator.

The responses of $\sqrt{\Delta_+{}^2 +\Delta_-{}^2}$
are $h\sqrt2$, $h\sqrt2$, $h$ and $h$.
```
Perhaps the most notable aspect is the use of \Delta_+{}^2 in order to stagger the subscript and superscript.

5.15: These are some potential solutions:
```
$$G_\rho = \dot F_\rho
   = \bigcup_{\epsilon>0}F_{\rho+\epsilon}
   = \bigcup_{\epsilon>0}G_{\rho+\epsilon}$$
$$d(X_i,X)\rightarrow 0\Rightarrow W^{(n)}_k (X_i)
    \to W^{(n)}_k(Y),\,\forall n,k$$
```

```
$$\gamma_z(h) =
  {(\gamma*K)_h-(\gamma*K)_0\over A^2(Z)}$$
$$C^\ast(k) =
  {\sum_{\lambda=1}^g A(Z_\lambda)
  \cdot C^\ast_\lambda(k)
  \over \sum_{\lambda=1}^g A(Z_\lambda)}$$
$${\partial\over\partial t}
    \overline{\int_{-h}^\zeta\rho U_\alpha\,dz}
  = {-\partial\over\partial x_\beta}
    \overline{\int_{-h}^\zeta(\rho u_\alpha
    u_\beta+p\delta_{\alpha\beta})\,dz}
  + \overline{(p)_{z=-h}
    {\partial h\over\partial x_\alpha}}$$
$$r^2={\int_{-\infty}^\infty w(x)c^2(x)\,dx
  \over\int_{-\infty}^\infty c^2(x)\,dx}$$
$$\int\!\!\!\int fg \le
  \sqrt{\int\!\!\!\int f^2 \int\!\!\!\int g^2}$$
$$p(1)p(z\vert1)+p(2)p(z\vert2)$$
$$p(h|r)=\sum_z q(z|r)q(z+h|r)$$
$${e^{-m'/2}\over {\sqrt{2\pi}\,\sigma_1}^{m'}}\cdot
  {e^{-m''/2}\over {\sqrt{2\pi}\,\sigma_1}^{m''}}
 ={e^{-m/2}\over {\sqrt{2\pi}\,}^m
  \sigma_1^{m'}\sigma_2^{m''}}$$
$$f_\delta(x,y)\equiv
  f(x,y)-f(x+\delta x,y+\delta y)$$
$$\exists j:k<j\le N:X_k>0\land X_j>0\land
  \lnot(\exists i:k<i<j:X_i>0)$$
```

These solutions often look more difficult than the equations on which they are based. It is often very straightforward to read these out directly. Apart from ensuring that the braces are balanced properly, and deciding which of the commands should be used to obtain | or :, they tend to fall out. Note the equivalence of \vert and |, and of * and \ast. The choice of nomenclature is usually determined by the 'meaning' or your preference. In this instance, three \!s were used to draw the integral signs together. This always looks rather crude to me. You may also observe that sometimes the use of \over lends itself to chaos.

6.1: Taking them one at a time:
{\OE }dipus: the space after the \OE 'delimits' the command. It therefore is ignored. Multiple spaces would be similarly ignored.
\OE{}dipus: the {} terminates the \OE command.
\OE {dipus}: again the space delimits the command. And even if

it did not, the {dipus} is braced.

\O{E}dipus: not what we wanted: ØEdipus. Who is he/she?

{\OE} dipus: placing the \OE within braces has the effect of terminating the command: therefore the space is seen.

6.2: The implicit kerning (hidden in the `tfm` files) is present in \OE dipus but in none of the others. But what is the difference? The kern between Œ and d (in Computer Modern Roman 10 point) is zero anyway! While it is 'philosophically' correct to write \OE dipus, in this instance it makes no difference.

6.3: A parsimonious solution is

```
Zde se v\v semo\v zn\v e sna\v z\'\i\ m\v e p\v
reluvit, abych z\accent23ustal je\v st\v e n\v ekolik
m\v es\'\i c\accent23u a napsal je\v st\v e jednu
operu. Hay\i r! \.I\c s \"oyle de\u gil. B\"uy\"u\u
g\"u k\"u\c c\"u\u g\"une takilmay\i\ pek severdi.
Ce f\^ut d'ores et d\'ej\'a une id\'ee
d\'eg\'en\'er\'ee et ambig\"ue.
${\mit\Gamma}\varepsilon\iota\acute o\ \sigma
o\upsilon$\it!
```

One thing to watch is the need to write \accent23u for ů (later we shall find out that there are ways to abbreviate this by giving it its own definition). The words in 'greek' are typeset in maths mode. It is possible to access the characters directly by quoting their position in the font table. This is really only worthwhile if you have to write a lot of greek. Note that there will be no kerning (it looks rather loose here, emphasising that these really are mathematical symbols).

6.4: This one is much more difficult. The simplest solution assumes that only a few 'foreign' words are present. In which case, using \- is probably sufficient. This assumes you know where to put the hyphens. TₑX3 has introduced a new capability to switch between languages through a \language command. However, this assumes that the version of TₑX you are using will have been built 'knowing' about the languages you wish to use. At the time of writing this book, this is not yet true. In fact, there is not yet agreement on what languages are to be supported. Since \language is set equal to an integer value between zero and 255, there is a restriction (!) on the number of languages which can be supported simultaneously. Hyphenation patterns are available for less than a dozen languages (one of the notable missing languages is english, which turns out to have rather different hyphenation rules from american-english).

6.5: The recommendation to reset the area of the text will save you from output which goes outside the area of the usually obtainable paper sizes. If you use a screen previewer it may permit you to view outside the 'normal' area.

TEX by default sets up a text area of 6.5 inches wide by 8.9 inches deep. When the \magstep is processed, the 'inch' is also expanded. However, things are not this simple. If we do not have an \hsize and \vsize following the \magstep, TEX will not modify the sizes. Loosely, the idea is that they have been set up already, before the \magstep came into play. On the other hand, the \baselineskip, \parindent, \parskip and a host of other distances *will* be changed by the \magstep. Since the default size is totally unsuited to the A4 paper size used outside the United States (how ironic that the United States should retain Imperial measures), you would normally change the \hsize and \vsize to
\hsize6.25truein
\vsize9.5truein
The true is there to make life much easier. It is then possible to change the \magstep without having to change the text size. While this is better suited to the A4 page size, it is still not satisfactory. If we use the default 10 point cmr with TEX's default, or this suggested A4 alternative, the 'measure' is far to great. I would contend that \magstep1 with the suggested size is about right, although it represents over 70 characters to the line and therefore over 15 words: this is rather greater than that recommended by the 'average' typographer. It merely represents a balance between the tyranny of the A4 page (designed with typewriters in mind) and the available typographic resources. Increasing the \magstep to 2 seems to give a rather childish appearance.

6.6: The error generated is
! Incompatible magnification (1440);
 the previous value will be retained (1200).
once the subsequent \magnification is encountered. It says it all, except that you should recall that the figures 1440 and 1200 are the 'scales' given in Figure 6.3.

6.7: The first decision is what to call the sans serif fonts. This is a possible solution:

```
\font\ssu cmss10
\font\ssi cmssi10
\font\ssb cmssbx10
\ssu
```
In very general terms, type should seek to be
unobtrusive. It should never {\ssb dominate} the
text. At some {\ssi subtle\/} levels it may manage
to influence the reader.

In LATₑX, sans serif upright is denoted by \sf and is available by
default. The sans serif fonts in TₑX are said to have been mainly
the work of Richard Southall. They appear not to have ligatures,
in the sense that ffl and ffi are not joined. Nevertheless, they are
supported by TₑX as ligatures. There are noticeable differences in
the second f. The 'ligatured' fi and fl do look rather similar to fi
and fl, but there is the equivalent of a kern of about −0.08 points
between the ligatured characters (in cmss10).

6.8: This is for you.

6.9: There can be no cut and dried answers here. But it is difficult
to argue that TₑX and far less Knuth, are responsible. TₑX merely
looks for the relevant TₑX font metrics. If those metrics are not
available, it suggests that you are using a font without a tfm. For
example
```
! Font \rm=times10 not loadable:
                        Metric (TFM) file not found.
```
implies that there is no suitable information. This could be just
because TₑX could not find the information, perhaps the tfm file
is present but in the wrong directory or folder. In general, there is
a well defined set of places where TₑX will look for the tfm files,
but you should consult whatever local documentation you have.
Because computer operating systems vary so widely, TₑX deliberately eschews any statements about how the implementation
should be organised.

This merely touches on the running of TₑX itself: it does not
address what happens when 'visible' output is generated. For
example, we may happily write
```
\magnification\magstephalf
\font\quaint cmff10 scaled\magstep1
```
TₑX is quite content with this. It can find the tfm files for cmff10
and merely scales up the distances embodied there by the equivalent of one and a half magsteps (a 'scale' of 1314). When the
resulting dvi file is passed to some driver that driver will be unable

to find a suitable output font. What it does now is the interesting bit. And to find the answer you will either have to experiment, or read the documentation. Some drivers will substitute an existing 'default' font (usually with rather unpleasing results), while others will simply give up (with even less satisfactory results), or leave a space (that is, substitute an 'empty' character for each of the unavailable characters). Joachim Schrod (1990) comments 'we strongly recommend not to scale bitimage characters to the desired size within the driver', and continues 'either the document is important, when the desired font should be created by META-FONT, or it is a document for which this small work is too still too much, and another font can be chosen'.

6.10: In general, you will obtain the error message:
```
! Missing number, treated as zero.
<to be read again>
```
This is not very explicit. But at this point we cannot give a very good account of the problem that TEX has encountered, nor its solution. Once you have read the next chapter, come back and look at the following explanation.

The command \magstep is defined in plain as
```
\def\magstep#1{\ifcase#1 1000\or 1200\or 1440\or 1728
    \or 2074\or 2488\fi\relax}
```
In other words, when \magnification is used, it would be perfectly happy with some number. The use of \magstep merely restricts the possible values to the ones which are provided in the normal Computer Modern family. There is nothing truly sacrosanct in these values. But this does reveal why using a value for \magstep of over 5 leads to some problems. A more robust version could be
```
\def\magstep#1{\ifcase#1 1000\or 1200\or 1440\or 1728
    \or 2074\or 2488\else 2488
    \message{You are asking too much!}\fi\relax}
```
Without the \message there would be no evidence that TEX had over-ridden your request for \magstep6. It turns out that there are commands which may be inserted before \magnification despite what has been said. But don't do it often.

There are implementations of TEX which will allow higher \magsteps. If you have METAFONT you may easily generate the equivalent of higher \magsteps, or even 'partial' \magsteps, like the generally available \magstephalf. This is actually a separate definition in its own right:

```
\def\magstephalf{1095 }
```
If you wanted `\magsteponeandahalf` you would need a similar definition.

6.11: According to my calculations it is not a linear relationship. 'Smaller' sizes tend to be 'broader' than a simple linear relationship would suggest. In terms of readability that makes sense. The short measure makes this exercise tricky. The best way to tackle it is by placing the text in a box and finding out the length of that box (see Chapter 9).

6.12: It is strictly linear in practice as well as theory. The readibility is your decision though.

6.13: Can you really see any differences?

7.1: Naturally, the expansion is rather terse, but in the examples given below, it is even more terse, since they are expressed in a single line.

```
\show\"              macro:          #1->{\accent "7F #1}.
```
the command `\"` is a macro or command, which uses the underlying `\accent` command. The `#1` indicates that the command has a single argument (to be discussed in Chapter 10).

```
\show\alpha         \mathchar"10B.
```
a mathematical character of type `\mathchar`. The `"10B` used here is a way of specifying a position in a font.

```
\show\it            macro:          ->\fam \itfam \tenit .
```
another command, but this time without an argument (like the commands which will be discussed in this chapter). The expanded commands may be tested with `\show` to find out if they too expand.

```
\show\par           \par.
```
this is a fundamental command which may not be further expanded.

```
\show\what          \what=undefined.
```
this is not a command at all. T_EX usefully tells us.

```
\show\bye           \outer macro:
                    ->\par \vfill \supereject \end .
```
another command, this time of type `\outer`.

```
\show\baselineskip\baselineskip.
```
another fundamental command.

7.2: On the face of it, it could suggest that the structure of the universe is a little less complex than the structure of text. Or perhaps that we have not yet discerned the underlying simplicity.

7.3: The characters are 'expanded' by `\show` to reflect their 'meanings' as determined by their `\catcode`.

```
\show#              macro parameter character #.
\show&              alignment tab character &.
\show{              begin-group character {.
\show a             the letter a.
```

If you modify the category code of a character, its meaning, according to `\show` will also change.

7.4: As usual, there are lots of ways to do this.

```
\def\degree{$^\circ$}
```

will only work in 'text'. It is tempting to try to use the 'small circle' accent, but it does not look quite as nice, and it is in any case much more tricky to manipulate.

By the end of this chapter you will be able to test the 'mode', and have something which works in both maths and text:

```
\def\degree{\ifmmode^\circ\else$^\circ$\fi}
```

Making commands robust is almost always a worth while task, but testing is often more demanding than writing.

7.5: The most awkward part of this is to find convenient names for these particles: perhaps this would do

```
\def\taun{$\bar\nu_\tau$}   %tau-neutrino
\def\muon{$\bar\nu_\mu$}    %muon-neutrino
\def\kaon{$K^+$}            %positive kaon
\def\ppion{$\pi^+$}         %positive pion
\def\npion{$\pi^-$}         %negative pion
```

These would not work in a 'maths' mode. Should you need to write expressions where maths mode would be the intuitive way to do it, it will again be necessary to adopt the `\ifmmode` test. In looking at these expressions I again feel that a superscripted plus sign looks far too large.

It would be nice to be able to call the negative and positive pions as `\pion+` and `\pion-`. This is indeed possible, but not until the end of Chapter 10, when we would be able to say

```
\def\pion#1{$\if#1+\pi^+\else\if#1-\pi^-\else
                    \errmessage{mistake}\fi\fi$}
```

The `\errmessage` is not covered until Chapter 22, but its use is probably intuitive. The argument is tested to see whether it is a - or a +, and the appropriate action is taken. If it is not one of these two options, then an error message is generated. A much simpler solution is

```
\def\pion#1{$\pi\if#1+^+\else^-\fi$}
```

but writing `\pion=` would give π^-. Perhaps not what we wanted.

The error message here does not assist greatly, but it is possible to specify particular messages to help:
```
\newhelp\helppion{pion must be followed by + or -!}
\def\pion#1{$\if#1+\pi^+\else\if#1-\pi^-\else
   \errhelp\helppion\errmessage{pion mistake}\fi\fi$}
```
Now if you use `\pion=` there will be the message `pion mistake`, but in addition, requesting help at the `?` prompt will yield
```
\pion must be followed by + or -!
```
The `\` is always inserted in the help message.

7.6: TEX continues to read until it finds the first non-blank 'token'. Unless that is the first character of a one of the acceptable 'dimensions', TEX will complain that it has encountered an
```
! Illegal unit of measure (pt inserted).
```
This may raise two questions: first, has TEX really inserted `pt`? and, have we lost the character that TEX read in, but found unsatisfactory. It is easy to verify what happend: a suitable dimension is inserted (although it is much better to correct its absence, or when you come to run this again, you will again be interupted by the error message); and the character is still output. We lose nothing. There are variations to be considered too. What happens if the first character is legal, but the second is not?

One other thing to note. If we
```
\def\pt{pt}
```
then it is acceptable to say `\dimen0=10\sp`. The command `\sp` is read and expands to an acceptable sequence.

7.7: TEX interprets the `sp`, the `Pt` or the `in` as quite acceptable abbreviations for (in this case) scaled points, points and inches. Note that these abbreviations need not be delimited by spaces, nor need they be in lower case. Of course this also means that the 'abbreviation' is absorbed by TEX and is not passed to output.

This feature of TEX can lend itself to errors that appear sporadic. If somehow `\dimen0=10` is followed by a word like `special`, TEX will be content. The `sp` is thought of as the abbreviation for 'scaled point'. True, on output we will only find 'ecial', but this may not be noticed immediately. On the other hand, following the `\dimen=10` by an unacceptable pair of characters will gencrate an immediate error.

7.8: When you show the value of `\hsize`, or any other dimension, it will be shown in terms of points. When we assign the value to a counter, it is transferred as the number of scaled points, since that is what TEX is really working in. However, when the dimension is displayed, it is displayed as a number followed by a decimal point. But it is still an integer value. For example

```
\count1\hsize
\divide\count1 by 65536
\showthe\count1
\showthe\hsize
```

would apparently yield two values which should have the same numeric value. But \hsize will be in points and have some numbers after the decimal point, while \count1 will be an integer followed by a decimal point.

7.9: It's up to you, but once you have read the explanation below, fix it.

7.10: For example

```
\newcount\minleft
\newcount\milhour
\def\miltime{\milhour=\time
 \divide\milhour by 60
 \minleft=\milhour
 \multiply\minleft by -60
 \advance\minleft by\time
 \ifnum\milhour<10 0\fi
 \number\milhour:\ifnum\minleft<10 %
                0\fi\relax\number\minleft}
```

Unfortunately it is not possible to include the \newcounts within the definition.

7.11: This is one solution:

```
\newcount\minleft
\newcount\timehour
\def\thetime{\timehour=\time
  \divide\timehour by60 %gives 24 hour part of clock
  \minleft=\timehour
  \multiply\minleft by-60 %
  \advance\minleft by\time    %minutes after hour
  \ifnum\time>720\advance\timehour by-12\fi\relax
  \number\timehour:\ifnum\minleft<10 %
                 0\fi\relax\number\minleft
  \ifnum\time>720~p.m.\else~a.m.\fi}
```

but many variations are possible.

7.12: This is fairly direct:

```
\def\today{%
 \count10=\year
 \advance\count10 by-1900
 \number\day/\number\month/\number\count10}
```

We might quibble that if we were running TEX between 1900 and 1909, the dates would come out with only one digit in the year part. To do this more generally, we really want to implement a modulus function. Then *year* mod 100 would give the year part. Then allow for the first decade of any century. The arithmetically inclined might enjoy this. The rest of us will remember to change the command on January 1st, 2000.

7.13: This is a very longwinded way, but it does work:

```
\def\today{\ifcase\month\or
    January\or    February\or    March\or    April\or
    May\or        June\or        July\or     August\or
    September\or  October\or November\or December\fi
\space\number\day
\ifcase\day\or st\or nd\or rd\or th\or th\or
 th\or th\or th\or th\or st\or nd\or rd\or th\or
 th\or th\or th\or th\or th\or st\or nd\or rd\or
 th\or th\or th\or th\or
 th\or th\or st\or nd\fi, \number\year}
```

The real purists might like to raise the 'st', 'nd', 'rd' and 'th', and perhaps even turn them into italics.

We Librans don't believe too much in astrology, but the basic structure of this could be to calculate the day within the year:

```
\def\dayofyear{\count10=\ifcase\month\or0\or30\or59\or
 90\or120\or151\or181\or212\or243\or273\or304\or334\fi
 \advance\count10 by\day
 \count11\year
 \divide\count11 by 4
 \multiply\count11 by 4
 \advance\count11 by-\year
 \multiply\count11 by-1
 \advance\count10 by\ifcase\count11 1\else0\fi\relax
 \the\count10}
```

and use this against a table of the beginning of each star sign. Lots of \ifnums, nested quite a few times. The computing aware will recall that rather than 12 or so comparisons, you only need at most 3.

7.14: If we only ever use colons in text, this would do:

```
\catcode`\:\active
\def:{\kern0.25em\char'72{}}
```

The `\kern` is unbreakable (unlike an `\hskip` of the same amount). The colon has to be addressed indirectly through its position in the coding scheme, rather than as a :, otherwise we would have a rather recursive definition. Another way round this is

```
\def\Colon{:}
\catcode`\:\active
\def:{\kern0.25em\Colon{}}
```

but at the loss of some of TEX's registers. The null brace `{}` ensures that we do not have to follow each colon with \␣.

If colons may still be used in maths, then

```
\catcode`\:\active
\def:{\ifmmode\char'72\else\kern0.25em\char'72{}\fi}
```

would be a more robust definition. Fortunately, although TEX already uses the maths colon in a particular non-punctuation form, by referencing it as `\char'72`, TEX still sees it in the same way.

8.1: To do this you have to find a way of making the delimited maths big. Perhaps the easiest way is by judicious use of `\over` to create an expression with some vertical extent.

8.2: Unfortunately you have to assign the larger sizes yourself:

```
$$ \bigl\vert \left\vert x \right\vert
  + \left\vert y \right\vert \bigr\vert $$
```

The `\left` and `\right` before the `\vert`s are superfluous, although they do help to explain what is going on. They could have been simple `\vert`s or even just |.

8.3: In order to make the parentheses smaller, it is necessary to do it manually, through `\big`, `\bigg` etc.:

```
$$\biggl( \sum_{k=1}^n A_k \biggr)$$
```

This is rather inflexible and hardly in the spirit of 'declarative' markup

8.4: This set of equations can be made easier by defining a new operator, which TEX does not have by default:

```
\def\minimize{\mathop{\rm minimize}\nolimits}
$$W_0=\lim_{R\to0}\pi R^2q_0$$
$${h\over L_0}={h\over L}\tanh{2\pi h\over L}$$
$${v\over u}=-\tanh k(h+ y)\cot k x$$
$$p_{ij}^{(r+1)}=\min_{h=1}^n\left[\max_{k=1}^m
        c(i,j;h,k)p_{hk}^{(r)}\right]$$
```

```
$$\minimize\{\hat{\vec f^t}[C]^t[C]\hat{\vec f}\}$$
$$\lim_{x\to 0}\ln(1+x)=x$$
$$M=\log\nolimits_{10}{A\over A_0}$$
```
The `\hat` accent is centred over its 'group'. Ensuring that the t superscript is not taken into account in $\hat{\vec f}^t$ requires some extra attention. One solution could be

```
\hat{\vec f}{}^t
```
but that is neither intuitive nor attractive.

8.5: This should be fairly straightforward, especially in view of the 'rules' worked out in Exercise 5.2, and the way that `\limits` and `\nolimits` work.

8.6: There is a small cheat in this exercise, since you probably don't yet know how to set the text of 'k times' quite properly. But don't let that detract:

```
$$B=\underbrace{
  \left({1\over k}B\right)\oplus
  \left({1\over k}B\right)\oplus\ldots
  \left({1\over k}B\right)}_{\hbox{$k$ times}}
 =\left({1\over k}B\right)^{\oplus k}$$
```
There are other ways to handle the 'k times', but the `\hbox` is probably preferred. Here, the operator $\oplus$ means 'dilation'. In which case it might have been a good idea to rename it.

8.7: The way it was done here was:

```
$$ a_{\hbox{red}}   + a_{\hbox{green}}
 + a_{\hbox{blue}} = a_{\hbox{white}} $$
$$ {\rm colour} \propto
 b_{\rm intensity},b_{\rm spectra},b_{\rm hue}$$
```
If we want to control the level of the baselines, we have to do an extra bit of work. There are ways to do this with struts, but a quick and dirty way is to use `\mathstrut`:

```
$$ a_{\hbox{red\mathstrut}} + a_{\hbox{green\mathstrut}}
   + a_{\hbox{blue\mathstrut}} = a_{\hbox{white}} $$
$$ {\rm colour}
    \propto b_{\rm intensity\mathstrut},
           b_{\rm spectra\mathstrut},
           b_{\rm hue\mathstrut}$$
```
to give

$$a_{\rm red} + a_{\rm green} + a_{\rm blue} = a_{\rm white}$$

$$\mathrm{colour} \propto b_{\rm intensity}, b_{\rm spectra}, b_{\rm hue}$$

What is the \mathstrut? We will meet \struts later, but in this context a maths strut is equivalent to inserting a character which is of maximum height and maximum depth, but of no width. This ensures that the baselines are kept consistent. By amazing coincidence, the parentheses (in the Computer Modern typeface) have this maximum height and depth. The use of a maths strut ensures that the correct size is chosen for sub- and superscripts.

8.8: The default value of \mathsurround is 0 point. In other words, the maths is treated as just another word, with no 'extra' space inserted. It is interesting that the value of \mathsurround may be changed within a paragraph, and only influences the paragraph from where it occurs.

8.9: This works much as you would expect. The other font changes to the greek symbols usually end up with an omega of some kind. The only major exception is if you try to use \cal. The 'bold' version of omega is unslanted. Rather oddly, \it works with \Omega just as well as \mit. The necessity of \mit becomes apparent in sub and super scripts.

8.10: Whether we are in text or display, the subscripted \it will generate messages like
! \scriptfont 4 is undefined
while the \mit form will be swallowed without complaint. But the inter-letter spacing will be a mite unsatisfactory. Even I can see that *wave* is unpleasant. At least the \mit form is reduced in size – that in fact is what is going wrong with the \it form: TEX is trying to find a smaller \it, which it just does not have – in truth, it does have it (somewhere), it just does not have it defined in this context. If we really want to use \it, pop it in an \hbox. But then the phrase will be rendered in whatever the text part thinks \it is: probably as 10 point. The other difference you might note is that \it and \mit are two slightly different fonts.

8.11: They may be used in script and scriptscript styles. So too can \bf. The experiments are worth while.

8.12: The 'only' real problem is ensuring that the font changes are grouped:
$$B\equiv B'\iff B\buildrel{\cal I}\over=B'$$
$${\bf f}(N+1)=\rho{\bf f}(N)+{\bf v}(N+1)$$
$${\cal Q}[f]
  =1\;{\rm if}\;\sum_{\cal I}a_i{\cal P}_i[f]\ge t$$

but note the manual control over spacing in that very last example. Since the 'if' is text, and not an operator or relation, it needs 'textual' spacing around it. We can achieve this with the maths spacing given in Figure 8.3. Another possibility is to say
`\hbox{ if }`
which takes care of the spacing, and the change into the upright font.

   The 'text' part was
```
Let ${\cal O}$ be an operation that takes pictures
into  pictures. We say that the property ${\cal P}$
is  {\it invariant\/} under ${\cal O}$ if
${\cal P}[{\cal O}[f]]={\cal P}[f]$ for all $f$.
```
An alternative to that last expression is to set it all in \cal, escaping into \mit when required:
```
$\cal P[O[{\mit f}]]=P[{\mit f}]$
```
Although this is shorter, it is less 'obvious' to read.

8.13: Experiment reveals the defaults very swiftly. Adjusting the value of \hsize saves you having to create some elaborate long equation. You may be relieved that the equation number is placed so that it does not 'interfere' with the equation itself. In the case of \eqno the number is placed after the equation, but \leqno places it before.

8.14: The 'text' is treated as if it were a maths equation (in fact this is one way to cheat and place some extra information there instead of a number (see Exercise 11.16). The point here though is that the text looks unsatisfactory: in order to make it 'real' text, place it in an \hbox, or write \rm Eq.6. If you really wanted to mark the equation as Eq. 6, you could have to write something like
```
\eqno\hbox{Eq. 6}
```
Although all the examples will have used a form like \eqno(1), the parentheses are not needed at all: \eqno1 is satisfactory: but there will be no parentheses around the number when the equation is typeset. We could as easily have written \eqno[3] if we wanted square brackets instead. This perhaps helps to reveal that what TEX does is take everything between the \eqno and the closing $$ and treat that as the 'number'.

8.15: This is a strategy:
```
The predicates of $\chi_S$ are Boolean functions of
the Boolean variables $P_1,\ldots,P_N$. For example,
```

the predicate ``$\vert S\vert=1$'' (``there is only
one 1 inχ_S'') corresponds to the function
$$\bigvee_{i=1}^N(\bar{P}_1 \wedge \cdots$$
$$\wedge \bar{P}_{i-1} \wedge P_i$$
$$\wedge \bar{P}_{i+1} \wedge\cdots$$
$$\wedge \bar{P}_{N}) $$
where the overbars denote logical negation.
and
In this chapter, Σ denotes a picture; subsets
of Σ are denoted by $S, T,\ldots$\thinspace,
and points by $P,Q,\dots$\thinspace.
An alternative is to place a maths 'thinspace', \, between the
dots and the closing \$. I might even be inclined to leave out the
last \thinspace. and let the third dot of the ellipsis do the job.

8.16: This is the solution used here:
The condition $B_x^2\subset X^c$ is always fulfilled,
and the eroded set Y is the locus of the points x,
such that B_x is included in$X$:
$$Y=\lbrace x\colon B_x\subset X\rbrace$$
and
Finally, let $S_n(K_0;K_1,\ldots\,,K_n)$ denote the
probability that X misses the compact set K_0,
but hits the other compact sets $K_1,\ldots\,,K_n$.
\def\Sup{\mathop{\rm Sup}\nolimits}%
$$\Lambda(x)=$$
$$\Sup\{\lambda\mathbin\colon x\in \psi_\lambda(x)\}$$
Both \colon and : would give the same end product when used
with \mathbin.

9.1: The presence of the command \' disables the 'natural' kerning between the v and the é. As a consequence, the two letters are
about 0.3 pt more widely spaced (in cmr10).

If you really have TEX3, you may be able to type véritable,
and TEX will accept it. It is possible however that the é will be
translated into \'e behind your back and the natural kerning will
again be lost. Part of this exercise is to encourage you to read
the documentation which should have been supplied with your
implemertation of TEX.

9.2: The spacing between letters is fixed through the tfm files.
The only thing that can spread is the space between words. If
there is punctuation in the box, the space after full stops and commas will stretch differently, by default. If the glue between words

stretches at the rate of 1, after a comma, glue stretches at the rate of 1.25, and after a full stop, 3. Investigate the characteristics of colons, semi-colons, exclamation and question marks.

9.3: Counter-intuitively, the explicitly kerned word is 'longer' than the one where we do nothing. The \kern is not cumulative.

9.4: Copying the TEX logo:
```
\def\DeK{D\kern-0.1667em
        \lower0.5ex\hbox{E}\kern-0.125emK}
```
perhaps some further adjustment is appropriate.

9.5: In order to force TEX into horizontal mode at this point you can precede the \copy by \leavevmode, or less explicity, \indent or \noindent. Much less elegantly, an \hskip0pt would also have the desired effect, although \kern0pt would not.

9.6: Again, it all depends in which mode TEX starts out. A further alternative might be
```
hello
\hbox{A title}
\hbox{A subtitle}
```
where the 'hello' would have switched TEX into horizontal mode.

9.7: Intuitively we might expect the height of the larger box to be equivalent to the height and depth of 'one' plus the height of 'eight'. This is not correct. The two vertical boxes are still placed on 'normal' baselines, thus the height is the amount of the baseline plus the height of 'one'. If we manually switch off the interlineskip using the command \nointerlineskip then the boxes will be placed as close together as they will go. The descender on the 'g' of 'eight' maintains the same depth for the boxes.

9.8: The first box (the \vbox) will have a large height, the extent of which will depend on the number of lines set, the second box (the \vtop) will have a height which is determined by the tallest letter on the first line (a capital letter in this case). The depth of the first box will be small, but not zero, since the last letter in the paragraph has a descender. The depth of the other box will be large, again depending on the number of lines set.

9.9: The alterations to the size of the box are most easily accomplished by placing \hsize within the \vbox. If you write \vbox to 72pc where 72 picas is likely to be greater than the vertical extent of the text, TEX will generate some underfull box messages.

If there is more than one paragraph, it will likely insert more space than you would anticipate between the paragraphs.

9.10: It all depends on whether TEX is in vertical or horizontal mode. Forcing them into an \hbox ensures that we are in 'restricted' horizontal mode, and they come out side by side (even if they are too large for the line length).

9.11: This is just to get you used to extracting the relevant information from the masses that TEX divulges.

9.12: Let's make some assumptions: first that we know the \baselineskip. If we can ensure that there is a full height ascender in the first line and a full depth descender in the last line (and we can always engineer this), then we can calculate the full extent of the paragraph. Dividing this by the \baselineskip will give the number of lines (within the limitations of integer arithmetic). We are also assuming that there is no display maths in this paragraph.

By modifying the \hsize of the vertical box containing the paragraph, we may eventually hit upon a combination that does what we want. Here, the use of \unhcopy may be useful.

A way of finding out what might be a good starting point would be to fit all the text into a single \hbox with the \hsize set to \maxdimen. This is the maximum dimension which may occur in TEX, and should accomodate all but the most extreme paragraphs. Dividing the typeset width of this box by n will give a good starting value for our real \hsize. Of course, this does not take into account the flexibility of inter word spaces, and TEX's ability to hyphenate, which may be expected to make the estimate different from the 'true' value.

The command \prevgraf records the number of lines in the most recent paragraph. This could be used to confirm that you have indeed managed to make the desired number of lines, n.

There are ways to make TEX loop, so in theory we could set up a command which would keep setting this paragraph with different values of \hsize until we get the desired configuration. But given all the possible things that TEX can do, it might never come out with the 'right' answer, given our initial constraints, and may loop endlessly, forever unsatisfied...

9.13: It probably does what you want, but it also does a bit extra, leaving the characters 'ch' somewhere in your text (as you asked).

9.14: TEX reads this as
`\vskip 1in Plus-fours`
which is quite legal, up to the 'f' of four. The syntax of a `\vskip` allows for a `plus` followed by a `minus` dimension. The 'Plus' of 'Plus-fours' implies to TEX that there will soon be a dimension which it will recognise. The hyphen does nothing to dispel this, since TEX thinks it is a minus sign. The 'f' is totally unexpected, and leads to disaster. What is the solution? The immediate solution is to write something like
`\vskip 1in\relax Plus-fours`
but the better solution is never to write `\vskip` expressions explicitly. They should be hidden away in macros (together with their `\relax`). Another solution, which emphasises that a `plus` must occur before a `minus`, is
`\vskip 1in minus0pt Plus-fours`
but that's obscure.

9.15: Even the small amounts of extra white space become quite noticeable and change the 'texture' of the page. With paragraphs this is perhaps excusable, although if you become used to a small (or no) gap between paragraphs when you read a book, encountering a paragraph which is separated from its predecessor by more space can be off-putting and raises questions of 'Why?' In the case of books, printers will generally attempt to make the position of lines on either side of a page identical so that the 'shadow' of the ink on the other face affects the printed parts of the face you are reading, and not the white parts. Small changes in the distance between the lines on successive pages would make this impossible.

9.16: The idea here is that we manipulate the vertical fills: it seems straightforward that
`\null`
`\vfill\vfill`
`  lots of text`
`\vfill\vfill\vfill`
`\end`
will do the job. This is not quite the case. Firstly, `\end` *appears* to have its own `\vfill` associated with it. But note that replacing `\end` by `\bye` gives the same result. Closer examination of the definition of `\bye` reveals a `\supereject`. Placing this `\supereject` before the `\end` has the effect of eliminating this unwanted vertical fill. An `\eject` has just the same effect (except that an extra page is created).

There is another way to tackle this, which avoids these machinations. Although there is no `\vfilll` by default, it is not difficult to define one:
`\def\vfilll{\vskip0pt plus 1filll \relax}`
This massive vertical fill overrides everything else, and gives us just what we want. Equally,
`\null`
`\vskip0pt plus 2filll\relax`
` lots of text`
`\vskip0pt plus 3filll`
`\end`
would do it (except that I don't like to see explicit `\vskips`).

To eliminate the `\null` before the vertical skip, we could use a feature of TEX3, `\topglue`:
`\topglue0pt plus 2filll\relax`
` lots of text`
`\vskip0pt plus 3filll`
Again, these explicit commands should be hidden.

9.17: This is a variation on an earlier exercise. It may not be possible. The notion is that you experiment with the `\hsize` values associated with the `\vbox`es until they both have the same vertical extent. The trivial solution is to fix the horizontal extent of one of the blocks, and then set the other vertical box to this vertical extent. If the commands like `\baselineskip`, `\lineskip`, or `\parskip` are given some extra skip, they will expand to make the text the required length. In this context it might be what you want. Good luck.

9.18: The simplistic approach of
`\leavevmode\rlap{\hskip\hsize$\Leftarrow$}`
does something suitable, but the `\hskip` starts after the indentation of the paragraph (remember, this is to be used at the beginning of a paragraph), and therefore there will be horizontal white space of width `\parindent` between the text and the arrow. A clumsy way of removing this is by
`\hskip-\parindent`
These commands really ought to be encapsulated in a command; no-one wants to see things like this in their text (or to type it in).

10.1: The use of `\show` indicates that `\leftline` is
`\line {#1\hss }`
and pursuing this further, `\line` is `\show`n to be

`\hbox to\hsize`
The use of `\hss` rather than `\hfil` ensures that when the `\hbox` is set it may exceed the dimensions of `\hsize`. It is therefore much more flexible than if we had merely included `\hfil` or `\hfill`.

10.2: The use of `\show\repeat` should tell you. It is already defined. It is a command needed for the `\loop` structure. It is perhaps less obvious that `\iterate` and `\body` have already been defined and that it would be dangerous to redefine them.

10.3: This restriction simplifies the syntax of the definition. The definition merely has a # followed by a single digit. If it was more complex, it would have been harder to program. Since it is possible to include 'template' items, once we get to #10 it could appear as #1 delimited by a 0. My major surprise is that the limit is not 8, numbered from 0 to 7.

10.4: One noticeable way is with diacriticals. While `\&` does not require to be followed by a command space, since it is a self-contained command which does not have to be delimited, writing something which looks very similar, `\'` reads on to the next character, ignoring spaces. If we were to look at the definitions driving most diacriticals, they would be seen to be commands which have one argument. Thus, until the argument is found, all intervening spaces are consumed and ignored.

10.5: The important part of this is the way the `\proclaim` is delimited:
`\def\proclaim #1. #2\par`
We expect the first argument to be terminated by a full stop, and the second to go as far as a `\par` or (more likely) a blank line.
1 The number of spaces will make no difference in this context.
2 Something may go wrong. If the first argument starts with an alphabetic character you will have an undefined command. If it is non-alphabetic, or braced, there will be no error. The space in the definition between the name and the # symbol is not a delimiter.
3 No problem there. Provided there is at least one space, the results will be satisfactory.
4 The template is not satisfied, and probably TEX will complain that it has encountered a 'runaway argument', and that the paragraph ended before the `\proclaim` was complete. Later, when you encounter `\long`, you will see a way around this, but at present, the argument to a command may not include a `\par`

or a blank line. TEX was busy reading away until it encountered the sequence .␣: of course, if the argument has two sentences, the end of the first sentence will have just that sequence, and will be understood as the template.

5 Similar results to the previous case. In these last two cases, the template is not satisfied, and the argument likely will appear to have 'run away'. You may obtain something, but not what was intended.

10.6: Again TEX will complain about a runaway argument, but this time it will indicate that a 'forbidden control sequence' has been encountered. It turns out that \bye is defined as \outer. This is explained later, but basically it means that these commands may not appear within the definitions of other commands. You could take it apart and encapsulate its contents, though. Or redefine without the prefix \outer.

10.7: The notion here is that everything between the command \eatme and the next asterisk will be the argument to the command, and will be thrown away.[delimiter!command]

10.8: This will do:
\def\<#1>{\leavevmode\hbox{$\langle$#1\/$\rangle$}}
Another alternative is to use the < and > symbols from the typewriter font:
\def\<#1>{\leavevmode\hbox{{\tt<}#1\/{\tt>}}}
The italic correction is a prophylactic measure. The notion of 'italic correction' is rather odd. The way that TEX handles characters is not really to place a box around a character: there is a box, but a slanted (or italic) character may very well 'lean' out of the box. When such letters are assembled into a word they will appear to overlap one another (from the point of view of a rectangular grid). When a slanted or italic word ends and is followed by an 'upright' font, it may appear that the tops of the last letter of the italic word and the first letter of the upright word are too close together. In order to 'correct' this, TEX has an italic correction which adds a little space. In very general terms, the italic correction of a letter is zero (even upright fonts have italic corrections). In general though, you really need the correction only when you are dealing with letters which have ascenders. But rather than choose, it is easier to put it in every time, even though it may not be needed.

10.9: This one is too difficult for me.

10.10: I'm not going to worry about the italic correction. If we look first at the definition of `\rm`, `\bf`, and so on, it can be extended:

```
\def\rm{\fam0 \tenrm\let\em\it}
\def\it{\fam\itfam\tenit\let\em\rm}
\def\sl{\fam\slfam\tensl\let\em\rm}
\def\bf{\fam\bffam\tenbf\let\em\it}
```

The reference to `\fam` is something required by maths, so we can just 'ignore' it here. It is necessary to add something which ensures that `\em` changes in context: the `\let` will do this.

This is not a particularly elaborate definition, but it may be sufficient.

10.11: There are lots of solutions. For example:

```
\def\sectionhead#1#2#3\par{\dimen0\hsize
 \advance\dimen0 by-5.5pc
 \halign to\hsize{%
   \hbox to 1.5pc{\bf##\hfil}\hskip0.5pc
   &\vtop{\raggedright\hsize 3pc\noindent##}%
                              \hskip0.5pc
   &\vtop{\hsize\dimen0\noindent ##}\cr
   #1&#2&#3\cr}
\bigskip\noindent}
```

This is a little more rigid than the one shown in the text, but works nonetheless.

10.12: Only you can do this. I know how to do it on most of the machines I use.

10.13: The most critical ones are those which effectively prevent you from allocating new counts, dimensions, skips, boxes, ifs, and token strings from within another command. Apart from those, `\+`, `\proclaim`, `\beginsection`, and `\bye` are also outer. The first of these is usually used with the tabbing commands, which will be covered in Chapter 13. Some people are foolhardy enough to redefine the way allocation is done (for example, Hoenig, 1988, redefines the way that `\newbox` is used, so that he has greater flexibility in some aspects of page make-up).

10.14: The delimiting space is removed from the definition.

```
\def\start#1{{\bf #1}}
\everypar{\start}
```

TₑX now looks for the first token.

10.15: 3.

10.16: There will be no error message at all. It is quite a legal definition, although not the one you want:

```
\def\one\bgroup x\egroup\def\two{y}
```

In other words, there is a template of `\bgroup x\egroup\def\two`. TEX is defining `\one` as y, although actually referring to `\one` will probably generate an error.

10.17: First, the boxed mini page, divided into a beginning and end:

```
\long\def\beginBoxit#1#2{\vbox\bgroup\hrule
  \hbox\bgroup\vrule\kern3pt
        \vbox\bgroup\kern3pt\vbox\bgroup\hsize
                #1\noindent\strut#2}
\def\endBoxit{\egroup\kern3pt\egroup\kern3pt
                \vrule\egroup\hrule\egroup}
```

This is just an unravelling where lots of { } pairs are translated into `\bgroup \egroup` pairs. To centre this, put it into a `\centerline`. Perhaps a better structure would be to introduce `\begincentre \endcentre`. Since this boxed mini page is a suitable box, it is relatively easy to place two (or more) within an `\hbox to\hsize` (just like a `\centerline`), provided of course that the boxes are not bigger than `\hsize`. If the boxed mini pages are separated by `\hss` rather than `\hfil`, there will be no complaints at all. I prefer to use fractional `\hsize` values:

```
\line{%
 \beginBoxit{0.45\hsize}{\raggedright\tolerance1000
 Years afterwards she could bring the whole scene
 ...
 the melancholy music of the song.}\endBoxit
\hss
 \beginBoxit{0.5\hsize}
 {But the tune {\it isn't\/} his own invention.
 ...
 but no tears came into her eyes.}\endBoxit}
```

11.1: For example

```
$$A=-C
    \left\vert\matrix{z_0-f&y_0\cr c&b\cr}\right\vert
\Big/ \left\vert\matrix{x_0&y_0\cr a&b\cr}\right\vert
                                \eqno(20)$$
```

The only awkward part may be finding the size of the / symbol.

11.2: The second expression is the one using \matrix. In the first case, the terms are separated by a \quad:

```
$${\cal C}=[R\quad G\quad B]$$
$${\cal C}=[\matrix{R&G&B\cr}]$$
```

Even though they hardly look different, it is easier for someone else to read the 'raw' input and understand the meaning. The typography does not contain all the information.

11.3: I think I prefer the second one, but the addition of some 'thick space' to the first one does give something acceptable:

```
$$\left\lbrace\matrix{c_0 & \ldots& c_n\hfill     \cr
              c_1 & \ldots& c_{n+1}           \cr
       \;\vdots\hfill & \ddots& \;\vdots\hfill\cr
              c_n & \ldots& c_{2n}\hfill   \cr}
  \right\rbrace\eqno(11.3)$$
```

Not only is this a fair amount of extra effort, but the attention to typography could obscure the relative simplicity of the expression.

11.4: The straightforward approach of

```
$${\bf f}=\left[\matrix{
    f_e(0)\cr
    f_e(1)\cr
    \vdots\cr
 f_e(M-1)\cr}\right]$$
```

would give

$$\mathbf{f} = \begin{bmatrix} f_e(0) \\ f_e(1) \\ \vdots \\ f_e(M-1) \end{bmatrix}$$

To reproduce the example it is necessary to try to align the f_e terms by using \hfill to left justify them. This tends to put the \vdots too far to the left. There are a number of ways to rectify this: for example, the \vdots could be preceded by ; but in order to make the dots align with the 0 and 1 a little extra adjustment is required; for example, \hbox to 5pt{\hfill$\vdots$\hfill}. You might think that since you are in maths mode and that the mu is a mathematical unit you could have used, say, \hbox to 9mu; not so: \hskip, \kern, and \hbox, although legal in maths, may use any dimension *except* mu!

This is becoming too complicated. A reasonable alternative might be to abandon the desire to align through the 'digits' and just use, say, \;\vdots.

11.5: In this case, `\phantom{-}` was inserted in order to align the terms. The 'problem' with the brackets in the first vector is induced from two factors: the lack of descenders or subscripts; and the elements being capital letters: the brackets are positioned in the general assumption that they will be suitable for a general group of letters, with some ascenders and descenders. A selection which contains only capitals, and therefore no descenders, will look 'high' in contrast to the brackets.

11.6: Since the same term is repeated, rather than keep typing it in, it can be defined:
```
\def\part#1{\displaystyle{\partial s(u)\over\partial u}
           \bigg\vert_{u=b_{#1}}}
```
The equation then simplifies to:
```
$$[S_b]=\left[\matrix{
    \part1&&&0\cr
         &\part2\cr
         &&\ddots\cr
         0&&&\part{N^2}\cr}\right]$$
```
The definition could be inserted after the first `$$`, but it would be local to that display equation.

11.7: Taking a simplistic approach:
```
$$\left\Vert \matrix{
\rm small\hfill&\rm smaller\hfill&\rm smallest\hfill\cr
\rm sum\hfill &\rm summer\hfill &\rm summit\hfill\cr}
\right\Vert$$
```
but it might be much 'better' to place each piece of text in its own `\hbox`:
```
$$\left\Vert \matrix{
\hbox{small}\hfill&\hbox{smaller}\hfill
                        &\hbox{smallest}\hfill\cr
\hbox{sum}\hfill   &\hbox{summer}\hfill
                        &\hbox{summit}\hfill   \cr}
\right\Vert$$
```
And perhaps even better to make a local definition of:
```
\def\h#1{\hbox{#1}\hfill}
```
to make the expression a little tidier.

11.8: This should be straightforward:
```
$$h_1(y)=\int_{-1/2n}^{1/2n}n^2dx=
\cases{n&for $\vert y\vert\le1/2n$\cr
       0&otherwise\cr}\eqno{214}$$
```

The only interest is in the ability to attach an equation number, and its location.

11.9: There is (as usual) more than one answer. The one chosen was to move into the slanted font before the display equation: `{\sl$$`, remembering of course to close the braces after the closing `$$`. Alternatively, insert `\sl` before the `if` and the `otherwise.`: you might like to quibble about the presence of the full stop there, or argue whether it ought to be in `\sl` or the default `\rm` font.

11.10: If we take this naively, we will write something like:
```
$$z'=\cases{
{z_K-z_1\over b-a}(z-a)+z_1&for $a\le z\le b$\cr
 z_1&for $z<a$\cr
 z_K&for $z>b$\cr}$$
```
In that case, the $\frac{z_K-z_1}{b-a}$ term is out of scale with the others. To rectify this, write
```
$$z'=\cases{\displaystyle
{z_K-z_1\over b-a}(z-a)+z_1&for $a\le z\le b$\cr
...
```
This does tend to emphasize the advantage of knowing what goes on under the surface.

11.11: Apart from the use of `\displaystyle`, the main issue here is to insert a phantom copy of $-\dfrac{1}{Z_3^*}$ on the bottom line of the 2×2 matrix to add depth (perhaps too much depth!). But if `\phantom` is used, the width of the expression is included in the positioning of the entry. In this case, the correct phantom is a `\vphantom`:
```
$$\pmatrix{Q_{02}\cr \eta_{02}}=
  \pmatrix{-1&\displaystyle-{1\over Z^*_3}\cr
 0&1\vphantom{\displaystyle-{1\over Z^*_3}}\cr}
  \pmatrix{Q_{01}\cr \eta_{01}\cr}$$
```
The last `\cr` in a `\pmatrix` or `\matrix` may be omitted with impunity. Delving into their definitions reveals a `\crcr` which allows this behaviour.

11.12: The only imagination required in the first of these two is to introduce a little extra space, perhaps with a `\quad`:
```
$$\eqalign{
H(j,k)=0, &\quad j=1,2,\ldots,8\cr
H(257-j,257-k)=0, &\quad k=17,18,\ldots,256\cr}
                              \eqno(221)$$
```
The second example contains a little 'trick' in order to encourage

the \vdots to align with the =:
```
$$\eqalign{{\bf f}_1 &
                        =(f_{11},f_{12},\ldots,f_{1m}),\cr
       {\bf f}_2 &=(f_{21},f_{22},\ldots,f_{2m}),\cr
                 &\phantom{=}\llap{\vdots}\cr
       {\bf f}_M &=(f_{M1},f_{M2},\ldots,f_{Mm}).\cr}
\eqno(9.84)$$
```
The punctuation appears in the original.

11.13: Using \left and \right works surprisingly well, but not perfectly:

$$
\sigma^2(x,y) = \frac{1}{(2X+1)(2Y+1)} \sum_{m=-X}^{X} \sum_{m=-Y}^{Y} \{ [\bar{g}(x+m,y+n) \\
- w(x+m,y+n)p(x+m,y+n)] \\
- \left[\bar{g}(x,y) - \overline{w(x,y)p(x,y)}\right] \}^2
$$

Although each alignment 'cell' is balanced correctly with use of \left. and \right. when appropriate, this simplistic use leads to uneven delimiters. Both the large braces *and* the square brackets contain expressions which extends over more than one 'row'. TEX is unable to keep track of this. Here, we should have used the family of **big** delimiters.

Note also that the \left. at the beginning of the second and third equation lines is before the \null-. If we write -\left.w, there will be space between the minus and the non-existent parenthesis, and also between the parenthesis and the w. Not what we meant.

11.14: The point of this exercise is to demonstrate that the definition of \displaylines includes \hfils. Over-riding these with \hfill may sometimes be required in order to place equation correctly. The \quads would not really be needed if we used \hfil:
```
$$\displaylines{\sigma^2(x,y)
   ={1\over(2X+1)(2Y+1)}
     \sum_{m=-X}^X\sum_{m=-Y}^Y\Bigl\{
     \bigl[\bar g(x+m,y+n)\hfil\cr
     \hfil\null-w(x+m,y+n)p(x+m,y+n)\bigr]\hfil\cr
     \hfil\null-\Bigl[\bar g(x,y)
    -\overline{w(x,y)p(x,y)} \Bigr]\Bigr\}^2\cr}$$
```

which results in

$$\sigma^2(x,y) = \frac{1}{(2X+1)(2Y+1)} \sum_{m=-X}^{X} \sum_{m=-Y}^{Y} \left\{ \left[\bar{g}(x+m,y+n) \right. \right.$$
$$\left. - w(x+m,y+n)p(x+m,y+n) \right]$$
$$\left. - \left[\bar{g}(x,y) - \overline{w(x,y)p(x,y)} \right] \right\}^2$$

The first line of this equation is almost 4 inches (about 284 pt) wide. In other words, we may have to take some of the physical constraints into account when we decide how to divide up an equation over more than one line.

11.15: This is rather lengthy, but one of the two approaches could be to use `\displayline`:
```
$$\displaylines{\quad\underbrace{
   -D\left\{u{\partial\over\partial x}
 \left[\omega\over D\right]+v{\partial\over\partial y}
 \left[\omega\over D\right]\right\}}
     _{\hbox{non-linear term}}
=   \underbrace{
  {\partial\over\partial y}\left[R_x\over\rho D\right]
   -{\partial\over\partial x}
                      \left[R_y\over\rho D\right]}
   _{\hbox{frictional term}}        \hfill\cr
\hfill{}+\underbrace{
  -{\partial\over\partial y}\left\{{1\over\rho D}
    \left[{\partial\over\partial x}S_{xx}
 +{\partial\over\partial y}S_{xy}\right]\right\}
 +{\partial\over\partial x}\left\{{1\over\rho D}
    \left[{\partial\over\partial x}S_{xy}
 +{\partial\over\partial y}S_{yy}\right]\right\}}
   _{\hbox{forcing term}}\quad\cr}$$
```
Although `\eqalign` is possible, it does not seem very natural.

11.16: The differences in setting are not noticeable, unless the text width is large enough that the second line is not really required. The command `\eqno` has the pleasing feature that it staggers the 'equation number' if it would overlap the equation.

```
$$\displaylines{
   \int_{-\infty}^\infty\int_{-\infty}^\infty
           m(\alpha-x,\beta-y)R_{gg}(x,y)dx\,dy
                        =R_{fg}(\alpha,\beta),\cr
   \hfill -\infty<\alpha<\infty,\
                        -\infty<\beta<\infty\ (33) \cr}
$$
```
and
```
$$\int_{-\infty}^\infty\int_{-\infty}^\infty
           m(\alpha-x,\beta-y)R_{gg}(x,y)dx\,dy
                        =R_{fg}(\alpha,\beta),
   \eqno{-\infty<\alpha<\infty,\
                        -\infty<\beta<\infty\ (33)}
$$
```
This seems an abuse of the concept 'equation number'. One way
to rationalise is to rename \eqno to something plausible.

11.17: One tempting solution is to exploit the use of \hfil in the
definition of \displaylines:
```
$$\displaylines{\quad{\textstyle{1\over2}}[g(x-1,y+1)
                +g(x+1,y+1)+g(x-1,y)\hfill\cr
  \hfil{}+g(x+1,y)+g(x-1,y-1)+g(x+1,y-1)]\hfill\cr
  \hfill{}-[g(x,y+1)+g(x,y)+g(x,y-1)]\quad\cr
\noalign{\hbox{at $(x,y)$.}}}}
$$
```
noting that the last piece of 'text' is included as part of the equa-
tion in order to ensure that there would be no intervening page
break. If you attempt something like this, you may very well end
up with some odd vertical spacing on the page. TEX may have to
exploit any glue which occurs between paragraphs (and displays).

The other example could use an \eqalignno:
```
$$\eqalignno{
   K(y) &=(2\pi)^{1/2}e^{-y^2/2},&(6.11a)\cr
   K(y) &=[\pi(1+y^2)]^{-1},&(6.11b)       \cr
\noalign{\hbox{and}}}
   K(y) &=\cases{1-\vert y\vert,&$\vert y\vert\le1$,\cr
   0,    &$\vert y\vert>1$.\cr}&(6.11c)    \cr}$$
```
Further 'alternatives' might be to \vbox the section which is to
be held together.

11.18: Adjusting the delimiter commands, for example to a 'null'
value:

```
\delimiterfactor1000
\delimitershortfall0pt
```
would yield

$$[\mathbf{R} \quad \mathbf{G} \quad \mathbf{B}] \begin{bmatrix} 2/\sqrt{6} & -1/\sqrt{6} & -1/\sqrt{6} \\ 0 & 1/\sqrt{2} & -1/\sqrt{2} \\ 1/\sqrt{3} & 1/\sqrt{3} & 1/\sqrt{3} \end{bmatrix} = [M_1 \quad M_2 \quad M_3]$$

$$\begin{pmatrix} Q_{02} \\ \eta_{02} \end{pmatrix} = \begin{pmatrix} -1 & -\dfrac{1}{Z_3^*} \\ 0 & 1 \end{pmatrix} \begin{pmatrix} Q_{01} \\ \eta_{01} \end{pmatrix}$$

$$P = \begin{bmatrix} 1 & 0 \\ \dfrac{1}{d} & 1 \end{bmatrix}$$

This does seem to illustrate that the delimiter commands are essential to the way in which TEX has been written. With the null values we have very unsatisfactory setting.

Many other publishers seem to set matrices in a similar way to Addison Wesley.

12.1: The `\hang` sets up hanging indentation for the next paragraph. The `\noindent` ensures that the first line of the paragraph is not indented at all. By default, `\hang` implies `\hangafter1`, that is to say, the hanging starts after the first line in the paragraph. Therefore the first line is set 'normally', using the currently set paragraph indentation. Note of course that if `\parindent` is set to zero (points, inches, etc.) these things will not have any effect at all.

12.2: It should be straightforward to experiment here. The use of `\everypar` is needed to make the modifications apply to each paragraph, since the way they normally work is to apply only to the current paragraph:
```
\everypar={\hangindent=20pt\hangafter=3}
```
Note that it is necessary to 'group' the commands which you wish to associate with the `\everypar`. To switch this off again you have two main choices. Either group the whole block in some way, so that the action of the `\everypar` is 'local' rather than permanent from the point at which it is set up, or set it back to the default by,
```
\everypar={}
```

There is an interesting, if potentially frustrating, consequence of the way that \everypar works. It attaches the commands to the first token which changes the mode from vertical to horizontal. Besides implying that the commands (like \kern) which do not have that effect will not, by themselves, have the \everypar commands attached to them, it also implies that a paragraph beginning

```
{\bf This} paragraph...
```

will not be formatted in the manner expected. The extra commands are attached to This. They are therefore inside a group, and they are not in operation when the paragraph ends and the formatting takes place.

12.3: In this instance, it was accomplished by:

```
{\hangindent30pt\noindent
{\bf Zahir:} beings or things possessing the property
of being unforgettable; in Arabic, 'notorious' or
'visible'. See Borges,  {\sl The Zahir}.\par}
```

This is dreadfully explicit and cumbersome. No-one would want to have to type that all the time. An alternative might be:

```
\def\entry#1:#2\par{%
              \hangindent30pt\noindent{\bf#1:} #2\par}
```

where each of the entries in the bibliography would look like:

```
\entry Rachel: one of the vessels in the universal
novel, Moby Dick; ''{\sl She was  Rachel, weeping
for her lost children, because they were not.}''

\entry Holkham: windswept and expansive: a fascinating
landscape of algal flats, small islands of windblown
sand, pine trees, and a slowly disintegrating whale.
```

With more effort and subtlety (and a deeper appreciation of how TEX puts paragraphs together), it would also be possible to use \everypar, thus eliminating the need for \entry.

12.4: A broad description is to place two boxes side by side: the first box contains the large letter, while the second contains the paragraph, with a suitable notch cut out of the corner. By boxing the initial letter suitably, its width can be calculated. One of the weaknesses of the \magstep structure of Computer Modern is that it is difficult to arrange fonts which are two or three times the base size. In order to have something approximately suitable, cmr17 has been scaled to about the right size. Perhaps \magstep3

would have been better still:
```
\font\bf cmr17 scaled\magstep2
\def\drop#1#2\par{\setbox0\hbox{\bf#1}%
  \setbox1\vtop{\hangafter-2\hangindent\wd0\noindent
                                  #2\strut}
  \hbox to\hsize{\vtop{\noindent\lower12pt\box0}%
                              \kern-\hsize\copy1}\par}
\drop Zahir: beings or things possessing the property
of being unforgettable; in Arabic, `notorious' or
`visible'. See Borges,  {\sl The Zahir.}
```

The extent of the `\hangafter` was determined manually, with reference to the chosen font. Similarly, the `\lower`ing of the box containing the initial letter was also determined with reference to the size of the initial, and the knowledge that the current `\base-lineskip` is 12 points. The `\strut` is there just in case the last line does not have a descender. There are countless improvements which could be made to this definition.

12.5: As usual, the answer is in the grouping:
```
\def\beginnarrow{\bgroup\smallskip\narrower}
\def\endnarrow{\smallskip\egroup}
```
Since the extent of the narrowing is equivalent to the paragraph indent, I would be inclined to add a `\parindent1.5\parindent` (or similar). The following paragraph, which starts indented, does not then seem at first like a continuation of the narrowed section. Not usually a problem, unless you write really short paragraphs!

The `\smallskips` could be `\pars`, or something else. At least if they are at least `\smallskips` there is a chance that the sliver of white space will alert the reader to the fact that this 'exceptional' bit of text has ended.

12.6: One strategy is:
```
\newcount\numi      \newcount\numii
\def\nitem{\par\hang\nindent}
\def\nindent{\indent\llap{%
    \global\advance\numi by 1\relax
          \number\numi\enspace}\ignorespaces}
\def\niindent{\indent\llap{%
    \global\advance\numii by 1\relax
      \romannumeral\numii\enspace}\ignorespaces}
\def\nitemitem{\par\indent
              \hangindent2\parindent\niindent}
```

where two counters are defined, \numi and \numii, to account for the two levels. This approach requires that we also have two different analogues of \textindent, here named \nindent and \niindent. In order to switch the counters off at the end of a list, it will be necessary to reset them by \numi=0 and \numii=0, noting that since their \advance was \global, simply grouping them is not sufficient. Of course it matters little whether you

\def\endnitem{\numi=0\relax\numii=0\relax}

or

\def\beginitem{\numi=0\relax\numii=0\relax}

provided that the counters are indeed reset before the next list using \numi or \numii starts.

12.7: One way to do this is to keep track of the 'depth' of the itemization, as well as numbering the items. Using \leftskip seemed easier than modifying the existing structure of \item and \itemitem. It does have its own problems (as you will note if you omit the \bgroup \egroup pair or a strategic \par).

```
\newcount\itemlevel      \newcount\numb
\def\beginitem{\bgroup\par\numb0
  \advance\leftskip by \parindent
  \global\advance\itemlevel by 1
 \def\item{\advance\numb by 1
   \par\noindent\llap{\number\numb
                            \enspace}\ignorespaces}}
\def\enditem{\global\advance\itemlevel by-1
                            \par\egroup}
```

The more subtle (or adventurous) would wish to use a different symbol for first-level itemization, second level, and so on, or to number the items as 1, 1.1, 1.2, 2, 2.1, and so on.

12.8: In essence this was covered in two of the previous exercises. The main point is to abandon the existing \item structure and replace it with one controlled like \narrower.

12.9: If it is omitted, TEX keeps adding more and more material into this insert. Since this has to be accumulated somewhere, the most likely thing that will happen is that you will find the message that TEX has run out of capacity and that you should seek the help of a guru. Ignore this. As usual, the path to enlightenment comes from within. On the other hand, you might encounter \bye or \end, where TEX will chastise you for being in internal vertical mode – in other words, an insert.

12.10: The first one
`\long\def\foot#1#2{\hang\footnote{#1}{\eightpoint#2}}`
is not braced correctly, and the `\hang` is used by the paragraph
in which the footnote is included, with disquieting results. Adding
an extra pair of braces helps, but still does not do what we want.

The second attempt,
`\long\def\foot#1#2{\footnote{#1}{\eightpoint\hang#2}}`
results in all the text of the first paragraph being 'hung', but
subsequent paragraphs are set in the normal style.

12.11: Go ahead and try it.

12.12: This may be done fairly simply by creating a new counter
and remembering to increment it each time the footnote is used:
`\newcount\footcount`
`\long\def\foot#1{\global\advance\footcount by1`
  `\footnote{$^{\number\footcount}$}{#1}}`
If you were writing a book, you might have to reset the counter
at the beginning of each chapter.

12.13: You don't have to. The default action of `\footline` is to
do just that. As noted, `\footline` is a token string:
`\footline={\hss\tenrm\folio\hss}`
Examining `\folio` will provide something like
`\def\folio{\ifnum\pageno<0 \romannumeral-\pageno`
          `\else\number\pageno \fi}`
The `\pageno` has to be negated since `\romannumeral` will only
provide a Roman numeral when it is given a positive value. With
a negative value, nothing appears. And of course, TEX keeps track
of these page numbers by maintaining them as negative values. Of
course, `\advance` simply increments a value: it is not an addition
operation.

12.14: There are two components here. One straightforward way
to ensure that some text is not broken is to have it in restricted
horizontal mode – in other words, in an `\hbox`. To have the full
stops treated as abbreviation symbols, use `\frenchspacing`. In
the case of Prof. R. A. Bailey, it is only the full stop of Prof.
which would be thought to be a full stop. The attraction of the
`\hbox` and `\frenchspacing` approach is that it would be possible
to write something like
`\def\name#1{\hbox{\frenchspacing#1}}`
The other alternatives to `\frenchspacing`, writing `Prof.{} R.`
`A. Bailey` or `Prof.\ R. A. Bailey`, are slightly less attractive,

since they demand that you (or whoever else is typing in) have to think more. To have to tell people that 'if a full point is used as an abbreviation do one thing, otherwise, do something else' requires extra thinking. What's the point in thinking about trivia when some convenient, explicit command can take care of the decision-making process – and correctly every time?

12.15: Just how might we tackle this? We might just try to measure it, but that is a rather hit and miss approach. Recall that it is possible to examine the contents of a box, including the glue, by \showbox. If we then examine the contents of an \hbox which contains a question mark followed by space, we can see what sort of glue is inserted. If we also have a normal space, we have something with which to compare it. It would probably be wise to increase the value of \showboxbreadth.

```
\showboxbreadth10
\setbox0\hbox{Hello? I said.}
\showbox0
\setbox0\hbox{Hello. I said.}
\showbox0
\setbox0\hbox{Hello! I said.}
\showbox0
```

The default value of \showboxbreadth is 5. The information which TEX provides would have come to an end before we find the interesting stuff.

12.16: This is perhaps most noticeable with a bold font, or with one larger than 10 point. Close examination of \dots reveals that it is defined with reference to mathematical notions. Even the font is specified as a maths font. This seems curious. If we can work out how \dots is defined, it should be possible to change that definition so that it is appropriate to the current font.

In order to unravel \dots, we can use \show. This will reveal that it is currently defined as

```
\def\dots{\relax \ifmmode \ldots \else
                            $\m@th \ldots \,$\fi}
```

This leads us to ask what \m@th is, and then what \ldots really is. You may be able to pursue \m@th, but first you will have to find out how to make @ be treated by TEX as a letter (it is all in the category codes), otherwise \show will not help you here. It turns out that all this command is doing is ensuring that \mathsurround is zero. A moment's reflection will show why that is needed in this definition. Working out what happens with \ldots is more involved. But let's not be too literal, and think intuitively. The \, helps give it away. Effectively, \ldots is a string of dots separated by \,. In maths, \, is 3 mu. There are 18 mu to the em. This is an interesting example of the longevity of the dead hand of 'real' type. Traditionally, all Monotype typefaces (in which tradition Computer Modern has been wrought) were created on a grid of 9 (or later, 18) units to the em. The finest 'gradation' was 1 unit. This enforced grid did lead to some infelicities in Monotype designs, and it is curious that Knuth enshrined this odd scale in typeface design when he was in no way restricted to such crude units. The gap in a thin space is therefore $3/18$ em, or 0.16667 em. Since the em is font related, we can be reasonably happy that it will introduce a suitable gap in (say) cmr17, or any other font for which the em is not 10 points. The mu is of course related to the fonts used in maths.

After all this, a suitable definition could be

```
\def\dots{\relax
  \ifmmode \ldots
  \else.\kern0.16667em.\kern0.16667em.\kern0.16667em
  \fi}
```

If we know the definition \thinspace we may be pleased to note that it is a kern of 0.16667 em. Coincidence? Why \kerns? (For an answer, if you need one, see Exercise 7.14.)

12.17: There never are enough underused characters. But since " should never really be used, except as \", it will do, without too much ambiguity:

```
\catcode'\"\active
\def"{\hfil\break}
```

A more natural candidate might be <, but that could create problems in maths. Of course, since we can test for maths mode, there are ways around this, which you can no doubt work out by now. An example of an exercise within an exercise...

12.18: It will happen soon enough.

12.19: The \enskip is a variety of \hskip. It may therefore only occur sensibly within horizontal mode. If it is at the beginning of a paragraph, where TEX would be in vertical mode, TEX will switch to horizontal mode. An \enspace, on the other hand, is defined through a \kern. In horizontal mode, a \kern will generate a horizontal movement; in vertical mode, a vertical movement. And as indicated, right at the beginning of a paragraph, we are in vertical mode.

13.1: The fixed width of the columns may lead to something like
Jan van Eyck   Albrecht Dürer Pieter Bruegel   Jeroen Bosch
Filippo Lippi   Piero della Fran~~Domenico~~cesca Ghirlandaio ~~Andrea~~ Mantegna
Note that no error message is issued.

13.2: Most of the clues are there. Perhaps the only real issues are
recalling the need for \struts and \vtop rather than \vbox. But
other issues include adjusting \tolerance so that the tighter measure which will be employed does not lead to too many demands
being placed on TEX. Perhaps the standard \parindent is also
inappropriate in this context.

13.3: The entries behave as if they were each grouped. But unfortunately there is no way to have the desired effect percolate down
the 'column'. Each entry has to be edited manually:

```
\+\hfil\bf Name\hfil & \hfil Office Address\hfil &
\hfil Phone\hfil&\cr
\+\bf James J. Florio & 23 S. White Horse Pike,
Somerdale 08083 & 609-627-8222\cr
\+\bf William J. Hughes & 2920 Atlantic Ave.,
Atlantic City 08401 & 609-345-4844\cr
```

and so on all the way down.

13.4: We have to adjust each of the relevant entries, but there are
some other things to be considered. To have a reasonable interval
between the chapter numbers and the titles, we could manually
insert (say) a \quad, but a less cumbersome alternative could be
to introduce another column in the \settabs which was a quad
wide. This means that there has to be an additional & in the table
too. To justify the page numbers correctly, simply preceding them
with an \hfill is not sufficient, and we should introduce an extra
& in both the \settabs line and all the entries.

```
\settabs\+LXXXVIII&\quad&The Pequod Meets the Samuel
          Enderby of London\quad & 999\cr
\+\hfill I      && Loomings        &\hfill   1&\cr
\+\hfill II     && The Carpet Bag  &\hfill   9&\cr
\+\hfill III    && The Spouter Inn &\hfill  16&\cr
\+\hfill        && .               & .        \cr
\+\hfill CXXXV  && The Chase -- Third Day &\hfill 806&
                                               \cr
\+             && Epilogue         &\hfill 825&\cr
```

It is wise to remove any spaces after the numerals (you should be
able to work out why, but the key thing is to be consistent).

13.5: It really does not matter whether the `\settabs` is inside or outside the `$$` or even the `\vbox`. But without the `$$` it will be left justified.

13.6: This is achieved in several ways, including the use of display maths and the use of `\centerline`, replacing `\+` by `\tabalign`.

13.7: On the face of it, what we want to do is to cast various bits into maths so that the spacing is handled correctly. An alternative, which requires a bit less work, is to modify the definitions of = and `\circ`:

```
\catcode'\=\active
\def={$\null\mathrel\char'075\null$}
\def\circle{$\null\circ\null$}
```

To redefine the = it was first made active, but it cannot then be used in its own definition without recursion. But we can address it by its position in the font table. It just happens to be position 75 (octal). Note too that just to make the point we describe it as a maths relation. If the `\null`s are omitted, these two relations will not be spaced 'correctly' (or rather, like mathematical relations). We also remove the spaces in the expression of the example:

```
\+column&=\bf Id\cr
\+table &=&\bf Transpose\circle\cr
\+      & &(\bf all $i$: Insert{\rm []&place=first\cr
\+      & &                        &element=word({\bf
                                    Arabic}($i$))])\circle\cr
\+      & &(\bf all $i$:
        Layout{\rm[dimension=horizontal\dots])}\circle\cr
\+      & &\bf Layout{\rm[dimension=vertical\dots]}\cr
```

This requires quite a lot of attention to detail, and if it was required regularly, it would be a good case for a specially written program which would input the algorithm and output suitable TEX commands.

14.1: In general terms this means surrounding each # with `\hfil` or `\hfill`. For example:

```
\halign{\hfil#\hfil&\hfil#\hfil&\hfil#\hfil\cr
```

14.2: One way could be:

```
\halign{\hfil#\quad&#\hfil\quad&\hfil#\cr
```

To some extent this simplifies the entries:

```
I  & Loomings       & 1\cr
II & The Carpet Bag & 9\cr
```

```
CXXXV & The Case -- Third Day & 806\cr
    & Epilogue        & 825\cr
```
But the use of 'trailing' space should be consistent, especially for
right-justified entries, otherwise these generally unwanted spaces
may be included, and the alignments will be incorrect.

14.3: Here is some of it:
```
\centerline{\vbox{\def\rt{\omit\hfil}
\halign {\quad#\hfil&\quad\hfil#\quad\cr
\multispan2
      \hfil Some London Transport Statistics\hfil\cr
\multispan2\hfil \it(Year 1964)\hfil\cr
\noalign{\smallskip}
\omit Railway route miles\hfil\cr
Tube                  & 244\cr
Sub-surface           & 66\cr
Surface               & 156\cr
\noalign{\medskip}
\omit Passenger Traffic -- railway\hfil\cr
Journeys              &\rt 674 million\cr
Average length        &\rt 4.55 miles\cr
Passenger miles       &\rt 3,066 million\cr
\noalign{\smallskip}
\omit Passenger Traffic -- road\hfil\cr
Journeys              &\rt 2,252 million\cr
Average length        &\rt 2.26 miles\cr
Passenger miles       &\rt 5.094 million\cr
\noalign{\medskip}
\omit Vehicles\hfil   & 12,521\cr
Railway motor cars    &  2,905\cr
```
Again, consistency is crucial.

14.4: While this is possible, it seems a lot more work. It starts
like this:
```
$$\vbox{%
\settabs\+Passenger Traffic -- Railway\quad 9.999
                                    million&\cr
\+\hfill Some London Transport Statistics\hfill&\cr
\+\hfill\it(Year 1964)\hfill&\cr
\settabs\+Passenger Traffic -- Railway\quad&9.999
                                    million&\cr
```

```
\smallskip
\+Railway route miles\cr
\+\quad Tube                 &\hfill 244\quad&\cr
\+\quad Sub-surface         &\hfill  66\quad&\cr
\+\quad Surface             &\hfill 156\quad&\cr
\medskip
\+Passenger Traffic -- railway\cr
\+\quad Journeys            &\hfill 674 million&\cr
\+\quad Average length      &\hfill 4.55 miles&\cr
\+\quad Passenger miles     &\hfill 3,066 million&\cr
\smallskip
\+Passenger Traffic -- road\cr
\+\quad Journeys            &\hfill  2,252 million&\cr
\+\quad Average length      &\hfill  2.26 miles&\cr
\+\quad Passenger miles     &\hfill  5.094 million&\cr
\medskip
\+Vehicles                  &\hfill 12,521\quad&\cr
\+\quad Railway motor cars  &\hfill  2,905\quad&\cr
\+\quad Railway trailer cars &\hfill  1,269\quad&\cr
\+\quad Total railway       &\hfill  4,174\quad&\cr
\+\quad Omnibuses           &\hfill  8,347\quad&\cr
\medskip
\+Staff                     &\hfill 73,739\quad&\cr
```

As usual with \settabs the difficulties arise when you need to
centre an entry over several columns. Apart from that, all the
extra \hfill and \quad entries make the individual lines look very
unwieldy. They could of course be simplified into a local definition.
In fact,

```
\def\rt#1{&\hfill#1\quad&\cr}
```

could be quite helpful.

14.5: The following preamble does a fair job:

```
\centerline{\vbox{\def\rt{\omit\hfil}\tabskip0pt
  \halign spread 1em
  {\quad#\hfil\tabskip1em&\hfil#\quad\tabskip0pt\cr
```

The choice of 1 em is rather arbitrary.

14.6: All spaces between words disappear. In an emergency they
could be reinserted with ⌴; fortunately spaces used to delimit commands still delimit commands. But really this is something which
should be kept firmly under control.

14.7: What is a footnote then, except a type of bottom insert?

The problem then arises on how to manage both footnotes and some sort of bottom insert.

14.8: Using `\openup1\jot` gives the same effect.

14.9: Once `\boxit` has been defined, the table could be centred and boxed by
`\centerline{\boxit{\vbox{\halign`
but equally, it could be centred through a maths display.

14.10: The original was given by
`\centerline{\vbox{%`
`\def\sw{\llap{$\vcenter{\hbox{\tt WEAVE}}$}$\swarrow$}`
`\def\se{$\searrow$\rlap{$\vcenter{\hbox{\tt TANGLE}}$}}`
`  \halign{&#\cr`
`    \multispan3\hfil{\tt WEB} document\hfil\cr`
`    \hfil\sw&\qquad&\se\hfil\cr`
`    \hfil Pascal source&&\TeX\ document\hfil\cr`
`}}}`
There is a lot of rather exceptional stuff in here, not least the use of `\vcenter`, which has the knock-on effect of having to be in maths mode, and therefore the text must be placed in an `\hbox`. And then they are `\rlap`ped or `\llap`ped. Undoubtedly there are other ways too.

15.1: The basic table is given by
`\centerline{\vbox{{\tabskip 0in\hsize0.5\hsize`
`\offinterlineskip`
`\halign to\hsize{%`
`\strut\vrule#\tabskip1in plus1in minus1in&#\hfil&\vrule`
`    #&\hfil#&\vrule#&\hfil#&\vrule#&\hfil$#$&\vrule`
`    #\tabskip0in\cr`
`\noalign{\hrule}`
`  &\multispan7\hfil 1970 Federal Budget`
`                                        Transfers\hfil&\cr`
`  &\multispan7\hfil (in billions of dollars)\hfil&\cr`
`\noalign{\hrule}`
`  &\omit\hfil State\hfil&`
`    &\omit\hidewidth Taxes\hidewidth&`
`      &\omit\hidewidth Money\hidewidth&`
`        &\omit\hidewidth Net\hidewidth&\cr`
`  &&&\omit\hidewidth collected\hidewidth&`
`    &\omit\hidewidth spent\hidewidth&&&\cr`

```
\noalign{\hrule}
  &New York&&22.91&&21.35&&-1.56&\cr
  &New Jersey&&8.33&&6.96&&-1.37&\cr
  &Connecticut&&4.12&&3.10&&-1.02&\cr
  &Maine&&0.74&&0.67&&-0.07&\cr
  &California&&22.29&&22.42&&+0.13&\cr
  &New Mexico&&0.70&&1.49&&+0.79&\cr
  &Georgia&&3.30&&4.28&&+0.98&\cr
  &Mississippi&&1.15&&2.32&&+1.17&\cr
  &Texas&&9.33&&11.13&&+1.80&\cr
\noalign{\hrule}}}}}
```

The rest is up to you.

15.2: The first part of this one should be left to you. The second part is much more interesting. The & has a special meaning to TEX; it is the alignment tab. If we look at its category code, it has the value 4. It is possible to convert any other symbol to take a category code. For example,

```
\catcode'\174=4
```

turns the vertical bar into another alignment tab. An equally attractive alternative is to turn the keyboard's own tab character into an alignment tab. This is a shade more difficult, but it has some appeal. Firstly we have to know how to represent the tab character. In the 'standard' ASCII character set, the usual notation is to call tab HT. This is located in what TEX knows as position ^^09. The four characters ^^ab are read as if ab are any of the 'lower-case hexadecimal digits' 0–9, and a–f. An example will help to describe how to employ this knowledge. The way that \catcode allocations works is to indicate that a particular character has a particular code. The simplest method is to say

```
\catcode'\^^09=4
```

This new notation was introduced with TEX3 in order to handle the increase in character set from 128 to 256. Before that time it would have been sufficient to say

```
\catcode'\^^I=4
```

since this corresponded to the original way of referencing this position. Fortunately, both notations work (except in a rather arcane and abstruse way that should never have to worry you). All existing commands should work, and any new ones should use the new notation.

15.3: Reproducing the table is a matter of following the rules developed so far. In order to tackle the second part, building on

Figure 15.1, you need again to use the definition of \vspan. All that need be done is to surround the text 'State' and 'Net' by \vspans:

```
&\omit\hfil\vspan2{State}\hfil&
&\omit\hidewidth Taxes\hidewidth&
&\omit\hidewidth Money\hidewidth&
&\omit\hidewidth\vspan2{Net}\hidewidth&\cr
```

The \omit\hidewidth...\hidewidth could be better encapsulated in a command.

15.4: They are indeed small. In many printing systems, the spread of ink would mean they were even less discernible.

15.5: This can be redesigned either from scratch, or, much more simply, by omitting and \omitting. It is slightly irritating that some of the preamble includes vertical rules, but that almost all of these are to be \omitted. But it makes the preamble so simple...

15.6: This turns out to be quite simple:

```
\offinterlineskip
\halign{\vrule\strut\quad#\hfill\quad\vrule
              &\quad$#$\hfil&\quad$#$\hfil\vrule\cr
\omit\hfil\vrule&\multispan2\hrulefill\cr
\omit\hfil\vrule
  &\omit\hfil\bigstrut$\Delta H/\hbox{Jmol}^{-1}$\hfil
              &\omit\hfil$T/{\rm K}$\hfil\vrule\cr
\noalign{\hrule}
 Eistreicher and Schnerr & 18992     & 237.3\cr
 Giauque and Powell      & 20406\pm17 & 239.10\pm0.05\cr
 Equation  of State      & 20427     & 239.166\cr
\noalign{\hrule}
}
```

Note the assumption that \bigstrut has been defined somewhere. The table works reasonably without the standard definition of \strut. This is one nice example where the omission of a \vrule leads to a small bite out of the rules. Replacing the first line of the table with

```
\omit\hfil&\multispan2\hrulefill\cr
```

leaves a small irregularity.

Since all the columns contain numbers with the same magnitude, the effort to align around some imagined decimal point is equivalent to left justifying them.

16.1: In addition to defining \partline, define a \thinline which is very similar, but uses a modified definition of `\hrulefill`:

```
\font\small=cmr7
\centerline{\vbox{%
  \offinterlineskip
  \def\partline{\omit&\multispan2\hrulefill\cr}
  \def\thinline{\omit&\multispan2\leaders
          \hrule height0.2pt depth0pt\hfill\cr}
  \halign{\small#\quad&\vrule\strut\enspace\hfil
                        #&#\hfil\enspace\vrule\cr
    \omit&\multispan2\strut\hfil Stack\hfil\cr
          \partline
    1&46&\cr  \thinline
    2&23&\cr  \thinline
    3&15&\cr  \thinline
    4&6&.5\cr \thinline
    5&2&.1\cr \partline}}}
```

Perhaps a tidier table would have thicker bounding rules and default thickness 'internal' rules.

16.2: This may be done with one of the leader commands, but trying to make these work well within the `\tabalign` will be stressful. If, however, we are using a command based on `\line`, it will be sufficient to write:

```
\line{Loomings\dotfill1}
\line{The Carpet Bag\dotfill9}
```

This could be encapsulated into a more structured command, like `\entry{Loomings}{1}`, which offers advantages should we decide to handle the table of contents in a different format.

16.3: The following command corresponds to the 'standard' form:

```
\def\dotfill{\cleaders\hbox{%
                \kern.833333pt.\kern.833333pt}\hfill}
```

but without the restriction to the maths style. It has the limitation that if the font being used does not have the same size of full stop as `cmr10` or `cmsy10`, it will give a wider version. Since we probably want the dots to appear to be based on the same grid, no matter what the font, the following could be used:

```
\def\dotfill{\cleaders\hbox to4.444456pt{%
                          \hfil.\hfil}\hfill}
```

In some circumstances, and especially if the fonts were very large, such as `cmr17`, or in a different style, this should be rethought and a more suitable form created.

16.4: Although it is possible to infer that the answer is 'nothing good', it is even more instructive to see just how bad it really is. If you have already typed in this example, rather than edit it, just switch off \normalbaselines and \strut:
```
\let\normalbaselines\relax
\let\strut\relax
```
It can often be useful to turn off commands in this way.

16.5: This requires that you go ahead and experiment.

16.6: The alternatives are: the \multispan:
```
\multispan6{$^\ast$(first quarter only)\hfil}\cr
```
which is shown. A hidden problem here would be that if the text of the 'note' is greater than the width of the table, it will control the table width. With the use of \tabskip the table may go sadly awry. Secondly, we might use \noalign:
```
\noalign{\noindent\strut$^\ast$ (first quarter only)}
```
where the \strut is just added so that the spacing is adequate. Equally a \smallskip might be inserted as part of the \noalign. If the text is long, it might be better to include it in a \vtop, controlling the width by an 'internal' \hsize, but remember to insert \normalbaselines too. Lastly, the \vfootnote:
```
\vfootnote{$^\ast$}{(first quarter only)}
```
which, unlike the other two constructs, should follow the table, and not be part of it. This may generate a problem: inserts may not be placed within inserts. A \vfootnote is still an insert – it comes out at the bottom of the page, like a 'normal' footnote, and if you try to include it within a \topinsert, or a \midinsert, TeX will complain. It is possible then to have an 'inserted' table on one page, and the footnote on another.

16.7: The stock is always given as a range, and the en-dash, which is used to indicate a numeric range, could have been manipulated in the preamble, first having made the category code of – that of an alignment tab. Similarly, the decimal point could also become an alignment tab. Although the preamble looks awkward, once the 'stubs' are handled, the body of the table itself is more 'natural'. The elements would be:
```
\catcode'\.4    \catcode'\-4 % - and . as tabs
\centerline{\vbox{\offinterlineskip
   \halign{\strut\vrule\quad\hfil#\quad
     &\vrule\quad\hfil#\char'173-#-#\hfil\quad
     &\vrule\quad\hfil#\char'56.#\quad\vrule\cr
```

Where do these `\char'173` and `\char'56` come from? They are
a way of referring to particular characters when they are in some
way inaccessible. Having recategorized the - and ., they will not
translate into their 'normal' meaning. The particular syntax of the
`\char` command requires that it is followed by a number, which
may be in decimal, octal, or hexadecimal format. The `\char'173`
is an octal format. The alternatives here are `\char124` (decimal)
and `\char"7C` (hexadecimal), for the en-dash symbol. The decimal
point is given by `\char'56`. You can work out the decimal and
hexadecimal equivalents yourself.

16.8: Taking these separately, the left-hand table may be tackled
by using `\vspan` yet again, but actually boxing its entry on three
sides. Having said that, it mostly falls out:

```
\def\boxed#1{\vbox{%
   \hrule\hbox{\vrule height 14pt depth 9pt#1}\hrule}}
%                       14pt=\ht\strutbox+5.5pt
%                       9pt=\dp\strutbox+5.5pt
\offinterlineskip
\halign{%
\vrule\strut\enspace#\hfil
      &\enspace#\hfil
                   &\enspace#\hfil\vrule             \cr
\noalign{\hrule}
January&   February&                        March\cr
   April&       May&\vspan3{\boxed{\quad Month\quad}}\cr
   June&       July&                              \cr
 August& September&                               \cr
October&   November&                     December\cr
\noalign{\hrule}}
```

The definition of `\boxed` contains a `\vrule` to a particular height
and depth. Provided the height and depth do not exceed the total
vertical space available here (the equivalent of three baselines),
not too much will go wrong. The asymmetry of the height and
depth ensures that the text is apparently correctly placed.

The right-hand example is really a re-run of Figure 15.4. It
should not pose too many problems.

Placing the two tables side by side is just a matter of placing
them both in vertical boxes and, for example, enclosing them in
`\line`, separating them by some suitable space (or glue).

18.1: The length of the standard font names, as used by T_EX,
reflects the maximum length of file names on some varieties of

computer equipment. It is a simple technological constraint. While it has simplified portability, it is sometimes irritating. Some comments on font file names can be found in Berry (1990).

18.2: Over to you.

18.3: Since \oldstyle places us in family 1, it should be obvious that it will take its characters from the Math Italic fonts. Thus we obtain an A and a 9 from that font: *A9*. On the other hand, the \cal has the effect of turning on family 2, and therefore we take the characters from the symbol fonts. That is fine for the A, but the corresponding character for the 9 is not a numeral: *A∃*.

18.4: The \cal command can be extended just like \rm:
\def\cal{\fam2\tensy}
But be careful: don't try to write \cal Beware the Ides of March!.

18.5: Firstly, to change the progression, assume that the appropriate 8 and 6 point fonts have been set up, with names consistent with the ones we currently use:
```
\textfont0=\tenrm \scriptfont0=\eightrm
                  \scriptscriptfont1=\sixrm
\textfont1=\teni  \scriptfont1=\eightsy
                  \scriptscriptfont1=\sixsy
```
Family 2 can stay the way it is.

To restrain the diminution in size to only one jump, make the \scriptscriptfont the same as the \scriptfont. There is no way to extend the progression of script styles to more levels, short of rewriting parts of TEX. (But don't call it TEX!)

18.6: For \tenpoint we could add
```
\tenBig#1{{\hbox{$\left#1\vbox to11.5pt{}\right.
                                    \n@space$}}}
\tenbigg#1{{\hbox{$\left#1\vbox to14.5pt{}\right.
                                    \n@space$}}}
\tenBigg#1{{\hbox{$\left#1\vbox to17.5pt{}\right.
                                    \n@space$}}}
```
with the notion that we also say:
```
\let\Big\tenBig
\let\bigg\tenbigg
\let\Bigg\tenBigg
```
and that we may also wish to set up some \nineBig, \ninebigg, and similar commands.

18.7: The essence of this is
```
\font\tensc=cmcsc10
\newfam\scfam
\def\sc{\fam\scfam\tensc}
\textfont\scfam=\tensc
```
Problems start to arise when we want `\sc` to work as part of a `\ninepoint` command. It is possible to fudge a 9 point version through `cmr9` for the capitals, and something smaller, say `cmr6` or `cmr5` for the small capitals, but it is not quite right, conceptually, aesthetically, or typographically.

18.8: Assuming that the progression in size is just to increase by 3 pt each time:
```
\def\BIG#1{{\hbox{$\left#1\vbox to20.5pt{}\right.
                                       \n@space$}}}
\def\BIGG#1{{\hbox{$\left#1\vbox to23.5pt{}\right.
                                       \n@space$}}}
```
after setting the `\catcode` of @ appropriately. If you adopt the `\tenpoint` command, you would be using a strategy more similar to that used in Exercise 18.6.

18.9: This is just routine substitution, for the most part.

18.10: Disaster! The `\ifcase` falls off the end. Go back to Exercise 6.10.

18.11: This is a possible solution:
```
\def\raggedright{\ifnum\fam=\ttfam
  \rightskip0pt plus1fil\hyphenchar\font-1
                 \else
  \rightskip0pt plus2em \spaceskip0.3333em
                        \xspaceskip0.5em
                 \fi}
```
I do not really see why the interword spaces should be standardized for 'ordinary' fonts. Failing to do so usually permits the right margin to be fairly smooth. An alternative, to ensure that the margin is ragged, is to discourage hyphenation, say with `\hyphenpenalty100`.

18.12: A possible solution is
```
\def\centre{\rightskip   0pt plus 1fill
            \leftskip    0pt plus 1fill
            \parfillskip 0pt \relax}
```
Although it is difficult to see why you might want to do this, it

does illustrate that you may also manipulate the very last line in a paragraph. It is not unusual to require the last line to be centred, while the remainder of the paragraph is set flush right as normal. Set the following:

```
\rightskip   0pt plus -1fil
\leftskip    0pt plus 1fil
\parfillskip 0pt plus 2fil \relax
```

This is perhaps rather subtle and needs some thought.

18.13: It is easy enough to interrogate TEX to find the value of these dimensions, and to interpolate some plausible value. Again, the important fact is that this is possible. An alternative is to alter the `tfm` files, but that enters a different dimension altogther.

19.1: There are three main reasons for attempting this exercise. Firstly, it helps to bring out the relationship between upper- and lower-case characters a little better; the 'offset' is a little clearer. Secondly, as 256 character and 'virtual fonts' become more generally available, it will be slightly easier to organize and display a 16×16 table than an 8×32 table (cf. Ferguson, 1990). And lastly, once a table like this is created, it is very useful when you need to create a font table for any arbitrary font.

19.2: I make it about six or seven words.

19.3: The property list tends to be quite long. It does emphasize the fact that it is possible to edit it with a normal text editor: this gives you the power to modify the font characteristics in order to create a new `tfm`, and perhaps to contemplate creating a whole new property list. Virtual fonts have additional features, including the capability to include something like a `\special` – this is very powerful, and only slightly explored, as yet.

19.4: This is not quite as easy as it sounds. Firstly, you cannot just use TEX itself. You have to use `INITEX`. Once you have eliminated the preloaded fonts and created the new format file, you may find that the font memory statistics do not appear. Production versions of TEX are not compelled to register all (or any) of the `\tracingstats` details.

19.5: If all we need is to be able to say METAFONT, then

```
\font\mf=logo10
\def\MF{{\rm{\mf META}\-{\mf FONT}}}
```

will do. Omitting the explicit hyphenation,

```
\def\MF{{\mf METAFONT}}
```

is fine until T_EX tries to hyphenate the word. Since there is no
hyphen character in the font, you will have a message to the effect
that there is a missing character. On the other hand, you could
argue that the logo should not be hyphenated at all. There are
several ways to guarantee that it is not hyphenated. However,
what if we need to say **METAFONT** or *METAFONT*? Although it
is possible to create a general command, \MF, which would respond
to the style of the surrounding text, is it worth the effort?

20.1: In the very simplest case this is just a matter of putting
another \boxit around \box255:
\output={\shipout\boxit{\boxit{\box255}}}
The other definition, \Boxit, is rather more difficult to handle in
this case. A dip into the definition may indicate why. Specifying
the box width correctly is more difficult. A slight shortcoming is
that the box sits outside the text, as defined through the \hsize
and \vsize. A more rigorous approach would reduce the \hsize
by the amount of the \kerns and the width of the rules.

20.2: Since the most convenient place to obtain \box255 is in the
middle of an output routine, you need to embed the \vsplit and
the \showthe within the \output:
\output={\setbox254\vsplit255 to0.5\vsize
          \showthe\dp254\showthe\ht254
          \showthe\dp255\showthe\ht255}
Note that this cheats, since we are not actually attempting any
output at all. It is worth repeating this experiment by changing
the value of \hsize to ensure that the total number of lines is odd
and even. It might also be worth reminding yourself of the options
like \scrollmode, \nonstopmode, and \batchmode, introduced in
Chapter 3.

20.3: There are other strategies to achieve this, but this is simple
and effective. You may detect deficiencies (depending on just what
sizes and text characteristics you employ), which we will attempt
to rectify later.

20.4: This requirement embroiders slightly, by simply placing a
vertical rule between the boxes:
\output={\setbox254\vsplit255 to0.5\vsize
\shipout\hbox{\vtop{\unvbox254}\quad
    \vrule\quad\vtop{\unvbox255}}}
Do ensure that you check how 'incomplete' pages are handled by
this sort of approach.

20.5: This evolves the structure used so far:

```
\newdimen\pageheight   \pageheight3in
    %\pageheight is to be the total height of the text
\newdimen\pagewidth    \pagewidth6in
    %\pagewidth is to be the full width of the text
\newdimen\gutter        \gutter10pt
    %\gutter: gap between the column and the rule
\hsize\pagewidth
\advance\hsize by-0.4pt
       %\vrule is 0.4pt wide
\advance\hsize by-2\gutter
\divide\hsize by2 \vsize2\pageheight
       %manipulating the underlying \hsize & \vsize
%
\output={\setbox254\vsplit255 to0.5\vsize
\shipout\hbox{\vtop{\unvbox254}\hskip\gutter\vrule
    \hskip\gutter\vtop{\unvbox255}}}
```

This even has some internal documentation! Normally the 'gutter' is the total distance between columns, rather than the definition used here (effectively half the normal distance).

20.6: The 'normal' \footline and \headline were introduced in Chapter 12. The following is crude, but starts to outline the steps:

```
\output{\shipout\vbox{\line{\the\headline}%
  \smallskip\box255\smallskip
  \line{\the\footline}}\advancepageno}
```

This yields no headline, since by default the headline is null. However the footline will have the page number. To change the furniture:

```
\headline{\tensl experiment\hss}
\footline{\tensl\hss\folio}
```

would be sufficient.

20.7: The first is fairly straightforward, since 5 on 6 is just half of the default. You could work it out from the clues given, or you could be intuitive and guess that the dimensions could be reduced proportionately:

```
\hsize2in              \vsize2in
\baselineskip6pt
\font\smallrm cmr5  \smallrm
%
\footline{\smallrm\folio}
```

```
\def\makeheadline{\vbox to 0pt {\vskip -11.25pt
    \line{\vbox to 4.25pt{}\the\headline
                                }\vss}\nointerlineskip}
\def\makefootline{\baselineskip12pt
    \line{\the\footline}}
%
\output{\shipout%
  \vbox{\makeheadline\box255\makefootline}%
                        \advancepageno}
```

Let us assume we select 14.4 on 17: the use of 14.4 is so that we can pick up a font like cmr12 scaled to \magstep1. This is not a simple factoring this time, so we have to tackle it quite logically. Firstly, the footline, since it is easiest:

```
\footline{\largerm\folio}
\def\makefootline{\baselineskip34pt
                \line{\the\footline}}
```

If we unravel the relationships embedded in the description, the first vertical skip, v is given by:

$$v = 2 \times b - t + h$$

where b is the \baselineskip, t is the \topskip, and h is the height of a strut in the font used for the document. The \baselineskip is 17 pt, the \topskip should be increased to a value like 14.4 pt, and the height of a strut in the 14.4 pt font will be about 10.8 pt. In case this last value seems like a rabbit conjured out of a hat, it is the height of a parenthesis in the 14.4 pt font, and was found by interrogating a box containing that character. This gives us

```
\topskip14.4pt
\def\makeheadline{\vbox to 0pt {\vskip -30.4pt
\line{\vbox to 10.8pt{}\the\headline}\vss}%
                        \nointerlineskip}
```

I would be inclined to round measurements to full point values.

20.8: Solutions include

```
\headline{\vbox{\offinterlineskip
  \hrule\line{\sl\hbox to0.9\hsize{%
  \vrule\hfill\strut Making Pages\hfill\vrule}
  \hfill\folio\hfill\vrule} \hrule}}
```

and

```
\headline{\vbox{\offinterlineskip
  \line{\sl Making Pages \strut\hfill \folio}\hrule}}
```

If the vertical extent of these headlines was much larger, it would be necessary to modify the accompanying \makeheadline.

20.9: Adopting the double columning given above, it would be almost enough to write:

```
\def\makeheadline{\vbox to 0pt{\vskip -22.5pt
    \hbox to\pagewidth{%
    \vbox to8.5pt{}\the\headline}\vss}\nointerlineskip}
\def\makefootline{\baselineskip24pt
    \hbox to\pagewidth{\the\footline}}
```

The change is to replace the 'normal' reference to \line by an \hbox to \pagewidth. Make sure that this has been assigned an appropriate value.

However, the position of the footline may be unsatisfactory. The total page depth is simply the depth of its box. If the page has only a single column, which might not be of the full depth, this becomes very obvious. Some way must be found of ensuring that the depth is correct. Possible strategies include reboxing to the 'correct' size:

```
\vtop to0.5\vsize{\unvbox255\vfil}
```

or including a vertical rule of the appropriate depth.

20.10: One way to find the depth of the page is to

```
\setbox\page\vbox{\unvbox255\bigskip}
```

where \page is a box in which the built up page is accumulated. The \bigskip is to build in an extra 'line' to ensure that the left hand box is a shade larger than the right (when we come to split). The whole structure looks like:

```
\newbox\page
\newdimen\pagewidth        \pagewidth2\hsize
\advance\pagewidth by10pt
\output{\setbox\page\vbox{\unvbox255\bigskip}%
  \setbox254\vsplit\page to0.5\ht\page
  \shipout
  \vbox{\hbox to\pagewidth{\the\headline}\smallskip
  \hbox to\pagewidth{\vtop{\unvbox254}\hfil
                    \vtop{\unvbox\page}%
                    \vrule depth0.5\vsize width0pt}%
  \smallskip\hbox to\pagewidth{\the\footline}}%
                              \advancepageno}
```

This brings in many of the points which have been mentioned in other exercises, but not necessarily fleshed out in full. There are lots of other solutions.

20.11: The default page size is 8.9 in, and the default maximum extent of a page which can have footnotes is 8 in. If we assume that no more than half the page height should be taken up by footnotes,

```
\dimen\footins=0.5\vsize
```

would give a more flexible approach.

20.12: Setting in a different style is trivial, since all that needs to happen is a modification to the definition of `\margindetail`. A change in font characteristics might also require that the `\strut` in `\margin` also changes, but if a command like `\ninepoint`, introduced in Chapter 18, is used, that should have been tackled correctly. Changing the position is not difficult either:

```
\newdimen\marginht                                  %
\marginht\vsize                                     %
\def\pagecontents{\ifvoid\topins\else\unvbox\topins\fi
   \dimen0=\dp255
   \ifvoid\margins \else                            %
   \marginht\ht255                                  %
   \advance\marginht by-\ht\margins                 %
   \divide\marginht by2                             %
   \rlap{\kern1.01\hsize\vbox to0pt                  %
                   {\kern\marginht\box\margins\vss}}%
   \fi
\unvbox255
   \ifvoid\footins\else
   \vskip\skip\footins\footnoterule\unvbox\footins\fi}
```

The main changes are indicated by the `%`, but the key part is in the `\rlap`, where the `\kern` positions the marginal text.

20.13: With multiple columns, the inserted material should presumably be inserted around the 'edges' of the whole text. That tends to make two columns a practical maximum. On the other hand, the usual function of marginal information is to assist in the draft stages of manuscript development. Bits of overwriting may be acceptable at that stage. If marginal information is being used at the final stages, it will possibly be part of the page furniture. Some books place page numbers, or even a chapter key on the outside margin – such information might be better handled in ways other than the approach to marginal inserts suggested here. An explicit box on the right or left would be a suitable strategy in such cases. Once you analyse what the function is, a solution usually pops up (or can be dragged up).

20.14: The marginal note is rather crude. Notes on the left have the disadvantage that they tend to look rather far away, unless they have been organized in a ragged left form, and because they tend to be quite narrow, overfull boxes tend to abound. But it is not difficult to modify the definition:

```
\def\leftnote#1{#1\vadjust{\vbox to 0pt{%
   \vss\hbox to\hsize{\hskip-1.1in %
   \vbox{\hsize1truein\overfullrule0pt\noindent
         \ninepoint#1}\hss}\vskip\strutdepth}}}
```

where the principal difference is the \hskip.

If we wished to use marginal inserts on the left or right, allowing an \ifodd\pageno to control the position, the suggested solution to Exercise 20.12 could be modified by changing the \rlap to:

```
\ifodd\pageno
\rlap{\kern1.01\hsize\vbox to0pt
            {\kern\marginht\box\margins \vss}}%
\else
\llap{\vbox to0pt
            {\kern\marginht\box\margins \vss}}%
\fi
```

but this will suffer from being related only to the page, and not to the position of the individual insert reference.

20.15: Yes, it can be done, but it is possible that the two overlap. Ensuring that they do not would be very tricky.

21.1: This is straightforward. Perhaps it is the definition of strut that should be changed.

21.2: The simplest way to inhibit hyphenation is by setting \pretolerance10000, although an alternative is to disallow hyphens in a font through \hyphenchar\tenrm-1. Making the penalty associated with a hyphen very large (say, 10,000), should have a similar effect, but I do not have as much confidence in it. If the page is narrow, it will be necessary to adjust the \tolerance figure.

21.3: The cynical answer is 'too many', but it all depends. I really do not find it makes all that much difference. Counter-intuitively, fewer hyphens are sometimes required when the line measure is reduced.

21.4: Although they will both work, \looseness has the nicer feature that you ask for the effect you want (which may or may not be achieved), while \linepenalty is rather less specific, and is not local. The default value for \linepenalty has to be changed quite markedly before it seems to have an effect.

21.5: Obviously, when \looseness succeeds the interword spacing must have been reduced or increased. If the paragraph length is changed by just one line, I just cannot see the change. This is hardly surprising, since the interword spacing should still be within the required range. If the paragraph is lengthened by one line, T_EX does seem to tend to place the last part of a hyphenated word in the last line. This does not look good, but perhaps it is the best that can be done. To eliminate this, you could try adjusting \finalhyphendemerits, but placing the last word in an \hbox is infallible (if ugly).

21.6: As hinted from time to time, the multiplicity of parameters, tolerances, penalties, and demerits makes it very difficult to guage the interactions. If all words were exactly the same length and hyphenated in exactly the same way, it might be possible to see what is going on, but fortunately, no language is like that.

21.7: One way in which this might occur is if, by removing a word, a paragraph of four lines is shortened to three lines: if it had been divided over two pages, as two lines and two lines, it will now have to be presented as a block of three lines, and will have to be placed at the top of the next page. So the document will end up apparently one line longer (at least – but who knows what other effects may be lurking later?). See Mittelbach, 1991, for some other ways this might happen. Naturally, the setting of parameters such as the \clubpenalty and \widowpenalty are paramount in determining whether a single line may exist at the top or bottom of a page.

21.8: This is another time where experimentation is essential.

21.9: It forces a page break after the line containing the \vadjust. The \vadjust is handled in vertical mode and therefore does not interfere with line breaking.

21.10: In the very trivial case, a paragraph may be longer than an individual page.

21.11: A very large memory version of T_EX might handle it. A non-trivial answer has nothing to do with any of the \break commands: in order to ensure that a paragraph ends flush right, the \parfillskip can be set to zero. If the next paragraph is begun

with a \noindent, there will be no obvious break. We must also
ensure that the \parskip is zero; for example:
\def\subtle{{\parfillskip0pt\par\parskip0pt\noindent}}
The only worry might be the 'extra' braces around the definition.
But reflect a moment. We only want these values and commands
to have local action. Therefore...

21.12: The following may do as an example:
```
\def\section#1{\goodbreak\vskip2ex plus 1ex%
                \centerline{\bf #1}%
                \nobreak\vskip1ex\nobreak
                \par\noindent\ignorespaces}
```
This should ensure that the section title stays with the first few
lines of the text that follow.

22.1: Some experimentation needed.

22.2: If we use \read16 to\version, TEX will respond with
\version=
which may save having to write out a message, although if this is
encountered in a production environment, I would prefer to have
a message than such a terse prompt.

22.3: Again, some experimentation will be needed. Ensure that
you use \section several times, in positions which are close to
page breaks. Similary, the effect of an \immediate close of the file
is best noticed when a section occurs close to the end of the text.

22.4: The following commands will accomplish the initial task of
creating a file with index entries and the relevant page number.
As a check, the \write-1 will echo the index entries to the screen.
```
\newwrite\idx
\immediate\openout\inx=\jobname.idx
\def\index#1{#1%
  \write-1  \expandafter{#1:\folio}%
  \write\idx\expandafter{#1:\folio}}
```
Much more work needs to be done to turn the file into an index.

22.5: Taking this at face value, commands are expanded, just
as indicated in the text. After some experimentation trying to
supress the expansion, you might end up with:
```
\newwrite\inx
\immediate\openout\inx=\jobname.idx
\def\index#1{{#1}\def\save{\noexpand#1}%
  \write\inx\expandafter{\save:\folio}}
```

which manages to give something a little more attractive, but,
while this manages to suppress the expansion if the command is
the first item in an entry (like `\index{\TeX}`), it fails when there
is another token before the command.

An alternative is to use token strings:

```
\newtoks\intox
\newwrite\inx\immediate\openout\inx=\jobname.idx
\def\index#1{{#1}\intox={#1}%
    \immediate\write\inx{\the\intox:\folio}}
```

but that does not illustrate `\expandafter`, although it conveniently suppresses the expansion.

23.1: The question more or less spells out what to do:

```
\catcode'\_\active
\def_{\ifmmode\sb\else{\tt\char'137}\fi}
```

The major disadvantage is that the underscore is only available in
the typewriter font. If this was very unsatisfactory, a horizontal
rule tuned to the particular font might be a reasonable alternative.

23.2: This solution goes a little further than merely calculating
the values in the table: it attempts to format them acceptably:

```
\newcount\lhs        %the left hand sides, 1 to \uptomax
\newcount\by         %as in 'multiplied by'
\newcount\answer     %to store \lhs times \by
\newdimen\lhswd \newdimen\bywd \newdimen\answerwd
                     %their maximum widths
\newcount\upto       %a local counter
\newcount\uptomax    %max value to be multiplied by \by
\def\multiplication #1 times #2.{\by#1 \uptomax#2
\setbox0\hbox{$\number\uptomax$}   \lhswd\wd0
              %greatest width of left hand side
\setbox0\hbox{$\number\by$}        \bywd\wd0
              %greatest width of multiplier
\answer\by    \multiply\answer by\uptomax
\setbox0\hbox{$\number\answer$}    \answerwd\wd0
              %greatest width of highest value
\advance\uptomax by1
\loop \advance\upto by1 \advance\lhs by1
  \ifnum\upto<\uptomax
    \answer\lhs \multiply\answer by\by\centerline{$
      \hbox to\lhswd{\hfil\number\lhs} \times
      \hbox to\bywd{\hfil\number\by}    =
      \hbox to\answerwd{\hfil\number\answer}$}\repeat}
```

This may then be invoked by `\multiplication 11 times 17.` or similar. It would be convenient to be able to prepare more complex tables than this (perhaps emulating Babbage's difference engine), but TEX's restriction to integer arithmetic makes this a real chore. A solution is to create the tables through some conventional programming language, embedding the TEX commands required. This file could then be `\input` to TEX.

23.3: Although the following has many of the characteristics of a steam-roller, it is serviceable and robust:

```
\def\ut#1{\mathchoice
%displaystyle
   {\vtop{\offinterlineskip\halign{##\crcr
   $\hfil\displaystyle{#1}\hfil$\cr
   \noalign{\vskip1pt}
   $\hfil\displaystyle\char'176\hfil$\cr}}}
%textstyle
   {\smash
   {\vtop{\offinterlineskip\halign{##\crcr
   $\hfil\textstyle{#1}\hfil$\cr
   \noalign{\vskip1pt}
   $\hfil\textstyle\char'176\hfil$\cr}}}
   {\textstyle\vphantom{#1}}}
%scriptstyle
   {\vtop{\offinterlineskip\halign{##\crcr
   $\hfil\scriptstyle{#1}\hfil$\cr
   \noalign{\vskip0.7pt}
   $\scriptstyle\hfil\char'176\hfil$\cr}}}
%scriptscriptstyle
   {\vtop{\offinterlineskip\halign{##\crcr
   $\hfil\scriptscriptstyle{#1}\hfil$\cr
   \noalign{\vskip0.5pt}
   $\scriptscriptstyle\hfil\char'176\hfil$\cr}}}}
```

The hard-wired `\vskip` values could be improved upon (at the very least). The `\crcr` commands are sheer overkill. This command is the same as `\cr`, except that it is ignored after either `\noalign` or `\cr`. It is therefore most useful in creating commands where `\cr` might be inserted by mistake when they are employed. A genuine and valid use can be found if you unravel the complexities of `\matrix`. It is a feature which could be used to advantage in the creation of table commands, where the body of the table is effectively an argument to a command containing the alignment preamble. Since in normal circumstances \cr\cr is equivalent to two 'rows', it could lead to the insertion of unwanted vertical space in the table.

23.4: The major change is to find a way of discarding the first character. This will do the job:

```
\def\testing{\futurelet\next\switch}
\def\switch{\ifx\next T
  \def\action##1{\bf}
    \else
  \def\action##1{\sl}
    \fi
 \action}
```

It requires the introduction of a new local command which is then invoked at the end. This is rather more flexible than the simple form introduced originally.

23.5: One preferred way is to extend the previous structures slightly:

```
\def\test{\futurelet\next\switch}
\def\switch{\ifx\next *
  \def\action##1##2{\bf##2}}
    \else
  \def\action##1{\sl##1}}
    \fi
 \action}
```

which allows us to write:

```
\test*{asterisk form}
\test{no asterisk}
```

A rather sly alternative is to change the category code of * so that \fred and \fred* may both be defined. Why is this not a good idea?

Index